2017

Astrological Ephemeris

with Planetary Hours

COMPILED BY

J J GAMBLE

Artwork by: Charlotte Watts

It is suggested the word *almanac* derives from a Greek word meaning *calendar*. However, that word appears only once in antiquity, by Eusebius who quotes Porphyry as to the Coptic Egyptian use of astrological charts ("almenichiaká").

MOON PHASES

New Moon:

The Moon is 0 deg – 45 deg ahead of the Sun.
It rises at dawn and sets at sunset. The period is exact for 3 ½ days during which it is invisible.

Waxing Crescent:

The Moon is 45 – 90 deg ahead of the Sun
It rises mid-morning and sets after sunset. This period is 3 ½ - 7 days after the exact New Moon.

The First Quarter:

The Moon is 90–135 deg ahead of the Sun
It rises and noon and sets after midnight. It is 7 – 10 ½ days after the exact New Moon.

Waxing Gibbous:

The Moon is 135-180 deg ahead of the Sun
It rises mid-afternoon and sets at approx. 3am. This period is 10 ½ days after the New Moon.

Full Moon:

The Moon is 180-225 deg ahead of the Sun.
It rises at sunset and sets at dawn. This period is 14-17 ½ days after the New Moon.

Waning Gibbous or Disseminating:

The Moon is 225-270 deg ahead of the Sun. It rises mid-evening and sets mid-morning. It is 3 ½ - 7 days after the exact Full Moon.

Last Quarter:

The Moon is 270-315 deg ahead of the Sun.
It rises at midnight and sets at noon. This period is 7 – 10 ½ days after the exact Full Moon.

Waning Crescent or Balsamic:

The Moon is 315-360 deg ahead of the Sun. It rises at approx. 3am and sets mid-afternoon. This period is 10 ½ days after the exact Full Moon.

Void of Course Moons

The Moon is *void of course* during the time between making its last major aspect to a planet in one sign and its entry into the next sign. The duration of this period can be as little as a few seconds or more than two days. The exact moment the Moon enters the new sign ends the void of course period.

Planets Out Of Bounds

Planets that are out of bounds have been documented to behave in a way such that the characteristics of the planet are especially well developed even extreme in nature. By definition, an OOB planet is one that exceeds 23 degrees 27 minutes either North or South of the equator.

Seasons

Northern Hemisphere

Spring - March, April, May
Vernal equinox to summer solstice

Summer - June, July, August
Summer solstice to autumn equinox

Autumn - September, October, November
Autumn equinox to winter solstice

Winter – December, January, February
Winter solstice to vernal equinox

Solstice: This is the time when the Sun is either closest to, or furthest from the Equator. Winter solstice is the longest night, Summer Solstice is the longest day.

Equinox: This is when the Sun crosses the Equator and day and night are of equal length and occurs around the 21st March & 23rd September each year.

Measurements of Time

Mean Sidereal Day

The period of time during which the earth makes one revolution on its axis relative to a particular star – 23h 56m 4.09s

Mean Solar Day

The period of time during which the earth makes one revolution on its axis relative to the sun – 24h 00m 0.59s

The Year

The earth revolves round the sun in 365 days 5 hours 48 minutes and 45 seconds. A calendar year is therefore usually 365 days. Leap years deal with the accumulation of the surplus time.

Leap Year

Leap years are those years divisible by 4 without a remainder.

International Dateline

A modified meridian of 180 degrees longitude from north to south in the Pacific forms the International Dateline. When crossing this line, the date moves on by one day if travelling westward and back by one day if travelling eastward.

Moonrise and Set will vary according to location

Planetary data set for midnight GMT
and where applicable is inclusive of British Summer Time

Planetary Hours And Angelic Rulerships

Planet	Archangel	Day	Dominion
Sun	Michael	Sunday	Beloved Of God
Moon	Gabriel	Monday	Power of God
Mercury	Raphael	Tuesday	Messenger of God
Venus	Anael	Wednesday	Queen of God
Mars	Samael	Thursday	Warrier of God
Jupiter	Sachiel	Friday	King of the Gods
Saturn	Cassiel	Saturday	Father of Time

Primary Rulerships

Michael – Physical healing, exercise, group or community work

Gabriel – Intuition, psychic power, feminine health, domestic matters

Samael – Masculine energy, physical courage, sport, craftsmanship

Raphael – Writing, communication, mental healing, memory

Sachiel – Business, trade, investments, banking, insurance politics

Anael – Love, marriage, friendship, artistic creation, friendship

Cassiel – Land, agriculture, property, legal matters, study, timekeeping

The Daily Hours

The Daily Hours - or Horai in Greek, Horae in Latin - were how the Ancients marked the various points in the day. The Christian monastic observance of the hours derives from the influence of the Greco-Roman timekeeping on the Jewish observation of daily prayers around the time of Christ. These hours are not equal periods of time, exactly one twenty-fourth of the day, instead they are even divisions of the hours of the day. Ceremonial magicians and astrologers use the daily hours to train their body's to the actual yearly cycle

The Horai

ANATOLIA: The dawn. Associated with beginnings and possibilities, driving away the darkness. Associated with aries.

MOUSIKA: Music-hour, associated with taurus. All gather for the morning practice of songs and chants that will be sung for the week's rituals. This need not last the entire period, and on some days may be cut short in order to do further work or chores.

GYMNASTIKA: Associated with gemini. The Greeks and Romans put a great store of importance into keeping the body healthy with exercise, an attitude which fell into disrepute in the Christian era of body-hatred.

NYMPHE: Water-hour, for bathing and showering after Gymnastika. Associated with cancer. Dishes and laundry should also be done at this time, as well as general cleaning.

MESEMBRIA: Lunch hour around noon. Associated with leo it begins with the meal Prayer honouring certain gods and festivals. Cleaning up after lunch until Sponde.

SPONDE: The first of the "libation horai", or ritual hours. Associated with virgo, the sign of Hestia, goddess of the Vestal virgins. The Sponde rituals run on the solar calendar. They need not take up the entire period; this will vary from day to day.

ELETE: First of the work-hours. For doing whatever work is necessary to the monastery. This might be agricultural or gardening, or repair, or cleaning and maintenance. Associated with Libra.

AKTE: Second of the work-hours. Associated with Scorpio. Elete's work can extend into Akte.

HESPERIS: Sacred evening "libation horai" before dusk. Associated with Sagittarius, the sign of religion.

DYSIS: Sunset, associated with endings and capricorn. The evening meal-hour, eaten communally and beginning with the meal prayer. Food will be dictated by the preceding Hesperis ritual.

ARKTOS: The hour after dark, associated with the Dead and the Ancestors, and aquarius. All work done during or after arktos should be of quiet contemplation, and silent work.

AUGE: First light. The hour before dawn, when ghosts walk. Associated with pisces. Breakfast is eaten communally; it should be simple and light. First prayers said. Announcements are made and work assignments given.

Sunday 1st January

Planets	**00:00 am**	**Moon**
Sun	10 cap 45	00.00 am - 11 aq 50
Mercury	03 cap 16	02.00 am - 12 aq 54
Venus	27 aq 29	04.00 am - 13 aq 57
Mars	09 pis 31	06.00 am - 15 aq 01
Jupiter	21 lib 08	08.00 am - 16 aq 05
Saturn	21 sag 22	10.00 am - 17 aq 09
Uranus	20 ar 33	12.00 pm - 18 aq 13
Neptune	09 pis 44	14.00 pm - 19 aq 17
Pluto	16 cap 56	16.00 pm - 20 aq 21
		18.00 pm - 21 aq 25
Oob		20.00 pm - 22 aq 29
		22.00 pm - 23 aq 33

Planetary Directions

Makemake retrograde
03 lib 52 at 15:06

Retrograde Planets

Mercury, Vesta, Eris,
Orcus, Sedna

Asteroids		**Dwarf Planets**	
Juno	19 sag 06	Eris	22 ar 32
Vesta	02 leo 18	Haumea	24 lib 36
Pallas	01 pis 05	Makemake	03 lib 52
Ceres	22 ar 37	Salacia	28 pis 53
Chiron	21 pis 06	Orcus	09 vir 02
N Node	04 vir32	Quaoar	29 sag 21
S Node	04 pis 32	Sedna	25 tau 12

Moon Phase: Crescent
Sunrise: 08:06 GMT
Sunset: 16:02
Moonrise: 09:46
Moonset: 19:43
Voc start:
Voc end:

Planetary and Angelic Hours

Sun	08:03	Jupiter	16:04
Venus	08:43	Mars	17:23
Mercury	09:23	Sun	18:43
Moon	10:03	Venus	20:03
Saturn	10:43	Mercury	21:23
Jupiter	11:23	Moon	22:43
Mars	12:03	Saturn	00:03
Sun	12:43	Jupiter	01:23
Venus	13:23	Mars	02:43
Mercury	14:03	Sun	04:03
Moon	14:43	Venus	05:23
Saturn	15:23	Mercury	06:43

New Years' Day

Aspects

Moon sextile Juno
Moon sextile Uranus
Moon trine Jupiter
Moon sextile Saturn
Moon sextile Eris
Moon sextile Ceres
Moon square Sedna
Mercury sextile Pallas
Mars conjunct Neptune
Jupiter sextile Saturn
Jupiter opposite Uranus
Saturn trine Uranus
Saturn square Chiron
Ceres conjunct Eris

Planets	**00:00 am**	**Moon**
Sun	11 cap 46	00.00 am - 24 aq 38
Mercury	02 cap 10	02.00 am - 25 aq 42
Venus	28 aq 34	04.00 am - 26 aq 47
Mars	10 pis 16	06.00 am - 27 aq 51
Jupiter	21 lib 15	08.00 am - 28 aq 56
Saturn	21 sag 29	10.00 am - 00 pis 01
Uranus	20 ar 33	12.00 pm - 01 pis 06
Neptune	09 pis 45	14.00 pm - 02 pis 11
Pluto	16 cap 58	16.00 pm - 03 pis 16
		18.00 pm - 04 pis 21
Oob		20.00 pm - 05 pis 27
		22.00 pm - 06 pis 32

Monday 2nd January

Planetary Directions

Moon into Pisces 09:58

Retrograde Planets

Mercury, Vesta, Eris, Makemake, Orcus, Sedna

Asteroids		**Dwarf Planets**	
Juno	19 sag 26	Eris	22 ar 32
Vesta	02 leo 05	Haumea	24 lib 37
Pallas	01 pis 21	Makemake	03 lib 52
Ceres	22 ar 45	Salacia	28 pis 54
Chiron	21 pis 07	Orcus	09 vir 01
N Node	04 vir 29	Quaoar	29 sag 23
S Node	04 pis 29	Sedna	25 tau 12

Moon Phase: Crescent
Sunrise: 08:06 GMT
Sunset: 16:03
Moonrise: 10:17
Moonset: 20:52
Voc start: 07:58
Voc end: 09:57

Planetary and Angelic Hours

Moon	08:03	Venus	16:05
Saturn	08:43	Mercury	17:24
Jupiter	09:23	Moon	18:44
Mars	10:03	Saturn	20:04
Sun	10:43	Jupiter	21:24
Venus	11:24	Mars	22:44
Mercury	12:04	Sun	00:04
Moon	12:44	Venus	01:23
Saturn	13:24	Mercury	02:43
Jupiter	14:04	Moon	04:03
Mars	14:44	Saturn	05:23
Sun	15:24	Jupiter	06:43

Aspects

Moon square Sedna
Moon conjunct Venus
Moon conjunct Pallas
Moon sextile Mercury
Mercury sextile Pallas
Jupiter sextile Saturn
Jupiter opposite Uranus
Saturn square Chiron
Saturn trine Eris
Uranus trine Juno
Ceres conjunct Eris

Planets	00:00 am	Moon
		00.00 am - 07 pis 37
Sun	12 cap 47	02.00 am - 08 pis 43
Mercury	01 cap 12	04.00 am - 09 pis 49
Venus	29 aq 39	06.00 am - 10 pis 54
Mars	11 pis 02	08.00 am - 12 pis 00
Jupiter	21 lib 21	10.00 am - 13 pis 06
Saturn	21 sag 35	12.00 pm - 14 pis 12
Uranus	20 ar 33	14.00 pm - 15 pis 18
Neptune	09 pis 46	16.00 pm - 16 pis 25
Pluto	17 cap 00	18.00 pm - 17 pis 31
		20.00 pm - 18 pis 38
Oob		22.00 pm - 19 pis 44

Tuesday 3rd January

Planetary Directions

Venus into Pisces
07:47

Retrograde Planets

Mercury, Vesta, Eris, Makemake, Orcus, Sedna

Asteroids		Dwarf Planets	
Juno	19 sag 46	Eris	22 ar 32
Vesta	01 leo 52	Haumea	24 lib 37
Pallas	01 pis 38	Makemake	03 lib 52
Ceres	22 ar 53	Salacia	28 pis 54
Chiron	21 pis 09	Orcus	09 vir 01
N Node	04 vir 29	Quaoar	29 sag 24
S Node	04 pis 29	Sedna	25 tau 11

Moon Phase: Crescent
Sunrise: 08:06 GMT
Sunset: 16:05
Moonrise: 10:45
Moonset: 22:03
Voc start:
Voc end:

Planetary and Angelic Hours			
Mars	08:03	Saturn	16:06
Sun	08:43	Jupiter	17:25
Venus	09:23	Mars	18:45
Mercury	10:03	Sun	20:05
Moon	10:44	Venus	21:25
Saturn	11:24	Mercury	22:44
Jupiter	12:04	Moon	00:04
Mars	12:44	Saturn	01:24
Sun	13:25	Jupiter	02:44
Venus	14:05	Mars	04:03
Mercury	14:45	Sun	05:23
Moon	15:25	Venus	06:43

Aspects

Moon conj. Neptune
Moon conjunct Mars
Sun sextile Moon
Moon sextile Pluto
Mercury sextile Venus
Moon square Juno
Moon square Saturn
Moon conjunct Chiron
Jupiter sextile Saturn
Jupiter opposite Uranus
Saturn square Chiron
Saturn trine Eris
Uranus trine Juno
Ceres conjunct Eris

Planets	00:00 am	Moon
Sun	13 cap 48	00.00 am - 20 pis 51
Mercury	00 cap 23	02.00 am - 21 pis 58
Venus	00 pis 43	04.00 am - 23 pis 05
Mars	11 pis 47	06.00 am - 24 pis 12
Jupiter	21 lib 27	08.00 am - 15 pis 19
Saturn	21 sag 42	10.00 am - 26 pis 26
Uranus	20 ar 34	12.00 pm - 27 pis 33
Neptune	09 pis 48	14.00 pm - 28 pis 41
Pluto	17 cap 02	16.00 pm - 29 pis 48
		18.00 pm - 00 ar 56
Oob		20.00 pm - 02 ar 04
		22.00 pm - 03 ar 12

Wednesday 4th January

Planetary Directions

Mercury rx into Sag 14:17
Moon into Aries 16:20

Retrograde Planets

Mercury, Vesta, Eris, Makemake, Orcus, Sedna

Asteroids		Dwarf Planets	
Juno	20 sag 07	Eris	22 ar 32
Vesta	01 leo 38	Haumea	24 lib 38
Pallas	01 pis 55	Makemake	03 lib 51
Ceres	23 ar 02	Salacia	28 pis 55
Chiron	21 pis 11	Orcus	09 vir 00
N Node	04 vir 30	Quaoar	29 sag 26
S Node	04 pis 30	Sedna	25 tau 11

Moon Phase: Crescent
Sunrise: 08:05 GMT
Sunset: 16:06
Moonrise: 11:11
Moonset: 23:15
Voc start: 16:14
Voc end: 16:19

Planetary and Angelic Hours			
Mercury	08:02	Sun	16:07
Moon	08:43	Venus	17:26
Saturn	09:23	Mercury	18:46
Jupiter	10:04	Moon	20:06
Mars	10:44	Saturn	21:25
Sun	11:24	Jupiter	22:45
Venus	12:05	Mars	00:05
Mercury	12:45	Sun	01:24
Moon	13:25	Venus	02:44
Saturn	14:06	Mercury	04:03
Jupiter	14:46	Moon	05:23
Mars	15:26	Saturn	06:43

Aspects

Moon conjunct Chiron
Moon square Saturn
Moon sextile Sedna
Moon square Mercury
Moon trine Vesta
Venus conjunct Pallas
Jupiter sextile Saturn
Jupiter opposite Uranus
Jupiter opposite Eris
Saturn square Chiron
Saturn trine Eris
Uranus trine Juno
Chiron square Juno
Ceres conjunct Eris

Planets	00:00 am	Moon
Sun	14 cap 49	00.00 am - 04 ar 20
Mercury	29 sag 45	02.00 am - 05 ar 28
Venus	01 pis 47	04.00 am - 06 ar 36
Mars	12 pis 32	06.00 am - 07 ar 45
Jupiter	21 lib 32	08.00 am - 08 ar 53
Saturn	21 sag 49	10.00 am - 10 ar 02
Uranus	20 ar 34	12.00 pm - 11 ar 11
Neptune	09 pis 49	14.00 pm - 12 ar 20
Pluto	17 cap 04	16.00 pm - 13 ar 29
		18.00 pm - 14 ar 38
Oob		20.00 pm - 15 ar 47
		22.00 pm - 16 ar 57

Thursday 5th January

Planetary Directions

Retrograde Planets

Mercury, Vesta, Eris, Makemake, Orcus, Sedna

Asteroids		Dwarf Planets	
Juno	20 sag 27	Eris	22 ar 32
Vesta	01 leo 24	Haumea	24 lib 38
Pallas	02 pis 12	Makemake	03 lib 51
Ceres	23 ar 11	Salacia	28 pis 55
Chiron	21 pis 13	Orcus	09 vir 00
N Node	04 vir 31	Quaoar	29 sag 28
S Node	04 pis 31	Sedna	25 tau 11

First Quarter: 19:47
Sunrise: 08:05 GMT
Sunset: 16:07
Moonrise: 11:37
Moonset: None
Voc start:
Voc end:

Planetary and Angelic Hours			
Jupiter	08:02	Moon	16:08
Mars	08:43	Saturn	17:27
Sun	09:23	Jupiter	18:47
Venus	10:04	Mars	20:06
Mercury	10:44	Sun	21:26
Moon	11:25	Venus	22:45
Saturn	12:05	Mercury	00:05
Jupiter	12:46	Moon	01:24
Mars	13:26	Saturn	02:44
Sun	14:07	Jupiter	04:03
Venus	14:47	Mars	05:23
Mercury	15:28	Sun	06:42

Aspects

Uranus trine Juno
Venus conjunct Pallas
Sun square Moon
Moon square Pluto
Jupiter sextile Saturn
Jupiter sextile Juno
Jupiter opposite Eris
Saturn square Chiron
Saturn trine Eris
Chiron square Juno
Ceres conjunct Eris

Planets	00:00 am	Moon
Sun	15 cap 51	00.00 am - 18 ar 06
Mercury	29 sag 17	02.00 am - 19 ar 16
Venus	02 pis 51	04.00 am - 20 ar 26
Mars	13 pis 17	06.00 am - 21 ar 36
Jupiter	21 lib 38	08.00 am - 22 ar 46
Saturn	21 sag 56	10.00 am - 23 ar 56
Uranus	20 ar 34	12.00 pm - 25 ar 06
Neptune	09 pis 51	14.00 pm - 26 ar 17
Pluto	17 cap 06	16.00 pm - 27 ar 27
		18.00 pm - 28 ar 38
Oob		20.00 pm - 29 ar 49
		22.00 pm - 01 tau 00

Friday 6th January

Planetary Directions

Moon into Taurus 20:18

Retrograde Planets

Mercury, Vesta, Eris, Makemake, Orcus, Sedna

Asteroids		Dwarf Planets	
Juno	20 sag 47	Eris	22 ar 32
Vesta	01 leo 10	Haumea	24 lib 39
Pallas	02 pis 29	Makemake	03 lib 51
Ceres	23 ar 20	Salacia	28 pis 56
Chiron	21 pis 15	Orcus	08 vir 59
N Node	04 vir 31	Quaoar	29 sag 28
S Node	04 pis 31	Sedna	25 tau 10

Moon Phase: Gibbous
Sunrise: 08:05 GMT
Sunset: 16:08
Moonrise: 12:04
Moonset: 00:29
Voc start: 18:41
Voc end: 20:17

Planetary and Angelic Hours

Venus	08:02	Mars	16:09
Mercury	08:42	Sun	17:29
Moon	09:23	Venus	18:48
Saturn	10:04	Mercury	20:07
Jupiter	10:44	Moon	21:27
Mars	11:25	Saturn	22:46
Sun	12:06	Jupiter	00:05
Venus	12:46	Mars	01:25
Mercury	13:27	Sun	02:44
Moon	14:07	Venus	04:03
Saturn	14:48	Mercury	05:23
Jupiter	15:29	Moon	06:42

12th Night - Epiphany

Aspects

Moon conjunct Uranus
Moon trine Juno
Moon opposite Jupiter
Moon trine Saturn
Moon conjunct Eris
Moon conjunct Ceres
Moon trine Mercury
Moon square Vesta
Moon sextile Pallas
Sun conjunct Pluto
Jupiter sextile Saturn
Jupiter sextile Juno
Jupiter opposite Eris
Saturn square Chiron
Chiron square Juno

Planets	00:00 am	Moon
Sun	16 cap 52	00.00 am - 02 tau 11
Mercury	28 sag 59	02.00 am - 03 tau 22
Venus	03 pis 54	04.00 am - 04 tau 33
Mars	14 pis 03	06.00 am - 05 tau 45
Jupiter	21 lib 43	08.00 am - 06 tau 56
Saturn	22 sag 02	10.00 am - 08 tau 08
Uranus	20 ar 35	12.00 pm - 09 tau 20
Neptune	09 pis 52	14.00 pm - 10 tau 32
Pluto	17 cap 08	16.00 pm - 11 tau 44
		18.00 pm - 12 tau 56
		20.00 pm - 14 tau 08
Oob		22.00 pm - 15 tau 20

Saturday 7th January

Retrograde Planets

Mercury, Vesta, Eris, Makemake, Orcus, Sedna

Asteroids		Dwarf Planets	
Juno	21 sag 07	Eris	22 ar 32
Vesta	00 leo 56	Haumea	24 lib 39
Pallas	02 pis 46	Makemake	03 lib 51
Ceres	23 ar 30	Salacia	28 pis 57
Chiron	21 Pis 17	Orcus	08 vir 58
N Node	04 vir 30	Quaoar	29 sag 31
S Node	04 pis 30	Sedna	25 tau 10

Moon Phase: Gibbous
Sunrise: 08:04 GMT
Sunset: 16:09
Moonrise: 12:34
Moonset: 01:45
Voc start:
Voc end:

Planetary and Angelic Hours

Saturn	08:02	Mercury	16:10
Jupiter	08:42	Moon	17:30
Mars	09:23	Saturn	18:49
Sun	10:04	Jupiter	20:08
Venus	10:45	Mars	21:27
Mercury	11:25	Sun	22:47
Moon	12:06	Venus	00:06
Saturn	12:47	Mercury	01:25
Jupiter	13:27	Moon	02:44
Mars	14:08	Saturn	04:03
Sun	14:49	Jupiter	05:23
Venus	15:30	Mars	06:42

Aspects

Moon sextile Pallas
Moon sextile Venus
Moon sextile Neptune
Moon sextile Mars
Moon trine Pluto
Sun conjunct Pluto
Jupiter sextile Saturn
Jupiter sextile Juno
Jupiter opposite Eris
Saturn conjunct Juno
Saturn square Chiron
Saturn trine Eris
Uranus trine Juno
Chiron square Juno

Planets	00:00 am	Moon
		00.00 am - 16 tau 33
Sun	17 cap 53	02.00 am - 17 tau 45
Mercury	28 sag 51	04.00 am - 18 tau 58
Venus	04 pis 57	06.00 am - 20 tau 11
Mars	14 pis 48	08.00 am - 21 tau 24
Jupiter	21 lib 49	10.00 am - 22 tau 36
Saturn	22 sag 09	12.00 pm - 23 tau 49
Uranus	20 ar 35	14.00 pm - 25 tau 03
Neptune	09 pis 54	16.00 pm - 26 tau 16
Pluto	17 cap 10	18.00 pm - 27 tau 29
		20.00 pm - 28 tau 42
Oob		22.00 pm - 29 tau 56

Sunday 8th January

Planetary Directions

Mercury direct
28 sag 50 at 09:43
Moon into Gemini
22:07

Retrograde Planets

Vesta, Eris, Makemake, Orcus, Sedna

Asteroids		Dwarf Planets	
Juno	21 sag 27	Eris	22 ar 32
Vesta	00 leo 41	Haumea	24 lib 39
Pallas	03 pis 04	Makemake	03 lib 51
Ceres	23 ar 40	Salacia	28 pis 57
Chiron	21 pis 19	Orcus	08 vir 58
N Node	04 vir 27	Quaoar	29 sag 32
S Node	04 pis 27	Sedna	25 tau 10

Moon Phase: Gibbous
Sunrise: 08:04 GMT
Sunset: 16:11
Moonrise: 13:09
Moonset: 03:02
Voc start: 02:22
Voc end: 22:00

Planetary and Angelic Hours

Sun	08:01	Jupiter	16:12
Venus	08:42	Mars	17:31
Mercury	09:23	Sun	18:50
Moon	10:04	Venus	20:09
Saturn	10:45	Mercury	21:18
Jupiter	11:26	Moon	22:47
Mars	12:06	Saturn	00:06
Sun	12:47	Jupiter	01:25
Venus	13:28	Mars	02:44
Mercury	14:09	Sun	04:03
Moon	14:50	Venus	05:22
Saturn	15:31	Mercury	06:42

Aspects

Moon trine Pluto
Sun trine Moon
Moon sextile Chiron
Moon conjunct Sedna
Moon sextile Vesta
Jupiter sextile Saturn
Jupiter sextile Juno
Jupiter opposite Eris
Saturn square Chiron
Saturn conjunct Juno
Saturn trine Eris
Chiron square Juno
Juno trine Eris

Planets	**00:00 am**	**Moon**
Sun	18 cap 54	00.00 am - 01 gem 09
Mercury	28 sag 52	02.00 am - 02 gem 23
Venus	06 pis 00	04.00 am - 03 gem 36
Mars	15 pis 33	06.00 am - 04 gem 50
Jupiter	21 lib 54	08.00 am - 06 gem 04
Saturn	22 sag 15	10.00 am - 07 gem 18
Uranus	20 ar 36	12.00 pm - 08 gem 31
Neptune	09 pis 55	14.00 pm - 09 gem 45
Pluto	17 cap 13	16.00 pm - 10 gem 59
		18.00 pm - 12 gem 13
Oob		20.00 pm - 13 gem 27
		22.00 pm - 14 gem 41

Monday 9th January

Planetary Directions

Eris direct
22 ar 32 at 16:49

Retrograde Planets

Vesta, Eris, Makemake, Orcus, Sedna

Asteroids		**Dwarf Planets**	
Juno	21 sag 48	Eris	22 ar 32
Vesta	00 leo 26	Haumea	24 lib 39
Pallas	03 pis 21	Makemake	03 lib 51
Ceres	23 ar 50	Salacia	28 pis 57
Chiron	21 pis 21	Orcus	08 vir 58
N Node	04 vir 22	Quaoar	29 sag 32
S Node	04 pis 22	Sedna	25 tau 10

Moon Phase: Gibbous
Sunrise: 08:03 GMT
Sunset: 16:12
Moonrise: 13:50
Moonset: 04:19
Voc start:
Voc end:

Planetary and Angelic Hours

Moon	08:01	Venus	16:13
Saturn	08:42	Mercury	17:32
Jupiter	09:23	Moon	18:51
Mars	10:04	Saturn	20:10
Sun	10:45	Jupiter	21:29
Venus	11:26	Mars	22:48
Mercury	12:07	Sun	00:07
Moon	12:48	Venus	01:26
Saturn	13:29	Mercury	02:44
Jupiter	14:10	Moon	04:03
Mars	14:51	Saturn	05:22
Sun	15:32	Jupiter	06:41

Aspects

Moon square Pallas
Moon square Venus
Moon square Neptune
Moon square Mars
Sun square Uranus
Mars sextile Pluto
Jupiter sextile Saturn
Jupiter sextile Juno
Jupiter opposite Eris
Saturn square Chiron
Saturn conjunct Juno
Saturn trine Eris
Chiron square Juno
Juno trine Eris

Planets	**00:00 am**	**Moon**
Sun	19 cap 55	00.00 am - 15 gem 55
Mercury	29 sag 01	02.00 am - 17 gem 09
Venus	07 pis 02	04.00 am - 18 gem 23
Mars	16 pis 18	06.00 am - 19 gem 37
Jupiter	21 lib 59	08.00 am - 20 gem 51
Saturn	22 sag 22	10.00 am - 22 gem 05
Uranus	20 ar 36	12.00 pm - 23 gem 19
Neptune	09 pis 57	14.00 pm - 24 gem 34
Pluto	17 cap 15	16.00 pm - 25 gem 48
		18.00 pm - 27 gem 02
Oob		20.00 pm - 28 gem 16
		22.00 pm - 29 gem 30

Tuesday 10th January

Planetary directions

Vesta rx into Cancer
18:21
Moon into Cancer
22:49

Retrograde Planets

Vesta, Makemake,
Orcus, Sedna

Asteroids		**Dwarf Planets**	
Juno	22 sag 08	Eris	22 ar 32
Vesta	00 leo 11	Haumea	24 lib 40
Pallas	03 pis 39	Makemake	03 lib 51
Ceres	24 ar 00	Salacia	28 pis 59
Chiron	21 pis 23	Orcus	08 vir 56
N Node	04 vir 15	Quaoar	29 sag 35
S Node	04 pis 15	Sedna	25 tau 09

Moon Phase: Gibbous
Sunrise: 08:03 GMT
Sunset: 16:14
Moonrise: 14:39
Moonset: 05:32
Voc start: 21:38
Voc end: 22:48

Planetary and Angelic Hours			
Mars	08:00	Saturn	16:14
Sun	08:41	Jupiter	17:33
Venus	09:23	Mars	18:52
Mercury	10:04	Sun	20:11
Moon	10:45	Venus	21:29
Saturn	11:26	Mercury	22:48
Jupiter	12:07	Moon	00:07
Mars	12:48	Saturn	01:26
Sun	13:30	Jupiter	02:45
Venus	14:11	Mars	04:03
Mercury	14:52	Sun	05:22
Moon	15:33	Venus	06:41

Aspects

Moon square Mars
Moon sextile Uranus
Moon square Chiron
Moon trine Jupiter
Moon opposite Juno
Moon opposite Saturn
Moon sextile Eris
Moon opp. Mercury
Sun square Uranus
Sun sextile Chiron
Mars sextile Pluto
Jupiter sextile Saturn
Jupiter sextile Juno
Jupiter opposite Eris
Saturn trine Eris
Juno trine Eris

Wednesday 11th January

Planets	00:00 am	Moon
Sun	20 cap 56	00.00 am - 00 can 43
Mercury	29 sag 18	02.00 am - 01 can 57
Venus	08 pis 04	04.00 am - 03 can 11
Mars	17 pis 04	06.00 am - 04 can 25
Jupiter	22 lib 04	08.00 am - 05 can 39
Saturn	22 sag 29	10.00 am - 06 can 52
Uranus	20 ar 37	12.00 pm - 08 can 06
Neptune	09 pis 59	14.00 pm - 09 can 19
Pluto	17 cap 17	16.00 pm - 10 can 33
		18.00 pm - 11 can 46
Oob		20.00 pm - 13 can 00
		22.00 pm - 14 can 13

Retrograde Planets

Vesta, Makemake, Orcus, Sedna

Asteroids		Dwarf Planets	
Juno	22 sag 28	Eris	22 ar 32
Vesta	29 can 56	Haumea	24 lib 40
Pallas	03 pis 56	Makemake	03 lib 51
Ceres	24 ar 11	Salacia	28 pis 59
Chiron	21 pis 25	Orcus	08 vir 56
N Node	04 vir 08	Quaoar	29 sag 37
S Node	04 pis 08	Sedna	25 tau 09

Moon Phase: Gibbous
Sunrise: 08:02 GMT
Sunset: 16:15
Moonrise: 15:38
Moonset: 06:38
Voc start:
Voc end:

Planetary and Angelic Hours			
Mercury	08:00	Sun	16:16
Moon	08:41	Venus	17:34
Saturn	09:22	Mercury	18:53
Jupiter	10:04	Moon	20:12
Mars	10:45	Saturn	21:30
Sun	11:26	Jupiter	22:49
Venus	12:08	Mars	00:07
Mercury	12:49	Sun	01:26
Moon	13:30	Venus	02;45
Saturn	14:12	Mercury	04:03
Jupiter	14:53	Moon	05:22
Mars	15:34	Saturn	06:40

Aspects

Saturn conjunct Juno
Juno trine Eris
Moon trine Pallas
Mars sextile Pluto
Saturn trine Eris
Sun sextile Chiron
Moon trine Venus
Moon trine Neptune
Sun square Jupiter
Sun square Eris
Venus conj. Neptune
Jupiter sextile Saturn
Jupiter sextile Juno
Jupiter opposite Eris

Planets	00:00 am	Moon
Sun	21 cap 57	00.00 am - 15 can 26
Mercury	29 sag 42	02.00 am - 16 can 39
Venus	09 pis 06	04.00 am - 17 can 52
Mars	17 pis 49	06.00 am - 19 can 05
Jupiter	22 lib 09	08.00 am - 20 can 17
Saturn	22 sag 35	10.00 am - 21 can 30
Uranus	20 ar 38	12.00 pm - 22 can 43
Neptune	10 pis 00	14.00 pm - 23 can 55
Pluto	17 cap 19	16.00 pm - 25 can 07
		18.00 pm - 26 can 19
Oob		20.00 pm - 27 can 31
		22.00 pm - 28 can 43

Thursday 12th January

Planetary Directions

Mercury re-enters Cap 14:04

Retrograde Planets

Vesta, Makemake, Orcus, Sedna

Asteroids		Dwarf Planets	
Juno	22 sag 48	Eris	22 ar 32
Vesta	29 can 41	Haumea	24 lib 41
Pallas	04 pis 14	Makemake	03 lib 50
Ceres	24 ar 22	Salacia	29 pis 00
Chiron	21 pis 27	Orcus	08 vir 55
N Node	04 vir 01	Quaoar	29 sag 38
S Node	04 pis 01	Sedna	25 tau 08

Full Moon: 11:35
Sunrise: 08:01 GMT
Sunset: 16:16
Moonrise: 16:44
Moonset: 07:35
Voc start: 11:33
Voc end:

Planetary and Angelic Hours			
Jupiter	07:59	Moon	16:17
Mars	08:40	Saturn	17:36
Sun	09:22	Jupiter	18:54
Venus	10:04	Mars	20:13
Mercury	10:45	Sun	21:31
Moon	11:27	Venus	22:49
Saturn	12:08	Mercury	00:08
Jupiter	12:50	Moon	01:26
Mars	13:31	Saturn	02:45
Sun	14:13	Jupiter	04:03
Venus	14:54	Mars	05:21
Mercury	15:36	Sun	06:40

Aspects

Moon opposite Pluto
Moon trine Mars
Sun square Jupiter
Moon square Uranus
Moon trine Chiron
Moon square Jupiter
Sun opposite Moon
Moon square Eris
Sun square Eris
Moon square Ceres
Moon sextile Sedna
Venus conj. Neptune
Moon conjunct Vesta
Jupiter sextile Saturn
Jupiter opposite Eris
Saturn trine Eris
Saturn conjunct Juno

Planets	00:00 am	Moon
		00.00 am - 29 can 55
Sun	22 cap 59	02.00 am - 01 leo 06
Mercury	00 cap 13	04.00 am - 02 leo 18
Venus	10 pis 07	06.00 am - 03 leo 29
Mars	18 pis 34	08.00 am - 04 leo 40
Jupiter	22 lib 13	10.00 am - 05 leo 51
Saturn	22 sag 42	12.00 pm - 07 leo 02
Uranus	20 ar 38	14.00 pm - 08 leo 13
Neptune	10 pis 02	16.00 pm - 09 leo 23
Pluto	17 cap 21	18.00 pm - 10 leo 34
		20.00 pm - 22 leo 44
Oob		22.00 pm - 12 leo 54

Friday 13th January

Planetary Directions

Moon into Leo 00:08

Retrograde Planets

Vesta, Makemake, Orcus, Sedna

Asteroids		Dwarf Planets	
Juno	23 sag 08	Eris	22 ar 32
Vesta	29 can 25	Haumea	24 lib 41
Pallas	04 pis 32	Makemake	03 lib 50
Ceres	24 ar 34	Salacia	29 pis 01
Chiron	21 pis 29	Orcus	08 vir 54
N Node	03 vir 56	Quaoar	29 sag 40
S Node	03 pis 56	Sedna	25 tau 08

Phase: Disseminating
Sunrise: 08:01 GMT
Sunset: 16:18
Moonrise: 17:55
Moonset: 08:22
Voc start: 00:07
Voc end:

Planetary and Angelic Hours			
Venus	07:58	Mars	16:19
Mercury	08:40	Sun	17:37
Moon	09:22	Venus	18:55
Saturn	10:03	Mercury	20:13
Jupiter	10:45	Moon	21:32
Mars	11:27	Saturn	22:50
Sun	12:08	Jupiter	00:08
Venus	12:50	Mars	01:26
Mercury	13:32	Sun	02:45
Moon	14:14	Venus	04:03
Saturn	14:55	Mercury	05:21
Jupiter	15:37	Moon	06:39

Aspects

Sun square Ceres
Jupiter sextile Saturn
Jupiter opposite Eris
Saturn conjunct Juno
Saturn trine Eris
Juno trine Eris

Planets	00:00 am	Moon
Sun	24 cap 00	00.00 am - 14 leo 04
Mercury	00 cap 49	02.00 am - 15 leo 14
Venus	11 pis 08	04.00 am - 16 leo 23
Mars	19 pis 19	06.00 am - 17 leo 32
Jupiter	22 lib 17	08.00 am - 18 leo 42
Saturn	22 sag 48	10.00 am - 19 leo 51
Uranus	20 ar 39	12.00 pm - 20 leo 59
Neptune	10 pis 04	14.00 pm - 22 leo 08
Pluto	17 cap 23	16.00 pm - 23 leo 17
		18.00 pm - 24 leo 25
Oob		20.00 pm - 25 leo 33
		22.00 pm - 26 leo 41

Saturday 14th January

Retrograde Planets
Vesta, Makemake, Orcus, Sedna

Asteroids		Dwarf Planets	
Juno	23 sag 28	Eris	22 ar 32
Vesta	29 can 09	Haumea	24 lib 41
Pallas	04 pis 50	Makemake	03 lib 50
Ceres	24 ar 45	Salacia	29 pis 02
Chiron	21 pis 31	Orcus	08 vir 53
N Node	03 vir 52	Quaoar	29 sag 41
S Node	03 pis 52	Sedna	25 tau 08

Phase: Disseminating
Sunrise: 08:00 GMT
Sunset: 16:19
Moonrise: 19:07
Moonset: 09:01
Voc start:
Voc end: 15:16

Planetary and Angelic Hours			
Saturn	07:58	Mercury	16:20
Jupiter	08:39	Moon	17:38
Mars	09:21	Saturn	18:56
Sun	10:03	Jupiter	20:14
Venus	10:45	Mars	21:32
Mercury	11:27	Sun	22:50
Moon	12:09	Venus	00:08
Saturn	12:51	Mercury	01:27
Jupiter	13:33	Moon	02:45
Mars	14:15	Saturn	04:03
Sun	14:56	Jupiter	05:21
Venus	15:38	Mars	06:39

Aspects

Moon trine Uranus
Moon sextile Jupiter
Moon trine Eris
Moon trine Saturn
Moon trine Juno
Moon trine Ceres
Moon square Sedna
Sun square Ceres
Sun trine Sedna
Jupiter sextile Saturn
Jupiter opposite Eris
Saturn conjunct Juno
Saturn trine Eris

Planets	**00:00 am**	**Moon**
Sun	25 cap 01	00.00 am - 27 leo 49
Mercury	01 cap 31	02.00 am - 28 leo 56
Venus	12 pis 08	04.00 am - 00 vir 04
Mars	20 pis 04	06.00 am - 01 vir 11
Jupiter	22 lib 22	08.00 am - 02 vir 18
Saturn	22 sag 54	10.00 am - 03 vir 25
Uranus	20 ar 40	12.00 pm - 04 vir 32
Neptune	10 pis 05	14.00 pm - 05 vir 38
Pluto	17 cap 25	16.00 pm - 06 vir 45
		18.00 pm - 07 vir 51
Oob		20.00 pm - 08 vir 57
		22.00 pm - 10 vir 03

Sunday 15th January

Planetary Directions

Moon into Virgo 03:53

Retrograde Planets

Vesta, Makemake, Orcus, Sedna

Asteroids		**Dwarf Planets**	
Juno	23 sag 47	Eris	22 ar 32
Vesta	28 can 54	Haumea	24 lib 41
Pallas	05 pis 08	Makemake	03 lib 49
Ceres	24 ar 57	Salacia	29 pis 03
Chiron	21 pis 34	Orcus	08 vir 52
N Node	03 vir 51	Quaoar	29 sag 44
S Node	03 pis 51	Sedna	25 tau 07

Phase: Disseminating
Sunrise: 07:59 GMT
Sunset: 16:21
Moonrise: 20:19
Moonset: 09:33
Voc start:
Voc end: 03:52

Planetary and Angelic Hours

Sun	07:57	Jupiter	16:22
Venus	08:39	Mars	17:40
Mercury	09:21	Sun	18:57
Moon	10:03	Venus	20:15
Saturn	10:45	Mercury	21:33
Jupiter	11:27	Moon	22:51
Mars	12:09	Saturn	00:09
Sun	12:51	Jupiter	01:27
Venus	13:33	Mars	02:45
Mercury	14:15	Sun	04:02
Moon	14:58	Venus	05:20
Saturn	15:40	Mercury	06:38

Aspects

Sun trine Sedna
Moon trine Mercury
Moon opposite Pallas
Moon opp. Neptune
Sun square Ceres
Mars conjunct Chiron
Jupiter sextile Saturn
Jupiter opposite Eris
Saturn trine Eris

Planets	**00:00 am**	**Moon**
		00.00 am - 11 vir 08
Sun	26 cap 02	02.00 am - 12 vir 14
Mercury	02 cap 17	04.00 am - 13 vir 19
Venus	13 pis 08	06.00 am - 14 vir 24
Mars	20 pis 49	08.00 am - 15 vir 29
Jupiter	22 lib 26	10.00 am - 16 vir 34
Saturn	23 sag 01	12.00 pm - 17 vir 39
Uranus	20 ar 41	14.00 pm - 18 vir 43
Neptune	10 pis 07	16.00 pm - 19 vir 48
Pluto	17 cap 27	18.00 pm - 20 vir 52
		20.00 pm - 21 vir 56
Oob		22.00 pm - 23 vir 00

Monday 16th January

Retrograde Planets

Vesta, Makemake, Orcus, Sedna

Asteroids		**Dwarf Planets**	
Juno	24 sag 07	Eris	22 ar 32
Vesta	28 can 38	Haumea	24 lib 41
Pallas	05 pis 26	Makemake	03 lib 49
Ceres	25 ar 09	Salacia	29 pis 04
Chiron	21 pis 36	Orcus	08 vir 51
N Node	03 vir 51	Quaoar	29 sag 46
S Node	03 pis 51	Sedna	25 tau 07

Phase: Disseminating
Sunrise: 07:58 GMT
Sunset: 16:23
Moonrise: 21:28
Moonset: 10:00
Voc start:
Voc end:

Planetary and Angelic Hours			
Moon	07:56	Venus	16:23
Saturn	08:38	Mercury	17:41
Jupiter	09:20	Moon	18:59
Mars	10:03	Saturn	20:16
Sun	10:45	Jupiter	21:34
Venus	11:27	Mars	22:52
Mercury	12:10	Sun	00:09
Moon	12:52	Venus	01:27
Saturn	13:34	Mercury	02:44
Jupiter	14:16	Moon	04:02
Mars	14:59	Saturn	05:20
Sun	15:41	Jupiter	06:37

Aspects

Moon opposite Venus
Moon trine Pluto
Moon opposite Mars
Moon opposite Chiron
Moon square Saturn
Moon square Juno
Mars conjunct Chiron
Jupiter sextile Saturn
Jupiter oposite Eris
Saturn trine Eris
Ceres trine Juno

Planets	00:00 am	Moon
		00.00 am - 24 vir 03
Sun	27 cap 03	02.00 am - 25 vir 07
Mercury	03 cap 08	04.00 am - 26 vir 10
Venus	14 pis 08	06.00 am - 27 vir 14
Mars	21 pis 34	08.00 am - 28 vir 17
Jupiter	22 lib 29	10.00 am - 29 vir 20
Saturn	23 sag 07	12.00 pm - 00 lib 23
Uranus	20 ar 42	14.00 pm - 01 lib 25
Neptune	10 pis 09	16.00 pm - 02 lib 28
Pluto	17 cap 29	18.00 pm - 03 lib 30
		20.00 pm - 04 lib 32
Oob		22.00 pm - 05 lib 35

Tuesday 17th January

Planetary Directions

Moon into Libra 11:16

Retrograde Planets

Vesta, Makemake, Orcus, Sedna

Asteroids		Dwarf Planets	
Juno	24 sag 27	Eris	22 ar 32
Vesta	28 can 22	Haumea	24 lib 42
Pallas	05 pis 44	Makemake	03 lib 49
Ceres	25 ar 21	Salacia	29 pis 05
Chiron	21 pis 38	Orcus	08 vir 50
N Node	03 vir 52	Quaoar	29 sag 47
S Node	03 pis 52	Sedna	25 tau 07

Phase: Disseminating
Sunrise: 07:57 GMT
Sunset: 16:24
Moonrise: 22:35
Moonset: 10:25
Voc start: 06:09
Voc end: 11:15

Planetary and Angelic Hours

Mars	07:55	Saturn	16:25
Sun	08:38	Jupiter	17:42
Venus	09:20	Mars	19:00
Mercury	10:02	Sun	20:17
Moon	10:45	Venus	21:35
Saturn	11:27	Mercury	22:52
Jupiter	12:10	Moon	00:09
Mars	12:52	Saturn	01:27
Sun	13:35	Jupiter	02:44
Venus	14:17	Mars	04:02
Mercury	15:00	Sun	05:19
Moon	15:42	Venus	06:37

Aspects

Moon square Juno
Moon trine Sedna
Mars conjunct Chiron
Sun trine Moon
Moon sextile Vesta
Jupiter opposite Eris
Moon square Mercury
Sun opposite Vesta
Mars square Saturn
Jupiter sextile Saturn
Saturn trine Eris
Ceres trine Juno

Planets	00:00 am	Moon
Sun	28 cap 04	00.00 am - 06 lib 37
Mercury	04 cap 02	02.00 am - 07 lib 39
Venus	15 pis 06	04.00 am - 08 lib 40
Mars	22 pis 19	06.00 am - 09 lib 42
Jupiter	22 lib 33	08.00 am - 10 lib 44
Saturn	23 sag 13	10.00 am - 11 lib 45
Uranus	20 ar 43	12.00 pm - 12 lib 46
Neptune	10 pis 11	14.00 pm - 13 lib 48
Pluto	17 cap 31	16.00 pm - 14 lib 49
		18.00 pm - 15 lib 50
Oob		20.00 pm - 16 lib 51
		22.00 pm - 17 lib 51

Wednesday 18th January

Retrograde Planets

Vesta, Makemake, Orcus, Sedna

Asteroids		Dwarf Planets	
Juno	24 sa 47	Eris	22 ar 32
Vesta	28 can 06	Haumea	24 lib 42
Pallas	06 pis 02	Makemake	03 lib 48
Ceres	25 ar 34	Salacia	29 pis 06
Chiron	21 pis 41	Orcus	08 vir 49
N Node	03 vir 54	Quaoar	29 sag 48
S Node	03 pis 54	Sedna	25 tau 06

Phase: Disseminating
Sunrise: 07:56 GMT
Sunset: 16:26
Moonrise: 23:41
Moonset: 10:49
Voc start:
Voc end:

Planetary and Angelic Hours			
Mercury	07:54	Sun	16:26
Moon	08:37	Venus	17:44
Saturn	09:20	Mercury	19:01
Jupiter	10:02	Moon	20:18
Mars	10:45	Saturn	21:35
Sun	11:28	Jupiter	22:53
Venus	12:10	Mars	00:10
Mercury	12:53	Sun	01:27
Moon	13:36	Venus	02:44
Saturn	14:18	Mercury	04:01
Jupiter	15:01	Moon	05:19
Mars	15:44	Saturn	06:36

Aspects

Sun opposite Vesta
Moon square Pluto
Mars square Saturn
Jupiter sextile Saturn
Jupiter opposite Eris
Saturn trine Eris
Ceres trine Juno

Planets	00:00 am	Moon
Sun	29 cap 05	00.00 am - 18 lib 52
Mercury	05 cap 00	02.00 am - 19 lib 53
Venus	16 pis 05	04.00 am - 20 lib 53
Mars	23 pis 05	06.00 am - 21 lib 54
Jupiter	22 lib 37	08.00 am - 22 lib 54
Saturn	23 sag 20	10.00 am - 23 lib 55
Uranus	20 ar 44	12.00 pm - 24 lib 55
Neptune	10 pis 12	14.00 pm - 25 lib 55
Pluto	17 cap 33	16.00 pm - 26 lib 55
		18.00 pm - 27 lib 55
		20.00 pm - 28 lib 55
Oob		22.00 pm - 29 lib 55

Thursday 19th January

Planetary Directions

Sun into Aq at 21:24
Moon into Scorpio 22:10

Retrograde Planets

Vesta, Makemake, Orcus, Sedna

Asteroids		Dwarf Planets	
Juno	25 sag 06	Eris	22 ar 32
Vesta	27 can 50	Haumea	24 lib 42
Pallas	06 pis 20	Makemake	03 lib 48
Ceres	25 ar 47	Salacia	29 pis 07
Chiron	21 pis 43	Orcus	08 vir 48
N Node	03 vir 55	Quaoar	29 sag 50
S Node	03 pis 55	Sedna	25 tau 06

Last Quarter: 22:14
Sunrise: 07:55 GMT
Sunset: 16:27
Moonrise: None
Moonset: 11:12
Voc start: 08:54
Voc end: 22:09

Planetary and Angelic Hours			
Jupiter	07:53	Moon	16:28
Mars	08:36	Saturn	17:45
Sun	09:19	Jupiter	19:02
Venus	10:02	Mars	20:19
Mercury	10:45	Sun	21:36
Moon	11:28	Venus	22:53
Saturn	12:11	Mercury	00:10
Jupiter	12:53	Moon	01:27
Mars	13:36	Saturn	02:44
Sun	14:19	Jupiter	04:01
Venus	15:02	Mars	05:18
Mercury	15:45	Sun	06:35

Aspects

Moon opposite Uranus
Moon opposite Eris
Moon conjunct Jupiter
Moon sextile Saturn
Mars square Saturn
Moon sextile Juno
Moon opposite Ceres
Moon square Vesta
Sun square Moon
Mercury sextile Pallas
Venus sextile Pluto
Jupiter sextile Saturn
Jupiter opposite Eris
Saturn trine Eris
Ceres trine Juno

Planets	00:00 am	Moon
Sun	00 aq 06	00.00 am - 00 sco 55
Mercury	06 cap 01	02.00 am - 01 sco 55
Venus	17 pis 03	04.00 am - 02 sco 54
Mars	23 pis 50	06.00 am - 03 sco 54
Jupiter	22 lib 40	08.00 am - 04 sco 54
Saturn	23 sag 26	10.00 am - 05 sco 53
Uranus	20 ar 45	12.00 pm - 06 sco 53
Neptune	10 pis 14	14.00 pm - 07 sco 52
Pluto	17 cap 35	16.00 pm - 08 sco 52
		18.00 pm - 09 sco 51
Oob		20.00 pm - 10 sco 51
		22.00 pm - 11 sco 50

Friday 20th January

Retrograde Planets

Vesta, Makemake, Orcus, Sedna

Asteroids		Dwarf Planets	
Juno	25 sag 26	Eris	22 ar 32
Vesta	27 can 34	Haumea	24 lib 42
Pallas	06 pis 39	Makemake	03 lib 47
Ceres	26 ar 00	Salacia	29 pis 08
Chiron	21 pis 46	Orcus	08 vir 47
N Node	03 vir 56	Quaoar	29 sag 51
S Node	03 pis 56	Sedna	25 tau 06

Moon Phase: Balsamic
Sunrise: 07:54 GMT
Sunset: 16:29
Moonrise: 00:44
Moonset: 11:36
Voc start:
Voc end:

Planetary and Angelic Hours			
Venus	07:52	Mars	16:30
Mercury	08:35	Sun	17:46
Moon	09:18	Venus	19:03
Saturn	10:02	Mercury	20:20
Jupiter	10:45	Moon	21:37
Mars	11:28	Saturn	22:54
Sun	12:11	Jupiter	00:10
Venus	12:54	Mars	01:27
Mercury	13:37	Sun	02:44
Moon	14:20	Venus	04:01
Saturn	15:03	Mercury	05:18
Jupiter	15:46	Moon	06:34

Aspects

Moon sextile Mercury
Moon trine Pallas
Venus sextile Pluto
Moon trine Neptune
Mercury sextile Pallas
Mars sextile Sedna
Jupiter sextile Saturn
Jupiter opposite Eris
Saturn trine Eris
Ceres trine Juno

Planets	00:00 am	Moon
		00.00 am - 12 sco 49
Sun	01 aq 07	02.00 am - 13 sco 49
Mercury	07 cap 04	04.00 am - 14 sco 48
Venus	18 pis 00	06.00 am - 15 sco 47
Mars	24 pis 35	08.00 am - 16 sco 46
Jupiter	22 lib 43	10.00 am - 17 sco 46
Saturn	23 sag 32	12.00 pm - 18 sco 45
Uranus	20 ar 46	14.00 pm - 19 sco 44
Neptune	10 pis 16	16.00 pm - 20 sco 44
Pluto	17 cap 37	18.00 pm - 21 sco 43
		20.00 pm - 22 sco 42
Oob		22.00 pm - 23 sco 41

Saturday 21st January

Retrograde Planets

Vesta, Makemake, Orcus, Sedna

Asteroids		Dwarf Planets	
Juno	25 sag 46	Eris	22 ar 32
Vesta	27 can 18	Haumea	24 lib 42
Pallas	06 pis 57	Makemake	03 lib 47
Ceres	26 ar 13	Salacia	29 pis 08
Chiron	21 pis 48	Orcus	08 vir 47
N Node	03 vir 55	Quaoar	29 sag 51
S Node	03 pis 55	Sedna	25 tau 06

Moon Phase: Balsamic
Sunrise: 07:53 GMT
Sunset: 16:31
Moonrise: 01:47
Moonset: 12:02
Voc start:
Voc end:

Planetary and Angelic Hours			
Saturn	07:51	Mercury	16:31
Jupiter	08:34	Moon	17:48
Mars	09:18	Saturn	19:04
Sun	10:01	Jupiter	20:21
Venus	10:44	Mars	21:38
Mercury	11:28	Sun	22:54
Moon	12:11	Venus	00:11
Saturn	12:55	Mercury	01:27
Jupiter	13:38	Moon	02:44
Mars	14:21	Saturn	04:00
Sun	15:05	Jupiter	05:17
Venus	15:48	Mars	06:33

Aspects

Moon sextile Pluto
Moon trine Venus
Mars sextile Sedna
Moon trine Chiron
Moon trine Mars
Moon opposite Sedna
Mercury sextile Pallas
Mars square Juno
Jupiter sextile Saturn
Jupiter opposite Eris
Ceres trine Juno
Ceres square Vesta

Planets	00:00 am	Moon
Sun	02 aq 08	00.00 am - 24 sco 41
Mercury	08 cap 10	02.00 am - 25 sco 40
Venus	18 pis 57	04.00 am - 26 sco 39
Mars	25 pis 20	06.00 am - 27 sco 39
Jupiter	22 lib 46	08.00 am - 28 sco 38
Saturn	23 sag 38	10.00 am - 29 sco 37
Uranus	20 ar 47	12.00 pm - 00 sag 37
Neptune	10 pis 18	14.00 pm - 01 sag 36
Pluto	17 cap 39	16.00 pm - 02 sag 35
		18.00 pm - 03 sag 35
Oob		20.00 pm - 04 sag 34
		22.00 pm - 05 sag 34

Sunday 22nd January

Planetary Directions

Moon into Sag 10:45
Haumea retrograde
24 lib 42 at 12:12

Retrograde Planets

Vesta, Makemake,
Orcus, Sedna

Asteroids		Dwarf Planets	
Juno	26 sag 05	Eris	22 ar 32
Vesta	27 can 02	Haumea	24 lib 42
Pallas	07 pis 16	Makemake	03 lib 47
Ceres	26 ar 27	Salacia	29 pis 09
Chiron	21 pis 51	Orcus	08 vir 47
N Node	03 vir 53	Quaoar	29 sag 53
S Node	03 pis 53	Sedna	25 tau 06

Moon Phase: Balsamic
Sunrise: 07:52 GMT
Sunset: 16:33
Moonrise: 02:48
Moonset: 12:31
Voc start: 01:23
Voc end: 10:44

Planetary and Angelic Hours

Sun	07:50	Jupiter	16:33
Venus	08:34	Mars	17:49
Mercury	09:17	Sun	19:06
Moon	10:01	Venus	20:22
Saturn	10:44	Mercury	21:38
Jupiter	11:28	Moon	22:55
Mars	12:11	Saturn	00:11
Sun	12:55	Jupiter	01:27
Venus	13:39	Mars	02:44
Mercury	14:22	Sun	04:00
Moon	15:06	Venus	05:16
Saturn	15:49	Mercury	06:33

Aspects

Moon opposite Sedna
Moon trine Mars
Moon trine Vesta
Sun sextile Moon
Mars square Juno
Mars trine Vesta
Mars sextile Sedna
Jupiter sextile Saturn
Jupiter opposite Eris
Ceres trine Juno
Ceres square Vesta

Planets	00:00 am	Moon
Sun	03 aq 09	00.00 am - 06 sag 33
Mercury	09 cap 19	02.00 am - 07 sag 33
Venus	19 pis 53	04.00 am - 08 sag 33
Mars	26 pis 04	06.00 am - 09 sag 33
Jupiter	22 lib 49	08.00 am - 10 sag 32
Saturn	23 sag 44	10.00 am - 11 sag 32
Uranus	20 ar 49	12.00 pm - 12 sag 32
Neptune	10 pis 20	14.00 pm - 13 sag 31
Pluto	17 cap 41	16.00 pm - 14 sag 31
		18.00 pm - 15 sag 31
Oob		20.00 pm - 16 sag 31
		22.00 pm - 17 sag 31

Monday 23rd January

Retrograde Planets

Vesta, Haumea, Makemake, Orcus, Sedna

Asteroids		Dwarf Planets	
Juno	26 sag 25	Eris	22 ar 32
Vesta	26 can 47	Haumea	24 lib 42
Pallas	07 pis 35	Makemake	03 lib 46
Ceres	26 ar 40	Salacia	29 pis 10
Chiron	22 pis 53	Orcus	08 vir 46
N Node	03 vir 49	Quaoar	29 sag 54
S Node	03 pis 49	Sedna	25 tau 06

Moon Phase: Balsamic
Sunrise: 07:51 GMT
Sunset: 16:34
Moonrise: 03:48
Moonset: 13:05
Voc start:
Voc end:

Planetary and Angelic Hours			
Moon	07:49	Venus	16:35
Saturn	08:33	Mercury	17:51
Jupiter	09:17	Moon	19:07
Mars	10:00	Saturn	20:23
Sun	10:44	Jupiter	21:39
Venus	11:28	Mars	22:55
Mercury	12:12	Sun	00:11
Moon	12:56	Venus	01:27
Saturn	13:39	Mercury	02:43
Jupiter	14:23	Moon	03:59
Mars	15:07	Saturn	05:16
Sun	15:51	Jupiter	06:32

Aspects

Moon square Pallas
Ceres square Vesta
Moon square Neptune
Mars trine Vesta
Mars square Juno
Mercury sext. Neptune
Jupiter sextile Saturn
Jupiter opposite Eris
Ceres trine Juno

Planets	**00:00 am**	**Moon**
Sun	04 aq 10	00.00 am - 18 sag 32
Mercury	10 cap 29	02.00 am - 19 sag 32
Venus	20 pis 49	04.00 am - 20 sag 32
Mars	26 pis 49	06.00 am - 21 sag 32
Jupiter	22 lib 51	08.00 am - 22 sag 33
Saturn	23 sag 50	10.00 am - 23 sag 33
Uranus	20 ar 50	12.00 pm - 24 sag 34
Neptune	10 pis 22	14.00 pm - 25 sag 34
Pluto	17 cap 43	16.00 pm - 26 sag 35
		18.00 pm - 27 sag 36
Oob		20.00 pm - 28 sag 37
		22.00 pm - 29 sag 38

Tuesday 24th January

Planetary Directions

Moon into Capricorn
22:44

Retrograde Planets

Vesta, Haumea, Makemake, Orcus, Sedna

Asteroids		**Dwarf Planets**	
Juno	26 sag 44	Eris	22 ar 33
Vesta	26 can 31	Haumea	24 lib 42
Pallas	07 pis 53	Makemake	03 lib 46
Ceres	26 ar 54	Salacia	29 pis 11
Chiron	21 pis 56	Orcus	08 vir 45
N Node	03 vir 44	Quaoar	29 sag 55
S Node	03 pis 44	Sedna	25 tau 06

Moon Phase: Balsamic
Sunrise: 07:50 GMT
Sunset: 16:36
Moonrise: 04:45
Moonset: 13:45
Voc start: 17:33
Voc end: 22:43

Planetary and Angelic Hours

Mars	07:48	Saturn	16:36
Sun	08:32	Jupiter	17:52
Venus	09:16	Mars	19:08
Mercury	10:00	Sun	20:24
Moon	10:44	Venus	21:40
Saturn	11:28	Mercury	22:56
Jupiter	12:12	Moon	00:11
Mars	12:56	Saturn	01:27
Sun	13:40	Jupiter	02:43
Venus	14:24	Mars	03:59
Mercury	15:08	Sun	05:15
Moon	15:52	Venus	06:31

Aspects

Moon trine Uranus
Moon square Venus
Moon square Chiron
Moon trine Eris
Moon sextile Jupiter
Moon conjunct Saturn
Moon conjunct Juno
Moon trine Ceres
Moon square Mars
Venus conjunct Chiron
Mars square Juno
Jupiter opposite Eris
Ceres trine Juno
Ceres square Vesta

Planets	00:00 am	Moon
Sun	05 aq 11	00.00 am - 00 cap 38
Mercury	11 cap 41	02.00 am - 01 cap 40
Venus	21 pis 44	04.00 am - 02 cap 41
Mars	27 pis 34	06.00 am - 03 cap 42
Jupiter	22 lib 54	08.00 am - 04 cap 43
Saturn	23 sag 56	10.00 am - 05 cap 45
Uranus	20 ar 51	12.00 pm - 06 cap 46
Neptune	10 pis 24	14.00 pm - 07 cap 48
Pluto	17 cap 45	16.00 pm - 08 cap 49
		18.00 pm - 09 cap 51
Oob		20.00 pm - 10 cap 53
		22.00 pm - 11 cap 54

Wednesday 25th January

Retrograde Planets

Vesta, Haumea, Makemake, Orcus, Sedna

Asteroids		Dwarf Planets	
Juno	27 sag 03	Eris	22 ar 33
Vesta	26 can 15	Haumea	24 lib 42
Pallas	08 pis 12	Makemake	03 lib 46
Ceres	27 ar 09	Salacia	29 pis 12
Chiron	21 pis 59	Orcus	08 vir 44
N Node	03 vir 39	Quaoar	29 sag 57
S Node	03 pis 39	Sedna	25 tau 05

Moon Phase: Balsamic
Sunrise: 07:48 GMT
Sunset: 16:38
Moonrise: 05:38
Moonset: 14:32
Voc start:
Voc end:

Planetary and Angelic Hours			
Mercury	07:46	Sun	16:38
Moon	08:31	Venus	17:54
Saturn	09:15	Mercury	19:09
Jupiter	09:59	Moon	20:25
Mars	10:44	Saturn	21:40
Sun	11:28	Jupiter	22:56
Venus	12:12	Mars	00:12
Mercury	12:57	Sun	01:27
Moon	13:41	Venus	02:43
Saturn	14:25	Mercury	03:58
Jupiter	15:09	Moon	05:14
Mars	15:54	Saturn	06:30

Aspects

Venus conjunct Chiron
Moon sextile Pallas
Moon sextile Neptune
Moon conj. Mercury
Mars square Juno
Jupiter opposite Eris
Ceres trine Juno
Vesta sextile Sedna

Planets	00:00 am	Moon
Sun	06 aq 12	00.00 am - 12 cap 56
Mercury	12 cap 56	02.00 am - 13 cap 58
Venus	22 pis 39	04.00 am - 15 cap 01
Mars	28 pis 19	06.00 am - 16 cap 03
Jupiter	22 lib 56	08.00 am - 17 cap 05
Saturn	24 sag 02	10.00 am - 18 cap 08
Uranus	20 ar 53	12.00 pm - 19 cap 10
Neptune	10 pis 26	14.00 pm - 20 cap 13
Pluto	17 cap 47	16.00 pm - 21 cap 15
		18.00 pm - 22 cap 18
Oob		20.00 pm - 23 cap 21
		22.00 pm - 24 cap 24

Thursday 26th January

Retrograde Planets

Vesta, Haumea, Makemake, Orcus, Sedna

Asteroids		Dwarf Planets	
Juno	27 sag 23	Eris	22 ar 33
Vesta	26 can 00	Haumea	24 lib 42
Pallas	08 pis 31	Makemake	03 lib 45
Ceres	27 ar 23	Salacia	29 pis 13
Chiron	22 pis 02	Orcus	08 vir 43
N Node	03 vir 34	Quaoar	29 sag 58
S Node	03 pis 34	Sedna	25 tau 05

Moon Phase: Balsamic
Sunrise: 07:47 GMT
Sunset: 16:39
Moonrise: 06:27
Moonset: 15:25
Voc start:
Voc end:

Planetary and Angelic Hours			
Jupiter	07:45	Moon	16:40
Mars	08:30	Saturn	17:55
Sun	09:14	Jupiter	19:10
Venus	09:59	Mars	20:26
Mercury	10:43	Sun	21:41
Moon	11:28	Venus	22:56
Saturn	12:12	Mercury	00:12
Jupiter	12:57	Moon	01:27
Mars	13:42	Saturn	02:43
Sun	14:26	Jupiter	03:58
Venus	15:11	Mars	05:13
Mercury	15:55	Sun	06:29

Aspects

Ceres trine Juno
Moon conjunct Pluto
Moon square Uranus
Moon sextile Chiron
Moon square Eris
Moon square Jupiter
Moon sextile Venus
Moon trine Sedna
Moon opposite Vesta
Venus square Saturn
Jupiter opposite Eris
Vesta sextile Sedna

Planets	00:00 am	Moon
Sun	07 aq 13	00.00 am - 25 cap 27
Mercury	14 cap 11	02.00 am - 26 cap 30
Venus	23 pis 32	04.00 am - 27 cap 33
Mars	29 pis 04	06.00 am - 28 cap 37
Jupiter	22 lib 58	08.00 am - 29 cap 40
Saturn	24 sag 08	10.00 am - 00 aq 44
Uranus	20 ar 54	12.00 pm - 01 aq 47
Neptune	10 pis 28	14.00 pm - 02 aq 51
Pluto	17 cap 49	16.00 pm - 03 aq 55
		18.00 pm - 04 aq 59
Oob		20.00 pm - 06 aq 03
		22.00 pm - 07 aq 07

Friday 27th January

Planetary Directions

Moon into Aquarius 08:37

Retrograde Planets

Vesta, Haumea, Makemake, Orcus, Sedna

Asteroids		Dwarf Planets	
Juno	27 sag 42	Eris	22 ar 33
Vesta	25 can 44	Haumea	24 lib 42
Pallas	08 pis 50	Makemake	03 lib 44
Ceres	27 ar 38	Salacia	29 pis 14
Chiron	22 pis 04	Orcus	08 vir 42
N Node	03 vir 29	Quaoar	00 cap 00
S Node	03 pis 29	Sedna	25 tau 05

Moon Phase: Balsamic
Sunrise: 07:46 GMT
Sunset: 16:41
Moonrise: 07:10
Moonset: 16:26
Voc start: 07:17
Voc end: 08:36

Planetary and Angelic Hours

Venus	07:44	Mars	16:41
Mercury	08:29	Sun	17:57
Moon	09:14	Venus	19:12
Saturn	09:58	Mercury	20:27
Jupiter	10:43	Moon	21:42
Mars	11:28	Saturn	22:57
Sun	12:13	Jupiter	00:12
Venus	12:57	Mars	01:27
Mercury	13:42	Sun	02:42
Moon	14:27	Venus	03:57
Saturn	15:12	Mercury	05:12
Jupiter	15:57	Moon	06:28

Aspects

Moon opposite Vesta
Moon square Ceres
Moon sextile Mars
Venus square Saturn
Venus sextile Sedna
Jupiter opposite Eris
Ceres trine Juno
Vesta sextile Sedna

Planets	**00:00 am**	**Moon**
Sun	08 aq 14	00.00 am - 08 aq 11
Mercury	15 cap 28	02.00 am - 09 aq 15
Venus	24 pis 25	04.00 am - 10 aq 20
Mars	29 pis 49	06.00 am - 11 aq 24
Jupiter	23 lib 00	08.00 am - 12 aq 29
Saturn	24 sag 13	10.00 am - 13 aq 33
Uranus	20 ar 56	12.00 pm - 14 aq 38
Neptune	10 pis 30	14.00 pm - 15 aq 43
Pluto	17 cap 51	16.00 pm - 16 aq 48
		18.00 pm - 17 aq 53
Oob		20.00 pm - 18 aq 58
		22.00 pm - 20 aq 03

Saturday 28th January

Planetary Directions

Mars into Aries
05:39

Retrograde Planets

Vesta, Haumea,
Makemake, Orcus,
Sedna

Asteroids		**Dwarf Planets**	
Juno	28 sag 01	Eris	22 ar 33
Vesta	25 can 29	Haumea	24 lib 41
Pallas	09 pis 09	Makemake	03 lib 44
Ceres	27 ar 53	Salacia	29 pis 15
Chiron	22 pis 07	Orcus	08 vir 41
N Node	03 vir 26	Quaoar	00 cap 01
S Node	03 pis 26	Sedna	25 tau 05

New Moon: 00:08
Sunrise: 07:44 GMT
Sunset: 16:43
Moonrise: 07:47
Moonset: 17:32
Voc start:
Voc end:

Planetary and Angelic Hours			
Saturn	07:43	Mercury	16:43
Jupiter	08:28	Moon	17:58
Mars	09:13	Saturn	19:13
Sun	09:58	Jupiter	20:28
Venus	10:43	Mars	21:43
Mercury	11:28	Sun	22:57
Moon	12:13	Venus	00:12
Saturn	12:58	Mercury	01:27
Jupiter	13:43	Moon	02:42
Mars	14:28	Saturn	03:57
Sun	15:13	Jupiter	05:12
Venus	15:58	Mars	06:26

Aspects

Sun conjunct Moon
Venus sextile Sedna
Venus trine Vesta
Moon sextile Uranus
Venus square Saturn
Jupiter opposite Eris
Ceres trine Juno
Vesta sextile Sedna

Planets	00:00 am	Moon
Sun	09 aq 15	00.00 am - 21 aq 08
Mercury	16 cap 47	02.00 am - 22 aq 14
Venus	25 pis 18	04.00 am - 23 aq 19
Mars	00 ar 34	06.00 am - 24 aq 25
Jupiter	23 lib 01	08.00 am - 25 aq 30
Saturn	24 sag 19	10.00 am - 26 aq 36
Uranus	20 ar 57	12.00 pm - 27 aq 42
Neptune	10 pis 32	14.00 pm - 28 aq 48
Pluto	17 cap 53	16.00 pm - 29 aq 54
		18.00 pm - 01 pis 00
Oob		20.00 pm - 02 pis 06
		22.00 pm - 03 pis 12

Sunday 29th January

Planetary Directions

Moon into Pisces 16:11

Retrograde Planets

Vesta, Haumea, Makemake, Orcus, Sedna

Asteroids		Dwarf Planets	
Juno	28 sag 20	Eris	22 ar 34
Vesta	25 can 14	Haumea	24 lib 41
Pallas	09 pis 28	Makemake	03 lib 43
Ceres	28 ar 08	Salacia	29 pis 16
Chiron	22 pis 10	Orcus	08 vir 40
N Node	03 vir 24	Quaoar	00 cap 02
S Node	03 pis 24	Sedna	25 tau 05

Moon Phase: Crescent
Sunrise: 07:43 GMT
Sunset: 16:45
Moonrise: 08:20
Moonset: 18:41
Voc start: 05:52
Voc end: 16:10

Planetary and Angelic Hours			
Sun	07:41	Jupiter	16:45
Venus	08:27	Mars	17:59
Mercury	09:12	Sun	19:14
Moon	09:57	Venus	20:29
Saturn	10:42	Mercury	21:43
Jupiter	11:28	Moon	22:58
Mars	12:13	Saturn	00:12
Sun	12:58	Jupiter	01:27
Venus	13:44	Mars	02:42
Mercury	14:29	Sun	03:56
Moon	15:14	Venus	05:11
Saturn	16:00	Mercury	06:25

Aspects

Moon sextile Eris
Moon trine Jupiter
Moon sextile Saturn
Moon square Sedna
Moon sextile Ceres
Moon sextile Juno
Vesta sextile Sedna
Mercury conjunct Pluto
Jupiter opposite Eris
Neptune conj. Pallas
Ceres trine Juno

Planets	00:00 am	Moon
Sun	10 aq 16	00.00 am - 04 pis 19
Mercury	18 cap 07	02.00 am - 05 pis 25
Venus	26 pis 09	04.00 am - 06 pis 32
Mars	01 ar 19	06.00 am - 07 pis 38
Jupiter	23 lib 03	08.00 am - 08 pis 45
Saturn	24 sag 25	10.00 am - 09 pis 52
Uranus	20 ar 59	12.00 pm - 10 pis 58
Neptune	10 pis 34	14.00 pm - 12 pis 05
Pluto	17 cap 55	16.00 pm - 13 pis 12
		18.00 pm - 14 pis 20
Oob		20.00 pm - 15 pis 27
		22.00 pm - 16 pis 34

Monday 30th January

Retrograde Planets

Vesta, Haumea, Makemake, Orcus, Sedna

Asteroids		Dwarf Planets	
Juno	28 sag 39	Eris	22 ar 34
Vesta	24 can 59	Haumea	24 lib 41
Pallas	09 pis 47	Makemake	03 lib 43
Ceres	28 ar 23	Salacia	29 pis 17
Chiron	22 pis 13	Orcus	08 vir 39
N Node	03 vir 24	Quaoar	00 cap 03
S Node	03 pis 24	Sedna	25 tau 05

Moon Phase: Crescent
Sunrise: 07:41 GMT
Sunset: 16:47
Moonrise: 08:49
Moonset: 19:53
Voc start:
Voc end:

Planetary and Angelic Hours			
Moon	07:40	Venus	16:47
Saturn	08:25	Mercury	18:01
Jupiter	09:11	Moon	19:15
Mars	09:57	Saturn	20:30
Sun	10:42	Jupiter	21:44
Venus	11:28	Mars	22:58
Mercury	12:13	Sun	00:13
Moon	12:59	Venus	01:27
Saturn	13:44	Mercury	02:41
Jupiter	14:30	Moon	03:55
Mars	15:16	Saturn	05:10
Sun	16:01	Jupiter	06:24

Aspects

Moon conjunct Pallas
Moon conj. Neptune
Moon sextile Pluto
Jupiter opposite Eris
Neptune conj. Pallas
Ceres trine Juno
Vesta sextile Sedna

Planets	00:00 am	Moon
Sun	11 aq 17	00.00 am - 17 pis 41
Mercury	19 cap 28	02.00 am - 18 pis 49
Venus	27 pis 00	04.00 am - 19 pis 56
Mars	02 ar 03	06.00 am - 21 pis 04
Jupiter	23 lib 04	08.00 am - 22 pis 11
Saturn	24 sag 30	10.00 am - 23 pis 29
Uranus	21 ar 00	12.00 pm - 24 pis 27
Neptune	10 pis 36	14.00 pm - 25 pis 35
Pluto	17 cap 57	16.00 pm - 26 pis 43
		18.00 pm - 27 pis 51
		20.00 pm - 28 pis 59
Oob		22.00 pm - 00 ar 07

Tuesday 31st January

Planetary Directions

Moon into Aries 21:47

Retrograde Planets

Vesta, Haumea, Makemake, Orcus, Sedna

Asteroids		Dwarf Planets	
Juno	28 sag 58	Eris	22 ar 34
Vesta	24 can 45	Haumea	24 lib 41
Pallas	10 pis 07	Makemake	03 lib 42
Ceres	28 ar 39	Salacia	29 pis 19
Chiron	22 pis 16	Orcus	08 vir 38
N Node	03 vir 24	Quaoar	00 cap 05
S Node	03 pis 24	Sedna	25 tau 05

Moon Phase: Crescent
Sunrise: 07:40 GMT
Sunset: 16:48
Moonrise: 09:17
Moonset: 21:06
Voc start: 17:35
Voc end: 21:46

Planetary and Angelic Hours

Mars	07:38	Saturn	16:48
Sun	08:24	Jupiter	18:02
Venus	09:10	Mars	19:16
Mercury	09:56	Sun	20:31
Moon	10:42	Venus	21:45
Saturn	11:28	Mercury	22:59
Jupiter	12:13	Moon	00:13
Mars	12:59	Saturn	01:27
Sun	13:45	Jupiter	02:41
Venus	14:31	Mars	03:55
Mercury	15:17	Sun	05:09
Moon	16:03	Venus	06:23

Aspects

Moon sextile Pluto
Moon sextile Mercury
Moon conjunct Chiron
Moon square Saturn
Moon trine Vesta
Moon sextile Sedna
Moon conjunct Venus
Moon square Juno
Mercury square Uranus
Jupiter opposite Eris
Neptune conj. Pallas
Ceres trine Juno
Vesta sextile Sedna

Planets	00:00 am	Moon
Sun	12 aq 18	00.00 am - 01 ar 15
Mercury	20 cap 50	02.00 am - 02 ar 24
Venus	27 pis 50	04.00 am - 03 ar 32
Mars	02 ar 48	06.00 am - 04 ar 41
Jupiter	23 lib 05	08.00 am - 05 ar 49
Saturn	24 sag 36	10.00 am - 06 ar 58
Uranus	21 ar 02	12.00 pm - 08 ar 07
Neptune	10 pis 38	14.00 pm - 09 ar 15
Pluto	17 cap 59	16.00 pm - 10 ar 24
		18.00 pm - 11 ar 33
Oob		20.00 pm - 12 ar 42
		22.00 pm - 13 ar 51

Wednesday 1st February

Retrograde Planets

Vesta, Haumea, Makemake, Orcus, Sedna

Asteroids		Dwarf Planets	
Juno	29 sag 17	Eris	22 ar 34
Vesta	24 can 30	Haumea	24 lib 41
Pallas	10 pis 26	Makemake	03 lib 41
Ceres	28 ar 54	Salacia	29 pis 20
Chiron	22 pis 19	Orcus	08 vir 37
N Node	03 vir 26	Quaoar	00 cap 06
S Node	03 pis 26	Sedna	25 tau 05

Moon Phase: Crescent
Sunrise: 07:38 GMT
Sunset: 16:50
Moonrise: 09:43
Moonset: 22:19
Voc start:
Voc end:

Planetary and Angelic Hours			
Mercury	07:37	Sun	16:50
Moon	08:23	Venus	18:04
Saturn	09:09	Mercury	19:18
Jupiter	09:55	Moon	20:31
Mars	10:41	Saturn	21:45
Sun	11:27	Jupiter	22:59
Venus	12:14	Mars	00:13
Mercury	13:00	Sun	01:27
Moon	13:46	Venus	02:40
Saturn	14:32	Mercury	03:54
Jupiter	15:18	Moon	05:08
Mars	16:04	Saturn	06:22

Imbolc

Aspects

Moon conjunct Mars
Mercury square Uranus
Neptune conj. Pallas
Sun sextile Moon
Mercury square Jupiter
Mercury sextile Chiron
Mercury square Eris
Venus square Juno
Jupiter opposite Eris
Ceres trine Juno
Vesta sextile Sedna

Planets	00:00 am	Moon
Sun	13 aq 19	00.00 am - 15 ar 00
Mercury	22 cap 13	02.00 am - 16 ar 10
Venus	28 pis 40	04.00 am - 17 ar 19
Mars	03 ar 33	06.00 am - 18 ar 28
Jupiter	23 lib 06	08.00 am - 19 ar 38
Saturn	24 sag 41	10.00 am - 20 ar 47
Uranus	21 ar 04	12.00 pm - 21 ar 57
Neptune	10 pis 40	14.00 pm - 23 ar 06
Pluto	18 cap 01	16.00 pm - 24 ar 16
		18.00 pm - 25 ar 26
		20.00 pm - 26 ar 36
Oob		22.00 pm - 27 ar 45

Thursday 2nd February

Retrograde Planets

Vesta, Haumea, Makemake, Orcus, Sedna

Asteroids		Dwarf Planets	
Juno	29 sag 36	Eris	22 ar 34
Vesta	24 can 16	Haumea	24 lib 41
Pallas	10 pis 45	Makemake	03 lib 41
Ceres	29 ar 10	Salacia	29 pis 21
Chiron	22 pis 22	Orcus	08 vir 36
N Node	03 vir 27	Quaoar	00 cap 07
S Node	03 pis 27	Sedna	25 tau 04

Moon Phase: Crescent
Sunrise: 07:37 GMT
Sunset: 16:52
Moonrise: 10:10
Moonset: 23:34
Voc start:16:50
Voc end:

Planetary and Angelic Hours			
Jupiter	07:35	Moon	16:52
Mars	08:22	Saturn	18:05
Sun	09:08	Jupiter	19:19
Venus	09:55	Mars	20:32
Mercury	10:41	Sun	21:46
Moon	11:27	Venus	22:59
Saturn	12:14	Mercury	00:13
Jupiter	13:00	Moon	01:26
Mars	13:46	Saturn	02:40
Sun	14:33	Jupiter	03:53
Venus	15:19	Mars	05:07
Mercury	16:06	Sun	06:20

Aspects

Mercury sextile Chiron
Moon square Pluto
Mercury square Eris
Moon conjunct Uranus
Moon conjunct Eris
Moon square Mercury
Moon opposite Jupiter
Mercury square Jupiter
Moon square Vesta
Moon trine Saturn
Moon conjunct Ceres
Moon trine Juno
Mercury opposite Vesta
Venus square Vesta
Jupiter opposite Eris
Neptune conj. Pallas

Planets	00:00 am	Moon
Sun	14 aq 20	00.00 am - 28 ar 55
Mercury	23 cap 37	02.00 am - 00 tau 05
Venus	29 pis 28	04.00 am - 01 tau 15
Mars	04 ar 17	06.00 am - 02 tau 25
Jupiter	23 lib 07	08.00 am - 03 tau 36
Saturn	24 sag 47	10.00 am - 04 tau 46
Uranus	21 ar 05	12.00 pm - 05 tau 56
Neptune	10 pis 42	14.00 pm - 07 tau 07
Pluto	18 cap 03	16.00 pm - 08 tau 17
		18.00 pm - 09 tau 27
Oob		20.00 pm - 10 tau 38
		22.00 pm - 11 tau 49

Friday 3rd February

Planetary Directions
Moon into Taurus 01:50
Venus into Aries 15:52
Juno into Cap 06:47

Retrograde Planets
Vesta, Haumea, Makemake, Orcus, Sedna

Asteroids		Dwarf Planets	
Juno	29 sag 54	Eris	22 ar 35
Vesta	24 can 02	Haumea	24 lib 40
Pallas	11 pis 05	Makemake	03 lib 40
Ceres	29 ar 27	Salacia	29 pis 22
Chiron	22 pis 25	Orcus	08 vir 35
N Node	03 vir 28	Quaoar	00 cap 08
S Node	03 pis 28	Sedna	25 tau 04

Moon Phase: Crescent
Sunrise: 07:35 GMT
Sunset: 16:54
Moonrise: 10:38
Moonset: None
Voc start: 01:49
Voc end:

Planetary and Angelic Hours			
Venus	07:34	Mars	16:54
Mercury	08:21	Sun	18:07
Moon	09:07	Venus	19:20
Saturn	09:54	Mercury	20:33
Jupiter	10:40	Moon	21:47
Mars	11:27	Saturn	23:00
Sun	12:14	Jupiter	00:13
Venus	13:00	Mars	01:26
Mercury	13:47	Sun	02:39
Moon	14:34	Venus	03:53
Saturn	15:20	Mercury	05:06
Jupiter	16:07	Moon	06:19

Aspects

Moon conjunct Ceres
Moon trine Juno
Mercury opposite Vesta
Moon sextile Neptune
Moon sextile Pallas
Venus square Juno
Mercury trine Sedna
Jupiter square Vesta
Jupiter opposite Eris
Neptune conj. Pallas
Ceres trine Juno

Planets	00:00 am	Moon
Sun	15 aq 21	00.00 am - 12 tau 59
Mercury	25 cap 03	02.00 am - 14 tau 10
Venus	00 ar 16	04.00 am - 15 tau 21
Mars	05 ar 02	06.00 am - 16 tau 31
Jupiter	23 lib 07	08.00 am - 17 tau 42
Saturn	24 sag 52	10.00 am - 18 tau 53
Uranus	21 ar 07	12.00 pm - 20 tau 04
Neptune	10 pis 44	14.00 pm - 21 tau 15
Pluto	18 cap 04	16.00 pm - 22 tau 26
		18.00 pm - 23 tau 37
Oob		20.00 pm - 24 tau 48
		22.00 pm - 25 tau 00

Saturday 4th February

Retrograde Planets

Vesta, Haumea, Makemake, Orcus, Sedna

Asteroids		Dwarf Planets	
Juno	00 cap 13	Eris	22 ar 35
Vesta	23 can 49	Haumea	24 lib 40
Pallas	11 pis 24	Makemake	03 lib 39
Ceres	29 ar 43	Salacia	29 pis 23
Chiron	22 pis 28	Orcus	08 vir 34
N Node	03 vir 29	Quaoar	00 cap 10
S Node	03 pis 29	Sedna	25 tau 04

First Quarter: 04:19
Sunrise: 07:33 GMT
Sunset: 16:56
Moonrise: 11:10
Moonset: 00:49
Voc start: 22:41
Voc end:

Planetary and Angelic Hours			
Saturn	07:32	Mercury	16:56
Jupiter	08:19	Moon	18:08
Mars	09:06	Saturn	19:21
Sun	09:53	Jupiter	20:34
Venus	10:40	Mars	21:47
Mercury	11:27	Sun	23:00
Moon	12:14	Venus	00:13
Saturn	13:01	Mercury	01:26
Jupiter	13:48	Moon	02:39
Mars	14:35	Saturn	03:52
Sun	15:22	Jupiter	05:05
Venus	16:09	Mars	06:18

Aspects

Mercury trine Sedna
Sun square Moon
Moon trine Pluto
Moon sextile Chiron
Moon sextile Vesta
Moon conjunct Sedna
Moon trine Mercury
Venus square Juno
Jupiter square Vesta
Jupiter opposite Eris
Neptune conj. Pallas
Ceres trine Juno

Planets	00:00 am	Moon
Sun	16 aq 22	00.00 am - 27 tau 11
Mercury	26 cap 29	02.00 am - 28 tau 22
Venus	01 ar 02	04.00 am - 29 tau 33
Mars	05 ar 47	06.00 am - 00 gem 45
Jupiter	23 lib 08	08.00 am - 01 gem 56
Saturn	24 sag 57	10.00 am - 03 gem 07
Uranus	21 ar 09	12.00 pm - 04 gem 19
Neptune	10 pis 46	14.00 pm - 05 gem 30
Pluto	18 cap 06	16.00 pm - 06 gem 42
		18.00 pm - 07 gem 53
Oob		20.00 pm - 09 gem 05
		22.00 pm - 10 gem 16

Sunday 5th February

Planetary Directions

Ceres into Taurus 00:14
Moon into Gemini 04:45

Retrograde Planets

Vesta, Haumea, Makemake, Orcus, Sedna

Asteroids		Dwarf Planets	
Juno	00 cap 31	Eris	22 ar 35
Vesta	23 can 36	Haumea	24 lib 40
Pallas	11 pis 44	Makemake	03 lib 39
Ceres	29 ar 59	Salacia	29 pis 25
Chiron	22 pis 31	Orcus	08 vir 33
N Node	03 vir 29	Quaoar	00 cap 11
S Node	03 pis 29	Sedna	25 tau 04

Moon Phase: Gibbous
Sunrise: 07:32 GMT
Sunset: 16:57
Moonrise: 11:47
Moonset: 02:04
Voc start:
Voc end: 04:44

Planetary and Angelic Hours			
Sun	07:31	Jupiter	16:57
Venus	08:18	Mars	18:10
Mercury	09:05	Sun	19:23
Moon	09:52	Venus	20:35
Saturn	10:40	Mercury	21:48
Jupiter	11:27	Moon	23:01
Mars	12:14	Saturn	00:13
Sun	13:01	Jupiter	01:26
Venus	13:48	Mars	02:38
Mercury	14:36	Sun	03:51
Moon	15:23	Venus	05:04
Saturn	16:10	Mercury	06:16

Aspects

Moon sextile Venus
Moon sextile Mars
Moon square Neptune
Moon square Pallas
Venus square Juno
Jupiter square Vesta
Jupiter opposite Eris
Chiron trine Vesta
Ceres trine Juno
Vesta square Eris

Planets	00:00 am	Moon
Sun	17 aq 23	00.00 am - 11 gem 28
Mercury	27 cap 56	02.00 am - 12 gem 39
Venus	01 ar 48	04.00 am - 13 gem 51
Mars	06 ar 31	06.00 am - 15 gem 03
Jupiter	23 lib 08	08.00 am - 16 gem 14
Saturn	25 sag 03	10.00 am - 17 gem 26
Uranus	21 ar 11	12.00 pm - 18 gem 37
Neptune	10 pis 48	14.00 pm - 19 gem 49
Pluto	18 cap 08	16.00 pm - 21 gem 01
		18.00 pm - 22 gem 12
		20.00 pm - 23 gem 24
Oob		22.00 pm - 24 gem 36

Monday 6th February

Planetary Directions

Jupiter retrograde
23 lib 08 at 06:53
Sedna direct
25 tau 04 at 13:39

Retrograde Planets

Vesta, Haumea, Makemake, Orcus, Sedna

Asteroids		Dwarf Planets	
Juno	00 cap 50	Eris	22 ar 36
Vesta	23 can 23	Haumea	24 lib 39
Pallas	12 pis 03	Makemake	03 lib 38
Ceres	00 tau 16	Salacia	29 pis 26
Chiron	22 pis 34	Orcus	08 vir 32
N Node	03 vir 27	Quaoar	00 cap 12
S Node	03 pis 27	Sedna	25 tau 04

Moon Phase: Gibbous
Sunrise: 07:30 GMT
Sunset: 16:59
Moonrise: 12:31
Moonset: 03:16
Voc start: 22:53
Voc end:

Planetary and Angelic Hours

Moon	07:29	Venus	16:59
Saturn	08:17	Mercury	18:11
Jupiter	09:04	Moon	19:24
Mars	09:52	Saturn	20:36
Sun	10:39	Jupiter	21:49
Venus	11:27	Mars	23:01
Mercury	12:14	Sun	00:13
Moon	13:02	Venus	01:26
Saturn	13:49	Mercury	02:38
Jupiter	14:37	Moon	03:50
Mars	15:24	Saturn	05:03
Sun	16:12	Jupiter	06:15

Aspects

Moon square Pallas
Sun trine Moon
Moon sextile Uranus
Moon sextile Eris
Moon square Chiron
Moon trine Jupiter
Moon opposite Saturn
Jupiter square Vesta
Jupiter opposite Eris
Chiron trine Vesta
Ceres trine Juno
Vesta square Eris

Planets	**00:00 am**	**Moon**
Sun	18 aq 23	00.00 am - 25 gem 47
Mercury	29 cap 24	02.00 am - 26 gem 59
Venus	02 ar 32	04.00 am - 28 gem 11
Mars	07 ar 16	06.00 am - 29 gem 22
Jupiter	23 lib 08	08.00 am - 00 can 34
Saturn	25 sag 08	10.00 am - 01 can 45
Uranus	21 ar 13	12.00 pm - 02 can 57
Neptune	10 pis 50	14.00 pm - 04 can 08
Pluto	18 cap 10	16.00 pm - 05 can 20
		18.00 pm - 06 can 31
Oob		20.00 pm - 07 can 43
		22.00 pm - 08 can 54

Tuesday 7th February

Planetary Directions

Moon into Cancer 07:03

Mercury into Aq at 09:36

Retrograde Planets

Jupiter, Vesta, Haumea, Makemake, Orcus

Asteroids		**Dwarf Planets**	
Juno	01 cap 08	Eris	22 ar 36
Vesta	23 can 10	Haumea	24 lib 39
Pallas	12 pis 23	Makemake	03 lib 37
Ceres	00 tau 33	Salacia	29 pis 27
Chiron	22 pis 37	Orcus	08 vir 31
N Node	03 vir 26	Quaoar	00 cap 13
S Node	03 pis 26	Sedna	25 tau 04

Moon Phase: Gibbous
Sunrise: 07:28 GMT
Sunset: 17:01
Moonrise: 13:24
Moonset: 04:23
Voc start:
Voc end: 07:02

Planetary and Angelic Hours

Mars	07:27	Saturn	17:01
Sun	08:15	Jupiter	18:13
Venus	09:03	Mars	19:25
Mercury	09:51	Sun	20:37
Moon	10:39	Venus	21:49
Saturn	11:26	Mercury	23:01
Jupiter	12:14	Moon	00:13
Mars	13:02	Saturn	01:25
Sun	13:50	Jupiter	02:37
Venus	14:38	Mars	03:49
Mercury	15:25	Sun	05:02
Moon	16:13	Venus	06:14

Aspects

Jupiter square Vesta
Moon sextile Ceres
Moon opposite Juno
Moon square Venus
Moon square Mars
Mercury square Ceres
Moon trine Neptune
Jupiter opposite Eris
Chiron trine Vesta
Ceres trine Juno
Vesta square Eris

Planets	00:00 am	Moon
Sun	19 aq 24	00.00 am - 10 can 06
Mercury	00 aq 53	02.00 am - 11 can 17
Venus	03 ar 16	04.00 am - 12 can 28
Mars	08 ar 00	06.00 am - 13 can 39
Jupiter	23 lib 08	08.00 am - 14 can 51
Saturn	25 sag 13	10.00 am - 16 can 02
Uranus	21 ar 15	12.00 pm - 17 can 13
Neptune	10 pis 53	14.00 pm - 18 can 24
Pluto	18 cap 12	16.00 pm - 19 can 35
		18.00 pm - 20 can 46
Oob		20.00 pm - 21 can 57
		22.00 pm - 23 can 07

Wednesday 8th February

Retrograde Planets

Jupiter, Vesta, Haumea, Makemake, Orcus

Asteroids		Dwarf Planets	
Juno	01 cap 27	Eris	22 ar 36
Vesta	22 can 58	Haumea	24 lib 39
Pallas	12 pis 43	Makemake	03 lib 37
Ceres	00 tau 50	Salacia	29 pis 28
Chiron	22 pis 40	Orcus	08 vir 29
N Node	03 vir 24	Quaoar	00 cap 14
S Node	03 pis 24	Sedna	25 tau 04

Moon Phase: Gibbous
Sunrise: 07:27 GMT
Sunset: 17:03
Moonrise: 14:25
Moonset: 05:22
Voc start: 21:59
Voc end:

Planetary and Angelic Hours			
Mercury	07:26	Sun	17:03
Moon	08:14	Venus	18:04
Saturn	09:02	Mercury	19:26
Jupiter	09:50	Moon	20:38
Mars	10:38	Saturn	21:50
Sun	11:26	Jupiter	23:02
Venus	12:14	Mars	00:13
Mercury	13:02	Sun	01:25
Moon	13:50	Venus	02:37
Saturn	14:38	Mercury	03:49
Jupiter	15:27	Moon	05:00
Mars	16:15	Saturn	06:12

Aspects

Moon trine Neptune
Moon trine Pallas
Moon opposite Pluto
Moon square Uranus
Moon square Eris
Moon trine Chiron
Moon conjunct Vesta
Moon square Jupiter
Sun sextile Uranus
Moon sextile Sedna
Jupiter square Vesta
Jupiter opposite Eris
Chiron trine Vesta
Ceres trine Juno
Vesta square Eris

Planets	**00:00 am**	**Moon**
Sun	20 aq 25	00.00 am - 24 can 18
Mercury	02 aq 23	02.00 am - 25 can 29
Venus	03 ar 58	04.00 am - 26 can 39
Mars	08 ar 45	06.00 am - 27 can 50
Jupiter	23 lib 07	08.00 am - 29 can 00
Saturn	25 sag 18	10.00 am - 00 leo 11
Uranus	21 ar 17	12.00 pm - 01 leo 21
Neptune	10 pis 55	14.00 pm - 02 leo 31
Pluto	18 cap 14	16.00 pm - 03 leo 41
		18.00 pm - 04 leo 51
Oob		20.00 pm - 06 leo 01
		22.00 pm - 07 leo 11

Thursday 9th February

Planetary Directions

Moon into Leo 09:41

Retrograde Planets

Jupiter, Vesta, Haumea, Makemake, Orcus

Asteroids		**Dwarf Planets**	
Juno	01 cap 45	Eris	22 ar 36
Vesta	22 can 46	Haumea	24 lib 38
Pallas	13 pis 02	Makemake	03 lib 36
Ceres	01 tau 07	Salacia	29 pis 30
Chiron	22 pis 43	Orcus	08 vir 28
N Node	03 vir 22	Quaoar	00 cap 15
S Node	03 pis 22	Sedna	25 tau 04

Moon Phase: Gibbous
Sunrise: 07:25 GMT
Sunset: 17:05
Moonrise: 15:32
Moonset: 06:13
Voc start:
Voc end: 09:40

Planetary and Angelic Hours			
Jupiter	07:24	Moon	17:04
Mars	08:12	Saturn	18:16
Sun	09:01	Jupiter	19:27
Venus	09:49	Mars	20:39
Mercury	10:37	Sun	21:50
Moon	11:26	Venus	23:02
Saturn	12:14	Mercury	00:13
Jupiter	13:03	Moon	01:25
Mars	13:51	Saturn	02:36
Sun	14:39	Jupiter	03:48
Venus	15:28	Mars	04:59
Mercury	16:16	Sun	06:11

Aspects

Moon sextile Sedna
Chiron trine Vesta
Moon square Ceres
Moon opp. Mercury
Moon trine Venus
Vesta square Eris
Sun sextile Uranus
Mercury sextile Venus
Jupiter square Vesta
Jupiter opposite Eris
Ceres trine Juno

Planets	00:00 am	Moon
Sun	21 aq 26	00.00 am - 08 leo 21
Mercury	03 aq 53	02.00 am - 09 leo 30
Venus	04 ar 39	04.00 am - 10 leo 40
Mars	09 ar 29	06.00 am - 11 leo 49
Jupiter	23 lib 07	08.00 am - 12 leo 58
Saturn	25 sag 23	10.00 am - 14 leo 08
Uranus	21 ar 19	12.00 pm - 15 leo 17
Neptune	10 pis 57	14.00 pm - 16 leo 25
Pluto	18 cap 15	16.00 pm - 17 leo 35
		18.00 pm - 18 leo 43
Oob		20.00 pm - 19 leo 52
		22.00 pm - 21 leo 00

Friday 10th February

Retrograde Planets

Jupiter, Vesta, Haumea, Makemake, Orcus

Asteroids		Dwarf Planets	
Juno	02 cap 03	Eris	22 ar 37
Vesta	22 can 35	Haumea	24 lib 38
Pallas	13 pis 22	Makemake	03 lib 35
Ceres	01 tau 25	Salacia	29 pis 31
Chiron	22 pis 46	Orcus	08 vir 27
N Node	03 vir 21	Quaoar	00 cap 17
S Node	03 pis 21	Sedna	25 tau 04

Moon Phase: Gibbous
Sunrise: 07:23 GMT
Sunset: 17:07
Moonrise: 16:43
Moonset: 06:55
Voc start:
Voc end:

Planetary and Angelic Hours			
Venus	07:22	Mars	17:06
Mercury	08:11	Sun	18:17
Moon	09:00	Venus	19:29
Saturn	09:48	Mercury	20:40
Jupiter	10:37	Moon	21:51
Mars	11:26	Saturn	23:02
Sun	12:14	Jupiter	00:13
Venus	13:03	Mars	01:25
Mercury	13:52	Sun	02:36
Moon	14:40	Venus	03:47
Saturn	15:29	Mercury	04:58
Jupiter	16:18	Moon	06:09

Aspects

Moon trine Mars
Mercury sextile Venus
Moon trine Uranus
Sun trine Jupiter
Sun sextile Eris
Moon sextile Jupiter
Moon trine Eris
Jupiter square Vesta
Jupiter opposite Eris
Chiron trine Vesta
Ceres trine Juno
Vesta square Eris

Planets	**00:00 am**	**Moon**
Sun	22 aq 26	00.00 am - 22 leo 09
Mercury	05 aq 25	02.00 am - 23 leo 17
Venus	05 ar 19	04.00 am - 24 leo 25
Mars	10 ar 14	06.00 am - 25 leo 33
Jupiter	23 lib 06	08.00 am - 26 leo 41
Saturn	25 sag 28	10.00 am - 27 leo 49
Uranus	21 ar 21	12.00 pm - 28 leo 57
Neptune	10 pis 59	14.00 pm - 00 vir 04
Pluto	18 cap 17	16.00 pm - 01 vir 12
		18.00 pm - 02 vir 19
Oob		20.00 pm - 03 vir 26
		22.00 pm - 04 vir 33

Saturday 11th February

Planetary Directions

Moon into Virgo 13:52

Retrograde Planets

Jupiter, Vesta, Haumea, Makemake, Orcus

Asteroids		**Dwarf Planets**	
Juno	02 cap 21	Eris	22 ar 37
Vesta	22 can 24	Haumea	24 lib 37
Pallas	13 pis 42	Makemake	03 lib 34
Ceres	01 tau 42	Salacia	29 pis 32
Chiron	22 pis 50	Orcus	08 vir 26
N Node	03 vir 20	Quaoar	00 cap 18
S Node	03 pis 20	Sedna	25 tau 04

Full Moon: 00:33
Sunrise: 07:21 GMT
Sunset: 17:08
Moonrise: 17:55
Moonset: 07:30
Voc start: 05:52
Voc end: 13:51

Planetary and Angelic Hours			
Saturn	07:20	Mercury	17:08
Jupiter	08:09	Moon	18:19
Mars	08:58	Saturn	19:30
Sun	09:47	Jupiter	20:41
Venus	10:36	Mars	21:52
Mercury	11:25	Sun	23:02
Moon	12:14	Venus	00:13
Saturn	13:03	Mercury	01:24
Jupiter	13:52	Moon	02:35
Mars	14:41	Saturn	03:46
Sun	15:30	Jupiter	04:57
Venus	16:19	Mars	06:08

Penumbral Lunar Eclipse visible in the UK at 00:43

Aspects

Sun opposite Moon
Moon trine Eris
Moon sextile Jupiter
Moon square Sedna
Moon trine Saturn
Sun trine Jupiter
Moon trine Ceres
Moon trine Juno
Mercury sextile Venus
Jupiter square Vesta
Chiron trine Vesta
Ceres trine Juno
Vesta square Eris

Planets	00:00 am	Moon
		00.00 am - 05 vir 40
Sun	23 aq 27	02.00 am - 06 vir 47
Mercury	06 aq 57	04.00 am - 07 vir 53
Venus	05 ar 58	06.00 am - 09 vir 00
Mars	10 ar 58	08.00 am - 10 vir 06
Jupiter	23 lib 05	10.00 am - 11 vir 12
Saturn	25 sag 33	12.00 pm - 12 vir 18
Uranus	21 ar 23	14.00 pm - 13 vir 24
Neptune	11 pis 01	16.00 pm - 14 vir 30
Pluto	18 cap 19	18.00 pm - 15 vir 36
		20.00 pm - 16 vir 41
Oob		22.00 pm - 17 vir 47

Sunday 12th February

Retrograde Planets

Jupiter, Vesta, Haumea, Makemake, Orcus

Asteroids		Dwarf Planets	
Juno	02 cap 39	Eris	22 ar 38
Vesta	22 can 13	Haumea	24 lib 37
Pallas	14 pis 02	Makemake	03 lib 33
Ceres	02 tau 00	Salacia	29 pis 34
Chiron	22 pis 53	Orcus	08 vir 25
N Node	03 vir 20	Quaoar	00 cap 19
S Node	03 pis 20	Sedna	25 tau 05

Phase: Disseminating
Sunrise: 07:19 GMT
Sunset: 17:10
Moonrise: 19:06
Moonset: 07:59
Voc start:
Voc end:

Planetary and Angelic Hours			
Sun	07:19	Jupiter	17:10
Venus	08:08	Mars	18:20
Mercury	08:57	Sun	19:31
Moon	09:46	Venus	20:42
Saturn	10:36	Mercury	21:52
Jupiter	11:25	Moon	23:03
Mars	12:14	Saturn	00:13
Sun	13:04	Jupiter	01:24
Venus	13:53	Mars	02:35
Mercury	14:42	Sun	03:45
Moon	15:31	Venus	04:56
Saturn	16:21	Mercury	06:06

Aspects

Moon opp. Neptune
Moon opposite Pallas
Moon trine Pluto
Sun square Sedna
Jupiter opposite Eris
Uranus square Vesta
Chiron trine Vesta
Ceres trine Juno
Vesta square Eris

Planets	00:00 am	Moon
Sun	24 aq 28	00.00 am - 18 vir 52
Mercury	08 aq 30	02.00 am - 19 vir 57
Venus	06 ar 35	04.00 am - 21 vir 02
Mars	11 ar 42	06.00 am - 22 vir 07
Jupiter	23 lib 04	08.00 am - 23 vir 11
Saturn	25 sag 37	10.00 am - 24 vir 16
Uranus	21 ar 25	12.00 pm - 25 vir 20
Neptune	11 pis 03	14.00 pm - 26 vir 25
Pluto	18 cap 21	16.00 pm - 27 vir 29
		18.00 pm - 28 vir 33
Oob		20.00 pm - 29 vir 37
		22.00 pm - 00 lib 41

Monday 13th February

Planetary Directions

Moon into Libra 20:43

Retrograde Planets

Jupiter, Vesta, Haumea, Makemake, Orcus

Asteroids		Dwarf Planets	
Juno	02 cap 57	Eris	22 ar 38
Vesta	22 can 02	Haumea	24 lib 36
Pallas	14 pis 22	Makemake	03 lib 33
Ceres	02 tau 18	Salacia	29 pis 35
Chiron	22 pis 56	Orcus	08 vir 24
N Node	03 vir 20	Quaoar	00 cap 20
S Node	03 pis 20	Sedna	25 tau 05

Phase: Disseminating
Sunrise: 07:17 GMT
Sunset: 17:12
Moonrise: 20:16
Moonset: 08:26
Voc start: 12:36
Voc end: 20:42

Planetary and Angelic Hours			
Moon	07:17	Venus	17:12
Saturn	08:06	Mercury	18:22
Jupiter	08:56	Moon	19:32
Mars	09:46	Saturn	20:42
Sun	10:35	Jupiter	21:53
Venus	11:25	Mars	23:03
Mercury	12:14	Sun	00:13
Moon	13:04	Venus	01:24
Saturn	13:53	Mercury	02:34
Jupiter	14:43	Moon	03:44
Mars	15:33	Saturn	04:54
Sun	16:22	Jupiter	06:05

Aspects

Moon sextile Vesta
Moon opposite Chiron
Moon trine Sedna
Moon square Saturn
Sun square Sedna
Sun sextile Saturn
Jupiter opposite Eris
Uranus square Vesta
Ceres trine Juno
Vesta square Eris

Planets	00:00 am	Moon
Sun	25 aq 28	00.00 am - 01 lib 44
Mercury	10 aq 05	02.00 am - 02 lib 48
Venus	07 ar 11	04.00 am - 03 lib 51
Mars	12 ar 27	06.00 am - 04 lib 54
Jupiter	23 lib 02	08.00 am - 05 lib 58
Saturn	25 sag 42	10.00 am - 07 :ib 01
Uranus	21 ar 27	12.00 pm - 08 lib 03
Neptune	11 pis 06	14.00 pm - 09 lib 06
Pluto	18 cap 22	16.00 pm - 10 lib 09
		18.00 pm - 11 lib 11
Oob		20.00 pm - 12 lib 14
		22.00 pm - 13 lib 06

Tuesday 14th February

Retrograde Planets

Jupiter, Vesta, Haumea, Makemake, Orcus

Asteroids		Dwarf Planets	
Juno	03 cap 15	Eris	22 ar 38
Vesta	21 can 53	Haumea	24 lib 36
Pallas	14 pis 42	Makemake	03 lib 32
Ceres	02 tau 36	Salacia	29 pis 36
Chiron	22 pis 59	Orcus	08 vir 23
N Node	03 vir 21	Quaoar	00 cap 21
S Node	03 pis 21	Sedna	25 tau 05

Phase: Disseminating
Sunrise: 07:16 GMT
Sunset: 17:14
Moonrise: 21:23
Moonset: 08:50
Voc start:
Voc end:

Planetary and Angelic Hours			
Mars	07:15	Saturn	17:13
Sun	08:05	Jupiter	18:23
Venus	08:55	Mars	19:33
Mercury	09:45	Sun	20:43
Moon	10:34	Venus	21:53
Saturn	11:24	Mercury	23:03
Jupiter	12:14	Moon	00:13
Mars	13:04	Saturn	01:23
Sun	13:54	Jupiter	02:33
Venus	14:44	Mars	03:43
Mercury	15:34	Sun	04:53
Moon	16:24	Venus	06:03

Valentines Day

Aspects

Moon square Juno
Sun sextile Saturn
Moon opposite Venus
Moon trine Mercury
Moon opposite Mars
Jupiter opposite Eris
Uranus square Vesta
Ceres trine Juno
Vesta square Eris

Wednesday 15th February

Planets	00:00 am	Moon
Sun	26 aq 29	00.00 am - 14 lib 18
Mercury	11 aq 39	02.00 am - 15 lib 20
Venus	07 ar 46	04.00 am - 16 lib 22
Mars	13 ar 11	06.00 am - 17 lib 24
Jupiter	23 lib 01	08.00 am - 18 lib 26
Saturn	25 sag 47	10.00 am - 19 lib 28
Uranus	21 ar 30	12.00 pm - 20 lib 29
Neptune	11 pis 08	14.00 pm - 21 lib 31
Pluto	18 cap 24	16.00 pm - 22 lib 32
		18.00 pm - 23 lib 33
Oob		20.00 pm - 24 lib 34
		22.00 pm - 25 lib 35

Retrograde Planets

Jupiter, Vesta, Haumea, Makemake, Orcus

Asteroids		Dwarf Planets	
Juno	03 cap 32	Eris	22 ar 39
Vesta	21 can 43	Haumea	24 lib 35
Pallas	15 pis 02	Makemake	03 lib 31
Ceres	02 tau 54	Salacia	29 pis 38
Chiron	23 pis 03	Orcus	08 vir 22
N Node	03 vir 21	Quaoar	00 cap 22
S Node	03 pis 21	Sedna	25 tau 05

Phase: Disseminating
Sunrise: 07:14 GMT
Sunset: 17:16
Moonrise: 22:28
Moonset: 09:14
Voc start:
Voc end:

Planetary and Angelic Hours			
Mercury	07:13	Sun	17:15
Moon	08:03	Venus	18:25
Saturn	08:53	Mercury	19:35
Jupiter	09:44	Moon	20:44
Mars	10:34	Saturn	21:54
Sun	11:24	Jupiter	23:04
Venus	12:14	Mars	00:13
Mercury	13:04	Sun	01:23
Moon	13:55	Venus	02:33
Saturn	14:45	Mercury	03:42
Jupiter	15:35	Moon	04:52
Mars	16:25	Saturn	06:02

Aspects

Moon square Pluto
Moon opposite Uranus
Moon square Vesta
Moon opposite Eris
Moon conjunct Jupiter
Moon sextile Saturn
Sun trine Moon
Mercury sextile Mars
Jupiter opposite Eris
Uranus square Vesta
Ceres trine Juno

Planets	**00:00 am**	**Moon**
Sun	27 aq 29	00.00 am - 26 lib 36
Mercury	13 aq 15	02.00 am - 27 lib 37
Venus	08 ar 19	04.00 am - 28 lib 38
Mars	13 ar 55	06.00 am - 29 lib 39
Jupiter	22 lib 59	08.00 am - 00 sco 40
Saturn	25 sag 51	10.00 am - 01 sco 40
Uranus	21 ar 32	12.00 pm - 02 sco 41
Neptune	11 pis 10	14.00 pm - 03 sco 41
Pluto	18 cap 26	16.00 pm - 04 sco 41
		18.00 pm - 05 sco 42
Oob		20.00 pm - 06 sco 42
		22.00 pm - 07 sco 42

Thursday 16th February

Planetary Directions

Moon into Scorpio
06:41

Retrograde Planets

Jupiter, Vesta, Haumea, Makemake, Orcus

Asteroids		**Dwarf Planets**	
Juno	03 cap 50	Eris	22 ar 39
Vesta	21 can 34	Haumea	24 lib 35
Pallas	15 pis 22	Makemake	03 lib 30
Ceres	03 tau 12	Salacia	29 pis 39
Chiron	23 pis 06	Orcus	08 vir 20
N Node	03 vir 22	Quaoar	00 cap 23
S Node	03 pis 22	Sedna	25 tau 05

Phase: Disseminating
Sunrise: 07:12 GMT
Sunset: 17:18
Moonrise: 23:32
Moonset: 09:38
Voc start: 01:53
Voc end: 06:40

Planetary and Angelic Hours

Jupiter	07:11	Moon	17:17
Mars	08:02	Saturn	18:26
Sun	08:52	Jupiter	19:36
Venus	09:43	Mars	20:45
Mercury	10:33	Sun	21:54
Moon	11:24	Venus	23:04
Saturn	12:14	Mercury	00:13
Jupiter	13:05	Moon	01:23
Mars	13:55	Saturn	02:32
Sun	14:46	Jupiter	03:41
Venus	15:36	Mars	04:51
Mercury	16:27	Sun	06:00

Aspects

Sun trine Moon
Uranus square Vesta
Moon opposite Ceres
Moon sextile Juno
Mercury sextile Mars
Jupiter opposite Eris
Cres trine Juno

Planets	00:00 am	Moon
Sun	28 aq 30	00.00 am - 08 sco 42
Mercury	14 aq 52	02.00 am - 09 sco 42
Venus	08 ar 51	04.00 am - 10 sco 42
Mars	14 ar 39	06.00 am - 11 sco 42
Jupiter	22 lib 57	08.00 am - 12 sco 42
Saturn	25 sag 56	10.00 am - 13 sco 41
Uranus	21 ar 34	12.00 pm - 14 sco 41
Neptune	11 pis 12	14.00 pm - 15 sco 41
Pluto	18 cap 28	16.00 pm - 16 sco 41
		18.00 pm - 17 sco 40
Oob		20.00 pm - 18 sco 40
		22.00 pm - 19 sco 39

Friday 17th February

Retrograde Planets

Jupiter, Vesta, Haumea, Makemake, Orcus

Asteroids		Dwarf Planets	
Juno	04 cap 07	Eris	22 ar 39
Vesta	21 can 25	Haumea	24 lib 34
Pallas	15 pis 42	Makemake	03 lib 29
Ceres	03 tau 31	Salacia	29 pis 41
Chiron	23 pis 09	Orcus	08 vir 19
N Node	03 vir 23	Quaoar	00 cap 24
S Node	03 pis 23	Sedna	25 tau 05

Phase: Disseminating
Sunrise: 07:10 GMT
Sunset: 17:19
Moonrise: None
Moonset: 10:03
Voc start: 19:37
Voc end:

Planetary and Angelic Hours			
Venus	07:09	Mars	17:19
Mercury	08:00	Sun	18:28
Moon	08:51	Venus	19:37
Saturn	09:42	Mercury	20:46
Jupiter	10:32	Moon	21:55
Mars	11:23	Saturn	23:04
Sun	12:14	Jupiter	00:13
Venus	13:05	Mars	01:22
Mercury	13:56	Sun	02:31
Moon	14:46	Venus	03:40
Saturn	15:37	Mercury	04:49
Jupiter	16:28	Moon	05:58

Aspects

Moon trine Neptune
Moon square Mercury
Moon trine Pallas
Moon sextile Pluto
Moon trine Vesta
Jupiter opposite Eris
Uranus square Vesta
Ceres trine Juno

Planets	00:00 am	Moon
		00.00 am - 20 sco 39
Sun	29 aq 30	02.00 am - 21 sco 38
Mercury	16 aq 29	04.00 am - 22 sco 38
Venus	09 ar 21	06.00 am - 23 sco 37
Mars	15 ar 23	08.00 am - 24 sco 37
Jupiter	22 lib 55	10.00 am - 25 sco 36
Saturn	26 sag 00	12.00 pm - 26 sco 36
Uranus	21 ar 37	14.00 pm - 27 sco 35
Neptune	11 pis 14	16.00 pm - 28 sco 34
Pluto	18 cap 29	18.00 pm - 29 sco 34
		20.00 pm - 00 sag 33
Oob		22.00 pm - 01 sag 32

Saturday 18th February

Planetary Directions

Sun into Pisces at 11:32
Moon into Sagittarius 18:53

Retrograde Planets

Jupiter, Vesta, Haumea, Makemake, Orcus

Asteroids		Dwarf Planets	
Juno	04 cap 25	Eris	22 ar 40
Vesta	21 can 17	Haumea	24 lib 34
Pallas	16 pis 03	Makemake	03 lib 28
Ceres	03 tau 49	Salacia	29 pis 42
Chiron	23 pis 13	Orcus	08 vir 18
N Node	03 vir 23	Quaoar	00 cap 25
S Node	03 pis 23	Sedna	25 tau 05

Last Quarter: 19:35
Sunrise: 07:08 GMT
Sunset: 17:21
Moonrise: 00:35
Moonset: 10:31
Voc start:
Voc end: 18:52

Planetary and Angelic Hours			
Saturn	07:07	Mercury	17:21
Jupiter	07:58	Moon	18:29
Mars	08:50	Saturn	19:38
Sun	09:41	Jupiter	20:47
Venus	10:32	Mars	21:56
Mercury	11:23	Sun	23:04
Moon	12:14	Venus	00:13
Saturn	13:05	Mercury	01:22
Jupiter	13:56	Moon	02:30
Mars	14:47	Saturn	03:39
Sun	15:38	Jupiter	04:48
Venus	16:29	Mars	05:57

Aspects

Moon trine Vesta
Moon trine Chiron
Moon opposite Sedna
Sun square Moon
Jupiter opposite Eris
Uranus square Vesta
Ceres trine Juno

Planets	00:00 am	Moon
Sun	00 pis 31	00.00 am - 02 sag 32
Mercury	18 aq 08	02.00 am - 03 sag 31
Venus	09 ar 50	04.00 am - 04 sag 31
Mars	16 ar 08	06.00 am - 05 sag 30
Jupiter	22 lib 53	08.00 am - 06 sag 29
Saturn	26 sag 04	10.00 am - 07 sag 29
Uranus	21 ar 39	12.00 pm - 08 sag 28
Neptune	11 pis 17	14.00 pm - 09 sag 28
Pluto	18 cap 31	16.00 pm - 10 sag 27
		18.00 pm - 11 sag 27
Oob		20.00 pm - 12 sag 26
		22.00 pm - 13 sag 26

Sunday 19th February

Retrograde Planets

Jupiter, Vesta, Haumea, Makemake, Orcus

Asteroids		Dwarf Planets	
Juno	04 cap 42	Eris	22 ar 40
Vesta	21 can 09	Haumea	24 lib 33
Pallas	16 pis 23	Makemake	03 lib 27
Ceres	04 tau 08	Salacia	29 pis 43
Chiron	23 pis 16	Orcus	08 vir 17
N Node	03 vir 23	Quaoar	00 cap 26
S Node	03 pis 23	Sedna	25 tau 05

Moon Phase: Balsamic
Sunrise: 07:06 GMT
Sunset: 17:23
Moonrise: 01:35
Moonset: 11:03
Voc start:
Voc end:

Planetary and Angelic Hours			
Sun	07:05	Jupiter	17:22
Venus	07:57	Mars	18:31
Mercury	08:48	Sun	19:39
Moon	09:40	Venus	20:48
Saturn	10:31	Mercury	21:56
Jupiter	11:22	Moon	23:04
Mars	12:14	Saturn	00:13
Sun	13:05	Jupiter	01:21
Venus	13:57	Mars	02:30
Mercury	14:48	Sun	03:38
Moon	15:40	Venus	04:47
Saturn	16:31	Mercury	05:55

Aspects

Moon trine Venus
Moon square Neptune
Jupiter opposite Eris
Uranus square Vesta
Uranus conjunct Eris
Ceres trine Juno

Planets	00:00 am	Moon
Sun	01 pis 31	00.00 am - 14 sag 25
Mercury	19 aq 47	02.00 am - 15 sag 25
Venus	10 ar 17	04.00 am - 16 sag 25
Mars	16 ar 52	06.00 am - 17 sag 24
Jupiter	22 lib 50	08.00 am - 18 sag 24
Saturn	26 sag 09	10.00 am - 19 sag 24
Uranus	21 ar 42	12.00 pm - 20 sag 24
Neptune	11 pis 19	14.00 pm - 21 sag 24
Pluto	18 cap 32	16.00 pm - 22 sag 24
		18.00 pm - 23 sag 24
Oob		20.00 pm - 24 sag 24
		22.00 pm - 25 sag 24

Monday 20th February

Retrograde Planets

Jupiter, Vesta, Haumea, Makemake, Orcus

Asteroids		Dwarf Planets	
Juno	04 cap 59	Eris	22 ar 41
Vesta	21 can 02	Haumea	24 lib 33
Pallas	16 pis 43	Makemake	03 lib 26
Ceres	04 tau 27	Salacia	29 pis 45
Chiron	23 pis 20	Orcus	08 vir 16
N Node	03 vir 23	Quaoar	00 cap 27
S Node	03 pis 23	Sedna	25 tau 05

Moon Phase: Balsamic
Sunrise: 07:04 GMT
Sunset: 17:25
Moonrise: 02:33
Moonset: 11:40
Voc start: 23:36
Voc end:

Planetary and Angelic Hours			
Moon	07:03	Venus	17:24
Saturn	07:55	Mercury	18:32
Jupiter	08:47	Moon	19:40
Mars	09:39	Saturn	20:48
Sun	10:30	Jupiter	21:57
Venus	11:22	Mars	23:05
Mercury	12:14	Sun	00:13
Moon	13:06	Venus	01:21
Saturn	13:57	Mercury	02:29
Jupiter	14:49	Moon	03:37
Mars	15:41	Saturn	04:45
Sun	16:32	Jupiter	05:53

Aspects

Moon trine Venus
Moon square Neptune
Jupiter opposite Eris
Uranus square Vesta
Uranus conjunct Eris
Ceres trine Juno

Planets	00:00 am	Moon
Sun	02 pis 32	00.00 am - 26 sag 24
Mercury	21 aq 28	02.00 am - 27 sag 25
Venus	10 ar 42	04.00 am - 28 sag 25
Mars	17 ar 36	06.00 am - 29 sag 25
Jupiter	22 lib 48	08.00 am - 00 cap 26
Saturn	26 lib 13	10.00 am - 01 cap 26
Uranus	21 ar 44	12.00 pm - 02 cap 27
Neptune	11 pis 21	14.00 pm - 03 cap 28
Pluto	18 cap 34	16.00 pm - 04 cap 29
		18.00 pm - 05 cap 30
Oob		20.00 pm - 06 cap 31
		22.00 pm - 07 cap 32

Tuesday 21st February

Planetary Directions

Moon into Capricorn 07:08

Retrograde Planets

Jupiter, Vesta, Haumea, Makemake, Orcus

Asteroids		Dwarf Planets	
Juno	05 cap 16	Eris	22 ar 41
Vesta	20 can 55	Haumea	24 lib 32
Pallas	17 pis 03	Makemake	03 lib 25
Ceres	04 tau 46	Salacia	29 pis 46
Chiron	23 pis 23	Orcus	08 vir 15
N Node	03 vir 23	Quaoar	00 cap 27
S Node	03 pis 23	Sedna	25 tau 06

Moon Phase: Balsamic
Sunrise: 17:02 GMT
Sunset: 17:27
Moonrise: 03:28
Moonset: 12:24
Voc start: 07:07
Voc end:

Planetary and Angelic Hours			
Mars	07:01	Saturn	17:26
Sun	07:54	Jupiter	18:34
Venus	08:46	Mars	19:41
Mercury	09:38	Sun	20:49
Moon	10:30	Venus	21:57
Saturn	11:22	Mercury	23:05
Jupiter	12:14	Moon	00:13
Mars	13:06	Saturn	01:20
Sun	13:58	Jupiter	02:28
Venus	14:50	Mars	03:36
Mercury	15:42	Sun	04:44
Moon	16:34	Venus	05:52

Aspects

Mercury sextile Uranus
Sun sextile Moon
Moon trine Ceres
Mercury sextile Eris
Moon conjunct Juno
Mercury trine Jupiter
Mars square Pluto
Jupiter opposite Uranus
Jupiter opposite Eris
Uranus square Vesta
Uranus conjunct Eris
Ceres trine Juno

Planets	00:00 am	Moon
Sun	03 pis 32	00.00 am - 08 cap 33
Mercury	23 aq 09	02.00 am - 09 cap 34
Venus	11 ar 06	04.00 am - 10 cap 35
Mars	18 ar 20	06.00 am - 11 cap 37
Jupiter	22 lib 45	08.00 am - 12 cap 39
Saturn	26 sag 17	10.00 am - 13 cap 40
Uranus	21 ar 47	12.00 pm - 14 cap 42
Neptune	11 pis 24	14.00 pm - 15 cap 44
Pluto	18 cap 36	16.00 pm - 16 cap 46
		18.00 pm - 17 cap 48
Oob		20.00 pm - 18 cap 50
		22.00 pm - 19 cap 52

Wednesday 22nd February

Retrograde Planets

Jupiter, Vesta, Haumea, Makemake, Orcus

Asteroids		Dwarf Planets	
Juno	05 cap 16	Eris	22 ar 41
Vesta	20 can 55	Haumea	24 lib 31
Pallas	17 pis 03	Makemake	03 lib 24
Ceres	04 tau 46	Salacia	29 pis 48
Chiron	23 pis 23	Orcus	08 vir 13
N Node	03 vir 23	Quaoar	00 cap 28
S Node	03 pis 23	Sedna	25 tau 06

Moon Phase: Balsamic
Sunrise: 07:00 GMT
Sunset: 17:28
Moonrise: 04:18
Moonset: 13:14
Voc start:
Voc end:

Planetary and Angelic Hours			
Mercury	06:59	Sun	17:28
Moon	07:52	Venus	18:35
Saturn	08:44	Mercury	19:43
Jupiter	09:37	Moon	20:50
Mars	10:29	Saturn	21:58
Sun	11:21	Jupiter	23:05
Venus	12:14	Mars	00:13
Mercury	13:06	Sun	01:20
Moon	13:58	Venus	02:28
Saturn	14:51	Mercury	03:35
Jupiter	15:43	Moon	04:42
Mars	16:35	Saturn	05:50

Aspects

Moon square Venus
Moon sextile Neptune
Mars square Pluto
Moon sextile Pallas
Moon conjunct Pluto
Moon square Mars
Jupiter opposite Eris
Moon opposite Vesta
Sun sextile Ceres
Moon square Uranus
Mercury square Sedna
Jupiter opposite Uranus
Uranus conjunct Eris
Pluto sextile Pallas
Ceres trine Juno

Planets	00:00 am	Moon
Sun	04 pis 33	00.00 am - 20 cap 55
Mercury	24 aq 51	02.00 am - 21 cap 57
Venus	11 ar 27	04.00 am - 23 cap 00
Mars	19 ar 04	06.00 am - 24 cap 03
Jupiter	22 lib 42	08.00 am - 25 cap 06
Saturn	26 sag 21	10.00 am - 26 cap 09
Uranus	21 ar 49	12.00 pm - 27 cap 12
Neptune	11 pis 26	14.00 pm - 28 cap 15
Pluto	18 cap 37	16.00 pm - 29 cap 19
		18.00 pm - 00 aq 22
Oob		20.00 pm - 01 aq 26
		22.00 pm - 02 aq 29

Thursday 23rd February

Planetary Directions

Moon into Aquarius
17:18

Retrograde Planets

Jupiter, Vesta,
Haumea, Makemake,
Orcus

Asteroids		Dwarf Planets	
Juno	05 cap 33	Eris	22 ar 42
Vesta	20 can 48	Haumea	24 lib 31
Pallas	17 pis 24	Makemake	03 lib 23
Ceres	05 tau 06	Salacia	29 pis 49
Chiron	23 pis 26	Orcus	08 vir 12
N Node	03 vir 23	Quaoar	00 cap 29
S Node	03 pis 23	Sedna	25 tau 06

Moon Phase: Balsamic
Sunrise: 06:58 GMT
Sunset: 17:30
Moonrise: 05:03
Moonset: 14:11
Voc start: 03:23
Voc end: 17:17

Planetary and Angelic Hours			
Jupiter	06:57	Moon	17:29
Mars	07:50	Saturn	18:37
Sun	08:43	Jupiter	19:44
Venus	09:35	Mars	20:51
Mercury	10:28	Sun	21:58
Moon	11:21	Venus	23:05
Saturn	12:13	Mercury	00:12
Jupiter	13:06	Moon	01:20
Mars	13:59	Saturn	02:27
Sun	14:51	Jupiter	03:34
Venus	15:44	Mars	04:41
Mercury	16:37	Sun	05:48

Aspects

Moon square Uranus
Moon square Jupiter
Moon square Eris
Mercury square Sedna
Moon sextile Chiron
Moon trine Sedna
Mercury sextile Saturn
Sun sextile Ceres
Sun sextile Juno
Mars square Vesta
Jupiter opposite Uranus
Jupiter opposite Eris
Uranus conjunct Eris
Pluto sextile Pallas
Ceres trine Juno

Planets	00:00 am	Moon
Sun	05 pis 33	00.00 am - 03 aq 33
Mercury	26 aq 34	02.00 am - 04 aq 37
Venus	11 ar 47	04.00 am - 05 aq 42
Mars	19 ar 48	06.00 am - 06 aq 46
Jupiter	22 lib 38	08.00 am - 07 aq 50
Saturn	26 sag 25	10.00 am - 08 aq 55
Uranus	21 ar 52	12.00 pm - 09 aq 59
Neptune	11 pis 28	14.00 pm - 11 aq 04
Pluto	18 cap 39	16.00 pm - 12 aq 09
		18.00 pm - 13 aq 14
Oob		20.00 pm - 14 aq 19
		22.00 pm - 15 aq 25

Friday 24th February

Retrograde Planets

Jupiter, Vesta, Haumea, Makemake, Orcus

Asteroids		Dwarf Planets	
Juno	05 cap 50	Eris	22 ar 42
Vesta	20 can 42	Haumea	24 lib 30
Pallas	17 pis 44	Makemake	03 lib 22
Ceres	05 tau 25	Salacia	29 pis 51
Chiron	23 pis 30	Orcus	08 vir 11
N Node	03 vir 23	Quaoar	00 cap 30
S Node	03 pis 23	Sedna	25 tau 06

Moon Phase: Balsamic
Sunrise: 06:56 GMT
Sunset: 17:32
Moonrise: 05:43
Moonset: 15:15
Voc start:
Voc end:

Planetary and Angelic Hours			
Venus	06:55	Mars	17:31
Mercury	07:48	Sun	18:38
Moon	08:41	Venus	19:45
Saturn	09:34	Mercury	20:52
Jupiter	10:27	Moon	21:59
Mars	11:20	Saturn	23:05
Sun	12:13	Jupiter	00:12
Venus	13:06	Mars	01:19
Mercury	13:59	Sun	02:26
Moon	14:52	Venus	03:33
Saturn	15:45	Mercury	04:40
Jupiter	16:38	Moon	05:47

Aspects

Moon square Ceres
Sun sextile Ceres
Moon sextile Venus
Sun sextile Juno
Mars square Vesta
Jupiter opposite Uranus
Jupiter opposite Eris
Uranus conjunct Eris
Pluto sextile Pallas
Ceres trine Juno

Planets	00:00 am	Moon
Sun	06 pis 34	00.00 am - 16 aq 30
Mercury	28 aq 18	02.00 am - 17 aq 36
Venus	12 ar 05	04.00 am - 18 aq 41
Mars	20 ar 31	06.00 am - 19 aq 47
Jupiter	22 lib 35	08.00 am - 20 aq 53
Saturn	26 sag 29	10.00 am - 21 aq 59
Uranus	21 ar 54	12.00 pm - 23 aq 06
Neptune	11 pis 30	14.00 pm - 24 aq 12
Pluto	18 cap 40	16.00 pm - 25 aq 19
		18.00 pm - 26 aq 25
Oob		20.00 pm - 27 aq 32
		22.00 pm - 28 aq 39

Saturday 25th February

Planetary Directions

Mercury into Pisces at 23:08

Retrograde Planets

Jupiter, Vesta, Haumea, Makemake, Orcus

Asteroids		Dwarf Planets	
Juno	06 cap 23	Eris	22 ar 43
Vesta	20 can 32	Haumea	24 lib 29
Pallas	18 pis 25	Makemake	03 lib 21
Ceres	06 tau 04	Salacia	29 pis 52
Chiron	23 pis 37	Orcus	08 vir 10
N Node	03 vir 23	Quaoar	00 cap 31
S Node	03 pis 23	Sedna	25 tau 06

Moon Phase: Balsamic
Sunrise: 06:54 GMT
Sunset: 17:34
Moonrise: 06:18
Moonset: 16:23
Voc start:18:11
Voc end:

Planetary and Angelic Hours			
Saturn	06:53	Mercury	17:33
Jupiter	07:47	Moon	18:39
Mars	08:40	Saturn	19:46
Sun	09:33	Jupiter	20:53
Venus	10:27	Mars	21:59
Mercury	11:20	Sun	23:06
Moon	12:13	Venus	00:12
Saturn	13:06	Mercury	01:19
Jupiter	14:00	Moon	02:25
Mars	14:53	Saturn	03:32
Sun	15:46	Jupiter	04:38
Venus	16:40	Mars	05:45

Aspects

Mars square Vesta
Moon sextile Mars
Moon sextile Uranus
Moon trine Jupiter
Moon sextile Eris
Moon square Sedna
Moon sextile Saturn
Pluto sextile Pallas
Sun sextile Juno
Moon conj. Mercury
Mars conjunct Uranus
Jupiter opposite Uranus
Jupiter opposite Eris
Uranus conjunct Eris
Ceres trine Juno

Planets	00:00 am	Moon
Sun	07 pis 34	00.00 am - 29 aq 46
Mercury	00 pis 03	02.00 am - 00 pis 53
Venus	12 ar 20	04.00 am - 02 pis 00
Mars	21 ar 15	06.00 am - 03 pis 08
Jupiter	22 lib 31	08.00 am - 04 pis 15
Saturn	26 sag 32	10.00 am - 05 pis 23
Uranus	21 ar 57	12.00 pm - 06 pis 31
Neptune	11 pis 33	14.00 pm - 07 pis 39
Pluto	18 cap 42	16.00 pm - 08 pis 47
		18.00 pm - 09 pis 55
Oob		20.00 pm - 11 pis 03
		22.00 pm - 12 pis 11

Sunday 26th February

Planetary Directions

Moon into Pisces 00:25

Retrograde Planets

Jupiter, Vesta, Haumea, Makemake, Orcus

Asteroids		Dwarf Planets	
Juno	06 cap 40	Eris	22 ar 43
Vesta	20 can 27	Haumea	24 lib 29
Pallas	18 pis 46	Makemake	03 lib 20
Ceres	06 tau 24	Salacia	29 pis 54
Chiron	23 pis 40	Orcus	08 vir 09
N Node	03 vir 23	Quaoar	00 cap 32
S Node	03 pis 23	Sedna	25 tau 07

New Moon: 15:00
Sunrise: 06:51 GMT
Sunset: 17:35
Moonrise: 06:50
Moonset: 17:35
Voc start:
Voc end: 00:24

Planetary and Angelic Hours

Sun	06:51	Jupiter	17:35
Venus	07:45	Mars	18:41
Mercury	08:39	Sun	19:47
Moon	09:32	Venus	20:53
Saturn	10:26	Mercury	22:00
Jupiter	11:19	Moon	23:06
Mars	12:13	Saturn	00:12
Sun	13:07	Jupiter	01:18
Venus	14:00	Mars	02:24
Mercury	14:54	Sun	03:31
Moon	15:47	Venus	04:37
Saturn	16:41	Mercury	05:43

Solar Eclipse 09:58
08 Pis 12

Aspects

Moon conj. Mercury
Moon sextile Ceres
Moon sextile Juno
Sun conjunct Moon
Moon conj. Neptune
Mars opposite Jupiter
Mars conjunct Uranus
Mars conjunct Eris
Jupiter opposite Uranus
Jupiter opposite Eris
Uranus conjunct Eris
Pluto sextile Pallas
Ceres trine Juno

Planets	00:00 am	Moon
Sun	08 pis 34	00.00 am - 13 pis 20
Mercury	01 pis 49	02.00 am - 14 pis 28
Venus	12 ar 34	04.00 am - 15 pis 37
Mars	21 ar 59	06.00 am - 16 pis 46
Jupiter	22 lib 28	08.00 am - 17 pis 55
Saturn	26 sag 36	10.00 am - 19 pis 04
Uranus	22 ar 00	12.00 pm - 20 pis 13
Neptune	11 pis 35	14.00 pm - 21 pis 22
Pluto	18 cap 43	16.00 pm - 22 pis 31
		18.00 pm - 23 pis 41
Oob		20.00 pm - 24 pis 50
		22.00 pm - 26 pis 00

Monday 27th February

Retrograde Planets

Jupiter, Vesta, Haumea, Makemake, Orcus

Asteroids		Dwarf Planets	
Juno	06 cap 56	Eris	22 ar 44
Vesta	20 can 23	Haumea	24 lib 28
Pallas	19 pis 06	Makemake	03 lib 19
Ceres	06 tau 44	Salacia	29 pis 55
Chiron	23 pis 44	Orcus	08 vir 08
N Node	03 vir 23	Quaoar	00 cap 32
S Node	03 pis 23	Sedna	25 tau 07

Moon Phase: Crescent
Sunrise: 06:49 GMT
Sunset: 17:37
Moonrise: 07:19
Moonset: 18:50
Voc start: 23:07
Voc end:

Planetary and Angelic Hours			
Moon	06:49	Venus	17:36
Saturn	07:43	Mercury	18:42
Jupiter	08:37	Moon	19:48
Mars	09:31	Saturn	20:54
Sun	10:25	Jupiter	22:00
Venus	11:19	Mars	23:06
Mercury	12:13	Sun	00:12
Moon	13:07	Venus	01:18
Saturn	14:01	Mercury	02:24
Jupiter	14:55	Moon	03:29
Mars	15:49	Saturn	04:35
Sun	16:42	Jupiter	05:41

Aspects

Mars conjunct Uranus
Moon sextile Pluto
Moon conjunct Pallas
Moon trine Vesta
Mars opposite Jupiter
Moon conjunct Chiron
Moon sextile Sedna
Moon square Saturn
Mars conjunct Eris
Jupiter opposite Uranus
Jupiter opposite Eris
Uranus conjunct Eris
Pluto sextile Pallas
Ceres trine Juno
Pallas trine Vesta

Planets	**00:00 am**	**Moon**
Sun	09 pis 35	00.00 am - 27 pis 10
Mercury	03 pis 37	02.00 am - 28 pis 20
Venus	12 ar 45	04.00 am - 29 pis 29
Mars	22 ar 43	06.00 am - 00 ar 39
Jupiter	22 lib 24	08.00 am - 01 ar 49
Saturn	26 sag 40	10.00 am - 03 ar 00
Uranus	22 ar 02	12.00 pm - 04 ar 10
Neptune	11 pis 37	14.00 pm - 05 ar 20
Pluto	18 cap 45	16.00 pm - 06 ar 30
		18.00 pm - 07 ar 41
Oob		20.00 pm - 08 ar 51
		22.00 pm - 10 ar 02

Tuesday 28th February

Retrograde Planets

Jupiter, Vesta, Haumea, Makemake, Orcus

Asteroids		**Dwarf Planets**	
Juno	07 cap 12	Eris	22 ar 44
Vesta	20 can 19	Haumea	24 lib 27
Pallas	19 pis 27	Makemake	03 lib 18
Ceres	07 tau 04	Salacia	29 pis 57
Chiron	23 pis 47	Orcus	08 vir 06
N Node	03 vir 23	Quaoar	00 cap 33
S Node	03 pis 23	Sedna	25 tau 07

Moon Phase: Crescent
Sunrise: 06:47 GMT
Sunset: 17:39
Moonrise: 07:46
Moonset: 20:06
Voc start:
Voc end: 04:51

Planetary and Angelic Hours			
Mars	06:47	Saturn	17:38
Sun	07:41	Jupiter	18:44
Venus	08:36	Mars	19:49
Mercury	09:30	Sun	20:55
Moon	10:24	Venus	22:00
Saturn	11:18	Mercury	23:06
Jupiter	12:13	Moon	00:12
Mars	13:07	Saturn	01:17
Sun	14:01	Jupiter	02:23
Venus	14:55	Mars	03:28
Mercury	15:50	Sun	04:34
Moon	16:44	Venus	05:39

Shrove Tuesday

Aspects

Mars conjunct Eris
Moon square Juno
Jupiter opposite Uranus
Jupiter opposite Eris
Uranus conjunct Eris
Ceres trine Juno
Pallas trine Vesta

Planets	00:00 am	Moon
Sun	10 pis 35	00.00 am - 11 ar 13
Mercury	05 pis 25	02.00 am - 12 ar 23
Venus	12 ar 55	04.00 am - 13 ar 34
Mars	23 ar 27	06.00 am - 14 ar 45
Jupiter	22 lib 20	08.00 am - 15 ar 56
Saturn	26 sag 43	10.00 am - 17 ar 07
Uranus	22 ar 05	12.00 pm - 18 ar 18
Neptune	11 pis 39	14.00 pm - 19 ar 29
Pluto	18 cap 46	16.00 pm - 20 ar 40
		18.00 pm - 21 ar 51
Oob		20.00 pm - 23 ar 02
		22.00 pm - 24 ar 13

Wednesday 1st March

Planetary Directions

Salacia into Aries 17:46

Retrograde Planets

Jupiter, Vesta, Haumea, Makemake, Orcus

Asteroids		Dwarf Planets	
Juno	07 cap 29	Eris	22 ar 45
Vesta	20 can 16	Haumea	24 lib 26
Pallas	19 pis 48	Makemake	03 lib 17
Ceres	07 tau 24	Salacia	29 pis 58
Chiron	23 pis 51	Orcus	08 vir 05
N Node	03 vir 22	Quaoar	00 cap 34
S Node	03 pis 22	Sedna	25 tau 07

Moon Phase: Crescent
Sunrise: 06:45 GMT
Sunset: 17:41
Moonrise: 08:13
Moonset: 21:22
Voc start:
Voc end:

Planetary and Angelic Hours			
Mercury	06:45	Sun	17:40
Moon	07:40	Venus	18:45
Saturn	08:34	Mercury	19:50
Jupiter	09:29	Moon	20:56
Mars	10:23	Saturn	22:01
Sun	11:18	Jupiter	23:06
Venus	12:12	Mars	00:11
Mercury	13:07	Sun	01:17
Moon	14:02	Venus	02:22
Saturn	14:56	Mercury	03:27
Jupiter	15:51	Moon	04:32
Mars	16:45	Saturn	05:38

Ash Wednesday
St David's Day

Aspects

Moon conjunct Venus
Moon square Pluto
Moon square Vesta
Moon conjunct Uranus
Moon opposite Jupiter
Moon conjunct Eris
Moon conjunct Mars
Sun conjunct Neptune
Mercury sextile Ceres
Mercury sextile Juno
Jupiter opposite Uranus
Uranus conjunct Eris
Ceres trine Juno
Pallas trine Vesta

Planets	00:00 am	Moon
Sun	11 pis 35	00.00 am - 25 ar 25
Mercury	07 pis 14	02.00 am - 26 ar 36
Venus	13 ar 01	04.00 am - 27 ar 47
Mars	24 ar 10	06.00 am - 28 ar 59
Jupiter	22 lib 16	08.00 am - 00 tau 10
Saturn	26 sag 47	10.00 am - 01 tau 21
Uranus	22 ar 08	12.00 pm - 02 tau 33
Neptune	11 pis 42	14.00 pm - 03 tau 44
Pluto	18 cap 48	16.00 pm - 04 tau 56
		18.00 pm - 06 tau 07
Oob		20.00 pm - 07 tau 19
		22.00 pm - 08 tau 30

Thursday 2nd March

Planetary Directions

Moon into Taurus
07:43

Retrograde Planets

Jupiter, Vesta, Haumea, Makemake, Orcus

Asteroids		Dwarf Planets	
Juno	07 cap 45	Eris	22 ar 45
Vesta	20 can 13	Haumea	24 lib 25
Pallas	20 pis 08	Makemake	03 lib 16
Ceres	07 tau 44	Salacia	00 ar 00
Chiron	23 pis 55	Orcus	08 vir 04
N Node	03 vir 21	Quaoar	00 cap 35
S Node	03 pis 21	Sedna	25 tau 08

Moon Phase: Crescent
Sunrise: 06:43 GMT
Sunset: 17:43
Moonrise: 08:42
Moonset: 22:39
Voc start: 02:18
Voc end: 07:42

Planetary and Angelic Hours			
Jupiter	06:43	Moon	17:42
Mars	07:38	Saturn	18:47
Sun	08:33	Jupiter	19:51
Venus	09:28	Mars	20:56
Mercury	10:22	Sun	22:01
Moon	11:17	Venus	23:06
Saturn	12:12	Mercury	00:11
Jupiter	13:07	Moon	01:16
Mars	14:02	Saturn	02:21
Sun	14:57	Jupiter	03:26
Venus	15:52	Mars	04:31
Mercury	16:47	Sun	05:36

Aspects

Ceres trine Juno
Moon trine Saturn
Sun conjunct Neptune
Pallas trine Vesta
Mercury sextile Juno
Mercury sextile Ceres
Moon trine Juno
Moon conjunct Ceres
Moon sextile Mercury
Jupiter opposite Uranus
Jupiter opposite Eris
Uranus conjunct Eris

Planets	**00:00 am**	**Moon**
Sun	12 pis 35	00.00 am - 09 tau 41
Mercury	09 pis 04	02.00 am - 10 tau 53
Venus	13 ar 06	04.00 am - 12 tau 05
Mars	24 ar 54	06.00 am - 13 tau 16
Jupiter	22 lib 11	08.00 am - 14 tau 28
Saturn	26 sag 50	10.00 am - 15 tau 39
Uranus	22 ar 11	12.00 pm - 16 tau 51
Neptune	11 pis 44	14.00 pm - 18 tau 02
Pluto	18 cap 49	16.00 pm - 19 tau 14
		18.00 pm - 20 tau 25
		20.00 pm - 21 tau 36
Oob		22.00 pm - 22 tau 48

Friday 3rd March

Retrograde Planets

Jupiter, Vesta, Haumea, Makemake, Orcus

Asteroids		**Dwarf Planets**	
Juno	08 cap 00	Eris	22 ar 46
Vesta	20 can 11	Haumea	24 lib 25
Pallas	20 pis 29	Makemake	03 lib 15
Ceres	08 tau 05	Salacia	00 ar 01
Chiron	23 pis 50	Orcus	08 vir 03
N Node	03 vir 20	Quaoar	00 cap 35
S Node	03 pis 20	Sedna	25 tau 08

Moon Phase: Crescent
Sunrise: 06:41 GMT
Sunset: 17:44
Moonrise: 09:13
Moonset: 23:54
Voc start: 15:20
Voc end:

Planetary and Angelic Hours			
Venus	06:41	Mars	17:43
Mercury	07:36	Sun	18:48
Moon	08:31	Venus	19:53
Saturn	09:26	Mercury	20:57
Jupiter	10:22	Moon	22:02
Mars	11:17	Saturn	23:06
Sun	12:12	Jupiter	00:11
Venus	13:07	Mars	01:16
Mercury	14:02	Sun	02:20
Moon	14:58	Venus	03:25
Saturn	15:53	Mercury	04:29
Jupiter	16:48	Moon	05:34

Aspects

Jupiter opposite Uranus
Moon sextile Neptune
Sun sextile Moon
Moon trine Pluto
Moon sextile Vesta
Moon sextile Pallas
Moon sextile Chiron
Mercury conj. Neptune
Jupiter opposite Eris
Uranus conjunct Eris
Ceres trine Juno
Pallas trine Vesta

Planets	00:00 am	Moon
Sun	13 pis 35	00.00 am - 23 tau 59
Mercury	10 pis 55	02.00 am - 25 tau 11
Venus	13 ar 08	04.00 am - 26 tau 22
Mars	25 ar 38	06.00 am - 27 tau 34
Jupiter	22 lib 07	08.00 am - 28 tau 45
Saturn	26 sag 53	10.00 am - 29 tau 56
Uranus	22 ar 14	12.00 pm - 01 gem 08
Neptune	11 pis 46	14.00 pm - 02 gem 19
Pluto	18 cap 50	16.00 pm - 03 gem 30
		18.00 pm - 04 gem 41
Oob		20.00 pm - 05 gem 53
		22.00 pm - 07 gem 04

Saturday 4th March

Planetary Directions

Venus retrograde
13 ar 08 at 09:09
Moon into Gemini
10:06

Retrograde Planets

Venus, Jupiter, Vesta, Haumea, Makemake, Orcus

Asteroids		Dwarf Planets	
Juno	08 cap 16	Eris	22 ar 46
Vesta	20 can 09	Haumea	24 lib 24
Pallas	20 pis 50	Makemake	03 lib 14
Ceres	08 tau 25	Salacia	00 ar 03
Chiron	24 pis 02	Orcus	08 vir 02
N Node	03 vir 19	Quaoar	00 cap 36
S Node	03 pis 19	Sedna	25 tau 08

Moon Phase: Crescent
Sunrise: 06:39 GMT
Sunset: 17:46
Moonrise: 09:48
Moonset: None
Voc start:
Voc end: 10:05

Planetary and Angelic Hours			
Saturn	06:39	Mercury	17:45
Jupiter	07:34	Moon	18:49
Mars	08:30	Saturn	19:54
Sun	09:25	Jupiter	20:58
Venus	10:21	Mars	22:02
Mercury	11:16	Sun	23:06
Moon	2:12	Venus	00:11
Saturn	13:07	Mercury	01:15
Jupiter	14:03	Moon	02:19
Mars	14:58	Saturn	03:24
Sun	15:54	Jupiter	04:28
Venus	16:50	Mars	05:32

Aspects

Moon sextile Chiron
Mercury conj. Neptune
Mars trine Saturn
Jupiter opposite Uranus
Jupiter opposite Eris
Uranus conjunct Eris
Ceres trine Juno

Planets	**00:00 am**	**Moon**
Sun	14 pis 36	00.00 am - 08 gem 15
Mercury	12 pis 47	02.00 am - 09 gem 26
Venus	13 ar 08	04.00 am - 10 gem 37
Mars	26 ar 21	06.00 am - 11 gem 48
Jupiter	22 lib 02	08.00 am - 12 gem 59
Saturn	26 sag 56	10.00 am - 14 gem 10
Uranus	22 ar 16	12.00 pm - 15 gem 21
Neptune	11 pis 49	14.00 pm - 16 gem 32
Pluto	18 cap 52	16.00 pm - 17 gem 42
		18.00 pm - 18 gem 53
Oob		20.00 pm - 20 gem 04
		22.00 pm - 21 gem 15

Sunday 5th March

Retrograde Planets

Venus, Jupiter, Vesta, Haumea, Makemake, Orcus

Asteroids		**Dwarf Planets**	
Juno	08 cap 32	Eris	22 ar 47
Vesta	20 can 08	Haumea	24 lib 23
Pallas	21 pis 10	Makemake	03 lib 13
Ceres	08 tau 46	Salacia	00 ar 05
Chiron	24 pis 05	Orcus	08 vir 01
N Node	03 vir 19	Quaoar	00 cap 37
S Node	03 pis 19	Sedna	25 tau 09

First Quarter: 11:33
Sunrise: 06:36 GMT
Sunset: 17:48
Moonrise: 10:30
Moonset: 01:07
Voc start:
Voc end:

Planetary and Angelic Hours			
Sun	06:36	Jupiter	17:47
Venus	07:32	Mars	18:51
Mercury	08:28	Sun	19:55
Moon	09:24	Venus	20:59
Saturn	10:20	Mercury	22:03
Jupiter	11:16	Moon	23:07
Mars	12:12	Saturn	00:11
Sun	13:07	Jupiter	01:14
Venus	14:03	Mars	02:18
Mercury	14:59	Sun	03:22
Moon	15:55	Venus	04:26
Saturn	16:51	Mercury	05:30

Aspects

Moon square Neptune
Moon sextile Venus
Moon square Mercury
Sun square Moon
Mars trine Saturn
Moon square Pallas
Moon trine Jupiter
Moon sextile Uranus
Sun conjunct Mercury
Moon sextile Eris
Jupiter opposite Uranus
Jupiter opposite Eris
Uranus conjunct Eris
Ceres trine Juno

Planets	**00:00 am**	**Moon**
Sun	15 pis 36	00.00 am - 22 gem 25
Mercury	14 pis 41	02.00 am - 23 gem 36
Venus	13 ar 05	04.00 am - 24 gem 46
Mars	27 ar 05	06.00 am - 25 gem 57
Jupiter	21 lib 57	08.00 am - 27 gem 07
Saturn	26 sag 59	10.00 am - 28 gem 17
Uranus	22 ar 19	12.00 pm - 29 gem 28
Neptune	11 pis 51	14.00 pm - 00 can 38
Pluto	18 cap 53	16.00 pm - 01 can 48
		18.00 pm - 02 can 58
Oob		20.00 pm - 04 can 08
		22.00 pm - 05 can 18

Monday 6th March

Planetary Directions

Moon into Cancer
12:55

Retrograde Planets

Venus, Jupiter, Vesta, Haumea, Makemake, Orcus

Asteroids		**Dwarf Planets**	
Juno	08 cap 47	Eris	22 ar 47
Vesta	20 can 07	Haumea	24 lib 22
Pallas	21 pis 31	Makemake	03 lib 12
Ceres	09 tau 06	Salacia	00 ar 06
Chiron	24 pis 09	Orcus	07 vir 59
N Node	03 vir 19	Quaoar	00 cap 37
S Node	03 pis 19	Sedna	25 tau 09

Moon Phase: Gibbous
Sunrise: 06:34 GMT
Sunset: 17:50
Moonrise: 11:19
Moonset: 02:15
Voc start: 08:21
Voc end: 12:54

Planetary and Angelic Hours			
Moon	06:34	Venus	17:48
Saturn	07:30	Mercury	18:52
Jupiter	08:27	Moon	19:56
Mars	09:23	Saturn	20:59
Sun	10:19	Jupiter	22:03
Venus	11:15	Mars	23:07
Mercury	12:11	Sun	00:10
Moon	13:08	Venus	01:14
Saturn	14:04	Mercury	02:18
Jupiter	15:00	Moon	03:21
Mars	15:56	Saturn	04:25
Sun	16:52	Jupiter	05:28

Aspects

Moon sextile Eris
Moon square Chiron
Moon opposite Saturn
Moon sextile Mars
Sun conjunct Mercury
Mars trine Saturn
Jupiter opposite Uranus
Jupiter opposite Eris
Uranus conjunct Eris
Ceres trine Juno

Planets	00:00 am	Moon
Sun	16 pis 36	00.00 am - 06 can 28
Mercury	16 pis 35	02.00 am - 07 can 38
Venus	13 ar 00	04.00 am - 08 can 48
Mars	27 ar 48	06.00 am - 09 can 58
Jupiter	21 lib 52	08.00 am - 11 can 08
Saturn	27 sag 02	10.00 am - 12 can 17
Uranus	22 ar 22	12.00 pm - 13 can 27
Neptune	11 pis 53	14.00 pm - 14 can 36
Pluto	18 cap 54	16.00 pm - 15 can 45
		18.00 pm - 16 can 55
Oob		20.00 pm - 18 can 04
		22.00 pm - 19 can 14

Tuesday 7th March

Planetary Directions

Vesta direct
20 can 07 at 09:34

Retrograde Planets

Venus, Jupiter, Haumea, Makemake, Orcus

Asteroids		Dwarf Planets	
Juno	09 cap 02	Eris	22 ar 48
Vesta	20 can 07	Haumea	24 lib 21
Pallas	21 pis 52	Makemake	03 lib 11
Ceres	09 tau 27	Salacia	00 ar 08
Chiron	24 pis 12	Orcus	07 vir 58
N Node	03 vir 20	Quaoar	00 cap 38
S Node	03 pis 20	Sedna	25 tau 09

Moon Phase: Gibbous
Sunrise: 06:32 GMT
Sunset: 17:51
Moonrise: 12:15
Moonset: 03:16
Voc start:
Voc end:

Planetary and Angelic Hours			
Mars	06:32	Saturn	17:50
Sun	07:29	Jupiter	18:53
Venus	08:25	Mars	19:57
Mercury	09:22	Sun	21:00
Moon	10:18	Venus	22:03
Saturn	11:15	Mercury	23:07
Jupiter	12:11	Moon	00:10
Mars	13:08	Saturn	01:13
Sun	14:04	Jupiter	02:17
Venus	15:01	Mars	03:20
Mercury	15:57	Sun	04:23
Moon	16:54	Venus	05:27

Aspects

Sun conjunct Mercury
Moon opposite Juno
Moon sextile Ceres
Moon trine Neptune
Moon square Venus
Sun trine Moon
Moon trine Mercury
Moon opposite Pluto
Moon conjunct Vesta
Mercury sextile Pluto
Jupiter opposite Uranus
Uranus conjunct Eris
Ceres trine Juno

Planets	00:00 am	Moon
Sun	17 pis 36	00.00 am - 20 can 23
Mercury	18 pis 30	02.00 am - 21 can 32
Venus	12 ar 52	04.00 am - 22 can 41
Mars	28 ar 32	06.00 am - 23 can 50
Jupiter	21 lib 47	08.00 am - 24 can 59
Saturn	27 sag 05	10.00 am - 26 can 08
Uranus	22 ar 25	12.00 pm - 27 can 16
Neptune	11 pis 55	14.00 pm - 28 can 25
Pluto	18 cap 55	16.00 pm - 29 can 34
		18.00 pm - 00 leo 42
Oob		20.00 pm - 01 leo 51
		22.00 pm - 02 leo 59

Wednesday 8th March

Planetary Directions

Moon into Leo 16:46

Retrograde Planets

Venus, Jupiter, Haumea, Makemake, Orcus

Asteroids		Dwarf Planets	
Juno	09 cap 18	Eris	22 ar 48
Vesta	20 can 07	Haumea	24 lib 20
Pallas	22 pis 13	Makemake	03 lib 10
Ceres	09 tau 48	Salacia	00 ar 09
Chiron	24 pis 16	Orcus	07 vir 57
N Node	03 vir 21	Quaoar	00 cap 38
S Node	03 pis 21	Sedna	25 tau 10

Moon Phase: Gibbous
Sunrise: 06:30 GMT
Sunset: 17:53
Moonrise: 13:19
Moonset: 04:08
Voc start: 14:59
Voc end: 16:45

Planetary and Angelic Hours			
Mercury	06:30	Sun	17:52
Moon	07:27	Venus	18:55
Saturn	08:24	Mercury	19:58
Jupiter	09:20	Moon	21:01
Mars	10:17	Saturn	22:04
Sun	11:14	Jupiter	23:07
Venus	12:11	Mars	00:10
Mercury	13:08	Sun	01:13
Moon	14:05	Venus	02:16
Saturn	15:01	Mercury	03:19
Jupiter	15:58	Moon	04:22
Mars	16:55	Saturn	05:25

Aspects

Moon square Jupiter
Moon trine Pallas
Moon square Uranus
Moon square Eris
Mercury sextile Pluto
Moon trine Chiron
Moon square Mars
Mercury trine Vesta
Sun sextile Pluto
Jupiter opposite Uranus
Uranus conjunct Eris
Ceres trine Juno

Planets	**00:00 am**	**Moon**
Sun	18 pis 36	00.00 am - 04 leo 07
Mercury	20 pis 25	02.00 am - 05 leo 15
Venus	12 ar 42	04.00 am - 06 leo 24
Mars	29 ar 15	06.00 am - 07 leo 32
Jupiter	21 lib 41	08.00 am - 08 leo 40
Saturn	27 sag 08	10.00 am - 09 leo 48
Uranus	22 ar 28	12.00 pm - 10 leo 55
Neptune	11 pis 58	14.00 pm - 12 leo 03
Pluto	18 cap 57	16.00 pm - 13 leo 11
		18.00 pm - 14 leo 18
Oob		20.00 pm - 15 leo 26
		22.00 pm - 16 leo 33

Thursday 9th March

Retrograde Planets

Venus, Jupiter, Haumea, Makemake, Orcus

Asteroids		**Dwarf Planets**	
Juno	09 cap 33	Eris	22 ar 49
Vesta	20 can 07	Haumea	24 lib 19
Pallas	22 pis 34	Makemake	03 lib 09
Ceres	10 tau 09	Salacia	00 ar 11
Chiron	24 pis 20	Orcus	07 vir 56
N Node	03 vir 22	Quaoar	00 cap 39
S Node	03 pis 22	Sedna	25 tau 10

Moon Phase: Gibbous
Sunrise: 06:27 GMT
Sunset: 17:55
Moonrise: 14:27
Moonset: 04:52
Voc start:
Voc end:

Planetary and Angelic Hours			
Jupiter	06:28	Moon	17:54
Mars	07:25	Saturn	18:56
Sun	08:22	Jupiter	19:59
Venus	09:19	Mars	21:02
Mercury	10:16	Sun	22:04
Moon	11:14	Venus	23:07
Saturn	12:11	Mercury	00:10
Jupiter	13:08	Moon	01:12
Mars	14:05	Saturn	02:15
Sun	15:02	Jupiter	03:18
Venus	15:59	Mars	04:20
Mercury	16:56	Sun	05:23

Aspects

Sun sextile Pluto
Moon square Ceres
Moon trine Venus
Sun trine Vesta
Mercury conj. Pallas
Jupiter opposite Uranus
Uranus conjunct Eris
Ceres trine Juno

Friday 10th March

Planets	00:00 am	Moon
Sun	19 pis 36	00.00 am - 17 leo 41
Mercury	22 pis 22	02.00 am - 18 leo 48
Venus	12 ar 29	04.00 am - 19 leo 55
Mars	29 ar 58	06.00 am - 21 leo 02
Jupiter	21 lib 36	08.00 am - 22 leo 09
Saturn	27 sag 11	10.00 am - 23 leo 16
Uranus	22 ar 31	12.00 pm - 24 leo 23
Neptune	12 pis 00	14.00 pm - 25 leo 30
Pluto	18 cap 58	16.00 pm - 26 leo 36
		18.00 pm - 27 leo 43
		20.00 pm - 28 leo 49
Oob		22.00 pm - 29 leo 56

Planetary Directions

Mars into Taurus 00:34
Moon into Virgo 22:08

Retrograde Planets

Venus, Jupiter, Haumea, Makemake, Orcus

Asteroids		Dwarf Planets	
Juno	09 cap 48	Eris	22 ar 49
Vesta	20 can 08	Haumea	24 lib 19
Pallas	22 pis 54	Makemake	03 lib 08
Ceres	10 tau 30	Salacia	00 ar 12
Chiron	24 pis 23	Orcus	07 vir 55
N Node	03 vir 23	Quaoar	00 cap 39
S Node	03 pis 23	Sedna	25 tau 10

Moon Phase: Gibbous
Sunrise: 06:25 GMT
Sunset: 17:56
Moonrise: 15:37
Moonset: 05:28
Voc start: 17:05
Voc end: 22:07

Planetary and Angelic Hours			
Venus	06:26	Mars	17:55
Mercury	07:23	Sun	18:58
Moon	08:21	Venus	20:00
Saturn	09:18	Mercury	21:02
Jupiter	10:15	Moon	22:05
Mars	11:13	Saturn	23:07
Sun	12:10	Jupiter	00:09
Venus	13:08	Mars	01:12
Mercury	14:05	Sun	02:14
Moon	15:03	Venus	03:16
Saturn	16:00	Mercury	04:19
Jupiter	16:58	Moon	05:21

Aspects

Moon sextile Jupiter
Mercury conj. Pallas
Moon trine Uranus
Moon trine Eris
Sun trine Vesta
Moon trine Saturn
Moon trine Mars
Mercury conj. Chiron
Uranus conjunct Eris
Ceres trine Juno

Planets	00:00 am	Moon
Sun	20 pis 36	00.00 am - 01 vir 02
Mercury	24 pis 19	02.00 am - 02 vir 08
Venus	12 ar 13	04.00 am - 03 vir 14
Mars	00 tau 42	06.00 am - 04 vir 20
Jupiter	21 lib 30	08.00 am - 05 vir 26
Saturn	27 sag 13	10.00 am - 06 vir 32
Uranus	22 ar 34	12.00 pm - 07 vir 38
Neptune	12 pis 02	14.00 pm - 08 vir 43
Pluto	18 cap 59	16.00 pm - 09 vir 49
		18.00 pm - 10 vir 54
Oob		20.00 pm - 12 vir 00
		22.00 pm - 13 vir 05

Saturday 11th March

Retrograde Planets

Venus, Jupiter, Haumea, Makemake, Orcus

Asteroids		Dwarf Planets	
Juno	10 cap 02	Eris	22 ar 50
Vesta	20 can 10	Haumea	24 lib 18
Pallas	23 pis 15	Makemake	03 lib 07
Ceres	10 tau 52	Salacia	00 ar 14
Chiron	24 Pis 27	Orcus	07 vir 54
N Node	03 vir 23	Quaoar	00 cap 40
S Node	03 pis 23	Sedna	25 tau 11

Moon Phase: Gibbous
Sunrise: 06:23 GMT
Sunset: 17:58
Moonrise: 16:48
Moonset: 05:59
Voc start:
Voc end:

Planetary and Angelic Hours			
Saturn	06:23	Mercury	17:57
Jupiter	07:21	Moon	18:59
Mars	08:19	Saturn	20:01
Sun	09:17	Jupiter	21:03
Venus	10:15	Mars	22:05
Mercury	11:12	Sun	23:07
Moon	12:10	Venus	00:09
Saturn	13:08	Mercury	01:11
Jupiter	14:06	Moon	02:13
Mars	15:04	Saturn	03:15
Sun	16:01	Jupiter	04:17
Venus	16:59	Mars	05:19

Aspects

Mercury conj. Chiron
Moon trine Juno
Moon trine Ceres
Moon opp. Neptune
Mercury square Saturn
Uranus conjunct Eris
Neptune sextile Ceres
Chiron conjunct Pallas
Ceres trine Juno

Planets	00:00 am
Sun	21 pis 36
Mercury	26 pis 17
Venus	11 ar 56
Mars	01 tau 25
Jupiter	21 lib 25
Saturn	27 sag 16
Uranus	22 ar 37
Neptune	12 pis 04
Pluto	19 cap 00
Oob	

Moon

00.00 am - 14 vir 10
02.00 am - 15 vir 15
04.00 am - 16 vir 20
06.00 am - 17 vir 25
08.00 am - 18 vir 30
10.00 am - 19 vir 35
12.00 pm - 20 vir 39
14.00 pm - 21 vir 44
16.00 pm - 22 vir 48
18.00 pm - 23 vir 53
20.00 pm - 24 vir 57
22.00 pm - 26 vir 01

Sunday 12th March

Retrograde Planets

Venus, Jupiter, Haumea, Makemake, Orcus

Asteroids		Dwarf Planets	
Juno	10 cap 17	Eris	22 ar 51
Vesta	20 can 11	Haumea	24 lib 17
Pallas	23 pis 36	Makemake	03 lib 05
Ceres	11 tau 13	Salacia	00 ar 16
Chiron	24 pis 30	Orcus	07 vir 52
N Node	03 vir 23	Quaoar	00 cap 40
S Node	03 pis 23	Sedna	25 tau 11

Full Moon: 14:54
Sunrise: 06:21 GMT
Sunset: 18:00
Moonrise: 17:58
Moonset: 06:27
Voc start:
Voc end:

Planetary and Angelic Hours

Sun	06:21	Jupiter	17:59
Venus	07:19	Mars	19:00
Mercury	08:17	Sun	20:02
Moon	09:16	Venus	21:04
Saturn	10:14	Mercury	22:05
Jupiter	11:12	Moon	23:07
Mars	12:10	Saturn	00:09
Sun	13:08	Jupiter	01:10
Venus	14:06	Mars	02:12
Mercury	15:04	Sun	03:14
Moon	16:02	Venus	04:16
Saturn	17:01	Mercury	05:17

Aspects

Moon trine Pluto
Moon sextile Vesta
Mercury square Saturn
Sun opposite Moon
Moon opposite Pallas
Moon opposite Chiron
Moon square Saturn
Uranus conjunct Eris
Neptune sextile Ceres
Chiron conjunct Pallas

Planets	00:00 am	Moon
Sun	22 pis 35	00.00 am - 27 vir 05
Mercury	28 pis 15	02.00 am - 28 vir 09
Venus	11 ar 35	04.00 am - 29 vir 13
Mars	02 tau 08	06.00 am - 00 lib 16
Jupiter	21 lib 19	08.00 am - 01 lib 20
Saturn	27 sag 18	10.00 am - 02 lib 24
Uranus	22 ar 40	12.00 pm - 03 lib 27
Neptune	12 pis 07	14.00 pm - 04 lib 30
Pluto	19 cap 01	16.00 pm - 05 lib 34
		18.00 pm - 06 lib 37
Oob		20.00 pm - 07 lib 40
		22.00 pm - 08 lib 43

Monday 13th March

Planetary Directions

Moon into Libra 05:29
Mercury into Aries at 21:08

Retrograde Planets

Venus, Jupiter, Haumea, Makemake, Orcus

Asteroids		Dwarf Planets	
Juno	10 cap 31	Eris	22 ar 51
Vesta	20 can 14	Haumea	24 lib 16
Pallas	23 pis 57	Makemake	03 lib 04
Ceres	11 tau 34	Salacia	00 ar 17
Chiron	24 pis 34	Orcus	07 vir 51
N Node	03 vir 22	Quaoar	00 cap 41
S Node	03 pis 22	Sedna	25 tau 12

Phase: Disseminating
Sunrise: 06:19 GMT
Sunset: 18:02
Moonrise: 19:06
Moonset: 06:52
Voc start: 02:36
Voc end: 05:28

Planetary and Angelic Hours			
Moon	06:19	Venus	18:00
Saturn	07:17	Mercury	19:02
Jupiter	08:16	Moon	20:03
Mars	09:14	Saturn	21:04
Sun	10:13	Jupiter	22:06
Venus	11:11	Mars	23:07
Mercury	12:10	Sun	00:09
Moon	13:08	Venus	01:10
Saturn	14:07	Mercury	02:11
Jupiter	15:05	Moon	03:13
Mars	16:03	Saturn	04:14
Sun	17:02	Jupiter	05:15

Aspects

Moon square Saturn
Moon opp. Mercury
Sun conjunct Pallas
Moon square Juno
Venus square Juno
Jupiter square Vesta
Uranus conjunct Eris
Neptune sextile Ceres
Chiron conjunct Pallas

Planets	00:00 am	Moon
Sun	23 pis 35	00.00 am - 09 lib 46
Mercury	00 ar 14	02.00 am - 10 lib 49
Venus	11 ar 13	04.00 am - 11 lib 51
Mars	02 tau 51	06.00 am - 12 lib 54
Jupiter	21 lib 13	08.00 am - 13 lib 56
Saturn	27 sag 20	10.00 am - 14 lib 59
Uranus	22 ar 43	12.00 pm - 16 lib 01
Neptune	12 pis 09	14.00 pm - 17 lib 03
Pluto	19 cap 02	16.00 pm - 18 lib 06
		18.00 pm - 19 lib 08
		20.00 pm - 20 lib 10
Oob		22.00 pm - 21 lib 11

Tuesday 14th March

Retrograde Planets

Venus, Jupiter, Haumea, Makemake, Orcus

Asteroids		Dwarf Planets	
Juno	10 cap 46	Eris	22 ar 52
Vesta	20 can 16	Haumea	24 lib 15
Pallas	24 pis 18	Makemake	03 lib 03
Ceres	11 tau 56	Salacia	00 ar 19
Chiron	24 pis 38	Orcus	07 vir 50
N Node	03 vir 19	Quaoar	00 cap 41
S Node	03 pis 19	Sedna	25 tau 12

Phase: Disseminating
Sunrise: 06:16 GMT
Sunset: 18:03
Moonrise: 20:13
Moonset: 07:15
Voc start:
Voc end:

Planetary and Angelic Hours			
Mars	06:17	Saturn	18:02
Sun	07:15	Jupiter	19:03
Venus	08:14	Mars	20:04
Mercury	09:13	Sun	21:05
Moon	10:12	Venus	22:06
Saturn	11:11	Mercury	23:07
Jupiter	12:09	Moon	00:08
Mars	13:08	Saturn	01:09
Sun	14:07	Jupiter	02:10
Venus	15:06	Mars	03:11
Mercury	16:04	Sun	04:12
Moon	17:03	Venus	05:13

Aspects

Moon square Juno
Moon opposite Venus
Neptune sextile Ceres
Venus square juno
Moon square Pluto
Moon square Vesta
Moon conjunct Jupiter
Sun conjunct Chiron
Sun conjunct Pallas
Moon opposite Uranus
Moon opposite Eris
Jupiter square Vesta
Uranus conjunct Eris
Chiron conjunct Pallas

Planets	00:00 am	Moon
Sun	24 pis 35	00.00 am - 22 lib 13
Mercury	02 ar 12	02.00 am - 23 lib 15
Venus	10 ar 48	04.00 am - 24 lib 17
Mars	03 tau 35	06.00 am - 25 lib 18
Jupiter	21 lib 07	08.00 am - 26 lib 20
Saturn	27 sag 23	10.00 am - 27 lib 21
Uranus	22 ar 46	12.00 pm - 28 lib 22
Neptune	12 pis 11	14.00 pm - 29 lib 24
Pluto	19 cap 04	16.00 pm - 00 sco 25
		18.00 pm - 01 sco 26
Oob		20.00 pm - 02 sco 27
		22.00 pm - 03 sco 28

Wednesday 15th March

Planetary Directions

Moon into Scorpio
15:11

Retrograde Planets

Venus, Jupiter, Haumea, Makemake, Orcus

Asteroids		Dwarf Planets	
Juno	11 cap 00	Eris	22 ar 52
Vesta	20 can 20	Haumea	24 lib 14
Pallas	24 pis 39	Makemake	03 lib 02
Ceres	12 tau 17	Salacia	00 ar 21
Chiron	24 pis 41	Orcus	07 vir 49
N Node	03 vir 16	Quaoar	00 cap 42
S Node	03 pis 16	Sedna	25 tau 12

Phase: Disseminating
Sunrise: 06:14 GMT
Sunset: 18:05
Moonrise: 21:18
Moonset: 07:39
Voc start: 10:05
Voc end: 15:10

Planetary and Angelic Hours			
Mercury	06:14	Sun	18:04
Moon	07:14	Venus	19:04
Saturn	08:13	Mercury	20:05
Jupiter	09:12	Moon	21:06
Mars	10:11	Saturn	22:07
Sun	11:10	Jupiter	23:07
Venus	12:09	Mars	00:08
Mercury	13:08	Sun	01:09
Moon	14:07	Venus	02:09
Saturn	15:06	Mercury	03:10
Jupiter	16:05	Moon	04:11
Mars	17:05	Saturn	05:12

Aspects

Moon opposite Uranus
Moon opposite Eris
Sun conjunct Pallas
Sun conjunct Chiron
Chiron conjunct Pallas
Moon sextile Saturn
Moon opposite Mars
Venus square Juno
Jupiter square Vesta
Uranus conjunct Eris
Neptune sextile Ceres
Neptune sextile Juno

Planets	**00:00 am**	**Moon**
Sun	25 pis 35	00.00 am - 04 sco 28
Mercury	04 ar 10	02.00 am - 05 sco 29
Venus	10 ar 21	04.00 am - 06 sco 30
Mars	04 tau 18	06.00 am - 07 sco 31
Jupiter	21 lib 00	08.00 am - 08 sco 31
Saturn	27 sag 25	10.00 am - 09 sco 32
Uranus	22 ar 50	12.00 pm - 10 sco 32
Neptune	12 pis 13	14.00 pm - 11 sco 32
Pluto	19 cap 05	16.00 pm - 12 sco 33
		18.00 pm - 13 sco 33
Oob		20.00 pm - 14 sco 33
		22.00 pm - 15 sco 33

Thursday 16th March

Retrograde Planets

Venus, Jupiter, Haumea, Makemake, Orcus

Asteroids		**Dwarf Planets**	
Juno	11 cap 14	Eris	22 ar 53
Vesta	20 can 23	Haumea	24 lib 13
Pallas	25 pis 00	Makemake	03 lib 01
Ceres	12 tau 39	Salacia	00 ar 22
Chiron	24 pis 45	Orcus	07 vir 48
N Node	03 vir 13	Quaoar	00 cap 43
S Node	03 pis 13	Sedna	25 tau 12

Phase: Disseminating
Sunrise: 06:12 GMT
Sunset: 18:07
Moonrise: 22:21
Moonset: 08:04
Voc start:
Voc end:

Planetary and Angelic Hours			
Jupiter	06:12	Moon	18:05
Mars	07:12	Saturn	19:06
Sun	08:11	Jupiter	20:06
Venus	09:11	Mars	21:07
Mercury	10:10	Sun	22:07
Moon	11:09	Venus	23:07
Saturn	12:09	Mercury	00:08
Jupiter	13:08	Moon	01:08
Mars	14:08	Saturn	02:08
Sun	15:07	Jupiter	03:09
Venus	16:06	Mars	04:09
Mercury	17:06	Sun	05:10

Aspects

Moon sextile Juno
Moon trine Neptune
Moon opposite Ceres
Sun square Saturn
Jupiter square Vesta
Uranus conjunct Eris
Neptune sextile Ceres
Neptune sextile Juno
Chiron conjunct Pallas

Planets	**00:00 am**	**Moon**
Sun	26 pis 34	00.00 am - 16 sco 33
Mercury	06 ar 08	02.00 am - 17 sco 33
Venus	09 ar 52	04.00 am - 18 sco 33
Mars	05 tau 01	06.00 am - 19 sco 33
Jupiter	20 lib 54	08.00 am - 20 sco 33
Saturn	27 sag 27	10.00 am - 21 sco 33
Uranus	22 ar 53	12.00 pm - 22 sco 33
Neptune	12 pis 16	14.00 pm - 23 sco 32
Pluto	19 cap 06	16.00 pm - 24 sco 32
		18.00 pm - 25 sco 32
Oob		20.00 pm - 26 sco 31
		22.00 pm - 27 sco 31

Friday 17th March

Retrograde Planets

Venus, Jupiter, Haumea, Makemake, Orcus

Asteroids		**Dwarf Planets**	
Juno	11 cap 27	Eris	22 ar 53
Vesta	20 can 27	Haumea	24 lib 12
Pallas	25 pis 21	Makemake	03 lib 00
Ceres	13 tau 01	Salacia	00 ar 24
Chiron	24 pis 48	Orcus	07 vir 47
N Node	03 vir 09	Quaoar	00 cap 42
S Node	03 pis 09	Sedna	25 tau 13

Phase: Disseminating
Sunrise: 06:09 GMT
Sunset: 18:08
Moonrise: 23:23
Moonset: 08:31
Voc start: 21:56
Voc end:

Planetary and Angelic Hours			
Venus	06:10	Mars	18:07
Mercury	07:10	Sun	19:07
Moon	08:09	Venus	20:07
Saturn	09:09	Mercury	21:07
Jupiter	10:09	Moon	22:07
Mars	11:09	Saturn	23:07
Sun	12:08	Jupiter	00:07
Venus	13:08	Mars	01:07
Mercury	14:08	Sun	02:08
Moon	15:08	Venus	03:08
Saturn	16:08	Mercury	04:08
Jupiter	17:07	Moon	05:08

St Patrick's Day

Aspects

Moon sextile Pluto
Uranus conjunct Eris
Moon trine Vesta
Moon trine Chiron
Moon trine Pallas
Sun square Saturn
Sun trine Moon
Jupiter square Vesta
Neptune sextile Juno
Chiron conjunct Pallas

Planets	00:00 am	Moon
Sun	27 pis 34	00.00 am - 28 sco 30
Mercury	08 ar 05	02.00 am - 29 sco 30
Venus	09 ar 22	04.00 am - 00 sag 29
Mars	05 tau 44	06.00 am - 01 sag 29
Jupiter	20 lib 48	08.00 am - 02 sag 28
Saturn	27 sag 29	10.00 am - 03 sag 28
Uranus	22 ar 56	12.00 pm - 04 sag 27
Neptune	12 pis 18	14.00 pm - 05 sag 27
Pluto	19 cap 07	16.00 pm - 06 sag 26
		18.00 pm - 07 sag 25
Oob		20.00 pm - 08 sag 25
		22.00 pm - 09 sag 24

Saturday 18th March

Planetary Directions

Moon into Sagittarius 03:00

Retrograde Planets

Venus, Jupiter, Haumea, Makemake, Orcus

Asteroids		Dwarf Planets	
Juno	11 cap 41	Eris	22 ar 54
Vesta	20 can 31	Haumea	24 lib 11
Pallas	25 pis 42	Makemake	02 lib 59
Ceres	13 tau 23	Salacia	00 ar 25
Chiron	24 pis 52	Orcus	07 vir 46
N Node	03 vir 06	Quaoar	00 cap 43
S Node	03 pis 06	Sedna	25 tau 14

Phase: Disseminating
Sunrise: 06:07 GMT
Sunset: 18:10
Moonrise: None
Moonset: 09:02
Voc start:
Voc end: 02:59

Planetary and Angelic Hours

Saturn	06:08	Mercury	18:09
Jupiter	07:08	Moon	19:08
Mars	08:08	Saturn	20:08
Sun	09:08	Jupiter	21:08
Venus	10:08	Mars	22:08
Mercury	11:08	Sun	23:07
Moon	12:08	Venus	00:07
Saturn	13:08	Mercury	01:07
Jupiter	14:08	Moon	02:07
Mars	15:08	Saturn	03:06
Sun	16:09	Jupiter	04:06
Venus	17:09	Mars	05:06

Aspects

Mercury conj. Venus
Moon trine Venus
Moon trine Mercury
Jupiter square Vesta
Uranus conjunct Eris
Neptune sextile Juno

Planets	**00:00 am**	**Moon**
Sun	28 pis 34	00.00 am - 10 sag 23
Mercury	10 ar 01	02.00 am - 11 sag 23
Venus	08 ar 50	04.00 am - 12 sag 22
Mars	06 tau 27	06.00 am - 13 sag 21
Jupiter	20 lib 41	08.00 am - 14 sag 21
Saturn	27 sag 31	10.00 am - 15 sag 20
Uranus	22 ar 59	12.00 pm - 16 sag 20
Neptune	12 pis 20	14.00 pm - 17 sag 19
Pluto	19 cap 08	16.00 pm - 18 sag 18
		18.00 pm - 19 sag 18
Oob		20.00 pm - 20 sag 17
		22.00 pm - 21 sag 17

Sunday 19th March

Retrograde Planets

Venus, Jupiter, Haumea, Makemake, Orcus

Asteroids		**Dwarf Planets**	
Juno	11 cap 54	Eris	22 ar 54
Vesta	20 can 36	Haumea	24 lib 10
Pallas	26 pis 03	Makemake	02 lib 57
Ceres	13 tau 45	Salacia	00 ar 27
Chiron	24 pis 56	Orcus	07 vir 45
N Node	13 vir 03	Quaoar	00 cap 43
S Node	03 pis 03	Sedna	25 tau 14

Phase: Disseminating
Sunrise: 06:05 GMT
Sunset: 18:12
Moonrise: 00:22
Moonset: 09:36
Voc start:
Voc end:

Planetary and Angelic Hours			
Sun	06:06	Jupiter	18:10
Venus	07:06	Mars	19:10
Mercury	08:06	Sun	20:09
Moon	09:07	Venus	21:09
Saturn	10:07	Mercury	22:08
Jupiter	11:08	Moon	23:07
Mars	12:08	Saturn	00:07
Sun	13:08	Jupiter	01:06
Venus	14:09	Mars	02:06
Mercury	15:09	Sun	03:05
Moon	16:10	Venus	04:04
Saturn	17:10	Mercury	05:04

Aspects

Moon square Neptune
Jupiter square Vesta
Moon sextile Jupiter
Moon trine Uranus
Moon trine Eris
Mercury square Juno
Uranus conjunct Eris
Neptune sextile Juno

Planets	00:00 am	Moon
Sun	29 pis 33	00.00 am - 22 sag 16
Mercury	11 ar 55	02.00 am - 23 sag 16
Venus	08 ar 16	04.00 am - 24 sag 16
Mars	07 tau 10	06.00 am - 25 sag 15
Jupiter	20 lib 34	08.00 am - 26 sag 15
Saturn	27 sag 32	10.00 am - 27 sag 15
Uranus	23 ar 02	12.00 pm - 28 sag 14
Neptune	12 pis 22	14.00 pm - 29 sag 14
Pluto	19 cap 09	16.00 pm - 00 cap 14
		18.00 pm - 01 cap 14
		20.00 pm - 02 cap 14
Oob		22.00 pm - 03 cap 14

Monday 20th March

Planetary Directions

Sun enters Aries 10:29

Moon into Capricorn 15:31

Retrograde Planets

Venus, Jupiter, Haumea, Makemake, Orcus

Asteroids		Dwarf Planets	
Juno	12 cap 08	Eris	22 ar 55
Vesta	20 can 41	Haumea	24 lib 09
Pallas	26 pis 24	Makemake	02 lib 56
Ceres	14 tau 07	Salacia	00 ar 29
Chiron	24 pis 59	Orcus	07 vir 44
N Node	03 vir 02	Quaoar	00 cap 43
S Node	03 pis 02	Sedna	25 tau 15

Last Quarter
Sunrise: 06:03 GMT
Sunset: 18:13
Moonrise: 01:18
Moonset: 10:16
Voc start: 10:37
Voc end: 15:30

Planetary and Angelic Hours			
Moon	06:03	Venus	18:12
Saturn	07:04	Mercury	19:11
Jupiter	08:05	Moon	20:10
Mars	09:05	Saturn	21:09
Sun	10:06	Jupiter	22:08
Venus	11:07	Mars	23:07
Mercury	12:08	Sun	00:06
Moon	13:08	Venus	01:06
Saturn	14:09	Mercury	02:05
Jupiter	15:10	Moon	03:04
Mars	16:11	Saturn	04:03
Sun	17:11	Jupiter	05:02

Vernal Equinox

Aspects

Moon trine Eris
Moon trine Uranus
Mercury square Juno
Moon square Chiron
Moon square Pallas
Moon conjunct Saturn
Sun square Moon
Jupiter square Vesta
Saturn square Pallas
Uranus conjunct Eris
Neptune sextile Juno

Planets	00:00 am	Moon
Sun	00 ar 33	00.00 am - 04 cap 14
Mercury	13 ar 48	02.00 am - 05 cap 14
Venus	07 ar 41	04.00 am - 06 cap 14
Mars	07 tau 53	06.00 am - 07 cap 15
Jupiter	20 lib 27	08.00 am - 08 cap 15
Saturn	27 sag 34	10.00 am - 09 cap 16
Uranus	23 ar 06	12.00 pm - 10 cap 16
Neptune	12 pis 24	14.00 pm - 11 cap 17
Pluto	19 cap 09	16.00 pm - 12 cap 17
		18.00 pm - 13 cap 18
		20.00 pm - 14 cap 19
Oob		22.00 pm - 15 cap 20

Tuesday 21st March

Retrograde Planets

Venus, Jupiter, Haumea, Makemake, Orcus

Asteroids		Dwarf Planets	
Juno	12 cap 21	Eris	22 ar 56
Vesta	20 can 47	Haumea	24 lib 08
Pallas	26 pis 45	Makemake	02 lib 55
Ceres	14 tau 29	Salacia	00 ar 30
Chiron	25 pis 03	Orcus	07 vir 42
N Node	03 vir 01	Quaoar	00 cap 44
S Node	03 pis 01	Sedna	25 tau 15

Moon Phase: Balsamic
Sunrise: 06:00 GMT
Sunset: 18:15
Moonrise: 02:10
Moonset: 11:03
Voc start:
Voc end:

Planetary and Angelic Hours			
Mars	06:01	Saturn	18:14
Sun	07:02	Jupiter	19:12
Venus	08:03	Mars	20:11
Mercury	09:04	Sun	21:10
Moon	10:05	Venus	22:09
Saturn	11:06	Mercury	23:07
Jupiter	12:07	Moon	00:06
Mars	13:08	Saturn	01:05
Sun	14:09	Jupiter	02:04
Venus	15:10	Mars	03:02
Mercury	16:12	Sun	04:01
Moon	17:13	Venus	05:00

Aspects

Moon square Venus
Moon trine Mars
Neptune sextile Juno
Moon sextile Neptune
Moon conjunct Juno
Moon trine Ceres
Moon square Mercury
Jupiter square Vesta
Saturn square Pallas
Uranus conjunct Eris

Planets	00:00 am	Moon
Sun	01 ar 33	00.00 am - 16 cap 21
Mercury	15 ar 38	02.00 am - 17 cap 22
Venus	07 ar 05	04.00 am - 18 cap 23
Mars	08 tau 35	06.00 am - 19 cap 25
Jupiter	20 lib 21	08.00 am - 20 cap 26
Saturn	27 sag 36	10.00 am - 21 cap 28
Uranus	23 ar 09	12.00 pm - 22 cap 30
Neptune	12 pis 27	14.00 pm - 23 cap 31
Pluto	19 cap 10	16.00 pm - 24 cap 33
		18.00 pm - 25 cap 35
Oob		20.00 pm - 26 cap 37
		22.00 pm - 27 cap 40

Wednesday 22nd March

Retrograde Planets

Venus, Jupiter, Haumea, Makemake, Orcus

Asteroids		Dwarf Planets	
Juno	12 cap 34	Eris	22 ar 56
Vesta	20 can 53	Haumea	24 lib 06
Pallas	27 pis 06	Makemake	02 lib 54
Ceres	14 tau 51	Salacia	00 ar 32
Chiron	25 pis 07	Orcus	07 vir 41
N Node	03 vir 02	Quaoar	00 cap 44
S Node	03 pis 02	Sedna	25 tau 16

Moon Phase: Balsamic
Sunrise: 05:58 GMT
Sunset: 18:17
Moonrise: 02:56
Moonset: 11:56
Voc start: 13:19
Voc end:

Planetary and Angelic Hours			
Mercury	05:59	Sun	18:15
Moon	07:00	Venus	19:14
Saturn	08:02	Mercury	20:12
Jupiter	09:03	Moon	21:11
Mars	10:04	Saturn	22:09
Sun	11:06	Jupiter	23:07
Venus	12:07	Mars	00:06
Mercury	13:08	Sun	01:04
Moon	14:10	Venus	02:03
Saturn	15:11	Mercury	03:01
Jupiter	16:13	Moon	04:00
Mars	17:14	Saturn	04:58

Aspects

Moon conjunct Pluto
Moon square Jupiter
Moon opposite Vesta
Moon square Eris
Moon square Uranus
Moon sextile Chiron
Moon sextile Pallas
Jupiter square Vesta
Saturn square Pallas
Uranus conjunct Eris
Neptune sextile Juno

Planets	**00:00 am**	**Moon**
Sun	02 ar 32	00.00 am - 28 cap 42
Mercury	17 ar 25	02.00 am - 29 cap 45
Venus	06 ar 28	04.00 am - 00 aq 47
Mars	09 tau 18	06.00 am - 01 aq 50
Jupiter	20 lib 14	08.00 am - 02 aq 53
Saturn	27 sag 37	10.00 am - 03 aq 56
Uranus	23 ar 12	12.00 pm - 04 aq 59
Neptune	12 pis 29	14.00 pm - 06 aq 03
Pluto	19 cap 11	16.00 pm - 07 aq 06
		18.00 pm - 08 aq 10
Oob		20.00 pm - 09 aq 14
		22.00 pm - 10 aq 18

Thursday 23rd March

Planetary Directions

Moon into Aquarius
02:29

Retrograde Planets

Venus, Jupiter,
Haumea, Makemake,
Orcus

Asteroids		**Dwarf Planets**	
Juno	12 cap 46	Eris	22 ar 57
Vesta	21 can 00	Haumea	24 lib 05
Pallas	27 pis 27	Makemake	02 lib 53
Ceres	15 tau 14	Salacia	00 ar 33
Chiron	25 pis 10	Orcus	07 vir 40
N Node	03 vir 04	Quaoar	00 cap 44
S Node	03 pis 04	Sedna	25 tau 16

Moon Phase: Balsamic
Sunrise: 05:56 GMT
Sunset: 18:19
Moonrise: 03:38
Moonset: 12:56
Voc start:
Voc end: 02:28

Planetary and Angelic Hours			
Jupiter	05:57	Moon	18:17
Mars	06:58	Saturn	19:15
Sun	08:0	Jupiter	20:13
Venus	09:02	Mars	21:11
Mercury	10:03	Sun	22:09
Moon	11:05	Venus	23:07
Saturn	12:07	Mercury	00:06
Jupiter	13:08	Moon	01:04
Mars	14:10	Saturn	02:02
Sun	15:12	Jupiter	03:00
Venus	16:14	Mars	03:58
Mercury	17:15	Sun	04:56

Aspects

Sun sextile Moon
Saturn square Pallas
Moon sextile Venus
Moon square Mars
Mercury opp. Jupiter
Mercury square Pluto
Jupiter square Pluto
Jupiter square Vesta
Uranus conjunct Eris
Neptune sextile Juno

Planets	**00:00 am**	**Moon**
Sun	03 ar 32	00.00 am - 11 aq 22
Mercury	19 ar 09	02.00 am - 12 aq 26
Venus	05 ar 51	04.00 am - 13 aq 30
Mars	10 tau 01	06.00 am - 14 aq 35
Jupiter	20 lib 07	08.00 am - 15 aq 40
Saturn	27 sag 39	10.00 am - 16 aq 45
Uranus	23 ar 15	12.00 pm - 17 aq 50
Neptune	12 pis 31	14.00 pm - 18 aq 55
Pluto	19 cap 12	16.00 pm - 20 aq 00
		18.00 pm - 21 aq 06
Oob		20.00 pm - 22 aq 11
		22.00 pm - 23 aq 17

Friday 24th March

Retrograde Planets

Venus, Jupiter, Haumea, Makemake, Orcus

Asteroids		**Dwarf Planets**	
Juno	12 cap 59	Eris	22 ar 58
Vesta	21 can 06	Haumea	24 lib 04
Pallas	27 pis 48	Makemake	02 lib 52
Ceres	15 tau 36	Salacia	00 ar 35
Chiron	25 pis 14	Orcus	07 vir 39
N Node	03 vir 06	Quaoar	00 cap 44
S Node	03 pis 06	Sedna	25 tau 17

Moon Phase: Balsamic
Sunrise: 05:54 GMT
Sunset: 18:20
Moonrise: 04:15
Moonset: 14:02
Voc start:
Voc end:

Planetary and Angelic Hours			
Venus	05:54	Mars	18:19
Mercury	06:56	Sun	19:16
Moon	07:58	Venus	20:14
Saturn	09:00	Mercury	21:12
Jupiter	10:02	Moon	22:10
Mars	11:04	Saturn	23:08
Sun	12:06	Jupiter	00:05
Venus	13:08	Mars	01:03
Mercury	14:10	Sun	02:01
Moon	15:13	Venus	02:59
Saturn	16:15	Mercury	03:56
Jupiter	17:17	Moon	04:54

Aspects

Mercury square Pluto
Moon square Ceres
Mercury opp. Jupiter
Moon trine Jupiter
Moon sextile Mercury
Moon sextile Eris
Moon sextile Uranus
Sun conjunct Venus
Mercury square Vesta
Jupiter square Pluto
Saturn square Pallas
Uranus conjunct Eris
Neptune sextile Juno

Planets	00:00 am	Moon
Sun	04 ar 31	00.00 am - 24 aq 23
Mercury	20 ar 49	02.00 am - 25 aq 29
Venus	05 ar 13	04.00 am - 26 aq 36
Mars	10 tau 44	06.00 am - 27 aq 42
Jupiter	19 lib 59	08.00 am - 28 aq 49
Saturn	27 sag 40	10.00 am - 29 aq 56
Uranus	23 ar 19	12.00 pm - 01 pis 03
Neptune	12 pis 33	14.00 pm - 02 pis 10
Pluto	19 cap 13	16.00 pm - 03 pis 18
		18.00 pm - 04 pis 25
Oob		20.00 pm - 05 pis 33
		22.00 pm - 06 pis 41

Saturday 25th March

Planetary Directions

Moon into Pisces 10:07

Retrograde Planets

Venus, Jupiter, Haumea, Makemake, Orcus

Asteroids		Dwarf Planets	
Juno	13 cap 11	Eris	22 ar 58
Vesta	21 can 13	Haumea	24 lib 03
Pallas	28 pis 10	Makemake	02 lib 51
Ceres	15 tau 58	Salacia	00 ar 37
Chiron	25 pis 17	Orcus	07 vir 38
N Node	03 vir 07	Quaoar	00 cap 44
S Node	03 pis 07	Sedna	25 tau 17

Moon Phase: Balsamic
Sunrise: 05:51 GMT
Sunset: 18:22
Moonrise: 04:47
Moonset: 15:12
Voc start: 05:55
Voc end: 10:06

Planetary and Angelic Hours

Saturn	05:52	Mercury	18:20
Jupiter	06:54	Moon	19:18
Mars	07:57	Saturn	20:15
Sun	08:59	Jupiter	21:13
Venus	10:01	Mars	22:10
Mercury	11:04	Sun	23:08
Moon	12:06	Venus	00:05
Saturn	13:08	Mercury	01:02
Jupiter	14:11	Moon	02:00
Mars	15:13	Saturn	02:57
Sun	16:16	Jupiter	03:55
Venus	17:18	Mars	04:52

Aspects

Moon sextile Saturn
Mercury square Vesta
Sun conjunct Venus
Mercury conj. Uranus
Mercury conjunct Eris
Jupiter square Pluto
Saturn square Pallas
Uranus conjunct Eris
Neptune sextile Juno

Planets	**00:00 am**	**Moon**
Sun	05 ar 31	01.00 am - 07 pis 49
Mercury	22 ar 56	03.00 am - 08 pis 57
Venus	04 ar 35	05.00 am - 10 pis 05
Mars	11 tau 26	07.00 am - 11 pis 14
Jupiter	19 lib 52	09.00 am - 12 pis 23
Saturn	27 sag 41	11.00 am - 13 pis 32
Uranus	23 ar 22	13.00 pm - 14 pis 41
Neptune	12 pis 35	15.00 pm - 15 pis 50
Pluto	19 cap 14	17.00 pm - 16 pis 59
		19.00 pm - 18 pis 09
Oob		21.00 pm - 19 pis 19
		23.00 pm - 20 pis 29

Sunday 26th March

Retrograde Planets

Venus, Jupiter, Haumea, Makemake, Orcus

Asteroids		**Dwarf Planets**	
Juno	13 cap 24	Eris	22 ar 59
Vesta	21 can 21	Haumea	24 lib 02
Pallas	28 pis 31	Makemake	02 lib 49
Ceres	16 tau 21	Salacia	00 ar 38
Chiron	25 pis 21	Orcus	07 vir 37
N Node	03 vir 07	Quaoar	00 cap 45
S Node	03 pis 07	Sedna	25 tau 18

Moon Phase: Balsamic
Sunrise: 06:49 BST
Sunset: 19:24
Moonrise: 06:17
Moonset: 17:26
Voc start:
Voc end:

Planetary and Angelic Hours			
Sun	06:50	Jupiter	19:22
Venus	07:52	Mars	20:19
Mercury	08:55	Sun	21:16
Moon	09:58	Venus	22:13
Saturn	11:00	Mercury	23:10
Jupiter	12:03	Moon	00:08
Mars	13:06	Saturn	01:05
Sun	14:08	Jupiter	02:02
Venus	15:11	Mars	02:59
Mercury	16:14	Sun	03:56
Moon	17:17	Venus	04:53
Saturn	18:19	Mercury	05:50

Mothering Sunday

Aspects

Moon sextile Mars
Moon conj. Neptune
Mercury conjunct Eris
Moon sextile Juno
Mercury conj. Uranus
Moon sextile Ceres
Moon sextile Pluto
Moon trine Vesta
Mars sextile Neptune
Jupiter square Pluto
Uranus conjunct Eris
Neptune sextile Juno

Planets	00:00 am	Moon
Sun	06 ar 30	01.00 am - 21 pis 39
Mercury	23 ar 57	03.00 am - 22 pis 49
Venus	03 ar 58	05.00 am - 23 pis 59
Mars	12 tau 09	07.00 am - 25 pis 10
Jupiter	19 lib 45	09.00 am - 26 pis 20
Saturn	27 sag 42	11.00 am - 27 pis 31
Uranus	23 ar 25	13.00 pm - 28 pis 42
Neptune	12 pis 37	15.00 pm - 29 pis 53
Pluto	19 cap 14	17.00 pm - 01 ar 04
		19.00 pm - 02 ar 16
		21.00 pm - 03 ar 27
Oob		23.00 pm - 04 ar 39

Monday 27th March

Planetary Directions

Moon into Aries 15:11

Retrograde Planets

Venus, Jupiter, Haumea, Makemake, Orcus

Asteroids		Dwarf Planets	
Juno	13 cap 36	Eris	23 ar 00
Vesta	21 can 29	Haumea	24 lib 01
Pallas	28 pis 52	Makemake	02 lib 48
Ceres	16 tau 44	Salacia	00 ar 40
Chiron	25 pis 24	Orcus	07 vir 36
N Node	03 vir 06	Quaoar	00 cap 45
S Node	03 pis 06	Sedna	25 tau 18

Moon Phase: Balsamic
Sunrise: 06:47 BST
Sunset: 19:25
Moonrise: 06:45
Moonset: 18:42
Voc start: 11:19
Voc end: 15:10

Planetary and Angelic Hours			
Moon	06:48	Venus	19:24
Saturn	07:51	Mercury	20:20
Jupiter	08:54	Moon	21:17
Mars	09:57	Saturn	22:14
Sun	11:00	Jupiter	23:11
Venus	12:03	Mars	00:08
Mercury	13:06	Sun	01:04
Moon	14:09	Venus	02:01
Saturn	15:12	Mercury	02:58
Jupiter	16:15	Moon	03:55
Mars	17:18	Saturn	04:52
Sun	18:21	Jupiter	05:48

Aspects

Moon conjunct Chiron
Moon square Saturn
Moon conjunct Pallas
Mars sextile Neptune
Moon conjunct Venus
Mars trine Juno
Jupiter square Pluto
Uranus conjunct Eris

Planets	**00:00 am**	**Moon**
Sun	07 ar 30	01.00 am - 05 ar 51
Mercury	25 ar 24	03.00 am - 07 ar 03
Venus	03 ar 21	05.00 am - 08 ar 15
Mars	12 tau 52	07.00 am - 09 ar 27
Jupiter	19 lib 38	09.00 am - 10 ar 39
Saturn	27 sag 43	11.00 am - 11 ar 51
Uranus	23 ar 39	13.00 pm - 13 ar 04
Neptune	12 pis 39	15.00 pm - 14 ar 16
Pluto	19 cap 15	17.00 pm - 15 ar 29
		19.00 pm - 16 ar 42
Oob		21.00 pm - 17 ar 54
		23.00 pm - 19 ar 07

Tuesday 28th March

Planetary Directions

Moon into Taurus
16:48

Retrograde Planets

Venus, Jupiter,
Haumea, Makemake,
Orcus

Asteroids		**Dwarf Planets**	
Juno	13 cap 47	Eris	23 ar 00
Vesta	21 can 37	Haumea	24 lib 00
Pallas	29 pis 13	Makemake	02 lib 47
Ceres	17 tau 06	Salacia	00 ar 42
Chiron	25 pis 28	Orcus	07 vir 35
N Node	03 vir 03	Quaoar	00 cap 45
S Node	03 pis 03	Sedna	25 tau 19

New Moon: 03:59
Sunrise: 06:44 BST
Sunset: 19:27
Moonrise: 07:13
Moonset: 20:01
Voc start:
Voc end:

Planetary and Angelic Hours			
Mars	06:45	Saturn	19:25
Sun	07:49	Jupiter	20:22
Venus	08:52	Mars	21:18
Mercury	09:55	Sun	22:15
Moon	10:59	Venus	23:11
Saturn	12:02	Mercury	00:08
Jupiter	13:05	Moon	01:04
Mars	14:09	Saturn	02:01
Sun	15:12	Jupiter	02:57
Venus	16:15	Mars	03:54
Mercury	17:19	Sun	04:50
Moon	18:22	Venus	05:47

Aspects

Sun conjunct Moon
Moon square Juno
Moon square Pluto
Moon opposite Jupiter
Mercury trine Saturn
Mars sextile Neptune
Mars trine Juno
Jupiter square Pluto
Uranus conjunct Eris

Planets	**00:00 am**	**Moon**
Sun	08 ar 29	01.00 am - 20 ar 20
Mercury	26 ar 46	03.00 am - 21 ar 34
Venus	02 ar 44	05.00 am - 22 ar 47
Mars	13 tau 34	07.00 am - 24 ar 00
Jupiter	19 lib 30	09.00 am - 25 ar 13
Saturn	27 sag 44	11.00 am - 26 ar 27
Uranus	23 ar 32	13.00 pm - 27 ar 40
Neptune	12 pis 42	15.00 pm - 28 ar 53
Pluto	19 cap 16	17.00 pm - 00 tau 07
		19.00 pm - 01 tau 21
Oob		21.00 pm - 02 tau 34
		23.00 pm - 03 tau 48

Wednesday 29th March

Retrograde Planets

Venus, Jupiter, Haumea, Makemake, Orcus

Asteroids		**Dwarf Planets**	
Juno	13 cap 59	Eris	23 ar 01
Vesta	21 can 46	Haumea	23 lib 59
Pallas	29 pis 34	Makemake	02 lib 46
Ceres	17 tau 29	Salacia	00 ar 43
Chiron	25 pis 32	Orcus	07 vir 34
N Node	02 vir 58	Quaoar	00 cap 45
S Node	02 pis 58	Sedna	25 tau 19

Moon Phase: Crescent
Sunrise: 06:42 BST
Sunset: 19:29
Moonrise: 07:41
Moonset: 21:20
Voc start: 13:06
Voc end: 16:47

Planetary and Angelic Hours			
Mercury	06:43	Sun	19:27
Moon	07:47	Venus	20:23
Saturn	08:50	Mercury	21:19
Jupiter	09:54	Moon	22:15
Mars	10:58	Saturn	23:11
Sun	12:01	Jupiter	00:08
Venus	13:05	Mars	01:04
Mercury	14:09	Sun	02:00
Moon	15:12	Venus	02:56
Saturn	16:16	Mercury	03:52
Jupiter	17:20	Moon	04:48
Mars	18:23	Saturn	05:45

Aspects

Moon square Vesta
Moon conjunct Eris
Moon conjunct Uranus
Moon conj. Mercury
Moon trine Saturn
Mercury trine Saturn
Mars trine Juno
Jupiter square Pluto
Uranus conjunct Eris

Planets	00:00 am	Moon
Sun	09 ar 28	01.00 am - 05 tau 02
Mercury	28 ar 02	03.00 am - 06 tau 15
Venus	02 ar 09	05.00 am - 07 tau 29
Mars	14 tau 17	07.00 am - 08 tau 43
Jupiter	19 lib 23	09.00 am - 09 tau 56
Saturn	27 sag 45	11.00 am - 11 tau 10
Uranus	23 ar 35	13.00 pm - 12 tau 24
Neptune	12 pis 44	15.00 pm - 13 tau 38
Pluto	19 cap 16	17.00 pm - 14 tau 52
		19.00 pm - 16 tau 05
Oob		21.00 pm - 17 tau 19
		23.00 pm - 18 tau 33

Thursday 30th March

Planetary Directions

Pallas into Aries 05:46

Retrograde Planets

Venus, Jupiter, Haumea, Makemake, Orcus

Asteroids		Dwarf Planets	
Juno	14 cap 10	Eris	23 ar 01
Vesta	21 can 55	Haumea	23 lib 58
Pallas	29 pis 55	Makemake	02 lib 45
Ceres	17 tau 52	Salacia	00 ar 45
Chiron	25 pis 35	Orcus	07 vir 33
N Node	02 vir 53	Quaoar	00 cap 45
S Node	02 pis 53	Sedna	25 tau 20

Moon Phase: Crescent
Sunrise: 06:40 BST
Sunset: 19:30
Moonrise: 08:12
Moonset: 22:39
Voc start:
Voc end:

Planetary and Angelic Hours			
Jupiter	06:41	Moon	19:28
Mars	07:45	Saturn	20:24
Sun	08:49	Jupiter	21:20
Venus	09:53	Mars	22:16
Mercury	10:57	Sun	23:12
Moon	12:01	Venus	00:08
Saturn	13:05	Mercury	01:03
Jupiter	14:09	Moon	01:59
Mars	15:13	Saturn	02:55
Sun	16:17	Jupiter	03:51
Venus	17:20	Mars	04:47
Mercury	18:24	Sun	05:43

Aspects

Moon sextile Neptune
Moon trine Juno
Moon conjunct Mars
Jupiter square Pluto
Moon conjunct Ceres
Moon trine Pluto
Mars trine Juno
Uranus conjunct Eris
Vesta square Eris

Planets	00:00 am	Moon
Sun	10 ar 28	01.00 am - 19 tau 47
Mercury	29 ar 12	03.00 am - 21 tau 00
Venus	01 ar 34	05.00 am - 22 tau 14
Mars	14 tau 59	07.00 am - 23 tau 27
Jupiter	19 lib 15	09.00 am - 24 tau 41
Saturn	27 sag 45	11.00 am - 25 tau 55
Uranus	23 ar 39	13.00 pm - 27 tau 08
Neptune	12 pis 46	15.00 pm - 28 tau 22
Pluto	19 cap 17	17.00 pm - 29 tau 35
		19.00 pm - 00 gem 48
Oob		21.00 pm - 02 gem 02
		23.00 pm - 03 gem 15

Friday 31st March

Planetary Directions

Quaoar rx at 10:08
Moon into Gemini 17:41
Mercury into Taurus at 18:31

Retrograde Planets

Venus, Jupiter, Haumea, Makemake, Orcus

Asteroids		Dwarf Planets	
Juno	14 cap 21	Eris	23 ar 02
Vesta	22 can 04	Haumea	23 lib 57
Pallas	00 ar 16	Makemake	02 lib 44
Ceres	18 tau 15	Salacia	00 ar 46
Chiron	25 pis 39	Orcus	07 vir 32
N Node	02 vir 47	Quaoar	00 cap 45
S Node	02 pis 47	Sedna	25 tau 21

Moon Phase: Crescent
Sunrise: 06:38 BST
Sunset: 19:32
Moonrise: 08:47
Moonset: 23:56
Voc start: 00:11
Voc end: 17:40

Planetary and Angelic Hours			
Venus	06:39	Mars	19:30
Mercury	07:43	Sun	20:26
Moon	08:47	Venus	21:21
Saturn	09:51	Mercury	22:17
Jupiter	10:56	Moon	23:12
Mars	12:00	Saturn	00:08
Sun	13:04	Jupiter	01:03
Venus	14:09	Mars	01:59
Mercury	15:13	Sun	02:54
Moon	16:17	Venus	03:50
Saturn	17:21	Mercury	04:45
Jupiter	18:26	Moon	05:41

Aspects

Moon sextile Vesta
Moon sextile Chiron
Moon sextile Pallas
Moon sextile Venus
Venus conjunct Pallas
Jupiter square Pluto
Uranus conjunct Eris
Pluto trine Ceres
Vesta square Eris

Planets	00:00 am	Moon
Sun	11 ar 27	01.00 am - 04 gem 28
Mercury	00 tau 16	03.00 am - 05 gem 41
Venus	01 ar 01	05.00 am - 06 gem 54
Mars	15 tau 42	07.00 am - 08 gem 07
Jupiter	19 lib 08	09.00 am - 09 gem 20
Saturn	27 sag 46	11.00 am - 10 gem 32
Uranus	23 ar 42	13.00 pm - 11 gem 45
Neptune	12 pis 48	15.00 pm - 12 gem 58
Pluto	19 cap 18	17.00 pm - 14 gem 10
		19.00 pm - 15 gem 23
Oob		21.00 pm - 16 gem 35
		23.00 pm - 17 gem 47

Saturday 1st April

Retrograde Planets

Venus, Jupiter, Haumea, Makemake, Orcus, Quaoar

Asteroids		Dwarf Planets	
Juno	14 cap 21	Eris	23 ar 03
Vesta	22 can 04	Haumea	23 lib 55
Pallas	00 ar 16	Makemake	02 lib 43
Ceres	18 tau 15	Salacia	00 ar 48
Chiron	25 pis 39	Orcus	07 vir 31
N Node	02 vir 42	Quaoar	00 cap 45
S Node	02 pis 42	Sedna	25 tau 21

Moon Phase: Crescent
Sunrise: 06:35 BST
Sunset: 19:34
Moonrise: 09:27
Moonset: None
Voc start:
Voc end:

Planetary and Angelic Hours			
Saturn	06:36	Mercury	19:32
Jupiter	07:41	Moon	20:27
Mars	08:46	Saturn	21:22
Sun	09:50	Jupiter	22:17
Venus	10:55	Mars	23:12
Mercury	11:59	Sun	00:08
Moon	13:04	Venus	01:03
Saturn	14:09	Mercury	01:58
Jupiter	15:13	Moon	02:53
Mars	16:18	Saturn	03:48
Sun	17:22	Jupiter	04:44
Venus	18:27	Mars	05:39

April Fool's Day

Aspects

Venus conjunct Pallas
Sun sextile Moon
Moon square Neptune
Moon trine Jupiter
Jupiter square Pluto
Uranus conjunct Eris
Pluto trine Ceres
Vesta square Eris

Planets	00:00 am	Moon
Sun	12 ar 26	01.00 am - 18 gem 59
Mercury	01 tau 14	03.00 am - 20 gem 11
Venus	00 ar 30	05.00 am - 21 gem 23
Mars	16 tau 24	07.00 am - 22 gem 35
Jupiter	19 lib 00	09.00 am - 23 gem 47
Saturn	27 sag 46	11.00 am - 24 gem 58
Uranus	23 ar 45	13.00 pm - 26 gem 10
Neptune	12 pis 50	15.00 pm - 27 gem 21
Pluto	19 cap 18	17.00 pm - 28 gem 32
		19.00 pm - 29 gem 44
Oob		21.00 pm - 00 can 55
		23.00 pm - 02 can 06

Sunday 2nd April

Planetary Directions

Moon into Cancer 19:27

Retrograde Planets

Venus, Jupiter, Haumea, Makemake, Orcus, Quaoar

Asteroids		Dwarf Planets	
Juno	14 cap 43	Eris	23 ar 03
Vesta	22 can 24	Haumea	23 lib 54
Pallas	00 ar 59	Makemake	02 lib 42
Ceres	19 tau 01	Salacia	00 ar 50
Chiron	25 pis 46	Orcus	07 vir 30
N Node	02 vir 38	Quaoar	00 cap 45
S Node	02 pis 38	Sedna	25 tau 22

Moon Phase: Crescent
Sunrise: 06:33 BST
Sunset: 19:35
Moonrise: 10:15
Moonset: 01:08
Voc start: 15:42
Voc end: 19:26

Planetary and Angelic Hours

Sun	06:34	Jupiter	19:33
Venus	07:39	Mars	20:28
Mercury	08:44	Sun	21:23
Moon	09:49	Venus	22:18
Saturn	10:54	Mercury	23:13
Jupiter	11:59	Moon	00:08
Mars	13:04	Saturn	01:03
Sun	14:09	Jupiter	01:57
Venus	15:14	Mars	02:52
Mercury	16:19	Sun	03:47
Moon	17:23	Venus	04:42
Saturn	18:28	Mercury	05:37

Aspects

Moon trine Jupiter
Moon sextile Eris
Moon sextile Uranus
Moon square Chiron
Moon opposite Saturn
Pluto trine Ceres
Moon square Venus
Moon square Pallas
Moon sextile Mercury
Jupiter square Pluto
Uranus conjunct Eris
Vesta square Eris

Planets	00:00 am	Moon
Sun	13 ar 25	01.00 am - 03 can 16
Mercury	02 tau 05	03.00 am - 04 can 27
Venus	00 ar 00	05.00 am - 05 can 38
Mars	17 tau 06	07.00 am - 06 can 48
Jupiter	18 lib 52	09.00 am - 07 can 58
Saturn	27 sag 47	11.00 am - 09 can 09
Uranus	23 ar 49	13.00 pm - 10 can 19
Neptune	12 pis 52	15.00 pm - 11 can 29
Pluto	19 cap 19	17.00 pm - 12 can 39
		19.00 pm - 13 can 48
Oob		21.00 pm - 14 can 58
		23.00 pm - 16 can 07

Monday 3rd April

Planetary Directions

Venus rx into Pisces
01:26

Retrograde Planets

Venus, Jupiter,
Haumea, Makemake,
Orcus, Quaoar

Asteroids		Dwarf Planets	
Juno	14 cap 54	Eris	23 ar 04
Vesta	22 can 35	Haumea	23 lib 53
Pallas	01 ar 20	Makemake	02 lib 40
Ceres	19 tau 24	Salacia	00 ar 51
Chiron	25 pis 49	Orcus	07 vir 29
N Node	02 vir 36	Quaoar	00 cap 45
S Node	02 pis 36	Sedna	25 tau 22

First Quarter: 19:40
Sunrise: 06:31 BST
Sunset: 19:37
Moonrise: 11:10
Moonset: 02:12
Voc start:
Voc end:

Planetary and Angelic Hours			
Moon	06:32	Venus	19:35
Saturn	07:37	Mercury	20:30
Jupiter	08:42	Moon	21:24
Mars	09:48	Saturn	22:19
Sun	10:53	Jupiter	23:13
Venus	11:58	Mars	00:08
Mercury	13:03	Sun	01:02
Moon	14:09	Venus	01:57
Saturn	15:14	Mercury	02:51
Jupiter	16:19	Moon	03:46
Mars	17:24	Saturn	04:41
Sun	18:30	Jupiter	05:35

Aspects

Moon trine Neptune
Sun square Moon
Moon opposite Juno
Sun square Juno
Moon sextile Mars
Jupiter square Pluto
Uranus conjunct Eris
Pluto trine Ceres
Vesta square Eris

Planets	**00:00 am**	**Moon**
Sun	14 ar 24	01.00 am - 17 can 17
Mercury	02 tau 49	03.00 am - 18 can 26
Venus	29 pis 32	05.00 am - 19 can 35
Mars	17 tau 49	07.00 am - 20 can 44
Jupiter	18 lib 45	09.00 am - 21 can 53
Saturn	27 sag 47	11.00 am - 23 can 02
Uranus	23 ar 52	13.00 pm - 24 can 10
Neptune	12 pis 54	15.00 pm - 25 can 19
Pluto	19 cap 19	17.00 pm - 26 can 27
		19.00 pm - 27 can 36
Oob		21.00 pm - 28 can 44
		23.00 pm - 29 can 52

Tuesday 4th April

Planetary Directions

Moon into Leo 23:14

Retrograde Planets

Venus, Jupiter,
Haumea, Makemake,
Orcus, Quaoar

Asteroids		**Dwarf Planets**	
Juno	15 cap 04	Eris	23 ar 05
Vesta	22 can 45	Haumea	23 lib 52
Pallas	01 ar 41	Makemake	02 lib 39
Ceres	19 tau 47	Salacia	00 ar 53
Chiron	25 pis 53	Orcus	07 vir 29
N Node	02 vir 36	Quaoar	00 cap 45
S Node	02 pis 36	Sedna	25 tau 23

Moon Phase: Gibbous
Sunrise: 06:29 BST
Sunset: 19:39
Moonrise: 12:12
Moonset: 03:07
Voc start: 21:45
Voc end: 23:13

Planetary and Angelic Hours			
Mars	06:30	Saturn	19:37
Sun	07:35	Jupiter	20:31
Venus	08:41	Mars	21:25
Mercury	09:46	Sun	22:19
Moon	10:52	Venus	23:14
Saturn	11:58	Mercury	00:08
Jupiter	13:03	Moon	01:02
Mars	14:09	Saturn	01:56
Sun	15:14	Jupiter	02:50
Venus	16:20	Mars	03:45
Mercury	17:25	Sun	04:39
Moon	18:31	Venus	05:33

Aspects

Moon sextile Mars
Moon square Jupiter
Moon opposite Pluto
Moon sextile Ceres
Moon conjunct Vesta
Moon square Eris
Moon square Uranus
Moon trine Chiron
Sun square Juno
Moon trine Venus
Mars trine Pluto
Jupiter square Pluto
Uranus square Vesta
Uranus conjunct Eris
Pluto trine Ceres
Vesta square Eris

Planets	00:00 am	Moon
Sun	15 ar 23	01.00 am - 01 leo 00
Mercury	03 tau 27	03.00 am - 02 leo 08
Venus	29 pis 06	05.00 am - 03 leo 15
Mars	18 tau 31	07.00 am - 04 leo 23
Jupiter	18 lib 37	09.00 am - 05 leo 31
Saturn	27 sag 47	11.00 am - 06 leo 38
Uranus	23 ar 56	13.00 pm - 07 leo 45
Neptune	12 pis 56	15.00 pm - 08 leo 52
Pluto	19 cap 20	17.00 pm - 09 leo 59
		19.00 pm - 11 leo 06
Oob		21.00 pm - 12 leo 13
		23.00 pm - 13 leo 20

Wednesday 5th April

Planetary Directions

Saturn retrograde
27 sag 47 at 06:06

Retrograde Planets

Venus, Jupiter, Haumea, Makemake, Orcus, Quaoar

Asteroids		Dwarf Planets	
Juno	15 cap 14	Eris	23 ar 05
Vesta	22 can 56	Haumea	23 lib 51
Pallas	02 ar 02	Makemake	02 lib 38
Ceres	20 tau 10	Salacia	00 ar 54
Chiron	25 pis 56	Orcus	07 vir 28
N Node	02 vir 37	Quaoar	00 cap 45
S Node	02 pis 37	Sedna	25 tau 24

Moon Phase: Gibbous
Sunrise: 06:26 BST
Sunset: 19:40
Moonrise: 13:18
Moonset: 03:53
Voc start:
Voc end:

Planetary and Angelic Hours			
Mercury	06:27	Sun	19:38
Moon	07:33	Venus	20:32
Saturn	08:39	Mercury	21:26
Jupiter	09:45	Moon	22:20
Mars	10:51	Saturn	23:14
Sun	11:57	Jupiter	00:08
Venus	13:03	Mars	01:02
Mercury	14:09	Sun	01:56
Moon	15:15	Venus	02:50
Saturn	16:21	Mercury	03:43
Jupiter	17:26	Moon	04:37
Mars	18:32	Saturn	05:31

Aspects

Moon trine Pallas
Moon square Mercury
Vesta square Eris
Sun square Juno
Venus square Saturn
Mars trine Pluto
Jupiter square Pluto
Uranus square Vesta
Uranus conjunct Eris

Planets	00:00 am	Moon
Sun	16 ar 22	01.00 am - 14 leo 27
Mercury	03 tau 57	03.00 am - 15 leo 33
Venus	28 pis 42	05.00 am - 16 leo 40
Mars	19 tau 13	07.00 am - 17 leo 46
Jupiter	18 lib 29	09.00 am - 18 leo 52
Saturn	27 sag 47	11.00 am - 19 leo 58
Uranus	23 ar 59	13.00 pm - 21 leo 04
Neptune	12 pis 58	15.00 pm - 22 leo 10
Pluto	19 cap 20	17.00 pm - 23 leo 16
		19.00 pm - 24 leo 22
Oob		21.00 pm - 25 leo 27
		23.00 pm - 26 leo 33

Thursday 6th April

Planetary Directions

Saturn retrograde
27 sag 47 at 06:06

Retrograde Planets

Venus, Jupiter, Saturn, Haumea, Makemake, Orcus, Quaoar

Asteroids		Dwarf Planets	
Juno	15 cap 24	Eris	23 ar 06
Vesta	23 can 08	Haumea	23 lib 50
Pallas	02 ar 23	Makemake	02 lib 37
Ceres	20 tau 34	Salacia	00 ar 56
Chiron	25 pis 59	Orcus	07 vir 27
N Node	02 vir 38	Quaoar	00 cap 44
S Node	02 pis 38	Sedna	25 tau 24

Moon Phase: Gibbous
Sunrise: 06:24 BST
Sunset: 19:42
Moonrise: 14:27
Moonset: 04:31
Voc start:
Voc end:

Planetary and Angelic Hours			
Jupiter	06:25	Moon	19:40
Mars	07:31	Saturn	20:33
Sun	08:38	Jupiter	21:27
Venus	09:44	Mars	22:21
Mercury	10:50	Sun	23:14
Moon	11:56	Venus	00:08
Saturn	13:03	Mercury	01:01
Jupiter	14:09	Moon	01:55
Mars	15:15	Saturn	02:49
Sun	16:21	Jupiter	03:42
Venus	17:27	Mars	04:36
Mercury	18:34	Sun	05:29

Aspects

Sun trine Moon
Mars trine Pluto
Moon sextile Jupiter
Moon square Mars
Moon square Ceres
Moon trine Eris
Moon trine Uranus
Moon trine Saturn
Venus square Saturn
Jupiter square Pluto
Uranus square Vesta
Uranus conjunct Eris
Vesta square Eris

Planets	00:00 am
Sun	17 ar 21
Mercury	04 tau 21
Venus	28 pis 21
Mars	19 tau 55
Jupiter	18 lib 22
Saturn	27 sag 47
Uranus	24 ar 02
Neptune	13 pis 00
Pluto	19 cap 21
Oob	

Moon

01.00 am - 27 leo 38
03.00 am - 28 leo 44
05.00 am - 29 leo 49
07.00 am - 00 vir 54
09.00 am - 01 vir 59
11.00 am - 03 vir 04
13.00 pm - 04 vir 09
15.00 pm - 05 vir 14
17.00 pm - 06 vir 18
19.00 pm - 07 vir 23
21.00 pm - 08 vir 28
23.00 pm - 09 vir 32

Friday 7th April

Planetary Directions

Moon into Virgo 05:20

Retrograde Planets

Venus, Jupiter, Saturn, Haumea, Makemake, Orcus, Quaoar

Asteroids		Dwarf Planets	
Juno	15 cap 34	Eris	23 ar 07
Vesta	23 can 20	Haumea	23 lib 48
Pallas	02 ar 45	Makemake	02 lib 36
Ceres	20 tau 57	Salacia	00 ar 57
Chiron	26 pis 03	Orcus	07 vir 26
N Node	02 vir 29	Quaoar	00 cap 44
S Node	02 Pis 39	Sedna	25 tau 25

Moon Phase: Gibbous
Sunrise: 06:22 BST
Sunset: 19:44
Moonrise: 15:36
Moonset: 05:03
Voc start: 01:16
Voc end: 05:19

Planetary and Angelic Hours			
Venus	06:23	Mars	19:42
Mercury	07:30	Sun	20:35
Moon	08:36	Venus	21:28
Saturn	09:43	Mercury	22:21
Jupiter	10:49	Moon	23:15
Mars	11:56	Saturn	00:08
Sun	13:02	Jupiter	01:01
Venus	14:09	Mars	01:54
Mercury	15:15	Sun	02:48
Moon	16:22	Venus	03:41
Saturn	17:28	Mercury	04:34
Jupiter	18:35	Moon	05:28

Aspects

Moon trine Saturn
Moon trine Mercury
Sun opposite Jupiter
Venus square Saturn
Mars conjunct Ceres
Uranus square Vesta
Uranus conjunct Eris
Vesta square Eris

Planets	00:00 am	Moon
Sun	18 ar 20	01.00 am - 10 vir 36
Mercury	04 tau 37	03.00 am - 11 vir 41
Venus	28 pis 01	05.00 am - 12 vir 45
Mars	20 tau 38	07.00 am - 13 vir 49
Jupiter	18 lib 14	09.00 am - 14 vir 53
Saturn	27 sag 47	11.00 am - 15 vir 57
Uranus	24 ar 06	13.00 pm - 17 vir 01
Neptune	13 pis 02	15.00 pm - 18 vir 05
Pluto	19 cap 21	17.00 pm - 19 vir 08
		19.00 pm - 20 vir 12
Oob		21.00 pm - 21 vir 16
		23.00 pm - 22 vir 19

Saturday 8th April

Retrograde Planets

Venus, Jupiter, Saturn, Haumea, Makemake, Orcus, Quaoar

Asteroids		Dwarf Planets	
Juno	15 cap 43	Eris	23 ar 07
Vesta	23 can 32	Haumea	23 lib 47
Pallas	03 ar 06	Makemake	02 lib 35
Ceres	21 tau 20	Salacia	00 ar 59
Chiron	26 pis 06	Orcus	07 vir 25
N Node	02 vir 39	Quaoar	00 cap 44
S Node	02 pis 39	Sedna	25 tau 25

Moon Phase: Gibbous
Sunrise: 06:20 BST
Sunset: 19:45
Moonrise: 16:45
Moonset: 05:30
Voc start:
Voc end:

Planetary and Angelic Hours			
Saturn	06:21	Mercury	19:43
Jupiter	07:28	Moon	20:36
Mars	08:35	Saturn	21:29
Sun	09:41	Jupiter	22:22
Venus	10:48	Mars	23:15
Mercury	11:55	Sun	00:08
Moon	13:02	Venus	01:01
Saturn	14:09	Mercury	01:54
Jupiter	15:16	Moon	02:47
Mars	16:23	Saturn	03:40
Sun	17:29	Jupiter	04:33
Venus	18:36	Mars	05:26

Aspects

Moon opp. Neptune
Moon trine Juno
Moon trine Pluto
Moon trine Mars
Venus square Saturn
Moon trine Ceres
Sun square Pluto
Moon sextile Vesta
Mars conjunct Ceres
Uranus square Vesta
Vesta square Eris

Planets	00:00 am	Moon
		01.00 am - 23 vir 23
Sun	19 ar 19	03.00 am - 24vir 26
Mercury	04 tau 47	05.00 am - 25 vir 29
Venus	27 pis 45	07.00 am - 26 vir 32
Mars	21 tau 20	09.00 am - 27 vir 36
Jupiter	18 lib 06	11.00 am - 28 vir 39
Saturn	27 sag 47	13.00 pm - 29 vir 42
Uranus	24 ar 09	15.00 pm - 00 vir 44
Neptune	13 pis 04	17.00 pm - 01 vir 47
Pluto	19 cap 21	19.00 pm - 02 vir 50
		21.00 pm - 03 vir 53
Oob		23.00 pm - 04 vir 55

Sunday 9th April

Planetary Directions

Moon into Libra 13:35

Retrograde Planets

Venus, Jupiter, Saturn, Haumea, Makemake, Orcus, Quaoar

Asteroids		Dwarf Planets	
Juno	15 cap 52	Eris	23 ar 08
Vesta	23 can 44	Haumea	23 lib 46
Pallas	03 ar 27	Makemake	02 lib 34
Ceres	21 tau 44	Salacia	01 ar 01
Chiron	26 pis 10	Orcus	07 vir 24
N Node	02 vir 37	Quaoar	00 cap 44
S Node	02 pis 37	Sedna	25 tau 26

Moon Phase: Gibbous
Sunrise: 06:17 BST
Sunset: 19:47
Moonrise: 17:53
Moonset: 05:55
Voc start: 09:21
Voc end: 13:34

Planetary and Angelic Hours			
Sun	06:19	Jupiter	19:45
Venus	07:26	Mars	20:37
Mercury	08:33	Sun	21:30
Moon	09:40	Venus	22:23
Saturn	10:47	Mercury	23:15
Jupiter	11:55	Moon	00:08
Mars	13:02	Saturn	01:01
Sun	14:09	Jupiter	01:53
Venus	15:16	Mars	02:46
Mercury	16:23	Sun	03:39
Moon	17:30	Venus	04:31
Saturn	18:38	Mercury	05:24

Aspects

Moon sextile Vesta
Sun square Pluto
Moon opposite Chiron
Moon opposite Venus
Moon square Saturn
Moon opposite Pallas
Venus square Saturn
Mars conjunct Ceres
Uranus square Vesta
Vesta square Eris

Planets	00:00 am	Moon
Sun	20 ar 18	01.00 am - 05 lib 58
Mercury	04 tau 50	03.00 am - 07 lib 00
Venus	27 pis 30	05.00 am - 08 lib 03
Mars	22 tau 02	07.00 am - 09 lib 05
Jupiter	17 lib 59	09.00 am - 10 lib 07
Saturn	27 sag 46	11.00 am - 11 lib 10
Uranus	24 ar 13	13.00 pm - 12 lib 12
Neptune	13 pis 06	15.00 pm - 13 lib 14
Pluto	19 cap 22	17.00 pm - 14 lib 16
		19.00 pm - 15 lib 28
Oob		21.00 pm - 16 lib 20
		23.00 pm - 17 lib 21

Monday 10th April

Planetary Directions

Mercury rx 04 tau 50 at 00:15

Retrograde Planets

Mercury, Venus, Jupiter, Saturn, Haumea, Makemake, Orcus, Quaoar

Asteroids		Dwarf Planets	
Juno	16 cap 01	Eris	23 ar 09
Vesta	23 can 57	Haumea	23 lib 45
Pallas	03 ar 48	Makemake	02 lib 33
Ceres	22 tau 07	Salacia	01 ar 02
Chiron	26 pis 13	Orcus	07 vir 23
N Node	02 vir 32	Quaoar	00 cap 44
S Node	02 pis 32	Sedna	25 tau 27

Moon Phase: Gibbous
Sunrise: 06:15 BST
Sunset: 19:49
Moonrise: 19:00
Moonset: 06:19
Voc start:
Voc end:

Planetary and Angelic Hours			
Moon	06:16	Venus	19:46
Saturn	07:24	Mercury	20:39
Jupiter	08:31	Moon	21:31
Mars	09:39	Saturn	22:23
Sun	10:46	Jupiter	23:16
Venus	11:54	Mars	00:08
Mercury	13:01	Sun	01:00
Moon	14:09	Venus	01:53
Saturn	15:16	Mercury	02:45
Jupiter	16:24	Moon	03:37
Mars	17:31	Saturn	04:30
Sun	18:39	Jupiter	05:22

Aspects

Mars conjunct Ceres
Moon square Juno
Moon conjunct Jupiter
Moon square Pluto
Venus square Saturn
Uranus square Vesta

Planets	00:00 am	Moon
		01.00 am - 18 lib 23
Sun	21 ar 17	03.00 am - 19 lib 25
Mercury	04 tau 47	05.00 am - 20 lib 27
Venus	27 pis 18	07.00 am - 21 lib 28
Mars	22 tau 44	09.00 am - 22 lib 30
Jupiter	17 lib 51	11.00 am - 23 lib 31
Saturn	27 sag 46	13.00 pm - 24 lib 32
Uranus	24 ar 16	15.00 pm - 25 lib 34
Neptune	13 pis 08	17.00 pm - 26 lib 35
Pluto	10 cap 22	19.00 pm - 27 lib 36
		21.00 pm - 28 lib 37
Oob		23.00 pm - 29 lib 38

Tuesday 11th April

Planetary Directions

Moon into Scorpio
23:42

Retrograde Planets

Mercury, Venus,
Jupiter, Saturn,
Haumea, Makemake,
Orcus, Quaoar

Asteroids		Dwarf Planets	
Juno	16 cap 10	Eris	23 ar 09
Vesta	24 can 09	Haumea	23 lib 44
Pallas	04 ar 09	Makemake	02 lib 32
Ceres	22 tau 31	Salacia	01 ar 04
Chiron	26 pis 16	Orcus	07 vir 23
N Node	02 vir 26	Quaoar	00 cap 44
S Node	02 pis 26	Sedna	25 tau 27

Full Moon: 07:09
Sunrise: 06:13 BST
Sunset: 19:50
Moonrise: 20:05
Moonset: 06:42
Voc start:19:18
Voc end: 23:41

Planetary and Angelic Hours			
Mars	06:14	Saturn	19:48
Sun	07:22	Jupiter	20:40
Venus	08:30	Mars	21:32
Mercury	09:38	Sun	22:24
Moon	10:46	Venus	23:16
Saturn	11:53	Mercury	00:08
Jupiter	13:01	Moon	01:00
Mars	14:09	Saturn	01:52
Sun	15:17	Jupiter	02:44
Venus	16:25	Mars	03:36
Mercury	17:32	Sun	04:28
Moon	18:40	Venus	05:20

Aspects

Moon square Pluto
Sun opposite Moon
Moon opposite Eris
Moon square Vesta
Moon opposite Uranus
Uranus square Vesta
Moon sextile Saturn
Sun conjunct Eris
Venus square Saturn
Venus conjunct Chiron
Mars conjunct Ceres
Mars sextile Vesta

Planets	**00:00 am**	**Moon**
Sun	22 ar 16	01.00 am - 00 sco 39
Mercury	04 tau 37	03.00 am - 01 sco 40
Venus	27 pis 08	05.00 am - 02 sco 41
Mars	23 tau 26	07.00 am - 03 sco 42
Jupiter	17 lib 43	09.00 am - 04 sco 43
Saturn	27 sag 46	11.00 am - 05 sco 44
Uranus	24 ar 19	13.00 pm - 06 sco 44
Neptune	13 pis 09	15.00 pm - 07 sco 45
Pluto	19 cap 22	17.00 pm - 08 sco 45
		19.00 pm - 09 sco 46
Oob		21.00 pm - 10 sco 46
		23.00 pm - 11 sco 47

Wednesday 12th April

Retrograde Planets

Mercury, Venus, Jupiter, Saturn, Haumea, Makemake, Orcus, Quaoar

Asteroids		**Dwarf Planets**	
Juno	16 cap 18	Eris	23 ar 10
Vesta	24 can 23	Haumea	23 lib 43
Pallas	04 ar 30	Makemake	02 lib 30
Ceres	22 tau 55	Salacia	01 ar 05
Chiron	26 pis 20	Orcus	07 vir 22
N Node	02 vir 17	Quaoar	00 cap 43
S Node	02 pis 17	Sedna	25 tau 28

Phase: Disseminating
Sunrise: 06:11 BST
Sunset: 19:52
Moonrise: 21:09
Moonset: 07:06
Voc start:
Voc end:

Planetary and Angelic Hours			
Mercury	06:12	Sun	19:50
Moon	07:20	Venus	20:41
Saturn	08:28	Mercury	21:33
Jupiter	09:36	Moon	22:25
Mars	10:45	Saturn	23:16
Sun	11:53	Jupiter	00:08
Venus	13:01	Mars	01:00
Mercury	14:09	Sun	01:52
Moon	15:17	Venus	02:43
Saturn	16:25	Mercury	03:35
Jupiter	17:33	Moon	04:27
Mars	18:42	Saturn	05:18

Aspects

Moon opp. Mercury
Sun conjunct Eris
Moon trine Neptune
Venus square Saturn
Venus conjunct Chiron
Mars conjunct Ceres
Mars sextile Vesta
Uranus square Vesta

Planets	00:00 am	Moon
Sun	23 ar 15	01.00 am - 12 sco 47
Mercury	04 tau 22	03.00 am - 13 sco 47
Venus	27 pis 01	05.00 am - 14 sco 48
Mars	24 tau 08	07.00 am - 15 sco 48
Jupiter	17 lib 36	09.00 am - 16 sco 48
Saturn	27 sag 45	11.00 am - 17 sco 48
Uranus	24 ar 43	13.00 pm - 18 sco 48
Neptune	13 pis 11	15.00 pm - 19 sco 48
Pluto	19 cap 23	17.00 pm - 20 sco 48
		19.00 pm - 21 sco 48
Oob		21.00 pm - 22 sco 48
		23.00 pm - 23 sco 48

Thursday 13th April

Retrograde Planets

Mercury, Venus, Jupiter, Saturn, Haumea, Makemake, Orcus, Quaoar

Asteroids		Dwarf Planets	
Juno	16 cap 26	Eris	23 ar 11
Vesta	24 can 36	Haumea	23 lib 41
Pallas	04 ar 52	Makemake	02 lib 29
Ceres	23 tau 18	Salacia	01 ar 07
Chiron	26 pis 23	Orcus	07 vir 21
N Node	02 vir 08	Quaoar	00 cap 43
S Node	02 pis 08	Sedna	25 tau 29

Phase: Disseminating
Sunrise: 06:09 BST
Sunset: 19:54
Moonrise: 22:12
Moonset: 07:32
Voc start:
Voc end:

Planetary and Angelic Hours			
Jupiter	06:10	Moon	19:51
Mars	07:18	Saturn	20:43
Sun	08:27	Jupiter	21:34
Venus	09:35	Mars	22:25
Mercury	10:44	Sun	23:17
Moon	11:52	Venus	00:08
Saturn	13:01	Mercury	01:00
Jupiter	14:09	Moon	01:51
Mars	15:18	Saturn	02:42
Sun	16:26	Jupiter	03:34
Venus	17:34	Mars	04:25
Mercury	18:43	Sun	05:16

Maundy Thursday

Aspects

Moon trine Neptune
Moon sextile Juno
Moon sextile Pluto
Moon opposite Ceres
Sun conjunct Uranus
Sun square Vesta
Moon opposite Mars
Moon trine Vesta
Venus square Saturn
Venus conjunct Chiron
Mars sextile Vesta
Jupiter square Juno
Uranus square Vesta

Planets	00:00 am	Moon
Sun	24 ar 14	01.00 am - 24 sco 48
Mercury	04 tau 00	03.00 am - 25 sco 47
Venus	26 pis 27	05.00 am - 26 sco 47
Mars	24 tau 49	07.00 am - 27 sco 47
Jupiter	17 lib 28	09.00 am - 28 sco 47
Saturn	27 sag 44	11.00 am - 29 sco 46
Uranus	24 ar 26	13.00 pm - 00 sag 46
Neptune	13 pis 13	15.00 pm - 01 sag 45
Pluto	19 cap 23	17.00 pm - 02 sag 45
		19.00 pm - 03 sag 44
Oob		21.00 pm - 04 sag 44
		23.00 pm - 05 sag 43

Friday 14th April

Planetary Directions

Moon into Sagittarius 11:27

Retrograde Planets

Mercury, Venus, Jupiter, Saturn, Haumea, Makemake, Orcus, Quaoar

Asteroids		Dwarf Planets	
Juno	16 cap 34	Eris	23 ar 11
Vesta	24 can 50	Haumea	23 lib 40
Pallas	05 ar 13	Makemake	02 lib 28
Ceres	23 tau 42	Salacia	01 ar 08
Chiron	26 pis 26	Orcus	07 vir 20
N Node	01 vir 58	Quaoar	00 cap 43
S Node	01 pis 58	Sedna	25 tau 29

Phase: Disseminating
Sunrise: 06:07 BST
Sunset: 19:55
Moonrise: 23:13
Moonset: 08:01
Voc start: 05:17
Voc end: 11:26

Planetary and Angelic Hours			
Venus	06:08	Mars	19:53
Mercury	07:17	Sun	20:44
Moon	08:25	Venus	21:35
Saturn	09:34	Mercury	22:26
Jupiter	10:43	Moon	23:17
Mars	11:52	Saturn	00:08
Sun	13:00	Jupiter	00:59
Venus	14:09	Mars	01:50
Mercury	15:18	Sun	02:41
Moon	16:27	Venus	03:32
Saturn	17:35	Mercury	04:24
Jupiter	18:44	Moon	05:15

Good Friday

Aspects

Moon opposite Mars
Moon trine Vesta
Mars sextile Vesta
Moon trine Chiron
Moon trine Venus
Sun conjunct Uranus
Sun square Vesta
Moon trine Pallas
Venus square Saturn
Venus conjunct Chiron
Mars sextile Chiron
Jupiter square Juno
Uranus square Vesta
Ceres sextile Vesta

Planets	00:00 am	Moon
Sun	25 ar 12	01.00 am - 06 sag 43
Mercury	03 tau 34	03.00 am - 07 sag 42
Venus	26 pis 54	05.00 am - 08 sag 42
Mars	25 tau 31	07.00 am - 09 sag 41
Jupiter	17 lib 20	09.00 am - 10 sag 40
Saturn	27 sag 43	11.00 am - 11 sag 40
Uranus	24 ar 30	13.00 pm - 12 sag 39
Neptune	13 pis 15	15.00 pm - 13 sag 38
Pluto	19 cap 23	17.00 pm - 14 sag 38
		19.00 pm - 15 sag 37
		21.00 pm - 16 sag 36
Oob		23.00 pm - 17 sag 36

Saturday 15th April

Planetary Directions

Venus direct
26 pis 54 at 11:18

Retrograde Planets

Mercury, Jupiter, Saturn, Haumea, Makemake, Orcus, Quaoar

Asteroids		Dwarf Planets	
Juno	16 cap 42	Eris	23 ar 12
Vesta	25 can 04	Haumea	23 lib 39
Pallas	05 ar 34	Makemake	02 lib 27
Ceres	24 tau 06	Salacia	01 ar 10
Chiron	26 pis 30	Orcus	07 vir 19
N Node	01 vir 49	Quaoar	00 cap 42
S Node	01 pis 49	Sedna	25 tau 30

Phase: Disseminating
Sunrise: 06:04 BST
Sunset: 19:57
Moonrise: None
Moonset: 08:34
Voc start:
Voc end:

Planetary and Angelic Hours

Saturn	06:06	Mercury	19:55
Jupiter	07:15	Moon	20:45
Mars	08:24	Saturn	21:36
Sun	09:33	Jupiter	22:27
Venus	10:42	Mars	23:18
Mercury	11:51	Sun	00:08
Moon	13:00	Venus	00:59
Saturn	14:09	Mercury	01:50
Jupiter	15:18	Moon	02:41
Mars	16:27	Saturn	03:31
Sun	17:36	Jupiter	04:22
Venus	18:46	Mars	05:13

Aspects

Moon square Neptune
Moon sextile Jupiter
Sun square Vesta
Venus sextile Mars
Venus square Saturn
Venus conjunct Chiron
Mars sextile Chiron
Mars sextile Vesta
Jupiter square Juno
Uranus square Vesta
Ceres sextile Vesta

Planets	00:00 am	Moon
Sun	26 ar 11	01.00 am - 18 sag 35
Mercury	03 tau 04	03.00 am - 19 sag 34
Venus	26 pis 54	05.00 am - 20 sag 33
Mars	26 tau 13	07.00 am - 21 sag 33
Jupiter	17 lib 13	09.00 am - 22 sag 32
Saturn	27 sag 42	11.00 am - 23 sag 31
Uranus	24 ar 33	13.00 pm - 24 sag 31
Neptune	13 pis 17	15.00 pm - 25 sag 30
Pluto	19 cap 23	17.00 pm - 26 sag 29
		19.00 pm - 27 sag 29
Oob		21.00 pm - 28 sag 28
		23.00 pm - 29 sag 28

Sunday 16th April

Retrograde Planets

Mercury, Jupiter, Saturn, Haumea, Makemake, Orcus, Quaoar

Asteroids		Dwarf Planets	
Juno	16 cap 49	Eris	23 ar 13
Vesta	25 can 18	Haumea	23 lib 38
Pallas	05 ar 55	Makemake	02 lib 26
Ceres	24 tau 30	Salacia	01 ar 11
Chiron	26 pis 33	Orcus	07 vir 19
N Node	01 vir 41	Quaoar	00 cap 42
S Node	01 pis 41	Sedna	25 tau 31

Phase: Disseminating
Sunrise: 06:02 BST
Sunset: 19:59
Moonrise: 00:10
Moonset: 09:11
Voc start: 19:26
Voc end:

Planetary and Angelic Hours			
Sun	06:04	Jupiter	19:56
Venus	07:13	Mars	20:47
Mercury	08:22	Sun	21:37
Moon	09:32	Venus	22:28
Saturn	10:41	Mercury	23:18
Jupiter	11:50	Moon	00:08
Mars	13:00	Saturn	00:59
Sun	14:09	Jupiter	01:49
Venus	15:19	Mars	02:40
Mercury	16:28	Sun	03:30
Moon	17:37	Venus	04:21
Saturn	18:47	Mercury	05:11

Easter Sunday

Aspects

Moon trine Eris
Moon trine Uranus
Mars sextile Chiron
Moon square Chiron
Sun trine Moon
Moon square Venus
Moon conjunct Saturn
Sun trine Saturn
Venus sextile Mars
Venus square Saturn
Venus conjunct Chiron
Jupiter square Juno
Uranus square Vesta
Ceres sextile Vesta

Planets	00:00 am	Moon
Sun	27 ar 10	01.00 am - 00 cap 27
Mercury	02 tau 29	03.00 am - 01 cap 25
Venus	26 pis 57	05.00 am - 02 cap 26
Mars	26 tau 55	07.00 am - 03 cap 25
Jupiter	17 lib 05	09.00 am - 04 cap 25
Saturn	27 sag 41	11.00 am - 05 cap 25
Uranus	24 ar 37	13.00 pm - 06 cap 24
Neptune	13 pis 19	15.00 pm - 07 cap 24
Pluto	19 cap 23	17.00 pm - 08 cap 24
		19.00 pm - 09 cap 23
Oob		21.00 pm - 10 cap 23
		23.00 pm - 11 cap 23

Monday 17th April

Planetary Directions

Moon into Capricorn 00:05

Retrograde Planets

Mercury, Jupiter, Saturn, Haumea, Makemake, Orcus, Quaoar

Asteroids		Dwarf Planets	
Juno	16 cap 56	Eris	23 ar 13
Vesta	25 can 33	Haumea	23 lib 37
Pallas	06 ar 16	Makemake	02 lib 25
Ceres	24 tau 54	Salacia	01 ar 13
Chiron	26 pis 36	Orcus	07 vir 18
N Node	01 vir 35	Quaoar	00 cap 42
S Node	01 pis 35	Sedna	25 tau 32

Phase: Disseminating
Sunrise: 06:00 BST
Sunset: 20:00
Moonrise: 01:03
Moonset: 09:55
Voc start:
Voc end: 00:04

Planetary and Angelic Hours

Moon	06:01	Venus	19:58
Saturn	07:11	Mercury	20:48
Jupiter	08:21	Moon	21:38
Mars	09:31	Saturn	22:28
Sun	10:40	Jupiter	23:18
Venus	11:50	Mars	00:08
Mercury	13:00	Sun	00:59
Moon	14:09	Venus	01:49
Saturn	15:19	Mercury	02:39
Jupiter	16:29	Moon	03:29
Mars	17:38	Saturn	04:19
Sun	18:48	Jupiter	05:09

Easter Monday

Aspects

Venus sextile Mars
Moon trine Mercury
Moon square Pallas
Sun trine Saturn
Jupiter square Juno
Moon sextile Neptune
Venus square Saturn
Venus conjunct Chiron
Mars sextile Chiron
Chiron trine Vesta
Ceres sextile Vesta

Planets	**00:00 am**	**Moon**
Sun	28 ar 08	01.00 am - 12 cap 23
Mercury	01 tau 52	03.00 am - 13 cap 23
Venus	27 pis 02	05.00 am - 14 cap 23
Mars	27 tau 36	07.00 am - 15 cap 23
Jupiter	16 lib 58	09.00 am - 16 cap 23
Saturn	27 sag 40	11.00 am - 17 cap 24
Uranus	24 ar 40	13.00 pm - 18 cap 24
Neptune	13 pis 20	15.00 pm - 19 cap 24
Pluto	19 cap 23	17.00 pm - 20 cap 25
		19.00 pm - 21 cap 25
Oob		21.00 pm - 22 cap 26
		23.00 pm - 23 cap 27

Tuesday 18th April

Retrograde Planets

Mercury, Jupiter, Saturn, Haumea, Makemake, Orcus, Quaoar

Asteroids		**Dwarf Planets**	
Juno	17 cap 03	Eris	23 ar 14
Vesta	25 can 48	Haumea	23 lib 36
Pallas	06 ar 37	Makemake	02 lib 24
Ceres	25 tau 17	Salacia	01 ar 14
Chiron	26 pis 39	Orcus	07 vir 17
N Node	01 vir 31	Quaoar	00 cap 41
S Node	01 pis 31	Sedna	25 tau 32

Phase: Disseminating
Sunrise: 05:58 BST
Sunset: 20:02
Moonrise: 01:52
Moonset: 10:45
Voc start:
Voc end:

Planetary and Angelic Hours			
Mars	05:59	Saturn	19:59
Sun	07:09	Jupiter	20:49
Venus	08:19	Mars	21:39
Mercury	09:29	Sun	22:29
Moon	10:39	Venus	23:19
Saturn	11:49	Mercury	00:09
Jupiter	12:59	Moon	00:58
Mars	14:09	Saturn	01:48
Sun	15:19	Jupiter	02:38
Venus	16:29	Mars	03:28
Mercury	17:39	Sun	04:18
Moon	18:49	Venus	05:07

Aspects

Moon sextile Neptune
Moon square Jupiter
Moon conjunct Juno
Moon conjunct Pluto
Moon square Eris
Moon square Uranus
Venus square Saturn
Venus conjunct Chiron
Jupiter square Juno
Saturn square Chiron
Chiron trine Vesta
Ceres sextile Vesta

Planets	00:00 am	Moon
		01.00 am - 24 cap 28
Sun	29 ar 07	03.00 am - 25 cap 28
Mercury	01 tau 12	05.00 am - 26 cap 29
Venus	27 pis 09	07.00 am - 27 cap 31
Mars	28 tau 18	09.00 am - 28 cap 32
Jupiter	16 lib 50	11.00 am - 29 cap 33
Saturn	27 sag 39	13.00 pm - 00 aq 34
Uranus	24 ar 44	15.00 pm - 01 aq 36
Neptune	13 pis 22	17.00 pm - 02 aq 38
Pluto	19 cap 23	19.00 pm - 03 aq 39
		21.00 pm - 04 aq 41
Oob		23.00 pm - 05 aq 43

Wednesday 19th April

Planetary Directions

Moon into Aquarius 11:52

Sun into Tau at 22:28

Retrograde Planets

Mercury, Jupiter, Saturn, Haumea, Makemake, Orcus, Quaoar

Asteroids		Dwarf Planets	
Juno	17 cap 10	Eris	23 ar 15
Vesta	26 can 03	Haumea	23 lib 34
Pallas	06 ar 58	Makemake	02 lib 23
Ceres	25 tau 41	Salacia	01 ar 16
Chiron	26 pis 42	Orcus	07 vir 17
N Node	01 vir 30	Quaoar	00 cap 41
S Node	01 pis 30	Sedna	25 tau 33

Last Quarter: 11:00
Sunrise: 05:56 BST
Sunset: 20:04
Moonrise: 02:34
Moonset: 11:42
Voc start: 10:56
Voc end: 11:51

Planetary and Angelic Hours			
Mercury	05:57	Sun	20:01
Moon	07:08	Venus	20:51
Saturn	08:18	Mercury	21:40
Jupiter	09:28	Moon	22:30
Mars	10:39	Saturn	23:19
Sun	11:49	Jupiter	00:09
Venus	12:59	Mars	00:58
Mercury	14:10	Sun	01:48
Moon	15:20	Venus	02:37
Saturn	16:30	Mercury	03:27
Jupiter	17:40	Moon	04:16
Mars	18:51	Saturn	05:04

Aspects

Moon square Uranus
Moon trine Ceres
Moon opposite Vesta
Moon sextile Chiron
Moon sextile Venus
Moon trine Mars
Sun square Moon
Moon square Mercury
Sun conjunct Mercury
Moon sextile Pallas
Venus square Saturn
Venus conjunct Chiron
Jupiter square Juno
Saturn square Chiron
Chiron sextile Ceres
Chiron trine Vesta
Ceres sextile Vesta

Thursday 20th April

Planets	00:00 am	Moon
Sun	00 tau 06	01.00 am - 06 aq 45
Mercury	00 tau 30	03.00 am - 07 aq 48
Venus	27 pis 18	05.00 am - 08 aq 50
Mars	29 tau 00	07.00 am - 09 aq 53
Jupiter	16 lib 43	09.00 am - 10 aq 55
Saturn	27 sag 38	11.00 am - 11 aq 58
Uranus	24 ar 47	13.00 pm - 13 aq 01
Neptune	13 pis 24	15.00 pm - 14 aq 04
Pluto	19 cap 23	17.00 pm - 15 aq 07
		19.00 pm - 16 aq 11
		21.00 pm - 17 aq 14
Oob		23.00 pm - 18 aq 18

Planetary Directions

Pluto retrograde
19 cap 23 at 13:49
Mercury rx-enters Aries
at 18:38

Retrograde Planets

Mercury, Jupiter, Saturn, Haumea, Makemake, Orcus, Quaoar

Asteroids		Dwarf Planets	
Juno	17 cap 16	Eris	23 ar 15
Vesta	26 can 18	Haumea	23 lib 34
Pallas	07 ar 19	Makemake	02 lib 23
Ceres	26 tau 05	Salacia	01 ar 16
Chiron	26 pis 46	Orcus	07 vir 17
N Node	01 vir 30	Quaoar	00 cap 41
S Node	01 pis 30	Sedna	25 tau 33

Moon Phase: Balsamic
Sunrise: 05:54 BST
Sunset: 20:05
Moonrise: 03:12
Moonset: 12:44
Voc start:
Voc end:

Planetary and Angelic Hours			
Jupiter	05:55	Moon	20:03
Mars	07:06	Saturn	20:52
Sun	08:16	Jupiter	21:41
Venus	09:27	Mars	22:30
Mercury	10:38	Sun	23:20
Moon	11:48	Venus	00:09
Saturn	12:59	Mercury	00:58
Jupiter	14:10	Moon	01:47
Mars	15:20	Saturn	02:36
Sun	16:31	Jupiter	03:26
Venus	17:41	Mars	04:15
Mercury	18:52	Sun	05:04

Aspects

Moon square Uranus
Moon trine Ceres
Moon opposite Vesta
Moon sextile Chiron
Moon sextile Venus
Moon trine Mars
Sun square Moon
Moon square Mercury
Sun conjunct Mercury
Moon sextile Pallas
Venus square Saturn
Venus conjunct Chiron
Jupiter square Juno
Saturn square Chiron
Chiron sextile Ceres
Chiron trine Vesta
Ceres sextile Vesta

Planets	00:00 am	Moon
Sun	01 tau 04	01.00 am - 19 aq 22
Mercury	29 ar 48	03.00 am - 20 aq 26
Venus	27 pis 30	05.00 am - 21 aq 30
Mars	29 tau 41	07.00 am - 22 aq 34
Jupiter	16 lib 36	09.00 am - 23 aq 38
Saturn	27 sag 37	11.00 am - 24 aq 43
Uranus	24 ar 50	13.00 pm - 25 aq 48
Neptune	13 pis 25	15.00 pm - 26 aq 53
Pluto	19 cap 23	17.00 pm - 27 aq 58
		19.00 pm - 29 aq 03
Oob		21.00 pm - 00 pis 09
		23.00 pm - 01 pis 15

Friday 21st April

Planetary Directions

Mars into Gemini 11:32
Moon into Pisces 20:43

Retrograde Planets

Mercury, Jupiter, Saturn, Pluto, Haumea, Makemake, Orcus, Quaoar

Asteroids		Dwarf Planets	
Juno	17 cap 22	Eris	23 ar 16
Vesta	26 can 34	Haumea	23 lib 32
Pallas	07 ar 41	Makemake	02 lib 21
Ceres	26 tau 30	Salacia	01 ar 19
Chiron	26 pis 49	Orcus	07 vir 15
N Node	01 vir 31	Quaoar	00 cap 40
S Node	01 pis 31	Sedna	25 tau 34

Moon Phase: Balsamic
Sunrise: 05:52 BST
Sunset: 20:07
Moonrise: 03:46
Moonset: 13:50
Voc start: 19:22
Voc end: 20:42

Planetary and Angelic Hours			
Venus	05:53	Mars	20:04
Mercury	07:04	Sun	20:53
Moon	08:15	Venus	21:42
Saturn	09:26	Mercury	22:31
Jupiter	10:37	Moon	23:20
Mars	11:48	Saturn	00:09
Sun	12:59	Jupiter	00:58
Venus	14:10	Mars	01:47
Mercury	15:21	Sun	02:36
Moon	16:32	Venus	03:24
Saturn	17:43	Mercury	04:13
Jupiter	18:53	Moon	05:02

Aspects

Moon sextile Eris
Moon sextile Uranus
Venus square Saturn
Ceres sextile Vesta
Moon square Ceres
Moon sextile Saturn
Moon sextile Mercury
Moon square Mars
Chiron sextile Ceres
Sun sextile Moon
Venus conjunct Chiron
Venus sextile Ceres
Venus trine Vesta
Jupiter square Juno
Saturn square Chiron
Chiron trine Vesta

Planets	00:00 am	Moon
Sun	02 tau 03	01.00 am - 02 pis 21
Mercury	29 ar 06	03.00 am - 03 pis 27
Venus	27 pis 43	05.00 am - 04 pis 33
Mars	00 gem 23	07.00 am - 05 pis 39
Jupiter	16 lib 28	09.00 am - 06 pis 46
Saturn	27 sag 35	11.00 am - 07 pis 53
Uranus	24 ar 54	13.00 pm - 09 pis 00
Neptune	13 pis 27	15.00 pm - 10 pis 07
Pluto	19 cap 23	17.00 pm - 11 pis 15
		19.00 pm - 12 pis 22
Oob		21.00 pm - 13 pis 30
		23.00 pm - 14 pis 38

Saturday 22nd April

Retrograde Planets

Mercury, Jupiter, Saturn, Pluto, Haumea, Makemake, Orcus, Quaoar

Asteroids		Dwarf Planets	
Juno	17 cap 28	Eris	23 ar 16
Vesta	26 can 50	Haumea	23 lib 31
Pallas	08 ar 02	Makemake	02 lib 20
Ceres	26 tau 54	Salacia	01 ar 20
Chiron	26 pis 52	Orcus	07 vir 15
N Node	01 vir 31	Quaoar	00 cap 39
S Node	01 pis 31	Sedna	25 tau 35

Moon Phase: Balsamic
Sunrise: 05:50 BST
Sunset: 20:09
Moonrise: 04:16
Moonset: 15:01
Voc start:
Voc end:

Planetary and Angelic Hours			
Saturn	05:51	Mercury	20:06
Jupiter	07:02	Moon	20:55
Mars	08:14	Saturn	21:43
Sun	09:25	Jupiter	22:32
Venus	10:36	Mars	23:20
Mercury	11:47	Sun	00:09
Moon	12:59	Venus	00:58
Saturn	14:10	Mercury	01:46
Jupiter	15:21	Moon	02:35
Mars	16:32	Saturn	03:23
Sun	17:44	Jupiter	04:12
Venus	18:55	Mars	05:01

Aspects

Chiron trine Vesta
Moon conj. Neptune
Mercury trine Saturn
Venus square Saturn
Venus sextile Ceres
Venus trine Vesta
Saturn square Chiron
Chiron sextile Ceres
Ceres sextile Vesta

Planets	00:00 am	Moon
Sun	03 tau 01	01.00 am - 15 pis 46
Mercury	28 ar 25	03.00 am - 16 pis 55
Venus	27 pis 59	05.00 am - 18 pis 03
Mars	01 gem 04	07.00 am - 19 pis 12
Jupiter	16 lib 21	09.00 am - 20 pis 21
Saturn	27 sag 33	11.00 am - 21 pis 30
Uranus	24 ar 57	13.00 pm - 22 pis 40
Neptune	13 pis 29	15.00 pm - 23 pis 49
Pluto	19 cap 23	17.00 pm - 24 pis 59
		19.00 pm - 26 pis 09
Oob		21.00 pm - 27 pis 19
		23.00 pm - 28 pis 30

Sunday 23rd April

Retrograde Planets

Mercury, Jupiter, Saturn, Pluto, Haumea, Makemake, Orcus, Quaoar

Asteroids		Dwarf Planets	
Juno	17 cap 34	Eris	23 ar 17
Vesta	27 can 06	Haumea	23 lib 30
Pallas	08 ar 23	Makemake	02 lib 19
Ceres	27 tau 18	Salacia	01 ar 21
Chiron	26 pis 55	Orcus	07 vir 14
N Node	01 vir 30	Quaoar	00 cap 39
S Node	01 pis 30	Sedna	25 tau 36

Moon Phase: Balsamic
Sunrise: 05:48 BST
Sunset: 20:10
Moonrise: 04:44
Moonset: 16:15
Voc start: 22:34
Voc end:

Planetary and Angelic Hours			
Sun	05:49	Jupiter	20:08
Venus	07:01	Mars	20:56
Mercury	08:12	Sun	21:44
Moon	09:24	Venus	22:33
Saturn	10:35	Mercury	23:31
Jupiter	11:47	Moon	00:09
Mars	12:58	Saturn	00:57
Sun	14:10	Jupiter	01:46
Venus	15:21	Mars	02:34
Mercury	16:33	Sun	03:22
Moon	17:45	Venus	04:11
Saturn	18:56	Mercury	04:59

St George's Day

Aspects

Moon sextile Juno
Moon sextile Pluto
Moon conjunct Chiron
Moon trine Vesta
Moon square Saturn
Moon sextile Ceres
Moon conjunct Venus
Mercury trine Saturn
Mercury square Vesta
Venus square Saturn
Venus sextile Ceres
Venus trine Vesta
Saturn square Chiron
Chiron sextile Ceres
Chiron trine Vesta

Planets	00:00 am	Moon
Sun	04 tau 00	01.00 am - 29 pis 40
Mercury	27 ar 45	03.00 am - 00 ar 51
Venus	28 pis 17	05.00 am - 02 ar 02
Mars	01 gem 46	07.00 am - 03 ar 13
Jupiter	16 lib 14	09.00 am - 04 ar 25
Saturn	27 sag 32	11.00 am - 05 ar 36
Uranus	25 ar 01	13.00 pm - 06 ar 48
Neptune	13 pis 30	15.00 pm - 08 ar 00
Pluto	19 cap 23	17.00 pm - 09 ar 12
		19.00 pm - 10 ar 24
Oob		21.00 pm - 11 ar 37
		23.00 pm - 12 ar 49

Monday 24th April

Planetary Directions

Moon into Aries 01:33

Retrograde Planets

Mercury, Jupiter, Saturn, Pluto, Haumea, Makemake, Orcus, Quaoar

Asteroids		Dwarf Planets	
Juno	17 cap 39	Eris	23 ar 18
Vesta	27 can 22	Haumea	23 lib 29
Pallas	08 ar 44	Makemake	02 lib 18
Ceres	27 tau 42	Salacia	01 ar 23
Chiron	26 pis 58	Orcus	07 vir 14
N Node	01 vir 27	Quaoar	00 cap 38
S Node	01 pis 27	Sedna	25 tau 37

Moon Phase: Balsamic
Sunrise: 05:46 BST
Sunset: 20:12
Moonrise: 05:11
Moonset: 17:32
Voc start:
Voc end: 01:32

Planetary and Angelic Hours			
Moon	05:47	Venus	20:09
Saturn	06:59	Mercury	20:57
Jupiter	08:11	Moon	21:45
Mars	09:23	Saturn	22:33
Sun	10:34	Jupiter	23:21
Venus	11:46	Mars	00:09
Mercury	12:58	Sun	00:57
Moon	14:10	Venus	01:45
Saturn	15:22	Mercury	02:33
Jupiter	16:34	Moon	03:21
Mars	17:46	Saturn	04:09
Sun	18:57	Jupiter	04:57

Aspects

Moon sextile Mars
Mercury trine Saturn
Mercury square Vesta
Moon conjunct Pallas
Venus sextile Ceres
Venus trine Vesta
Saturn square Chiron
Chiron trine Vesta
Ceres sextile Vesta

Planets	00:00 am	Moon
Sun	04 tau 58	01.00 am - 14 ar 02
Mercury	27 ar 07	03.00 am - 15 ar 15
Venus	28 pis 36	05.00 am - 16 ar 28
Mars	02 gem 27	07.00 am - 17 ar 41
Jupiter	16 lib 07	09.00 am - 18 ar 55
Saturn	27 sag 30	11.00 am - 20 ar 08
Uranus	25 ar 04	13.00 pm - 21 ar 22
Neptune	13 pis 32	15.00 pm - 22 ar 36
Pluto	19 cap 23	17.00 pm - 23 ar 50
		19.00 pm - 25 ar 04
Oob		21.00 pm - 26 ar 18
		23.00 pm - 27 ar 33

Tuesday 25th April

Retrograde Planets

Mercury, Jupiter, Saturn, Pluto, Haumea, Makemake, Orcus, Quaoar

Asteroids		Dwarf Planets	
Juno	17 cap 44	Eris	23 ar 18
Vesta	27 can 39	Haumea	23 lib 27
Pallas	09 ar 05	Makemake	02 lib 17
Ceres	28 tau 06	Salacia	01 ar 24
Chiron	27 pis 01	Orcus	07 vir 13
N Node	01 vir 22	Quaoar	00 cap 38
S Node	01 pis 22	Sedna	25 tau 37

Moon Phase: Balsamic
Sunrise: 05:44 BST
Sunset: 20:14
Moonrise: 05:39
Moonset: 18:52
Voc start: 22:52
Voc end:

Planetary and Angelic Hours			
Mars	05:45	Saturn	20:11
Sun	06:57	Jupiter	20:59
Venus	08:09	Mars	21:46
Mercury	09:22	Sun	22:34
Moon	10:34	Venus	23:22
Saturn	11:46	Mercury	00:09
Jupiter	12:58	Moon	00:57
Mars	14:10	Saturn	01:45
Sun	15:22	Jupiter	02:32
Venus	16:34	Mars	03:20
Mercury	17:47	Sun	04:08
Moon	18:59	Venus	04:55

Aspects

Moon opposite Jupiter
Moon square Juno
Moon square Pluto
Moon conjunct Eris
Moon conjunct Uranus
Moon conj. Mercury
Moon trine Saturn
Moon square Vesta
Mercury trine Saturn
Venus sextile Ceres
Saturn square Chiron
Chiron trine Vesta
Ceres sextile Vesta

Planets	**00:00 am**	**Moon**
Sun	05 tau 57	01.00 am - 28 ar 47
Mercury	26 ar 32	03.00 am - 00 tau 02
Venus	28 pis 57	05.00 am - 01 tau 17
Mars	03 gem 09	07.00 am - 02 tau 31
Jupiter	16 lib 00	09.00 am - 03 tau 46
Saturn	27 sag 28	11.00 am - 05 tau 01
Uranus	25 ar 07	13.00 pm - 06 tau 17
Neptune	13 pis 34	15.00 pm - 07 tau 32
Pluto	19 cap 23	17.00 pm - 08 tau 47
		19.00 pm - 10 tau 02
		21.00 pm - 11 tau 18
Oob		23.00 pm - 12 tau 33

Wednesday 26th April

Planetary Directions

Moon into Taurus
02:57

Retrograde Planets

Mercury, Jupiter, Saturn, Pluto, Haumea, Makemake, Orcus, Quaoar

Asteroids		**Dwarf Planets**	
Juno	17 cap 48	Eris	23 ar 19
Vesta	27 can 56	Haumea	23 lib 26
Pallas	09 ar 26	Makemake	02 lib 16
Ceres	28 tau 30	Salacia	01 ar 26
Chiron	27 pis 04	Orcus	07 vir 12
N Node	01 vir 14	Quaoar	00 cap37
S Node	01 pis 14	Sedna	25 tau 38

New Moon: 13:18
Sunrise: 05:42 BST
Sunset: 20:15
Moonrise: 06:08
Moonset: 20:13
Voc start:
Voc end: 02:56

Planetary and Angelic Hours			
Mercury	05:43	Sun	20:13
Moon	06:56	Venus	21:00
Saturn	08:08	Mercury	21:47
Jupiter	09:20	Moon	22:35
Mars	10:33	Saturn	23:22
Sun	11:45	Jupiter	00:09
Venus	12:58	Mars	00:57
Mercury	14:10	Sun	01:44
Moon	15:23	Venus	02:32
Saturn	16:35	Mercury	03:19
Jupiter	17:48	Moon	04:06
Mars	19:00	Saturn	04:54

Aspects

Sun conjunct Moon
Moon sextile Neptune
Mercury conj. Uranus
Venus sextile Ceres
Saturn square Chiron
Ceres sextile Vesta

Planets	**00:00 am**	**Moon**
Sun	06 tau 55	01.00 am - 13 tau 49
Mercury	26 ar 00	03.00 am - 15 tau 04
Venus	29 pis 20	05.00 am - 16 tau 20
Mars	03 gem 50	07.00 am - 17 tau 36
Jupiter	15 lib 53	09.00 am - 18 tau 51
Saturn	27 sag 26	11.00 am - 20 tau 07
Uranus	25 ar 11	13.00 pm - 21 tau 23
Neptune	13 pis 35	15.00 pm - 22 tau 38
Pluto	19 cap 23	17.00 pm - 23 tau 54
		19.00 pm - 25 tau 10
Oob		21.00 pm - 26 tau 26
		23.00 pm - 27 tau 41

Thursday 27th April

Retrograde Planets

Mercury, Jupiter, Saturn, Pluto, Haumea, Makemake, Orcus, Quaoar

Asteroids		**Dwarf Planets**	
Juno	17 cap 53	Eris	23 ar 20
Vesta	28 can 13	Haumea	23 lib 25
Pallas	09 ar 47	Makemake	02 lib 16
Ceres	28 tau 55	Salacia	01 ar 27
Chiron	27 pis 07	Orcus	07 vir 12
N Node	01 vir 05	Quaoar	00 cap37
S Node	01 pis 05	Sedna	25 tau 39

Moon Phase: Crescent
Sunrise: 05:40 BST
Sunset: 20:17
Moonrise: 06:41
Moonset: 21:33
Voc start:
Voc end:

Planetary and Angelic Hours			
Jupiter	05:41	Moon	20:14
Mars	06:54	Saturn	21:01
Sun	08:07	Jupiter	21:48
Venus	09:19	Mars	22:35
Mercury	10:32	Sun	23:23
Moon	11:45	Venus	00:10
Saturn	12:58	Mercury	00:57
Jupiter	14:10	Moon	01:44
Mars	15:23	Saturn	02:31
Sun	16:36	Jupiter	03:18
Venus	17:49	Mars	04:05
Mercury	19:01	Sun	04:52

Aspects

Moon trine Juno
Moon trine Pluto
Moon sextile Chiron
Moon sextile Vesta
Moon sextile Venus
Moon conjunct Ceres
Mercury conj. Uranus
Venus sextile Ceres
Saturn square Chiron
Ceres sextile Vesta

Planets	00:00 am	Moon
Sun	07 tau 54	01.00 am - 28 tau 57
Mercury	25 ar 32	03.00 am - 00 gem 13
Venus	29 pis 45	05.00 am - 01 gem 28
Mars	04 gem 31	07.00 am - 02 gem 44
Jupiter	15 lib 47	09.00 am - 04 gem 00
Saturn	27 sag 24	11.00 am - 05 gem 15
Uranus	25 ar 14	13.00 pm - 06 gem 31
Neptune	13 pis 37	15.00 pm - 07 gem 46
Pluto	19 cap 23	17.00 pm - 09 gem 01
		19.00 pm - 10 gem 16
Oob		21.00 pm - 11 gem 32
		23.00 pm - 12 gem 47

Friday 28th April

Planetary Directions

Venus re-enters Aries 14:14

Retrograde Planets

Mercury, Jupiter, Saturn, Pluto, Haumea, Makemake, Orcus, Quaoar

Asteroids		Dwarf Planets	
Juno	17 cap 57	Eris	23 ar 20
Vesta	28 can 30	Haumea	23 lib 24
Pallas	10 ar 08	Makemake	02 lib 15
Ceres	29 tau 19	Salacia	01 ar 28
Chiron	27 pis 10	Orcus	07 vir 11
N Node	00 vir 55	Quaoar	00 cap36
S Node	00 pis 55	Sedna	25 tau 40

Moon Phase: Crescent
Sunrise: 05:38 BST
Sunset: 20:19
Moonrise: 07:20
Moonset: 22:51
Voc start: 02:18
Voc end: 02:38

Planetary and Angelic Hours			
Venus	05:39	Mars	20:16
Mercury	06:52	Sun	21:03
Moon	08:05	Venus	21:49
Saturn	09:18	Mercury	22:36
Jupiter	10:31	Moon	23:23
Mars	11:44	Saturn	00:10
Sun	12:58	Jupiter	00:57
Venus	14:11	Mars	01:43
Mercury	15:24	Sun	02:30
Moon	16:37	Venus	03:17
Saturn	17:50	Mercury	04:04
Jupiter	19:03	Moon	04:51

Aspects

Moon conjunct Ceres
Moon sextile Venus
Moon conjunct Mars
Mercury conj. Uranus
Moon sextile Pallas
Moon square Neptune
Venus sextile Ceres
Saturn square Chiron
Ceres sextile Vesta

Saturday 29th April

Planets	00:00 am
Sun	08 tau 52
Mercury	25 ar 08
Venus	00 ar 12
Mars	05 gem 12
Jupiter	15 lib 40
Saturn	27 sag 22
Uranus	25 ar 18
Neptune	13 pis 38
Pluto	19 cap 22
Oob	

Moon

01.00 am - 14 gem 02
03.00 am - 15 gem 17
05.00 am - 16 gem 31
07.00 am - 17 gem 46
09.00 am - 19 gem 01
11.00 am - 20 gem 15
13.00 pm - 21 gem 30
15.00 pm - 22 gem 44
17.00 pm - 23 gem 58
19.00 pm - 25 gem 12
21.00 pm - 26 gem 26
23.00 pm - 27 gem 40

Planetary Directions

Ceres into Gemini 16:40

Retrograde Planets

Mercury, Jupiter, Saturn, Pluto, Haumea, Makemake, Orcus, Quaoar

Asteroids		Dwarf Planets	
Juno	18 cap 00	Eris	23 ar 21
Vesta	28 can 47	Haumea	23 lib 23
Pallas	10 ar 29	Makemake	02 lib 14
Ceres	29 tau 44	Salacia	01 ar 30
Chiron	27 pis 13	Orcus	07 vir 11
N Node	00 vir 45	Quaoar	00 cap36
S Node	00 pis 45	Sedna	25 tau 40

Moon Phase: Crescent
Sunrise: 05:36 BST
Sunset: 20:20
Moonrise: 08:06
Moonset: None
Voc start: 22:28
Voc end:

Planetary and Angelic Hours

Saturn	05:37	Mercury	20:17
Jupiter	06:51	Moon	21:04
Mars	08:04	Saturn	21:50
Sun	09:17	Jupiter	22:37
Venus	10:31	Mars	23:23
Mercury	11:44	Sun	00:10
Moon	12:57	Venus	00:56
Saturn	14:11	Mercury	01:43
Jupiter	15:24	Moon	02:29
Mars	16:37	Saturn	03:16
Sun	17:51	Jupiter	04:02
Venus	19:04	Mars	04:49

Aspects

Moon trine Jupiter
Moon sextile Eris
Moon sextile Mercury
Moon sextile Uranus
Moon square Chiron
Moon opposite Saturn
Mercury conj. Uranus
Venus sextile Ceres
Saturn square Chiron

Planets	**00:00 am**	**Moon**
Sun	09 tau 50	01.00 am - 28 gem 53
Mercury	24 ar 48	03.00 am - 00 can 07
Venus	00 ar 40	05.00 am - 01 can 20
Mars	05 gem 54	07.00 am - 02 can 33
Jupiter	15 lib 33	09.00 am - 03 can 46
Saturn	27 sag 20	11.00 am - 04 can 59
Uranus	25 ar 21	13.00 pm - 06 can 12
Neptune	13 pis 40	15.00 pm - 07 can 25
Pluto	19 cap 22	17.00 pm - 08 can 37
		19.00 pm - 09 can 49
Oob		21.00 pm - 11 can 02
		23.00 pm - 12 can 13

Sunday 30th April

Planetary Directions

Moon into Cancer
02:48

Retrograde Planets

Mercury, Jupiter, Saturn, Pluto, Haumea, Makemake, Orcus, Quaoar

Asteroids		**Dwarf Planets**	
Juno	18 cap 04	Eris	23 ar 22
Vesta	29 can 05	Haumea	23 lib 22
Pallas	10 ar 50	Makemake	02 lib 13
Ceres	00 gem 08	Salacia	01 ar 31
Chiron	27 pis 16	Orcus	07 vir 10
N Node	00 vir 38	Quaoar	00 cap35
S Node	00 pis 38	Sedna	25 tau 41

Moon Phase: Crescent
Sunrise: 05:34 BST
Sunset: 20:22
Moonrise: 09:00
Moonset: 00:02
Voc start:
Voc end: 02:47

Planetary and Angelic Hours			
Sun	05:35	Jupiter	20:19
Venus	06:49	Mars	21:05
Mercury	08:03	Sun	21:51
Moon	09:16	Venus	22:38
Saturn	10:30	Mercury	23:24
Jupiter	11:44	Moon	00:10
Mars	12:57	Saturn	00:56
Sun	14:11	Jupiter	01:43
Venus	15:24	Mars	02:29
Mercury	16:38	Sun	03:15
Moon	17:52	Venus	04:01
Saturn	19:05	Mercury	04:47

Aspects

Moon square Venus
Sun sextile Moon
Moon square Pallas
Saturn square Chiron
Moon trine Neptune
Mercury conj. Uranus
Venus sextile Ceres

Planets	00:00 am	Moon
Sun	10 tau 49	01.00 am - 13 can 25
Mercury	24 ar 33	03.00 am - 14 can 37
Venus	01 ar 09	05.00 am - 15 can 48
Mars	06 gem 35	07.00 am - 17 can 00
Jupiter	15 lib 27	09.00 am - 18 can 11
Saturn	27 sag 18	11.00 am - 19 can 22
Uranus	25 ar 24	13.00 pm - 20 can 32
Neptune	13 pis 41	15.00 pm - 21 can 43
Pluto	19 cap 22	17.00 pm - 22 can 54
		19.00 pm - 24 can 04
Oob		21.00 pm - 25 can 14
		23.00 pm - 26 can 24

Monday 1st May

Retrograde Planets

Mercury, Jupiter, Saturn, Pluto, Haumea, Makemake, Orcus, Quaoar

Asteroids		Dwarf Planets	
Juno	18 cap 07	Eris	23 ar 22
Vesta	29 can 23	Haumea	23 lib 21
Pallas	11 ar 11	Makemake	02 lib 12
Ceres	00 gem 32	Salacia	01 ar 32
Chiron	27 pis18	Orcus	07 vir 10
N Node	00 vir 33	Quaoar	00 cap34
S Node	00 pis 33	Sedna	25 tau 42

Moon Phase: Crescent
Sunrise: 05:32 BST
Sunset: 20:24
Moonrise: 10:01
Moonset: 01:02
Voc start: 21:22
Voc end:

Planetary and Angelic Hours			
Moon	05:34	Venus	20:21
Saturn	06:48	Mercury	21:06
Jupiter	08:01	Moon	21:52
Mars	09:15	Saturn	22:38
Sun	10:29	Jupiter	23:24
Venus	11:43	Mars	00:10
Mercury	12:57	Sun	00:56
Moon	14:11	Venus	01:42
Saturn	15:25	Mercury	02:28
Jupiter	16:39	Moon	03:14
Mars	17:53	Saturn	04:00
Sun	19:07	Jupiter	04:46

Beltane
May Bank Holiday

Aspects

Moon trine Neptune
Moon square Jupiter
Moon opposite Juno
Moon opposite Pluto
Moon square Eris
Moon square Mercury
Moon square Uranus
Moon trine Chiron
Mercury conjunct Eris
Venus sextile Ceres
Saturn square Chiron

Planets	**00:00 am**	**Moon**
Sun	11 tau 47	01.00 am - 27 can 34
Mercury	24 ar 22	03.00 am - 28 can 43
Venus	01 ar 40	05.00 am - 29 can 53
Mars	07 gem 16	07.00 am - 01 leo 02
Jupiter	15 lib 21	09.00 am - 02 leo 11
Saturn	27 sag 15	11.00 am - 03 leo 20
Uranus	25 ar 28	13.00 pm - 04 leo 29
Neptune	13 pis 42	15.00 pm - 05 leo 37
Pluto	19 cap 21	17.00 pm - 06 leo 46
		19.00 pm - 07 leo 54
Oob		21.00 pm - 09 leo 02
		23.00 pm - 10 leo 10

Tuesday 2nd May

Planetary Directions

Moon into Leo 05:12

Retrograde Planets

Mercury, Jupiter, Saturn, Pluto, Haumea, Makemake, Orcus, Quaoar

Asteroids		**Dwarf Planets**	
Juno	18 cap 10	Eris	23 ar 23
Vesta	29 can 41	Haumea	23 lib 20
Pallas	11 ar 32	Makemake	02 lib 11
Ceres	00 gem 57	Salacia	01 ar 34
Chiron	27 pis 21	Orcus	07 vir 10
N Node	00 vir 30	Quaoar	00 cap34
S Node	00 pis 30	Sedna	25 tau 43

Moon Phase: Crescent
Sunrise: 05:30 BST
Sunset: 20:25
Moonrise: 11:08
Moonset: 01:53
Voc start:
Voc end: 05:11

Planetary and Angelic Hours			
Mars	05:32	Saturn	20:22
Sun	06:46	Jupiter	21:08
Venus	08:00	Mars	21:53
Mercury	09:14	Sun	22:39
Moon	10:29	Venus	23:25
Saturn	11:43	Mercury	00:10
Jupiter	12:57	Moon	00:56
Mars	14:11	Saturn	01:42
Sun	15:25	Jupiter	02:27
Venus	16:40	Mars	03:13
Mercury	17:54	Sun	03:59
Moon	19:08	Venus	04:04

Aspects

Moon conjunct Vesta
Moon sextile Ceres
Moon trine Venus
Moon sextile Mars
Sun sextile Neptune
Moon trine Pallas
Mercury conjunct Eris
Venus sextile Ceres
Saturn square Chiron

Planets	00:00 am	Moon
Sun	12 tau 45	01.00 am - 11 leo 18
Mercury	24 ar 16	03.00 am - 12 leo 25
Venus	02 ar 12	05.00 am - 13 leo 33
Mars	05 gem 57	07.00 am - 14 leo 40
Jupiter	15 lib 15	09.00 am - 15 leo 47
Saturn	27 sag 13	11.00 am - 16 leo 54
Uranus	25 ar 31	13.00 pm - 18 leo 01
Neptune	13 pis 44	15.00 pm - 19 leo 08
Pluto	19 cap 21	17.00 pm - 20 leo 14
		19.00 pm - 21 leo 21
Oob		21.00 pm - 22 leo 27
		23.00 pm - 23 leo 33

Wednesday 3rd May

Planetary Directions

Vesta re-enters Leo 00:53

Mercury turns direct 24 ar 15 at 17:33

Retrograde Planets

Mercury, Jupiter, Saturn, Pluto, Haumea, Makemake, Orcus, Quaoar

Asteroids		Dwarf Planets	
Juno	18 cap 12	Eris	23 ar 24
Vesta	00 leo 00	Haumea	23 lib 18
Pallas	11 ar 52	Makemake	02 lib 10
Ceres	01 gem 21	Salacia	01 ar 35
Chiron	27 pis 24	Orcus	07 vir 09
N Node	00 vir 30	Quaoar	00 cap33
S Node	00 pis 30	Sedna	25 tau 43

First Quarter: 03:48
Sunrise: 05:28 BST
Sunset: 20:27
Moonrise: 12:18
Moonset: 02:34
Voc start:
Voc end:

Planetary and Angelic Hours			
Mercury	05:30	Sun	20:24
Moon	06:44	Venus	21:09
Saturn	07:59	Mercury	21:54
Jupiter	09:13	Moon	22:40
Mars	10:28	Saturn	23:25
Sun	11:42	Jupiter	00:11
Venus	12:57	Mars	00:56
Mercury	14:11	Sun	01:41
Moon	15:26	Venus	02:27
Saturn	16:40	Mercury	03:12
Jupiter	17:55	Moon	03:57
Mars	19:09	Saturn	04:43

Aspects

Moon trine Pallas
Sun square Moon
Moon sextile Jupiter
Moon trine Eris
Moon trine Mercury
Sun sextile Neptune
Moon trine Uranus
Mercury conjunct Eris
Venus sextile Ceres
Saturn square Chiron

Planets	00:00 am	Moon
Sun	13 tau 43	01.00 am - 24 leo 39
Mercury	24 ar 16	03.00 am - 25 leo 45
Venus	02 ar 46	05.00 am - 26 leo 51
Mars	08 gem 38	07.00 am - 27 leo 56
Jupiter	15 lib 09	09.00 am - 29 leo 02
Saturn	27 sag 10	11.00 am - 00 vir 07
Uranus	25 ar 34	13.00 pm - 01 vir 12
Neptune	13 pis 45	15.00 pm - 02 vir 17
Pluto	19 cap 21	17.00 pm - 03 vir 22
		19.00 pm - 04 vir 27
Oob		21.00 pm - 05 vir 31
		23.00 pm - 06 vir 36

Thursday 4th May

Planetary Directions

Moon into Virgo 10:47

Retrograde Planets

Jupiter, Saturn, Pluto, Haumea, Makemake, Orcus, Quaoar

Asteroids		Dwarf Planets	
Juno	18 cap 14	Eris	23 ar 24
Vesta	00 leo 18	Haumea	23 lib 17
Pallas	12 ar 13	Makemake	02 lib 09
Ceres	01 gem 46	Salacia	01 ar 36
Chiron	27 pis 27	Orcus	07 vir 09
N Node	00 vir 30	Quaoar	00 cap32
S Node	00 pis 30	Sedna	25 tau 44

Moon Phase: Gibbous
Sunrise: 05:27 BST
Sunset: 20:28
Moonrise: 13:27
Moonset: 03:08
Voc start: 05:35
Voc end: 10:46

Planetary and Angelic Hours

Jupiter	05:28	Moon	20:25
Mars	06:43	Saturn	21:10
Sun	07:58	Jupiter	21:56
Venus	09:12	Mars	22:41
Mercury	10:27	Sun	23:26
Moon	11:42	Venus	00:11
Saturn	12:57	Mercury	00:56
Jupiter	14:12	Moon	01:41
Mars	15:26	Saturn	02:26
Sun	16:41	Jupiter	03:11
Venus	17:56	Mars	03:56
Mercury	19:11	Sun	04:41

Aspects

Sun sextile Neptune
Moon trine Uranus
Moon trine Saturn
Moon square Ceres
Mercury conjunct Eris
Saturn square Chiron

Planets	00:00 am	Moon
Sun	14 tau 41	01.00 am - 07 vir 40
Mercury	24 ar 19	03.00 am - 08 vir 45
Venus	03 ar 21	05.00 am - 09 vir 49
Mars	09 gem 19	07.00 am - 10 vir 53
Jupiter	15 lib 03	09.00 am - 11 vir 57
Saturn	27 sag 08	11.00 am - 13 vir 01
Uranus	25 ar 38	13.00 pm - 14 vir 04
Neptune	13 pis 46	15.00 pm - 15 vir 08
Pluto	19 cap 20	17.00 pm - 16 vir 12
		19.00 pm - 17 vir 15
Oob		21.00 pm - 18 vir 18
		23.00 pm - 19 vir 22

Friday 5th May

Retrograde Planets

Jupiter, Saturn, Pluto, Haumea, Makemake, Orcus, Quaoar

Asteroids		Dwarf Planets	
Juno	18 cap 16	Eris	23 ar 25
Vesta	00 leo 37	Haumea	23 lib 16
Pallas	12 ar 34	Makemake	02 lib 09
Ceres	02 gem 11	Salacia	01 ar 37
Chiron	27 pis 29	Orcus	07 vir 08
N Node	00 vir 30	Quaoar	00 cap31
S Node	00 pis 30	Sedna	25 tau 45

Moon Phase: Gibbous
Sunrise: 05:25 BST
Sunset: 20:30
Moonrise: 14:36
Moonset: 03:36
Voc start:
Voc end:

Planetary and Angelic Hours			
Venus	05:26	Mars	20:27
Mercury	06:41	Sun	21:12
Moon	07:56	Venus	21:57
Saturn	09:12	Mercury	22:41
Jupiter	10:27	Moon	23:26
Mars	11:42	Saturn	00:11
Sun	12:57	Jupiter	00:56
Venus	14:12	Mars	01:41
Mercury	15:27	Sun	02:25
Moon	16:42	Venus	03:10
Saturn	17:57	Mercury	03:55
Jupiter	19:12	Moon	04:40

Aspects

Moon square Mars
Moon opp. Neptune
Sun trine Moon
Moon trine Juno
Moon trine Pluto
Saturn square Chiron

Planets	00:00 am	Moon
Sun	15 tau 39	01.00 am - 20 vir 25
Mercury	24 ar 28	03.00 am - 21 vir 28
Venus	03 ar 57	05.00 am - 22 vir 31
Mars	10 gem 00	07.00 am - 23 vir 34
Jupiter	14 lib 57	09.00 am - 24 vir 36
Saturn	27 sag 05	11.00 am - 25 vir 39
Uranus	25 ar 41	13.00 pm - 26 vir 42
Neptune	13 pis 48	15.00 pm - 27 vir 44
Pluto	19 cap 20	17.00 pm - 28 vir 47
		19.00 pm - 29 vir 49
Oob		21.00 pm - 00 lib 51
		23.00 pm - 01 lib 54

Saturday 6th May

Planetary Directions

Moon into Libra 19:21

Retrograde Planets

Jupiter, Saturn, Pluto, Haumea, Makemake, Orcus, Quaoar

Asteroids		Dwarf Planets	
Juno	18 cap 17	Eris	23 ar 25
Vesta	00 leo 56	Haumea	23 lib 15
Pallas	12 ar 55	Makemake	02 lib 08
Ceres	02 gem 35	Salacia	01 ar 39
Chiron	27 pis 32	Orcus	07 vir 08
N Node	00 vir 28	Quaoar	00 cap31
S Node	00 pis 28	Sedna	25 tau 46

Moon Phase: Gibbous
Sunrise: 05:23 BST
Sunset: 20:32
Moonrise: 15:44
Moonset: 04:01
Voc start: 13:41
Voc end: 19:20

Planetary and Angelic Hours			
Saturn	05:25	Mercury	20:28
Jupiter	06:40	Moon	21:13
Mars	07:55	Saturn	21:58
Sun	09:11	Jupiter	22:42
Venus	10:26	Mars	23:27
Mercury	11:41	Sun	00:11
Moon	12:57	Venus	00:56
Saturn	14:12	Mercury	01:40
Jupiter	15:27	Moon	02:25
Mars	16:43	Saturn	03:09
Sun	17:58	Jupiter	03:54
Venus	19:13	Mars	04:38

Aspects

Moon square Saturn
Moon opposite Chiron
Moon sextile Vesta
Moon trine Ceres
Saturn square Chiron

Planets	**00:00 am**	**Moon**
Sun	16 tau 37	01.00 am - 02 lib 56
Mercury	24 ar 41	03.00 am - 03 lib 58
Venus	04 ar 35	05.00 am - 05 lib 00
Mars	10 gem 41	07.00 am - 06 lib 02
Jupiter	14 lib 51	09.00 am - 07 lib 03
Saturn	27 sag 02	11.00 am - 08 lib 05
Uranus	25 ar 44	13.00 pm - 09 lib 07
Neptune	13 pis 49	15.00 pm - 10 lib 09
Pluto	19 cap 19	17.00 pm - 11 lib 10
		19.00 pm - 12 lib 12
Oob		21.00 pm - 13 lib 13
		23.00 pm - 14 lib 15

Sunday 7th May

Retrograde Planets

Jupiter, Saturn, Pluto, Haumea, Makemake, Orcus, Quaoar

Asteroids		**Dwarf Planets**	
Juno	18 cap 19	Eris	23 ar 26
Vesta	01 leo 15	Haumea	23 lib 14
Pallas	13 ar 16	Makemake	02 lib 07
Ceres	03 gem 00	Salacia	01 ar 40
Chiron	27 pis 35	Orcus	07 vir 08
N Node	00 vir 24	Quaoar	00 cap30
S Node	00 pis 24	Sedna	25 tau 47

Moon Phase: Gibbous
Sunrise: 05:21 BST
Sunset: 20:33
Moonrise: 16:50
Moonset: 04:24
Voc start:
Voc end:

Planetary and Angelic Hours			
Sun	05:23	Jupiter	20:30
Venus	06:39	Mars	21:14
Mercury	07:54	Sun	21:59
Moon	09:10	Venus	22:43
Saturn	10:25	Mercury	23:27
Jupiter	11:41	Moon	00:11
Mars	12:56	Saturn	00:56
Sun	14:12	Jupiter	01:40
Venus	15:28	Mars	02:24
Mercury	16:43	Sun	03:08
Moon	17:59	Venus	03:53
Saturn	19:14	Mercury	04:37

Aspects

Moon trine Ceres
Moon opposite Venus
Moon trine Mars
Moon opposite Pallas
Moon trine Jupiter
Sun trine Juno
Mercury conj. Uranus
Saturn square Chiron
Pluto conjunct Juno

Planets	00:00 am	Moon
Sun	17 tau 36	01.00 am - 15 lib 16
Mercury	24 ar 59	03.00 am - 16 lib 17
Venus	05 ar 13	05.00 am - 17 lib 18
Mars	11 gem 22	07.00 am - 18 lib 20
Jupiter	14 lib 46	09.00 am - 19 lib 21
Saturn	26 sag 59	11.00 am - 20 lib 22
Uranus	25 ar 47	13.00 pm - 21 lib 23
Neptune	13 pis 50	15.00 pm - 22 lib 24
Pluto	19 cap 19	17.00 pm - 23 lib 25
		19.00 pm - 24 lib 25
Oob		21.00 pm - 25 lib 26
		23.00 pm - 26 lib 27

Monday 8th May

Retrograde Planets

Jupiter, Saturn, Pluto, Haumea, Makemake, Orcus, Quaoar

Asteroids		Dwarf Planets	
Juno	18 cap 19	Eris	23 ar 27
Vesta	01 leo 34	Haumea	23 lib 13
Pallas	13 ar 36	Makemake	02 lib 06
Ceres	03 gem 25	Salacia	01 ar 41
Chiron	27 pis 37	Orcus	07 vir 07
N Node	00 vir 18	Quaoar	00 cap29
S Node	00 pis 18	Sedna	25 tau 47

Moon Phase: Gibbous
Sunrise: 05:20 BST
Sunset: 20:35
Moonrise: 17:56
Moonset: 04:47
Voc start: 23:58
Voc end:

Planetary and Angelic Hours			
Moon	05:21	Venus	20:32
Saturn	06:37	Mercury	21:16
Jupiter	07:53	Moon	22:00
Mars	09:09	Saturn	22:44
Sun	10:25	Jupiter	23:28
Venus	11:41	Mars	00:12
Mercury	12:56	Sun	00:56
Moon	14:12	Venus	01:40
Saturn	15:28	Mercury	02:24
Jupiter	16:44	Moon	03:08
Mars	18:00	Saturn	03:52
Sun	19:16	Jupiter	04:36

Aspects

Moon square Juno
Moon square Pluto
Moon opposite Eris
Sun trine Juno
Moon opp. Mercury
Moon opposite Uranus
Moon sextile Saturn
Sun trine Pluto
Mercury conj. Uranus
Jupiter opposite Pallas
Saturn square Chiron
Pluto conjunct Juno

Planets	00:00 am	Moon
Sun	18 tau 34	01.00 am - 27 lib 28
Mercury	25 ar 21	03.00 am - 28 lib 28
Venus	05 ar 53	05.00 am - 29 lib 29
Mars	12 gem 03	07.00 am - 00 sco 30
Jupiter	14 lib 40	09.00 am - 01 sco 30
Saturn	26 sag 57	11.00 am - 02 sco 31
Uranus	25 ar 51	13.00 pm - 03 sco 31
Neptune	13 pis 52	15.00 pm - 04 sco 31
Pluto	19 cap 18	17.00 pm - 05 sco 32
		19.00 pm - 06 sco 32
Oob		21.00 pm - 07 sco 32
		23.00 pm - 08 sco 33

Tuesday 9th May

Planetary Directions

Moon into Scorpio
06:01

Retrograde Planets

Jupiter, Saturn, Pluto, Haumea, Makemake, Orcus, Quaoar

Asteroids		Dwarf Planets	
Juno	18 cap 20	Eris	23 ar 27
Vesta	01 leo 54	Haumea	23 lib 12
Pallas	13 ar 57	Makemake	02 lib 06
Ceres	03 gem 49	Salacia	01 ar 42
Chiron	27 pis 40	Orcus	07 vir 07
N Node	00 vir 08	Quaoar	00 cap28
S Node	00 pis 08	Sedna	25 tau 48

Moon Phase: Gibbous
Sunrise: 05:18 BST
Sunset: 20:36
Moonrise: 19:00
Moonset: 05:10
Voc start:
Voc end: 06:00

Planetary and Angelic Hours

Mars	05:20	Saturn	20:33
Sun	06:36	Jupiter	21:17
Venus	07:52	Mars	22:01
Mercury	09:08	Sun	22:44
Moon	10:24	Venus	23:28
Saturn	11:40	Mercury	00:12
Jupiter	12:56	Moon	00:56
Mars	14:13	Saturn	01:39
Sun	15:29	Jupiter	02:23
Venus	16:45	Mars	03:07
Mercury	18:01	Sun	03:50
Moon	19:17	Venus	04:34

Aspects

Moon square Vesta
Sun trine Pluto
Mercury conj. Uranus
Jupiter opposite Pallas
Saturn trine Uranus
Saturn square Chiron
Pluto conjunct Juno

Planets	00:00 am	Moon
Sun	19 tau 32	01.00 am - 09 sco 33
Mercury	25 ar 48	03.00 am - 10 sco 33
Venus	06 ar 34	05.00 am - 11 sco 33
Mars	12 gem 44	07.00 am - 12 sco 33
Jupiter	14 lib 35	09.00 am - 13 sco 33
Saturn	26 sag 54	11.00 am - 14 sco 33
Uranus	25 ar 54	13.00 pm - 15 sco 33
Neptune	13 pis 53	15.00 pm - 16 sco 33
Pluto	19 cap 18	17.00 pm - 17 sco 33
		19.00 pm - 18 sco 33
Oob		21.00 pm - 19 sco 33
		23.00 pm - 20 sco 33

Wednesday 10th May

Planetary Directions

Juno retrograde
18 cap 20 at 00:06

Retrograde Planets

Jupiter, Saturn, Pluto, Juno, Haumea, Makemake, Orcus, Quaoar

Asteroids		Dwarf Planets	
Juno	18 cap 20	Eris	23 ar 28
Vesta	02 leo 13	Haumea	23 lib 11
Pallas	14 ar 18	Makemake	02 lib 05
Ceres	04 gem 14	Salacia	01 ar 43
Chiron	27 pis 42	Orcus	07 vir 07
N Node	29 leo 57	Quaoar	00 cap28
S Node	29 aq 57	Sedna	25 tau 49

Full Moon: 22:43
Sunrise: 05:16 BST
Sunset: 20:38
Moonrise: 20:03
Moonset: 05:35
Voc start: 22:42
Voc end:

Planetary and Angelic Hours			
Mercury	05:18	Sun	20:35
Moon	06:34	Venus	21:18
Saturn	07:51	Mercury	22:02
Jupiter	09:07	Moon	22:45
Mars	10:24	Saturn	23:29
Sun	11:40	Jupiter	00:12
Venus	12:56	Mars	00:56
Mercury	14:13	Sun	01:39
Moon	15:29	Venus	02:22
Saturn	16:46	Mercury	03:06
Jupiter	18:02	Moon	03:49
Mars	19:18	Saturn	04:33

Aspects

Mercury conj. Uranus
Moon trine Neptune
Jupiter opposite Pallas
Moon sextile Juno
Moon sextile Pluto
Sun opposite Moon
Mercury trine Saturn
Mars square Neptune
Saturn trine Uranus
Saturn square Chiron
Pluto conjunct Juno

Planets	**00:00 am**	**Moon**
Sun	20 tau 30	01.00 am - 21 sco 33
Mercury	26 ar 19	03.00 am - 22 sco 32
Venus	07 ar 15	05.00 am - 23 sco 32
Mars	13 gem 24	07.00 am - 24 sco 32
Jupiter	14 lib 30	09.00 am - 25 sco 31
Saturn	26 sag 51	11.00 am - 26 sco 31
Uranus	25 ar 57	13.00 pm - 27 sco 31
Neptune	13 pis 54	15.00 pm - 28 sco 30
Pluto	19 cap 17	17.00 pm - 29 sco 30
		19.00 pm - 00 sag 30
Oob		21.00 pm - 01 sag 29
		23.00 pm - 02 sag 29

Thursday 11th May

Planetary Directions

Moon in Sagittarius 18:00

Retrograde Planets

Jupiter, Saturn, Pluto, Juno, Haumea, Makemake, Orcus, Quaoar

Asteroids		**Dwarf Planets**	
Juno	18 cap 20	Eris	23 ar 28
Vesta	02 leo 33	Haumea	23 lib 10
Pallas	14 ar 39	Makemake	02 lib 04
Ceres	04 gem 39	Salacia	01 ar 45
Chiron	27 pis 45	Orcus	07 vir 07
N Node	29 leo 43	Quaoar	00 cap27
S Node	29 aq 43	Sedna	25 tau 50

Phase: Disseminating
Sunrise: 05:15 BST
Sunset: 20:40
Moonrise: 21:05
Moonset: 06:02
Voc start:
Voc end: 17:59

Planetary and Angelic Hours			
Jupiter	05:16	Moon	20:36
Mars	06:33	Saturn	21:19
Sun	07:50	Jupiter	22:03
Venus	09:06	Mars	22:46
Mercury	10:23	Sun	23:29
Moon	11:40	Venus	00:12
Saturn	12:56	Mercury	00:55
Jupiter	14:13	Moon	01:39
Mars	15:30	Saturn	02:22
Sun	16:46	Jupiter	03:05
Venus	18:03	Mars	03:48
Mercury	19:20	Sun	04:32

Aspects

Moon trine Chiron
Mars square Neptune
Mercury trine Saturn
Moon trine Vesta
Mercury conj. Uranus
Mars trine Jupiter
Mars sextile Pallas
Jupiter opposite Pallas
Saturn trine Uranus
Saturn square Chiron
Pluto conjunct Juno

Planets	00:00 am	Moon
Sun	21 tau 27	01.00 am - 03 sag 28
Mercury	26 ar 54	03.00 am - 04 sag 28
Venus	07 ar 58	05.00 am - 05 sag 27
Mars	14 gem 05	07.00 am - 06 sag 27
Jupiter	14 lib 25	09.00 am - 07 sag 26
Saturn	26 sag 47	11.00 am - 08 sag 25
Uranus	26 ar 00	13.00 pm - 09 sag 25
Neptune	13 pis 55	15.00 pm - 10 sag 24
Pluto	19 cap 17	17.00 pm - 11 sag 24
		19.00 pm - 12 sag 23
Oob		21.00 pm - 13 sag 22
		23.00 pm - 14 sag 22

Thursday 12th May

Retrograde Planets

Jupiter, Saturn, Pluto, Juno, Haumea, Makemake, Orcus, Quaoar

Asteroids		Dwarf Planets	
Juno	18 cap 19	Eris	23 ar 29
Vesta	02 leo 53	Haumea	23 lib 09
Pallas	14 ar 59	Makemake	02 lib 03
Ceres	05 gem 04	Salacia	01 ar 46
Chiron	27 pis 47	Orcus	07 vir 06
N Node	29 leo 29	Quaoar	00 cap26
S Node	29 aq 29	Sedna	25 tau 50

Phase: Disseminating
Sunrise: 05:13 BST
Sunset: 20:41
Moonrise: 22:04
Moonset: 06:03
Voc start:
Voc end:

Planetary and Angelic Hours			
Venus	05:15	Mars	20:38
Mercury	06:32	Sun	21:21
Moon	07:49	Venus	22:04
Saturn	09:06	Mercury	22:47
Jupiter	10:22	Moon	23:30
Mars	11:39	Saturn	00:13
Sun	12:56	Jupiter	00:55
Venus	14:13	Mars	01:38
Mercury	15:30	Sun	02:21
Moon	16:47	Venus	03:04
Saturn	18:04	Mercury	03:47
Jupiter	19:21	Moon	04:31

Aspects

Moon opposite Ceres
Moon trine Venus
Mars trine Jupiter
Moon square Neptune
Moon sextile Jupiter
Moon opposite Mars
Moon trine Pallas
Mercury trine Saturn
Mars square Neptune
Mars sextile Pallas
Jupiter opposite Pallas
Saturn trine Uranus
Pluto conjunct Juno

Planets	00:00 am	Moon
Sun	22 tau 25	01.00 am - 15 sag 21
Mercury	27 ar 32	03.00 am - 16 sag 20
Venus	08 ar 42	05.00 am - 17 sag 20
Mars	14 gem 46	07.00 am - 18 sag 19
Jupiter	14 lib 20	09.00 am - 19 sag 18
Saturn	26 sag 44	11.00 am - 20 sag 18
Uranus	26 ar 03	13.00 pm - 21 sag 17
Neptune	13 pis 56	15.00 pm - 22 sag 16
Pluto	19 cap 16	17.00 pm - 23 sag 15
		19.00 pm - 24 sag 15
Oob		21.00 pm - 25 sag 14
		23.00 pm - 26 sag 13

Saturday 13th May

Retrograde Planets

Jupiter, Saturn, Pluto, Juno, Haumea, Makemake, Orcus, Quaoar

Asteroids		Dwarf Planets	
Juno	18 cap 18	Eris	23 ar 30
Vesta	03 leo 13	Haumea	23 lib 08
Pallas	15 ar 20	Makemake	02 lib 03
Ceres	05 gem 28	Salacia	01 ar 47
Chiron	27 pis 50	Orcus	07 vir 06
N Node	29 leo 16	Quaoar	00 cap25
S Node	29 aq 16	Sedna	25 tau 51

Phase: Disseminating
Sunrise: 05:11 BST
Sunset: 20:43
Moonrise: 22:59
Moonset: 07:09
Voc start:
Voc end:

Planetary and Angelic Hours			
Saturn	05:13	Mercury	20:39
Jupiter	06:30	Moon	21:22
Mars	07:48	Saturn	22:05
Sun	09:05	Jupiter	22:47
Venus	10:22	Mars	23:30
Mercury	11:39	Sun	00:13
Moon	12:56	Venus	00:55
Saturn	14:13	Mercury	01:38
Jupiter	15:31	Moon	02:21
Mars	16:48	Saturn	03:04
Sun	18:05	Jupiter	03:46
Venus	19:22	Mars	04:29

Aspects

Moon trine Eris
Moon trine Uranus
Moon conjunct Saturn
Moon square Chiron
Mars sextile Pallas
Saturn trine Uranus
Pluto conjunct Juno

Planets	**00:00 am**	**Moon**
Sun	23 tau 23	01.00 am - 27 sag 13
Mercury	28 ar 15	03.00 am - 28 sag 12
Venus	09 ar 27	05.00 am - 29 sag 11
Mars	15 gem 27	07.00 am - 00 cap 11
Jupiter	14 lib 15	09.00 am - 01 cap 10
Saturn	26 sag 41	11.00 am - 02 cap 09
Uranus	26 ar 07	13.00 pm - 03 cap 09
Neptune	13 pis 57	15.00 pm - 04 cap 08
Pluto	19 cap 15	17.00 pm - 05 cap 08
		19.00 pm - 06 cap 07
Oob	Mars	21.00 pm - 07 cap 06
		23.00 pm - 08 cap 06

Sunday 14th May

Planetary Directions

Moon into Capricorn 06:38

Retrograde Planets

Jupiter, Saturn, Pluto, Juno, Haumea, Makemake, Orcus, Quaoar

Asteroids		**Dwarf Planets**	
Juno	18 cap 17	Eris	23 ar 30
Vesta	03 leo 34	Haumea	23 lib 07
Pallas	15 ar 40	Makemake	02 lib 02
Ceres	05 gem 53	Salacia	01 ar 48
Chiron	27 pis 52	Orcus	07 vir 06
N Node	29 leo 05	Quaoar	00 cap24
S Node	19 aq 05	Sedna	25 tau 52

Phase: Disseminating
Sunrise: 05:10 BST
Sunset: 20:44
Moonrise: 23:49
Moonset: 07:50
Voc start: 03:14
Voc end: 06:37

Planetary and Angelic Hours			
Sun	05:12	Jupiter	20:41
Venus	06:29	Mars	21:23
Mercury	07:47	Sun	22:06
Moon	09:04	Venus	22:48
Saturn	10:21	Mercury	23:31
Jupiter	11:39	Moon	00:13
Mars	12:56	Saturn	00:55
Sun	14:14	Jupiter	01:38
Venus	15:31	Mars	02:20
Mercury	16:48	Sun	03:03
Moon	18:06	Venus	03:45
Saturn	19:23	Mercury	04:28

Aspects

Moon square Chiron
Moon trine Mercury
Mars sextile Pallas
Saturn trine Uranus
Pluto conjunct Juno

Planets	00:00 am	Moon
Sun	24 tau 21	01.00 am - 09 cap 05
Mercury	29 ar 01	03.00 am - 10 cap 05
Venus	10 ar 12	05.00 am - 11 cap 05
Mars	16 gem 07	07.00 am - 12 cap 04
Jupiter	14 lib 11	09.00 am - 13 cap 04
Saturn	26 sag 38	11.00 am - 14 cap 03
Uranus	26 ar 10	13.00 pm - 15 cap 03
Neptune	13 pis 38	15.00 pm - 16 cap 03
Pluto	19 cap 15	17.00 pm - 17 cap 03
		19.00 pm - 18 cap 02
Oob	Mars	21.00 pm - 19 cap 02
		23.00 pm - 20 cap 02

Monday 15th May

Retrograde Planets

Jupiter, Saturn, Pluto, Juno, Haumea, Makemake, Orcus, Quaoar

Asteroids		Dwarf Planets	
Juno	18 cap 16	Eris	23 ar 31
Vesta	03 leo 54	Haumea	23 lib 06
Pallas	16 ar 01	Makemake	02 lib 01
Ceres	06 gem 18	Salacia	01 ar 49
Chiron	27 pis 54	Orcus	07 vir 06
N Node	28 leo 56	Quaoar	00 cap23
S Node	28 aq 56	Sedna	25 tau 53

Phase: Disseminating
Sunrise: 05:08 BST
Sunset: 20:46
Moonrise: None
Moonset: 08:38
Voc start:
Voc end:

Planetary and Angelic Hours			
Moon	05:10	Venus	20:42
Saturn	06:28	Mercury	21:24
Jupiter	07:46	Moon	22:07
Mars	09:03	Saturn	22:49
Sun	10:21	Jupiter	23:31
Venus	11:39	Mars	00:13
Mercury	12:56	Sun	00:55
Moon	14:14	Venus	01:38
Saturn	15:32	Mercury	02:20
Jupiter	16:49	Moon	03:02
Mars	18:07	Saturn	03:44
Sun	19:25	Jupiter	04:27

Aspects

Moon square Venus
Moon sextile Neptune
Moon square Jupiter
Moon square Pallas
Moon conjunct Juno
Moon conjunct Pluto
Mars sextile Pallas
Saturn trine Uranus

Planets	00:00 am	Moon
Sun	25 tau 19	01.00 am - 21 cap 02
Mercury	29 ar 51	03.00 am - 22 cap 02
Venus	10 ar 59	05.00 am - 23 cap 02
Mars	16 gem 48	07.00 am - 24 cap 02
Jupiter	14 lib 06	09.00 am - 25 cap 03
Saturn	26 sag 34	11.00 am - 26 cap 03
Uranus	26 ar 13	13.00 pm - 27 cap 03
Neptune	13 pis 59	15.00 pm - 28 cap 04
Pluto	19 cap 14	17.00 pm - 29 cap 04
		19.00 pm - 00 aq 05
Oob	Mars	21.00 pm - 01 aq 05
		23.00 pm - 02 aq 06

Tuesday 16th May

Planetary Directions
Mercury re-enters Taurus at 05:07
Moon into Aquarius 18:50

Retrograde Planets
Jupiter, Saturn, Pluto, Juno, Haumea, Makemake, Orcus, Quaoar

Asteroids		Dwarf Planets	
Juno	18 cap 14	Eris	23 ar 31
Vesta	04 leo 15	Haumea	23 lib 05
Pallas	16 ar 21	Makemake	02 lib 01
Ceres	07 gem 43	Salacia	01 ar 50
Chiron	27 pis 57	Orcus	07 vir 06
N Node	28 leo 49	Quaoar	00 cap22
S Node	28 aq 49	Sedna	25 tau 54

Phase: Disseminating
Sunrise: 05:07 BST
Sunset: 20:47
Moonrise: 00:34
Moonset: 09:32
Voc start: 11:22
Voc end: 18:49

Planetary and Angelic Hours			
Mars	05:09	Saturn	20:44
Sun	06:27	Jupiter	21:26
Venus	07:45	Mars	22:08
Mercury	09:02	Sun	22:50
Moon	10:20	Venus	23:32
Saturn	11:38	Mercury	00:14
Jupiter	12:56	Moon	00:56
Mars	14:14	Saturn	01:37
Sun	15:32	Jupiter	02:19
Venus	16:50	Mars	03:01
Mercury	18:08	Sun	03:43
Moon	19:26	Venus	04:25

Aspects

Moon square Eris
Sun trine Moon
Moon square Uranus
Moon sextile Chiron
Moon square Mercury
Mars sextile Pallas
Saturn trine Uranus

Planets	00:00 am	Moon
Sun	26 tau 17	01.00 am - 03 aq 07
Mercury	00 tau 44	03.00 am - 04 aq 08
Venus	11 ar 46	05.00 am - 05 aq 08
Mars	17 gem 28	07.00 am - 06 aq 10
Jupiter	14 lib 02	09.00 am - 07 aq 11
Saturn	26 sag 31	11.00 am - 08 aq 12
Uranus	26 ar 16	13.00 pm - 09 aq 13
Neptune	14 pis 00	15.00 pm - 10 aq 15
Pluto	19 cap 13	17.00 pm - 11 aq 16
		19.00 pm - 12 aq 18
Oob	Mars	21.00 pm - 13 aq 19
		23.00 pm - 14 aq 21

Wednesday 17th May

Retrograde Planets

Jupiter, Saturn, Pluto, Juno, Haumea, Makemake, Orcus, Quaoar

Asteroids		Dwarf Planets	
Juno	18 cap 12	Eris	23 ar 32
Vesta	04 leo 36	Haumea	23 lib 04
Pallas	17 ar 42	Makemake	02 lib 00
Ceres	07 gem 08	Salacia	01 ar 51
Chiron	28 pis 59	Orcus	07 vir 06
N Node	28 leo 46	Quaoar	00 cap21
S Node	28 aq 46	Sedna	25 tau 54

Phase: Disseminating
Sunrise: 05:06 BST
Sunset: 20:49
Moonrise: 01:13
Moonset: 10:31
Voc start:
Voc end:

Planetary and Angelic Hours			
Mercury	05:07	Sun	20:45
Moon	06:26	Venus	21:27
Saturn	07:44	Mercury	22:09
Jupiter	09:02	Moon	22:50
Mars	10:20	Saturn	23:32
Sun	11:38	Jupiter	00:14
Venus	12:56	Mars	00:56
Mercury	14:14	Sun	01:37
Moon	15:33	Venus	02:19
Saturn	16:51	Mercury	03:01
Jupiter	18:09	Moon	03:43
Mars	19:27	Saturn	04:24

Aspects

Moon opposite Vesta
Moon trine Ceres
Moon sextile Venus
Moon trine Jupiter
Sun sextile Chiron
Saturn trine Uranus

Planets	00:00 am	Moon
Sun	27 tau 15	01.00 am - 15 aq 23
Mercury	01 tau 40	03.00 am - 16 aq 25
Venus	12 ar 34	05.00 am - 17 aq 27
Mars	18 gem 09	07.00 am - 18 aq 30
Jupiter	13 lib 58	09.00 am - 19 aq 32
Saturn	26 sag 27	11.00 am - 20 aq 35
Uranus	26 ar 19	13.00 pm - 21 aq 37
Neptune	14 pis 01	15.00 pm - 22 aq 40
Pluto	19 cap 13	17.00 pm - 23 aq 43
		19.00 pm - 24 aq 46
Oob	Mars	21.00 pm - 25 aq 49
		23.00 pm - 26 aq 53

Thursday 18th May

Retrograde Planets

Jupiter, Saturn, Pluto, Juno, Haumea, Makemake, Orcus, Quaoar

Asteroids		Dwarf Planets	
Juno	18 cap 09	Eris	23 ar 32
Vesta	05 leo 57	Haumea	23 lib 03
Pallas	17 ar 02	Makemake	02 lib 00
Ceres	07 gem 33	Salacia	01 ar 52
Chiron	28 pis 01	Orcus	07 vir 06
N Node	28 leo 44	Quaoar	00 cap20
S Node	28 aq 44	Sedna	25 tau 55

Phase: Disseminating
Sunrise: 05:04 BST
Sunset: 20:50
Moonrise: 01:47
Moonset: 11:35
Voc start:
Voc end:

Planetary and Angelic Hours			
Jupiter	05:06	Moon	20:47
Mars	06:24	Saturn	21:28
Sun	07:43	Jupiter	22:10
Venus	09:01	Mars	22:51
Mercury	10:20	Sun	23:33
Moon	11:38	Venus	00:14
Saturn	12:56	Mercury	00:56
Jupiter	14:15	Moon	01:37
Mars	15:33	Saturn	02:19
Sun	16:51	Jupiter	03:00
Venus	18:10	Mars	03:42
Mercury	19:28	Sun	04:23

Aspects

Moon sextile Pallas
Moon trine Mars
Moon sextile Eris
Sun sextile Chiron
Moon sextile Uranus
Moon sextile Saturn
Sun square Moon
Venus opposite Jupiter
Saturn trine Uranus
Pallas square Juno

Planets	00:00 am	Moon
Sun	28 tau 12	01.00 am - 27 aq 56
Mercury	02 tau 39	03.00 am - 29 aq 00
Venus	13 ar 23	05.00 am - 00 pis 04
Mars	18 gem 49	07.00 am - 01 pis 08
Jupiter	13 lib 54	09.00 am - 02 pis 12
Saturn	26 sag 24	11.00 am - 03 pis 16
Uranus	26 ar 22	13.00 pm - 04 pis 21
Neptune	14 pis 02	15.00 pm - 05 pis 25
Pluto	19 cap 12	17.00 pm - 06 pis 30
		19.00 pm - 07 pis 35
Oob	Mars	21.00 pm - 08 pis 40
		23.00 pm - 09 pis 45

Friday 19th May

Planetary Directions

Moon into Pisces 04:52

Retrograde Planets

Jupiter, Saturn, Pluto, Juno, Haumea, Makemake, Orcus, Quaoar

Asteroids		Dwarf Planets	
Juno	18 cap 06	Eris	23 ar 33
Vesta	05 leo 18	Haumea	23 lib 02
Pallas	17 ar 23	Makemake	01 lib 59
Ceres	07 gem 58	Salacia	01 ar 53
Chiron	28 pis 03	Orcus	07 vir 06
N Node	28 leo 44	Quaoar	00 cap20
S Node	28 aq 44	Sedna	25 tau 56

Last Quarter: 01:35
Sunrise: 05:03 BST
Sunset: 20:51
Moonrise: 02:17
Moonset: 12:42
Voc start: 01:32
Voc end: 04:51

Planetary and Angelic Hours

Venus	05:05	Mars	20:48
Mercury	06:23	Sun	21:29
Moon	07:42	Venus	22:11
Saturn	09:00	Mercury	22:52
Jupiter	10:19	Moon	23:33
Mars	11:38	Saturn	00:14
Sun	12:56	Jupiter	00:56
Venus	14:15	Mars	01:37
Mercury	15:34	Sun	02:18
Moon	16:52	Venus	02:59
Saturn	18:11	Mercury	03:41
Jupiter	19:29	Moon	04:22

Aspects

Sun square Moon
Saturn trine Uranus
Moon sextile Mercury
Venus opposite Jupiter
Moon square Ceres
Pallas square Juno

Planets	**00:00 am**	**Moon**
		01.00 am - 10 pis 51
Sun	29 tau 10	03.00 am - 11 pis 57
Mercury	03 tau 42	05.00 am - 13 pis 03
Venus	14 ar 12	07.00 am - 14 pis 09
Mars	19 gem 30	09.00 am - 15 pis 15
Jupiter	13 lib 50	11.00 am - 16 pis 21
Saturn	26 sag 20	13.00 pm - 17 pis 28
Uranus	26 ar 25	15.00 pm - 18 pis 35
Neptune	14 pis 03	17.00 pm - 19 pis 42
Pluto	19 cap 11	19.00 pm - 20 pis 49
		21.00 pm - 21 pis 56
Oob	Mars	23.00 pm - 23 pis 04

Saturday 20th May

Planetary Directions

Sun into Gem at 21:31

Retrograde Planets

Jupiter, Saturn, Pluto, Juno, Haumea, Makemake, Orcus, Quaoar

Asteroids		**Dwarf Planets**	
Juno	18 cap 03	Eris	23 ar 34
Vesta	05 leo 39	Haumea	23 lib 01
Pallas	17 ar 43	Makemake	01 lib 59
Ceres	08 gem 23	Salacia	01 ar 54
Chiron	28 pis 05	Orcus	07 vir 06
N Node	28 leo 44	Quaoar	00 cap 19
S Node	28 aq 44	Sedna	25 tau 57

Moon Phase: Balsamic
Sunrise: 05:01 BST
Sunset: 20:53
Moonrise: 02:45
Moonset: 13:53
Voc start:
Voc end:

Planetary and Angelic Hours			
Saturn	05:03	Mercury	20:49
Jupiter	06:22	Moon	21:30
Mars	07:41	Saturn	22:11
Sun	09:00	Jupiter	22:53
Venus	10:19	Mars	23:34
Mercury	11:38	Sun	00:15
Moon	12:56	Venus	00:56
Saturn	14:15	Mercury	01:37
Jupiter	15:34	Moon	02:18
Mars	16:53	Saturn	02:59
Sun	18:12	Jupiter	03:40
Venus	19:31	Mars	04:21

Aspects

Moon conj. Neptune
Moon sextile Juno
Moon sextile Pluto
Moon square Mars
Pallas square Juno
Saturn trine Uranus

Planets	00:00 am	Moon
Sun	00 gem 08	01.00 am - 24 pis 11
Mercury	04 tau 48	03.00 am - 25 pis 19
Venus	15 ar 02	05.00 am - 26 pis 28
Mars	20 gem 10	07.00 am - 27 pis 36
Jupiter	13 lib 47	09.00 am - 28 pis 45
Saturn	26 sag 16	11.00 am - 29 pis 53
Uranus	26 ar 28	13.00 pm - 01 ar 02
Neptune	14 pis 04	15.00 pm - 02 ar 12
Pluto	19 cap 10	17.00 pm - 03 ar 21
		19.00 pm - 04 ar 31
Oob	Mars	21.00 pm - 05 ar 41
		23.00 pm - 06 ar 51

Sunday 21st May

Planetary Directions

Moon into Aries 11:11
Orcus direct
07 vir 05 at 13:44

Retrograde Planets

Jupiter, Saturn, Pluto, Juno, Haumea, Makemake, Orcus, Quaoar

Asteroids		Dwarf Planets	
Juno	17 cap 59	Eris	23 ar 34
Vesta	06 leo 01	Haumea	23 lib 00
Pallas	18 ar 04	Makemake	01 lib 58
Ceres	08 gem 48	Salacia	01 ar 55
Chiron	28 pis 08	Orcus	07 vir 05
N Node	28 leo 43	Quaoar	00 cap 18
S Node	28 aq 43	Sedna	25 tau 58

Moon Phase: Balsamic
Sunrise: 05:00 BST
Sunset: 20:54
Moonrise: 03:11
Moonset: 15:06
Voc start: 04:39
Voc end: 11:10

Planetary and Angelic Hours			
Sun	05:02	Jupiter	20:51
Venus	06:21	Mars	21:32
Mercury	07:40	Sun	22:12
Moon	08:59	Venus	22:53
Saturn	10:18	Mercury	23:34
Jupiter	11:37	Moon	00:15
Mars	12:56	Saturn	00:56
Sun	14:15	Jupiter	01:37
Venus	15:35	Mars	02:17
Mercury	16:54	Sun	02:58
Moon	18:13	Venus	03:39
Saturn	19:32	Mercury	04:20

Aspects

Moon sextile Sedna
Moon square Saturn
Moon conjunct Chiron
Sun sextile Moon
Moon trine Vesta
Mercury square Vesta
Saturn trine Uranus
Pluto square Pallas
Pallas square Juno

Planets	00:00 am	Moon
Sun	01 gem 06	01.00 am - 08 ar 01
Mercury	05 tau 56	03.00 am - 09 ar 11
Venus	15 ar 53	05.00 am - 10 ar 22
Mars	20 gem 51	07.00 am - 11 ar 33
Jupiter	13 lib 43	09.00 am - 12 ar 44
Saturn	26 sag 13	11.00 am - 13 ar 55
Uranus	26 ar 31	13.00 pm - 15 ar 07
Neptune	14 pis 05	15.00 pm - 16 ar 18
Pluto	19 cap 09	17.00 pm - 17 ar 30
		19.00 pm - 18 ar 42
Oob	Mars	21.00 pm - 19 ar 54
		23.00 pm - 21 ar 07

Monday 22nd May

Retrograde Planets

Jupiter, Saturn, Pluto, Juno, Haumea, Makemake, Quaoar

Asteroids		Dwarf Planets	
Juno	17 cap 55	Eris	23 ar 35
Vesta	06 leo 22	Haumea	22 lib 59
Pallas	18 ar 24	Makemake	01 lib 57
Ceres	09 gem 13	Salacia	01 ar 56
Chiron	28 pis 10	Orcus	07 vir 05
N Node	28 leo 39	Quaoar	00 cap 17
S Node	28 aq 39	Sedna	25 tau 58

Moon Phase: Balsamic
Sunrise: 04:59 BST
Sunset: 20:56
Moonrise: 03:38
Moonset: 16:23
Voc start:
Voc end:

Planetary and Angelic Hours			
Moon	05:01	Venus	20:52
Saturn	06:20	Mercury	21:33
Jupiter	07:39	Moon	22:13
Mars	08:59	Saturn	22:54
Sun	10:18	Jupiter	23:35
Venus	11:37	Mars	00:15
Mercury	12:56	Sun	00:56
Moon	14:16	Venus	01:36
Saturn	15:35	Mercury	02:17
Jupiter	16:54	Moon	02:58
Mars	18:14	Saturn	03:38
Sun	19:33	Jupiter	04:19

Aspects

Moon sextile Ceres
Moon opposite Jupiter
Mercury square Vesta
Moon conjunct Venus
Moon square Juno
Moon conjunct Pallas
Moon square Pluto
Moon sextile Mars
Saturn trine Uranus
Pluto square Pallas
Pallas square Juno

Planets	00:00 am	Moon
Sun	02 gem 03	01.00 am - 22 ar 20
Mercury	07 tau 07	03.00 am - 23 ar 32
Venus	16 ar 45	05.00 am - 24 ar 45
Mars	21 gem 31	07.00 am - 25 ar 59
Jupiter	13 lib 40	09.00 am - 27 ar 12
Saturn	26 sag 09	11.00 am - 28 ar 26
Uranus	26 ar 34	13.00 pm - 29 ar 39
Neptune	14 pis 06	15.00 pm - 00 tau 53
Pluto	19 cap 08	17.00 pm - 02 tau 07
		19.00 pm - 03 tau 22
Oob	Mars	21.00 pm - 04 tau 36
		23.00 pm - 05 tau 51

Tuesday 23rd May

Planetary Directions

Moon into Taurus
13:33

Retrograde Planets

Jupiter, Saturn, Pluto, Juno, Haumea, Makemake, Quaoar

Asteroids		Dwarf Planets	
Juno	17 cap 51	Eris	23 ar 35
Vesta	06 leo 44	Haumea	22 lib 58
Pallas	18 ar 44	Makemake	01 lib 57
Ceres	09 gem 38	Salacia	01 ar 57
Chiron	28 pis 12	Orcus	07 vir 06
N Node	28 leo 34	Quaoar	00 cap 16
S Node	28 aq 34	Sedna	25 tau 59

Moon Phase: Balsamic
Sunrise: 04:58 BST
Sunset: 20:57
Moonrise: 04:05
Moonset: 17:42
Voc start: 07:59
Voc end: 13:32

Planetary and Angelic Hours			
Mars	05:00	Saturn	20:53
Sun	06:19	Jupiter	21:34
Venus	07:39	Mars	22:14
Mercury	08:58	Sun	22:55
Moon	10:18	Venus	23:35
Saturn	11:37	Mercury	00:16
Jupiter	12:57	Moon	00:56
Mars	14:16	Saturn	01:36
Sun	15:35	Jupiter	02:17
Venus	16:55	Mars	02:57
Mercury	18:14	Sun	03:38
Moon	19:34	Venus	04:18

Aspects

Moon conjunct Eris
Moon trine Saturn
Moon conjunct Uranus
Moon square Vesta
Venus square Juno
Saturn trine Uranus
Pluto square Pallas

Planets	00:00 am	Moon
Sun	03 gem 01	01.00 am - 07 tau 05
Mercury	08 tau 21	03.00 am - 08 tau 20
Venus	17 ar 37	05.00 am - 09 tau 35
Mars	22 gem 11	07.00 am - 10 tau 50
Jupiter	13 lib 37	09.00 am - 12 tau 05
Saturn	26 sag 05	11.00 am - 13 tau 21
Uranus	26 ar 37	13.00 pm - 14 tau 36
Neptune	14 pis 06	15.00 pm - 15 tau 52
Pluto	19 cap 08	17.00 pm - 17 tau 08
		19.00 pm - 18 tau 24
		21.00 pm - 19 tau 40
Oob	Mars	23.00 pm - 20 tau 56

Wednesday 24th May

Planetary Directions

Moon into Gemini 13:16

Retrograde Planets

Jupiter, Saturn, Pluto, Juno, Haumea, Makemake, Quaoar

Asteroids		Dwarf Planets	
Juno	17 cap 46	Eris	23 ar 36
Vesta	07 leo 06	Haumea	22 lib 58
Pallas	19 ar 04	Makemake	01 lib 56
Ceres	10 gem 03	Salacia	01 ar 58
Chiron	28 pis 13	Orcus	07 vir 06
N Node	28 leo 25	Quaoar	00 cap 15
S Node	28 aq 25	Sedna	26 tau 00

Moon Phase: Balsamic
Sunrise: 04:57 BST
Sunset: 20:58
Moonrise: 04:36
Moonset: 19:04
Voc start: 20:08
Voc end:

Planetary and Angelic Hours			
Mercury	04:58	Sun	20:55
Moon	06:18	Venus	21:35
Saturn	07:38	Mercury	22:15
Jupiter	08:58	Moon	22:55
Mars	10:17	Saturn	23:36
Sun	11:37	Jupiter	00:16
Venus	12:57	Mars	00:56
Mercury	14:16	Sun	01:36
Moon	15:36	Venus	02:16
Saturn	16:56	Mercury	02:57
Jupiter	18:15	Moon	03:37
Mars	19:35	Saturn	04:17

Aspects

Moon square Vesta
Moon conj. Mercury
Pluto square Pallas
Venus square Juno
Moon sextile Neptune
Moon trine Juno
Moon trine Pluto
Venus square Pluto
Venus conjunct Pallas
Mars sextile Eris
Saturn trine Uranus

Planets	00:00 am	Moon
Sun	03 gem 59	01.00 am - 22 tau 12
Mercury	09 tau 38	03.00 am - 23 tau 28
Venus	18 ar 30	05.00 am - 24 tau 44
Mars	22 gem 51	07.00 am - 26 tau 00
Jupiter	13 lib 34	09.00 am - 27 tau 17
Saturn	26 sag 01	11.00 am - 28 tau 33
Uranus	26 ar 40	13.00 pm - 29 tau 50
Neptune	14 pis 07	15.00 pm - 01 gem 06
Pluto	19 cap 07	17.00 pm - 02 gem 23
		19.00 pm - 03 gem 39
Oob	Mars	21.00 pm - 04 gem 56
		22.00 pm - 06 gem 13

Thursday 25th May

Retrograde Planets

Jupiter, Saturn, Pluto, Juno, Haumea, Makemake, Quaoar

Asteroids		Dwarf Planets	
Juno	17 cap 41	Eris	23 ar 36
Vesta	07 leo 28	Haumea	22 lib 57
Pallas	19 ar 25	Makemake	01 lib 56
Ceres	10 gem 28	Salacia	01 ar 59
Chiron	28 pis 15	Orcus	07 vir 06
N Node	28 leo 15	Quaoar	00 cap 14
S Node	28 aq 15	Sedna	26 tau 01

New Moon: 20:46
Sunrise: 04:56 BST
Sunset: 21:00
Moonrise: 05:11
Moonset: 20:24
Voc start:
Voc end: 13:15

Planetary and Angelic Hours			
Jupiter	04:57	Moon	20:56
Mars	06:17	Saturn	21:36
Sun	07:37	Jupiter	22:16
Venus	08:57	Mars	22:56
Mercury	10:17	Sun	23:36
Moon	11:37	Venus	00:16
Saturn	12:57	Mercury	00:56
Jupiter	14:17	Moon	01:36
Mars	15:36	Saturn	02:16
Sun	16:56	Jupiter	02:56
Venus	18:16	Mars	03:36
Mercury	19:36	Sun	04:16

Super Moon

Aspects

Moon conjunct Sedna
Moon sextile Chiron
Venus square Pluto
Sun conjunct Moon
Moon sextile Vesta
Venus conjunct Pallas
Mars sextile Eris
Saturn trine Uranus
Pluto square Pallas

Planets	**00:00 am**	**Moon**
Sun	04 gem 56	01.00 am - 07 gem 29
Mercury	10 tau 57	03.00 am - 08 gem 46
Venus	19 ar 23	05.00 am - 10 gem 03
Mars	23 gem 32	07.00 am - 11 gem 19
Jupiter	13 lib 32	09.00 am - 12 gem 36
Saturn	25 sag 57	11.00 am - 13 gem 52
Uranus	26 ar 43	13.00 pm - 15 gem 09
Neptune	14 pis 08	15.00 pm - 16 gem 25
Pluto	19 cap 06	17.00 pm - 17 gem 42
		19.00 pm - 18 gem 58
Oob	Mars	21.00 pm - 20 gem 14
		23.00 pm - 21 gem 31

Friday 26th May

Retrograde Planets

Jupiter, Saturn, Pluto, Juno, Haumea, Makemake, Quaoar

Asteroids		**Dwarf Planets**	
Juno	17 cap 36	Eris	23 ar 37
Vesta	07 leo 50	Haumea	22 lib 56
Pallas	19 ar 45	Makemake	01 lib 56
Ceres	10 gem 53	Salacia	02 ar 00
Chiron	28 pis 17	Orcus	07 vir 06
N Node	28 leo 04	Quaoar	00 cap 13
S Node	28 aq 04	Sedna	26 tau 01

Moon Phase: Crescent
Sunrise: 04:54 BST
Sunset: 21:01
Moonrise: 05:53
Moonset: 21:40
Voc start:
Voc end:

Planetary and Angelic Hours			
Venus	04:56	Mars	20:57
Mercury	06:16	Sun	21:37
Moon	07:36	Venus	22:17
Saturn	08:57	Mercury	22:57
Jupiter	10:17	Moon	23:37
Mars	11:37	Saturn	00:16
Sun	12:57	Jupiter	00:56
Venus	14:17	Mars	01:36
Mercury	15:37	Sun	02:16
Moon	16:57	Venus	02:56
Saturn	18:17	Mercury	03:36
Jupiter	19:37	Moon	04:15

Aspects

Moon sextile Vesta
Mars sextile Eris
Moon conjunct Ceres
Moon trine Jupiter
Moon square Neptune
Venus conjunct Pallas
Moon sextile Pallas
Moon sextile Venus
Moon sextile Eris
Saturn trine Uranus
Pluto square Pallas

Planets	00:00 am	Moon
Sun	05 gem 54	01.00 am - 22 gem 47
Mercury	12 tau 19	03.00 am - 24 gem 03
Venus	20 ar 17	05.00 am - 25 gem 19
Mars	24 gem 12	07.00 am - 26 gem 35
Jupiter	13 lib 29	09.00 am - 27 gem 51
Saturn	25 sag 53	11.00 am - 29 gem 06
Uranus	26 ar 45	13.00 pm - 00 can 22
Neptune	14 pis 09	15.00 pm - 01 can 37
Pluto	19 cap 05	17.00 pm - 02 can 53
		19.00 pm - 04 can 08
Oob	Mars	21.00 pm - 08 can 23
		21.00 pm - 06 can 38

Saturday 27th May

Planetary Directions

Moon into Cancer
12:25

Retrograde Planets

Jupiter, Saturn, Pluto, Juno, Haumea, Makemake, Quaoar

Asteroids		Dwarf Planets	
Juno	17 cap 30	Eris	23 ar 37
Vesta	08 leo 13	Haumea	22 lib 55
Pallas	20 ar 05	Makemake	01 lib 55
Ceres	11 gem 18	Salacia	02 ar 01
Chiron	28 pis 19	Orcus	07 vir 06
N Node	27 leo 54	Quaoar	00 cap 11
S Node	27 aq 54	Sedna	26 tau 02

Moon Phase: Crescent
Sunrise: 04:53 BST
Sunset: 21:02
Moonrise: 06:44
Moonset: 22:49
Voc start: 07:18
Voc end: 12:24

Planetary and Angelic Hours

Saturn	04:55	Mercury	20:59
Jupiter	06:16	Moon	21:38
Mars	07:36	Saturn	22:18
Sun	08:56	Jupiter	22:57
Venus	10:16	Mars	23:37
Mercury	11:37	Sun	00:17
Moon	12:57	Venus	00:56
Saturn	14:17	Mercury	01:36
Jupiter	15:37	Moon	02:16
Mars	16:58	Saturn	02:55
Sun	18:18	Jupiter	03:35
Venus	19:38	Mars	04:15

Aspects

Moon sextile Eris
Moon conjunct Mars
Moon opposite Saturn
Moon sextile Uranus
Moon square Chiron
Mercury sext. Neptune
Venus conjunct Pallas
Mars opposite Saturn
Saturn trine Uranus

Planets	00:00 am	Moon
Sun	06 gem 52	01.00 am - 07 can 53
Mercury	13 tau 44	03.00 am - 09 can 08
Venus	21 ar 11	05.00 am - 10 can 22
Mars	24 gem 52	07.00 am - 11 can 37
Jupiter	13 lib 27	09.00 am - 12 can 51
Saturn	25 sag 49	11.00 am - 14 can 05
Uranus	26 ar 48	13.00 pm - 15 can 19
Neptune	14 pis 09	15.00 pm - 16 can 33
Pluto	19 cap 04	17.00 pm - 17 can 46
		19.00 pm - 19 can 00
Oob	Mars	21.00 pm - 20 can 13
		23.00 pm - 21 can 26

Sunday 28th May

Retrograde Planets

Jupiter, Saturn, Pluto, Juno, Haumea, Makemake, Quaoar

Asteroids		Dwarf Planets	
Juno	17 cap 24	Eris	23 ar 38
Vesta	08 leo 35	Haumea	22 lib 54
Pallas	20 ar 25	Makemake	01 lib 55
Ceres	11 gem 43	Salacia	02 ar 02
Chiron	28 pis 21	Orcus	07 vir 06
N Node	27 leo 45	Quaoar	00 cap 10
S Node	27 aq 45	Sedna	26 tau 03

Moon Phase: Crescent
Sunrise: 04:52 BST
Sunset: 21:03
Moonrise: 07:44
Moonset: 23:46
Voc start:
Voc end:

Planetary and Angelic Hours			
Sun	04:54	Jupiter	21:00
Venus	06:15	Mars	21:39
Mercury	07:35	Sun	22:19
Moon	08:56	Venus	22:58
Saturn	10:16	Mercury	23:38
Jupiter	11:37	Moon	00:17
Mars	12:57	Saturn	00:57
Sun	14:17	Jupiter	01:36
Venus	15:38	Mars	02:15
Mercury	16:58	Sun	02:55
Moon	18:19	Venus	03:34
Saturn	19:39	Mercury	04:14

Aspects

Mercury sext. Neptune
Moon square Jupiter
Moon trine Neptune
Moon sextile Mercury
Moon opposite Juno
Moon opposite Pluto
Moon square Pallas
Moon square Venus
Moon square Eris
Mars opposite Saturn

Planets	00:00 am	Moon
Sun	07 gem 49	01.00 am - 22 can 39
Mercury	15 tau 11	03.00 am - 23 can 52
Venus	22 ar 06	05.00 am - 25 can 04
Mars	25 gem 32	07.00 am - 26 can 16
Jupiter	13 lib 25	09.00 am - 27 can 29
Saturn	25 sag 45	11.00 am - 28 can 41
Uranus	26 ar 51	13.00 pm - 29 can 52
Neptune	14 pis 10	15.00 pm - 01 leo 04
Pluto	19 cap 03	17.00 pm - 02 leo 15
		19.00 pm - 03 leo 27
Oob	Mars	21.00 pm - 04 leo 38
		23.00 pm - 05 leo 48

Monday 29th May

Planetary Directions

Moon into Leo 13:12

Retrograde Planets

Jupiter, Saturn, Pluto, Juno, Haumea, Makemake, Quaoar

Asteroids		Dwarf Planets	
Juno	17 cap 17	Eris	23 ar 38
Vesta	08 leo 58	Haumea	22 lib 54
Pallas	20 ar 45	Makemake	01 lib 54
Ceres	12 gem 08	Salacia	02 ar 02
Chiron	28 pis 23	Orcus	07 vir 06
N Node	27 leo 39	Quaoar	00 cap 09
S Node	27 aq 39	Sedna	26 tau 04

Moon Phase: Crescent
Sunrise: 04:51 BST
Sunset: 21:04
Moonrise: 08:51
Moonset: None
Voc start: 07:58
Voc end: 13:11

Planetary and Angelic Hours			
Moon	04:53	Venus	21:01
Saturn	06:14	Mercury	21:40
Jupiter	07:35	Moon	22:19
Mars	08:55	Saturn	22:59
Sun	10:16	Jupiter	23:38
Venus	11:36	Mars	00:17
Mercury	12:57	Sun	00:57
Moon	14:18	Venus	01:36
Saturn	15:38	Mercury	02:15
Jupiter	16:59	Moon	02:55
Mars	18:20	Saturn	03:34
Sun	19:40	Jupiter	04:13

Spring Bank Holiday

Aspects

Moon square Eris
Moon sextile Sedna
Mars opposite Saturn
Moon square Uranus
Moon trine Chiron
Sun sextile Vesta
Mercury trine Juno
Venus conjunct Eris
Mars sextile Uranus
Jupiter trine Ceres

Planets	**00:00 am**	**Moon**
Sun	08 gem 47	01.00 am - 06 leo 59
Mercury	16 tau 41	03.00 am - 08 leo 09
Venus	23 ar 01	05.00 am - 09 leo 20
Mars	26 gem 12	07.00 am - 10 leo 30
Jupiter	13 lib 23	09.00 am - 11 leo 39
Saturn	25 sag 41	11.00 am - 12 leo 49
Uranus	26 ar 54	13.00 pm - 13 leo 59
Neptune	14 pis 10	15.00 pm - 15 leo 08
Pluto	19 cap 02	17.00 pm - 16 leo 17
		19.00 pm - 17 leo 26
Oob	Mars	21.00 pm - 18 leo 34
		23.00 pm - 19 leo 43

Tuesday 30th May

Retrograde Planets

Jupiter, Saturn, Pluto, Juno, Haumea, Makemake, Quaoar

Asteroids		**Dwarf Planets**	
Juno	17 cap 11	Eris	23 ar 39
Vesta	09 leo 21	Haumea	22 lib 53
Pallas	21 ar 05	Makemake	01 lib 54
Ceres	12 gem 33	Salacia	02 ar 03
Chiron	28 pis 24	Orcus	07 vir 06
N Node	27 leo 36	Quaoar	00 cap 08
S Node	27 aq 36	Sedna	26 tau 05

Moon Phase: Crescent
Sunrise: 04:51 BST
Sunset: 21:06
Moonrise: 10:02
Moonset: 00:33
Voc start:
Voc end:

Planetary and Angelic Hours			
Mars	04:52	Saturn	21:02
Sun	06:13	Jupiter	21:41
Venus	07:34	Mars	22:20
Mercury	08:55	Sun	22:59
Moon	10:16	Venus	23:39
Saturn	11:36	Mercury	00:18
Jupiter	12:57	Moon	00:57
Mars	14:18	Saturn	01:36
Sun	15:39	Jupiter	02:15
Venus	17:00	Mars	02:54
Mercury	18:20	Sun	03:33
Moon	19:41	Venus	04:12

Aspects

Sun sextile Moon
Moon conjunct Vesta
Mercury trine Juno
Moon sextile Ceres
Moon sextile Jupiter
Venus conjunct Eris
Moon square Mercury
Sun sextile Vesta
Moon trine Pallas
Mercury trine Pluto
Mars sextile Uranus
Jupiter trine Ceres

Planets	00:00 am	Moon
Sun	09 gem 44	01.00 am - 20 leo 51
Mercury	18 tau 13	03.00 am - 21 leo 59
Venus	23 ar 57	05.00 am - 23 leo 07
Mars	26 gem 52	07.00 am - 24 leo 15
Jupiter	13 lib 21	09.00 am - 25 leo 22
Saturn	25 sag 37	11.00 am - 26 leo 30
Uranus	26 ar 57	13.00 pm - 27 leo 37
Neptune	14 pis 11	15.00 pm - 28 leo 44
Pluto	19 cap 01	17.00 pm - 29 leo 51
		19.00 pm - 00 vir 57
Oob	Mars	21.00 pm - 02 vir 04
		23.00 pm - 03 vir 10

Wednesday 31st May

Planetary Directions

Moon into Virgo 17:16

Retrograde Planets

Jupiter, Saturn, Pluto, Juno, Haumea, Makemake, Quaoar

Asteroids		Dwarf Planets	
Juno	17 cap 04	Eris	23 ar 39
Vesta	09 leo 43	Haumea	22 lib 52
Pallas	21 ar 25	Makemake	01 lib 54
Ceres	12 gem 58	Salacia	02 ar 04
Chiron	28 pis 26	Orcus	07 vir 06
N Node	27 leo 35	Quaoar	00 cap 07
S Node	27 aq 35	Sedna	26 tau 05

Moon Phase: Crescent
Sunrise: 04:50 BST
Sunset: 21:07
Moonrise: 11:14
Moonset: 01:10
Voc start: 12:14
Voc end: 17:15

Planetary and Angelic Hours

Mercury	04:52	Sun	21:03
Moon	06:13	Venus	21:42
Saturn	07:34	Mercury	22:21
Jupiter	08:54	Moon	23:00
Mars	10:15	Saturn	23:39
Sun	11:36	Jupiter	00:18
Venus	12:57	Mars	00:57
Mercury	14:18	Sun	01:36
Moon	15:39	Venus	02:15
Saturn	17:00	Mercury	02:54
Jupiter	18:21	Moon	03:33
Mars	19:42	Saturn	04:12

Aspects

Moon trine Pallas
Mars sextile Uranus
Moon trine Eris
Moon trine Venus
Moon trine Saturn
Moon square Sedna
Moon trine Uranus
Moon sextile Mars
Mercury trine Pluto
Jupiter trine Ceres
Sun sextile Vesta
Venus trine Saturn
Mars square Chiron
Neptune square Ceres

Planets	00:00 am	Moon
Sun	10 gem 42	01.00 am - 04 vir 16
Mercury	19 tau 48	03.00 am - 05 vir 22
Venus	24 ar 34	05.00 am - 06 vir 28
Mars	27 gem 33	07.00 am - 07 vir 34
Jupiter	13 lib 19	09.00 am - 08 vir 39
Saturn	25 sag 33	11.00 am - 09 vir 44
Uranus	26 ar 59	13.00 pm - 10 vir 49
Neptune	14 pis 11	15.00 pm - 11 vir 54
Pluto	19 cap 00	17.00 pm - 12 vir 59
		19.00 pm - 14 vir 04
Oob	Mars	21.00 pm - 15 vir 08
		23.00 pm - 16 vir 13

Thursday 1st June

Retrograde Planets

Jupiter, Saturn, Pluto, Juno, Haumea, Makemake, Quaoar

Asteroids		Dwarf Planets	
Juno	16 cap 56	Eris	23 ar 40
Vesta	10 leo 06	Haumea	22 lib 51
Pallas	21 ar 44	Makemake	01 lib 53
Ceres	13 ge 24	Salacia	02 ar 05
Chiron	28 pis 27	Orcus	07 vir 07
N Node	27 leo 35	Quaoar	00 cap 06
S Node	27 aq 35	Sedna	26 tau 06

First Quarter: 13:43
Sunrise: 04:49 BST
Sunset: 21:08
Moonrise: 12:26
Moonset: 01:41
Voc start:
Voc end:

Planetary and Angelic Hours			
Jupiter	04:51	Moon	21:04
Mars	06:12	Saturn	21:43
Sun	07:33	Jupiter	22:22
Venus	08:54	Mars	23:01
Mercury	10:15	Sun	23:39
Moon	11:36	Venus	00:18
Saturn	12:58	Mercury	00:57
Jupiter	14:19	Moon	01:36
Mars	15:40	Saturn	02:15
Sun	17:01	Jupiter	02:54
Venus	18:22	Mars	03:32
Mercury	19:43	Sun	04:11

Aspects

Sun square Moon
Venus trine Saturn
Moon square Ceres
Moon opp. Neptune
Moon trine Juno
Mars square Chiron
Jupiter trine Ceres
Neptune square Ceres

Friday 2nd June

Planets	00:00 am	Moon
Sun	11 gem 39	01.00 am - 17 vir 17
Mercury	21 tau 25	03.00 am - 18 vir 21
Venus	25 ar 50	05.00 am - 19 vir 25
Mars	28 gem 13	07.00 am - 20 vir 29
Jupiter	13 lib 18	09.00 am - 21 vir 33
Saturn	25 sag 28	11.00 am - 22 vir 36
Uranus	27 ar 02	13.00 pm - 23 vir 40
Neptune	14 pis 12	15.00 pm - 24 vir 43
Pluto	18 cap 59	17.00 pm - 25 vir 46
		19.00 pm - 26 vir 49
		21.00 pm - 27 vir 52
Oob	Mars	23.00 pm - 28 vir 55

Retrograde Planets

Jupiter, Saturn, Pluto, Juno, Haumea, Makemake, Quaoar

Asteroids		Dwarf Planets	
Juno	16 cap 49	Eris	23 ar 40
Vesta	10 leo 30	Haumea	22 lib 51
Pallas	22 ar 04	Makemake	01 lib 53
Ceres	13 gem 49	Salacia	02 ar 05
Chiron	28 pis 29	Orcus	07 vir 07
N Node	27 leo 35	Quaoar	00 cap 05
S Node	27 aq 35	Sedna	26 tau 07

Moon Phase: Gibbous
Sunrise: 04:48 BST
Sunset: 21:09
Moonrise: 13:35
Moonset: 02:08
Voc start: 22:48
Voc end:

Planetary and Angelic Hours			
Venus	04:50	Mars	21:05
Mercury	06:11	Sun	21:44
Moon	07:33	Venus	22:23
Saturn	08:54	Mercury	23:01
Jupiter	10:15	Moon	23:40
Mars	11:36	Saturn	00:19
Sun	12:58	Jupiter	00:57
Venus	14:19	Mars	01:36
Mercury	15:40	Sun	02:15
Moon	17:01	Venus	02:53
Saturn	18:23	Mercury	03:32
Jupiter	19:44	Moon	04:11

Aspects

Moon trine Pluto
Moon trine Mercury
Mars square Chiron
Moon square Saturn
Moon trine Sedna
Moon opposite Chiron
Moon square Mars
Neptune square Ceres
Sun trine Jupiter
Venus conjunct Uranus
Jupiter trine Ceres

Planets	00:00 am	Moon
Sun	12 gem 37	01.00 am - 29 vir 58
Mercury	23 tau 04	03.00 am - 01 lib 00
Venus	26 ar 47	05.00 am - 02 lib 03
Mars	28 gem 53	07.00 am - 03 lib 05
Jupiter	13 lib 16	09.00 am - 04 lib 07
Saturn	25 sag 24	11.00 am - 05 lib 09
Uranus	27 ar 05	13.00 pm - 06 lib 12
Neptune	14 pis 12	15.00 pm - 07 lib 14
Pluto	18 cap 57	17.00 pm - 08 lib 15
		19.00 pm - 09 lib 17
Oob	Mars	21.00 pm - 10 lib 19
		23.00 pm - 11 lib 20

Saturday 3rd June

Planetary Directions

Moon into Libra 01:04

Retrograde Planets

Jupiter, Saturn, Pluto, Juno, Haumea, Makemake, Quaoar

Asteroids		Dwarf Planets	
Juno	16 cap 40	Eris	23 ar 41
Vesta	10 leo 53	Haumea	22 lib 50
Pallas	22 ar 24	Makemake	01 lib 53
Ceres	14 gem 14	Salacia	02 ar 06
Chiron	28 pis 30	Orcus	07 vir 07
N Node	27 leo 34	Quaoar	00 cap 04
S Node	27 aq 34	Sedna	26 tau 08

Moon Phase: Gibbous
Sunrise: 04:47 BST
Sunset: 21:10
Moonrise: 14:42
Moonset: 02:31
Voc start: 01:03
Voc end:

Planetary and Angelic Hours

Saturn	04:49	Mercury	21:06
Jupiter	06:11	Moon	21:45
Mars	07:32	Saturn	22:23
Sun	08:54	Jupiter	23:02
Venus	10:15	Mars	23:40
Mercury	11:36	Sun	00:19
Moon	12:58	Venus	00:57
Saturn	14:19	Mercury	01:36
Jupiter	15:41	Moon	02:15
Mars	17:02	Saturn	02:53
Sun	18:23	Jupiter	03:32
Venus	19:45	Mars	04:10

Aspects

Venus conjunct Uranus
Sun trine Jupiter
Moon sextile Vesta
Sun square Neptune
Moon conjunct Jupiter
Neptune square Ceres
Pallas conjunct Eris

Planets	00:00 am	Moon
Sun	13 gem 34	01.00 am - 12 lib 22
Mercury	24 tau 47	03.00 am - 13 lib 23
Venus	27 ar 45	05.00 am - 14 lib 25
Mars	29 gem 32	07.00 am - 15 lib 26
Jupiter	13 lib 15	09.00 am - 16 lib 27
Saturn	25 sag 20	11.00 am - 17 lib 28
Uranus	27 ar 07	13.00 pm - 18 lib 29
Neptune	14 pis 13	15.00 pm - 19 lib 30
Pluto	18 cap 56	17.00 pm - 20 lib 31
		19.00 pm - 21 lib 32
Oob	Mars	21.00 pm - 22 lib 33
		23.00 pm - 23 lib 33

Sunday 4th June

Planetary Directions

Mars into Cancer 17:16

Retrograde Planets

Jupiter, Saturn, Pluto, Juno, Haumea, Makemake, Quaoar

Asteroids		Dwarf Planets	
Juno	16 cap 32	Eris	23 ar 41
Vesta	11 leo 16	Haumea	22 lib 48
Pallas	22 ar 44	Makemake	01 lib 52
Ceres	14 gem 39	Salacia	02 ar 06
Chiron	28 pis 32	Orcus	07 vir 08
N Node	27 leo 30	Quaoar	00 cap 02
S Node	27 aq 30	Sedna	26 tau 09

Moon Phase: Gibbous
Sunrise: 04:47 BST
Sunset: 21:11
Moonrise: 15:47
Moonset: 02:54
Voc start:
Voc end:

Planetary and Angelic Hours			
Sun	04:49	Jupiter	21:07
Venus	06:10	Mars	21:46
Mercury	07:32	Sun	22:24
Moon	08:53	Venus	23:02
Saturn	10:15	Mercury	23:41
Jupiter	11:36	Moon	00:19
Mars	12:58	Saturn	00:58
Sun	14:20	Jupiter	01:36
Venus	15:41	Mars	02:14
Mercury	17:03	Sun	02:53
Moon	18:24	Venus	03:31
Saturn	19:46	Mercury	04:10

Aspects

Moon conjunct Jupiter
Sun trine Moon
Moon trine Ceres
Moon square Juno
Moon square Pluto
Sun square Neptune
Mercury conj. Sedna
Moon opposite Pallas
Moon opposite Eris
Sun conjunct Ceres
Moon sextile Saturn
Neptune square Ceres
Pallas conjunct Eris

Planets	**00:00 am**	**Moon**
Sun	14 gem 32	01.00 am - 24 lib 34
Mercury	26 tau 31	03.00 am - 25 lib 35
Venus	28 ar 43	05.00 am - 26 lib 35
Mars	00 can 12	07.00 am - 27 lib 36
Jupiter	13 lib 14	09.00 am - 28 lib 36
Saturn	25 sag 16	11.00 am - 29 lib 36
Uranus	27 ar 10	13.00 pm - 00 sco 37
Neptune	14 pis 13	15.00 pm - 01 sco 37
Pluto	18 cap 55	17.00 pm - 02 sco 37
		19.00 pm - 03 sco 37
Oob	Mars	21.00 pm - 04 sco 37
		23.00 pm - 05 sco 38

Monday 5th June

Planetary Directions

Moon into Scorpio
11:46

Retrograde Planets

Jupiter, Saturn, Pluto,
Juno, Haumea,
Makemake, Quaoar

Asteroids		**Dwarf Planets**	
Juno	16 cap 23	Eris	23 ar 42
Vesta	11 leo 40	Haumea	22 lib 48
Pallas	23 ar 03	Makemake	01 lib 52
Ceres	15 gem 04	Salacia	02 ar 08
Chiron	28 pis 33	Orcus	07 vir 08
N Node	27 leo 25	Quaoar	00 cap 01
S Node	27 aq 25	Sedna	26 tau 10

Moon Phase: Gibbous
Sunrise: 04:46 BST
Sunset: 21:12
Moonrise: 16:52
Moonset: 03:17
Voc start: 09:56
Voc end: 11:45

Planetary and Angelic Hours			
Moon	04:48	Venus	21:08
Saturn	06:10	Mercury	21:46
Jupiter	07:31	Moon	22:25
Mars	08:53	Saturn	23:03
Sun	10:15	Jupiter	23:41
Venus	11:36	Mars	00:20
Mercury	12:58	Sun	00:58
Moon	14:20	Venus	01:36
Saturn	15:41	Mercury	02:14
Jupiter	17:03	Moon	02:53
Mars	18:25	Saturn	03:31
Sun	19:47	Jupiter	04:09

Aspects

Moon sextile Saturn
Moon opposite Uranus
Moon opposite Venus
Moon trine Mars
Sun conjunct Ceres
Mercury sextile Chiron
Pallas conjunct Eris

Planets	00:00 am	Moon
Sun	15 gem 29	01.00 am - 06 sco 38
Mercury	28 tau 18	03.00 am - 07 sco 38
Venus	29 ar 41	05.00 am - 08 sco 38
Mars	00 can 52	07.00 am - 09 sco 37
Jupiter	13 lib 14	09.00 am - 10 sco 37
Saturn	25 sag 11	11.00 am - 11 sco 37
Uranus	27 ar 12	13.00 pm - 12 sco 37
Neptune	14 pis 14	15.00 pm - 13 sco 37
Pluto	18 cap 54	17.00 pm - 14 sco 37
		19.00 pm - 15 sco 36
Oob	Mars	21.00 pm - 16 sco 36
		23.00 pm - 17 sco 36

Tuesday 6th June

Planetary Directions
Venus into Taurus
08:27
Quaoar rx into Sag
22:26
Mercury into Gemini
23:16

Retrograde Planets
Jupiter, Saturn, Pluto,
Juno, Haumea,
Makemake, Quaoar

Asteroids		Dwarf Planets	
Juno	16 cap 14	Eris	23 ar 42
Vesta	12 leo 03	Haumea	22 lib 47
Pallas	23 ar 23	Makemake	01 lib 52
Ceres	15 gem 29	Salacia	02 ar 09
Chiron	28 pis 35	Orcus	07 vir 08
N Node	27 leo 16	Quaoar	29 sag 59
S Node	27 aq 16	Sedna	26 tau 11

Moon Phase: Gibbous
Sunrise: 04:46 BST
Sunset: 21:13
Moonrise: 17:55
Moonset: 03:40
Voc start:
Voc end:

Planetary and Angelic Hours

Mars	04:47	Saturn	21:09
Sun	06:09	Jupiter	21:47
Venus	07:31	Mars	22:25
Mercury	08:53	Sun	23:04
Moon	10:15	Venus	23:42
Saturn	11:36	Mercury	00:20
Jupiter	12:58	Moon	00:58
Mars	14:20	Saturn	01:36
Sun	15:42	Jupiter	02:14
Venus	17:04	Mars	02:52
Mercury	18:26	Sun	03:31
Moon	19:47	Venus	04:09

Aspects

Sun conjunct Ceres
Mercury sextile Chiron
Moon square Vesta
Moon trine Neptune
Moon sextile Juno
Moon sextile Pluto
Venus sextile Mars
Jupiter sextile Vesta
Pallas conjunct Eris

Planets	00:00 am	Moon
Sun	16 gem 27	01.00 am - 18 sco 35
Mercury	00 gem 08	03.00 am - 19 sco 35
Venus	00 tau 40	05.00 am - 20 sco 35
Mars	01 can 32	07.00 am - 21 sco 34
Jupiter	13 lib 13	09.00 am - 22 sco 34
Saturn	25 sag 07	11.00 am - 23 sco 33
Uranus	27 ar 15	13.00 pm - 24 sco 33
Neptune	14 pis 14	15.00 pm - 25 sco 32
Pluto	18 cap 53	17.00 pm - 26 sco 32
		19.00 pm - 27 sco 31
Oob	Mars	21.00 pm - 28 sco 31
		23.00 pm - 29 sco 30

Wednesday 7th June

Retrograde Planets

Jupiter, Saturn, Pluto, Juno, Haumea, Makemake, Quaoar

Asteroids		Dwarf Planets	
Juno	16 cap 05	Eris	23 ar 42
Vesta	12 leo 27	Haumea	22 lib 47
Pallas	23 ar 42	Makemake	01 lib 52
Ceres	15 gem 55	Salacia	02 ar 09
Chiron	28 pis 36	Orcus	07 vir 08
N Node	27 leo 06	Quaoar	29 sag 59
S Node	27 aq 06	Sedna	26 tau 11

Moon Phase: Gibbous
Sunrise: 04:46 BST
Sunset: 21:14
Moonrise: 18:57
Moonset: 04:06
Voc start: 01:35
Voc end: 23:59

Planetary and Angelic Hours			
Mercury	04:47	Sun	21:10
Moon	06:09	Venus	21:48
Saturn	07:31	Mercury	22:26
Jupiter	08:53	Moon	23:04
Mars	10:15	Saturn	23:42
Sun	11:37	Jupiter	00:20
Venus	12:58	Mars	00:58
Mercury	14:20	Sun	01:36
Moon	15:42	Venus	02:14
Saturn	17:04	Mercury	02:52
Jupiter	18:26	Moon	03:30
Mars	19:48	Saturn	04:08

Aspects

Pallas conjunct Eris
Moon sextile Pluto
Moon opposite Sedna
Moon trine Chiron
Venus sextile Mars
Jupiter sextile Vesta

Planets	**00:00 am**	**Moon**
Sun	17 gem 24	01.00 am - 00 sag 30
Mercury	01 gem 59	03.00 am - 01 sag 29
Venus	01 tau 39	05.00 am - 02 sag 28
Mars	02 can 12	07.00 am - 03 sag 28
Jupiter	13 lib 13	09.00 am - 04 sag 27
Saturn	25 sag 03	11.00 am - 05 sag 27
Uranus	27 ar 17	13.00 pm - 06 sag 26
Neptune	14 pis 14	15.00 pm - 07 sag 25
Pluto	18 cap 52	17.00 pm - 08 sag 25
		19.00 pm - 09 sag 24
Oob	Mars	21.00 pm - 10 sag 23
		23.00 pm - 11 sag 23

Thursday 8th June

Planetary Directions

Moon into Sagittarius 00:00

Retrograde Planets

Jupiter, Saturn, Pluto, Juno, Haumea, Makemake, Quaoar

Asteroids		**Dwarf Planets**	
Juno	15 cap 55	Eris	23 ar 43
Vesta	12 leo 51	Haumea	22 lib 47
Pallas	24 ar 02	Makemake	01 lib 52
Ceres	16 gem 20	Salacia	02 ar 09
Chiron	28 pis 37	Orcus	07 vir 09
N Node	26 leo 53	Quaoar	29 sag 58
S Node	26 aq 53	Sedna	26 tau 11

Moon Phase: Gibbous
Sunrise: 04:45 BST
Sunset: 21:14
Moonrise: 19:58
Moonset: 04:35
Voc start:
Voc end:

Planetary and Angelic Hours			
Jupiter	04:46	Moon	21:11
Mars	06:08	Saturn	21:49
Sun	07:30	Jupiter	22:27
Venus	08:53	Mars	23:05
Mercury	10:15	Sun	23:43
Moon	11:37	Venus	00:20
Saturn	12:59	Mercury	00:58
Jupiter	14:21	Moon	01:36
Mars	15:43	Saturn	02:14
Sun	17:05	Jupiter	02:52
Venus	18:27	Mars	03:30
Mercury	19:49	Sun	04:08

Aspects

Moon opp. Mercury
Jupiter sextile Vesta
Moon sextile Jupiter
Moon trine Vesta
Venus sextile Mars
Saturn trine Pallas
Pallas conjunct Eris

Planets	00:00 am	Moon
Sun	18 gem 21	01.00 am - 12 sag 22
Mercury	03 gem 54	03.00 am - 13 sag 22
Venus	02 tau 39	05.00 am - 14 sag 21
Mars	02 can 52	07.00 am - 15 sag 20
Jupiter	13 lib 13	09.00 am - 16 sag 20
Saturn	24 sag 58	11.00 am - 17 sag 19
Uranus	27 ar 20	13.00 pm - 18 sag 18
Neptune	14 pis 14	15.00 pm - 19 sag 18
Pluto	18 cap 50	17.00 pm - 20 sag 17
		19.00 pm - 21 sag 16
Oob	Mars	21.00 pm - 22 sag 16
		23.00 pm - 23 sag 15

Friday 9th June

Planetary Directions

Jupiter direct
13 lib 12 at 15:03

Retrograde Planets

Saturn, Pluto, Juno, Haumea, Makemake, Quaoar

Asteroids		Dwarf Planets	
Juno	15 cap 46	Eris	23 ar 43
Vesta	13 leo 15	Haumea	22 lib 46
Pallas	24 ar 21	Makemake	01 lib 52
Ceres	16 gem 45	Salacia	02 ar 10
Chiron	28 pis 38	Orcus	07 vir 09
N Node	26 leo 41	Quaoar	29 sag 57
S Node	26 aq 41	Sedna	26 tau 12

Full Moon: 14:11
Sunrise: 04:44 BST
Sunset: 21:15
Moonrise: 20:54
Moonset: 05:09
Voc start:
Voc end:

Planetary and Angelic Hours

Venus	04:46	Mars	21:12
Mercury	06:08	Sun	21:49
Moon	07:30	Venus	22:27
Saturn	08:52	Mercury	23:05
Jupiter	10:15	Moon	23:43
Mars	11:37	Saturn	00:21
Sun	12:59	Jupiter	00:59
Venus	14:21	Mars	01:36
Mercury	15:43	Sun	02:14
Moon	17:05	Venus	02:52
Saturn	18:27	Mercury	03:30
Jupiter	19:49	Moon	04:08

Micro Moon

Aspects

Moon sextile Jupiter
Moon trine Vesta
Moon square Neptune
Moon opposite Ceres
Sun opposite Moon
Venus sextile Mars
Moon trine Eris
Moon conjunct Saturn
Moon trine Pallas
Jupiter sextile Vesta
Saturn trine Pallas
Pallas conjunct Eris

Planets	00:00 am	Moon
Sun	19 gem 19	01.00 am - 24 sag 15
Mercury	05 gem 50	03.00 am - 25 sag 14
Venus	03 tau 58	05.00 am - 26 sag 13
Mars	03 can 31	07.00 am - 27 sag 13
Jupiter	13 lib 12	09.00 am - 28 sag 12
Saturn	24 sag 54	11.00 am - 29 sag 12
Uranus	27 ar 22	13.00 pm - 00 cap 11
Neptune	14 pis 15	15.00 pm - 01 cap 11
Pluto	18 cap 49	17.00 pm - 02 cap 10
		19.00 pm - 03 cap 10
Oob	Mars	21.00 pm - 04 cap 09
		23.00 pm - 05 cap 09

Saturday 10th June

Planetary Directions

Moon into Capricorn 12:37

Retrograde Planets

Saturn, Pluto, Juno, Haumea, Makemake, Quaoar

Asteroids		Dwarf Planets	
Juno	15 cap 35	Eris	23 ar 43
Vesta	13 leo 39	Haumea	22 lib 45
Pallas	24 ar 40	Makemake	01 lib 51
Ceres	17 gem 10	Salacia	02 ar 10
Chiron	28 pis 39	Orcus	07 vir 10
N Node	26 leo 29	Quaoar	29 sag 56
S Node	26 aq 29	Sedna	26 tau 13

Phase: Disseminating
Sunrise: 04:44 BST
Sunset: 21:16
Moonrise: 21:47
Moonset: 05:48
Voc start: 07:20
Voc end: 12:36

Planetary and Angelic Hours

Saturn	04:46	Mercury	21:12
Jupiter	06:08	Moon	21:50
Mars	07:30	Saturn	22:28
Sun	08:52	Jupiter	23:06
Venus	10:15	Mars	23:43
Mercury	11:37	Sun	00:21
Moon	12:59	Venus	00:59
Saturn	14:21	Mercury	01:37
Jupiter	15:43	Moon	02:14
Mars	17:06	Saturn	02:52
Sun	18:28	Jupiter	03:30
Venus	19:50	Mars	04:08

Aspects

Moon trine Pallas
Moon conjunct Saturn
Moon trine Uranus
Moon square Chiron
Saturn trine Pallas
Moon opposite Mars
Moon trine Venus
Venus sextile Mars
Jupiter sextile Vesta

Planets	**00:00 am**	**Moon**
Sun	20 gem 16	01.00 am - 06 cap 08
Mercury	07 gem 49	03.00 am - 07 cap 08
Venus	04 tau 39	05.00 am - 08 cap 08
Mars	04 can 11	07.00 am - 09 cap 07
Jupiter	13 lib 13	09.00 am - 10 cap 07
Saturn	24 sag 49	11.00 am - 11 cap 07
Uranus	27 ar 25	13.00 pm - 12 cap 06
Neptune	14 pis 15	15.00 pm - 13 cap 06
Pluto	18 cap 48	17.00 pm - 14 cap 06
		19.00 pm - 15 cap 06
Oob	Mars	21.00 pm - 16 cap 06
		23.00 pm - 17 cap 05

Sunday 11th June

Retrograde Planets

Saturn, Pluto, Juno, Haumea, Makemake, Quaoar

Asteroids		**Dwarf Planets**	
Juno	15 cap 25	Eris	23 ar 44
Vesta	14 leo 03	Haumea	22 lib 45
Pallas	25 ar 00	Makemake	01 lib 51
Ceres	17 gem 36	Salacia	02 ar 11
Chiron	28 pis 41	Orcus	07 vir 10
N Node	26 leo 18	Quaoar	29 sag 55
S Node	26 aq 18	Sedna	26 tau 14

Phase: Disseminating
Sunrise: 04:43 BST
Sunset: 21:17
Moonrise: 22:34
Moonset: 06:34
Voc start:
Voc end:

Planetary and Angelic Hours			
Sun	04:45	Jupiter	21:13
Venus	06:08	Mars	21:51
Mercury	07:30	Sun	22:28
Moon	08:52	Venus	23:06
Saturn	10:15	Mercury	23:44
Jupiter	11:37	Moon	00:21
Mars	12:59	Saturn	00:59
Sun	14:21	Jupiter	01:37
Venus	15:44	Mars	02:14
Mercury	17:06	Sun	02:52
Moon	18:28	Venus	03:30
Saturn	19:51	Mercury	04:07

Aspects

Moon square Jupiter
Moon sextile Neptune
Moon conjunct Juno
Moon conjunct Pluto
Venus sextile Mars
Saturn trine Pallas
Neptune sextile Juno

Planets	**00:00 am**	**Moon**
Sun	21 gem 13	01.00 am - 18 cap 05
Mercury	09 gem 50	03.00 am - 19 cap 05
Venus	05 tau 39	05.00 am - 20 cap 05
Mars	04 can 51	07.00 am - 21 cap 05
Jupiter	13 lib 13	09.00 am - 22 cap 05
Saturn	24 sag 45	11.00 am - 23 cap 05
Uranus	27 ar 27	13.00 pm - 24 cap 05
Neptune	14 pis 15	15.00 pm - 25 cap 06
Pluto	18 cap 47	17.00 pm - 26 cap 06
		19.00 pm - 27 cap 06
Oob	Mars	21.00 pm - 28 cap 06
		23.00 pm - 29 cap 07

Monday 12th June

Retrograde Planets

Saturn, Pluto, Juno, Haumea, Makemake, Quaoar

Asteroids		**Dwarf Planets**	
Juno	15 cap 14	Eris	23 ar 44
Vesta	14 leo 27	Haumea	22 lib 44
Pallas	25 ar 19	Makemake	01 lib 51
Ceres	18 gem 01	Salacia	02 ar 11
Chiron	28 pis 42	Orcus	07 vir 11
N Node	26 leo 10	Quaoar	29 sag 54
S Node	26 aq 10	Sedna	26 tau 14

Phase: Disseminating
Sunrise: 04:43 BST
Sunset: 21:17
Moonrise: 23:15
Moonset: 07:25
Voc start: 19:45
Voc end:

Planetary and Angelic Hours			
Moon	04:45	Venus	21:14
Saturn	06:07	Mercury	21:51
Jupiter	07:30	Moon	22:29
Mars	08:52	Saturn	23:06
Sun	10:15	Jupiter	23:44
Venus	11:37	Mars	00:22
Mercury	12:59	Sun	00:59
Moon	14:22	Venus	01:37
Saturn	15:44	Mercury	02:14
Jupiter	17:07	Moon	02:52
Mars	18:29	Saturn	03:30
Sun	19:51	Jupiter	04:07

Aspects

Moon conjunct Pluto
Moon square Eris
Moon square Pallas
Moon trine Sedna
Moon square Uranus
Moon sextile Chiron
Saturn trine Pallas
Saturn trine Eris
Neptune sextile Juno

Planets	00:00 am
Sun	22 gem 11
Mercury	11 gem 52
Venus	06 tau 40
Mars	05 can 30
Jupiter	13 lib 14
Saturn	24 sag 41
Uranus	27 ar 29
Neptune	14 pis 15
Pluto	18 cap 45
Oob	Mars

Moon
01.00 am - 00 aq 07
03.00 am - 01 aq 08
05.00 am - 02 aq 08
07.00 am - 03 aq 09
09.00 am - 04 aq 09
11.00 am - 05 aq 10
13.00 pm - 06 aq 11
15.00 pm - 07 aq 12
17.00 pm - 08 aq 13
19.00 pm - 09 aq 14
21.00 pm - 10 aq 15
23.00 pm - 11 aq 16

Tuesday 13th June

Planetary Directions

Moon into Aquarius 00:45

Retrograde Planets

Saturn, Pluto, Juno, Haumea, Makemake, Quaoar

Asteroids		Dwarf Planets	
Juno	15 cap 03	Eris	23 ar 45
Vesta	14 leo 52	Haumea	22 lib 44
Pallas	25 ar 38	Makemake	01 lib 51
Ceres	18 gem 26	Salacia	02 ar 12
Chiron	28 pis 43	Orcus	07 vir 11
N Node	26 leo 05	Quaoar	29 sag 52
S Node	26 aq 05	Sedna	26 tau 15

Phase: Disseminating
Sunrise: 04:43 BST
Sunset: 21:18
Moonrise: 23:51
Moonset: 08:23
Voc start:
Voc end: 00:44

Planetary and Angelic Hours			
Mars	04:45	Saturn	21:14
Sun	06:07	Jupiter	21:52
Venus	07:30	Mars	22:29
Mercury	08:52	Sun	23:07
Moon	10:15	Venus	23:44
Saturn	11:37	Mercury	00:22
Jupiter	13:00	Moon	00:59
Mars	14:22	Saturn	01:37
Sun	15:44	Jupiter	02:15
Venus	17:07	Mars	02:52
Mercury	18:29	Sun	03:30
Moon	19:52	Venus	04:07

Aspects

Moon square Venus
Mercury trine Jupiter
Sun sextile Eris
Moon trine Jupiter
Mercury sq. Neptune
Saturn trine Eris
Neptune sextile Juno

Planets	00:00 am	Moon
Sun	23 gem 08	01.00 am - 12 aq 17
Mercury	13 gem 57	03.00 am - 13 aq 18
Venus	07 tau 41	05.00 am - 14 aq 20
Mars	06 can 10	07.00 am - 15 aq 21
Jupiter	13 lib 14	09.00 am - 16 aq 22
Saturn	24 sag 36	11.00 am - 17 aq 24
Uranus	27 ar 32	13.00 pm - 18 aq 26
Neptune	14 pis 15	15.00 pm - 19 aq 27
Pluto	18 cap 44	17.00 pm - 20 aq 29
		19.00 pm - 21 aq 31
Oob	Mars	21.00 pm - 22 aq 33
		23.00 pm - 23 aq 35

Wednesday 14th June

Retrograde Planets

Saturn, Pluto, Juno, Haumea, Makemake, Quaoar

Asteroids		Dwarf Planets	
Juno	14 cap 52	Eris	23 ar 45
Vesta	15 leo 16	Haumea	22 lib 43
Pallas	25 ar 57	Makemake	01 lib 51
Ceres	18 gem 51	Salacia	02 ar 12
Chiron	28 pis 43	Orcus	07 vir 11
N Node	26 leo 02	Quaoar	29 sag 51
S Node	26 aq 02	Sedna	26 tau 16

Phase: Disseminating
Sunrise: 04:43 BST
Sunset: 21:18
Moonrise: None
Moonset: 09:25
Voc start:
Voc end:

Planetary and Angelic Hours			
Mercury	04:45	Sun	21:15
Moon	06:07	Venus	21:52
Saturn	07:30	Mercury	22:30
Jupiter	08:52	Moon	23:07
Mars	10:15	Saturn	23:45
Sun	11:37	Jupiter	00:22
Venus	13:00	Mars	01:00
Mercury	14:22	Sun	01:37
Moon	15:45	Venus	02:15
Saturn	17:07	Mercury	02:52
Jupiter	18:30	Moon	03:30
Mars	19:52	Saturn	04:07

Aspects

Moon trine Jupiter
Mercury sq. Neptune
Moon trine Mercury
Moon opposite Vesta
Moon trine Ceres
Sun sextile Eris
Mercury sextile Vesta
Moon sextile Eris
Sun trine Moon
Moon sextile Saturn
Sun opposite Saturn
Saturn trine Eris
Neptune sextile Juno

Planets	00:00 am	Moon
Sun	24 gem 05	01.00 am - 24 aq 38
Mercury	16 gem 03	03.00 am - 25 aq 40
Venus	08 tau 42	05.00 am - 26 aq 42
Mars	06 can 50	07.00 am - 27 aq 45
Jupiter	13 lib 15	09.00 am - 28 aq 48
Saturn	24 sag 32	11.00 am - 29 aq 50
Uranus	27 ar 34	13.00 pm - 00 pis 53
Neptune	14 pis 15	15.00 pm - 01 pis 56
Pluto	18 cap 43	17.00 pm - 02 pis 59
		19.00 pm - 04 pis 03
Oob	Mars	21.00 pm - 05 pis 06
		23.00 pm - 06 pis 09

Thursday 15th June

Planetary Directions

Moon into Pisces 11:18
Makemake direct
01 lib 51 at 23:07

Retrograde Planets

Saturn, Pluto, Juno, Haumea, Makemake, Quaoar

Asteroids		Dwarf Planets	
Juno	14 cap 41	Eris	23 ar 45
Vesta	15 leo 41	Haumea	22 lib 43
Pallas	26 ar 16	Makemake	01 lib 51
Ceres	19 gem 17	Salacia	02 ar 13
Chiron	28 pis 44	Orcus	07 vir 12
N Node	26 leo 01	Quaoar	29 sag 50
S Node	26 aq 01	Sedna	26 tau 17

Phase: Disseminating
Sunrise: 04:43 BST
Sunset: 21:19
Moonrise: 00:22
Moonset: 10:30
Voc start: 06:39
Voc end: 11:17

Planetary and Angelic Hours			
Jupiter	04:44	Moon	21:15
Mars	06:07	Saturn	21:53
Sun	07:30	Jupiter	22:30
Venus	08:52	Mars	23:08
Mercury	10:15	Sun	23:45
Moon	11:37	Venus	00:23
Saturn	13:00	Mercury	01:00
Jupiter	14:23	Moon	01:37
Mars	15:45	Saturn	02:15
Sun	17:08	Jupiter	02:52
Venus	18:30	Mars	03:30
Mercury	19:53	Sun	04:07

Aspects

Moon square Sedna
Moon sextile Pallas
Moon sextile Uranus
Sun opposite Saturn
Moon trine Mars
Saturn trine Eris
Neptune sextile Juno

Planets	00:00 am
Sun	25 gem 03
Mercury	18 gem 11
Venus	09 tau 44
Mars	07 can 29
Jupiter	13 lib 16
Saturn	24 sag 27
Uranus	27 ar 36
Neptune	14 pis 15
Pluto	18 cap 42
Oob	Mercury Mars

Moon
01.00 am - 07 pis 13
03.00 am - 08 pis 17
05.00 am - 09 pis 21
07.00 am - 10 pis 25
09.00 am - 11 pis 29
11.00 am - 12 pis 33
13.00 pm - 13 pis 38
15.00 pm - 14 pis 42
17.00 pm - 15 pis 47
19.00 pm - 16 pis 52
21.00 pm - 17 pis 57
23.00 pm - 19 pis 02

Friday 16th June

Planetary Directions

Neptune retrograde
14 pis 15 at 12:11

Retrograde Planets

Saturn, Pluto, Juno,
Haumea, Quaoar

Asteroids		Dwarf Planets	
Juno	14 cap 29	Eris	23 ar 46
Vesta	16 leo 05	Haumea	22 lib 42
Pallas	26 ar 35	Makemake	01 lib 51
Ceres	19 gem 42	Salacia	02 ar 13
Chiron	28 pis 45	Orcus	07 vir 13
N Node	26 leo 01	Quaoar	29 sag 49
S Node	26 aq 01	Sedna	26 tau 17

Phase: Disseminating
Sunrise: 04:43 BST
Sunset: 21:19
Moonrise: 00:50
Moonset: 11:38
Voc start:
Voc end:

Planetary and Angelic Hours

Venus	04:44	Mars	21:16
Mercury	06:07	Sun	21:53
Moon	07:30	Venus	22:31
Saturn	08:52	Mercury	23:08
Jupiter	10:15	Moon	23:45
Mars	11:38	Saturn	00:23
Sun	13:00	Jupiter	01:00
Venus	14:23	Mars	01:38
Mercury	15:45	Sun	02:15
Moon	17:08	Venus	02:52
Saturn	18:31	Mercury	03:30
Jupiter	19:53	Moon	04:07

Aspects

Moon trine Mars
Moon sextile Venus
Moon conj. Neptune
Moon sextile Juno
Mercury conj. Ceres
Moon sextile Pluto
Moon square Ceres
Sun sextile Pallas
Moon square Mercury
Jupiter square Juno
Saturn trine Eris
Uranus conjunct Pallas
Neptune sextile Juno

Planets	00:00 am	Moon
Sun	26 gem 00	01.00 am - 20 pis 07
Mercury	20 gem 20	03.00 am - 21 pis 13
Venus	10 tau 46	05.00 am - 22 pis 18
Mars	08 can 09	07.00 am - 23 pis 24
Jupiter	13 lib 17	09.00 am - 24 pis 30
Saturn	24 sag 23	11.00 am - 25 pis 35
Uranus	27 ar 38	13.00 pm - 26 pis 43
Neptune	14 pis 15	15.00 pm - 27 pis 49
Pluto	18 cap 40	17.00 pm - 28 pis 56
Oob	Mercury	19.00 pm - 00 ar 02
	Mars	21.00 pm - 01 ar 09
		23.00 pm - 02 ar 17

Saturday 17th June

Planetary Directions

Moon into Aries 18:55

Retrograde Planets

Saturn, Pluto, Juno, Haumea, Quaoar

Asteroids		Dwarf Planets	
Juno	14 cap 17	Eris	23 ar 46
Vesta	16 leo 30	Haumea	22 lib 42
Pallas	26 ar 54	Makemake	01 lib 51
Ceres	20 gem 07	Salacia	02 ar 14
Chiron	28 pis 46	Orcus	07 vir 13
N Node	26 leo 02	Quaoar	29 sag 48
S Node	26 aq 02	Sedna	26 tau 18

Last Quarter: 12:35
Sunrise: 04:43 BST
Sunset: 21:20
Moonrise: 01:15
Moonset: 12:49
Voc start: 12:32
Voc end: 18:54

Planetary and Angelic Hours

Saturn	04:44	Mercury	21:16
Jupiter	06:07	Moon	21:54
Mars	07:30	Saturn	22:31
Sun	08:52	Jupiter	23:08
Venus	10:15	Mars	23:46
Mercury	11:38	Sun	00:23
Moon	13:00	Venus	01:00
Saturn	14:23	Mercury	01:38
Jupiter	15:46	Moon	02:15
Mars	17:08	Saturn	02:52
Sun	18:31	Jupiter	03:30
Venus	19:54	Mars	04:07

Aspects

Moon square Mercury
Neptune sextile Juno
Moon square Saturn
Moon sextile Sedna
Sun square Moon
Moon conjunct Chiron
Sun sextile Uranus
Sun sextile Pallas
Jupiter square Juno
Saturn trine Eris
Uranus conjunct Pallas

Planets	00:00 am	Moon
Sun	26 gem 57	01.00 am - 03 ar 24
Mercury	22 gem 31	03.00 am - 04 ar 31
Venus	11 tau 48	05.00 am - 05 ar 39
Mars	08 can 48	07.00 am - 06 ar 47
Jupiter	13 lib 19	09.00 am - 07 ar 55
Saturn	24 sag 18	11.00 am - 09 ar 03
Uranus	27 ar 40	13.00 pm - 10 ar 12
Neptune	14 pis 15	15.00 pm - 11 ar 20
Pluto	18 cap 39	17.00 pm - 12 ar 29
Oob	Mercury	19.00 pm - 13 ar 38
	Mars	21.00 pm - 14 ar 47
		23.00 pm - 15 ar 57

Sunday 18th June

Retrograde Planets

Saturn, Neptune, Pluto, Juno, Haumea, Quaoar

Asteroids		Dwarf Planets	
Juno	14 cap 05	Eris	23 ar 46
Vesta	16 leo 55	Haumea	22 lib 41
Pallas	27 ar 12	Makemake	01 lib 51
Ceres	20 gem 32	Salacia	02 ar 14
Chiron	28 pis 47	Orcus	07 vir 14
N Node	26 leo 02	Quaoar	29 sag 47
S Node	26 aq 02	Sedna	26 tau 19

Moon Phase: Balsamic
Sunrise: 04:43 BST
Sunset: 21:20
Moonrise: 01:40
Moonset: 14:02
Voc start:
Voc end:

Planetary and Angelic Hours			
Sun	04:44	Jupiter	21:17
Venus	06:07	Mars	21:54
Mercury	07:30	Sun	22:31
Moon	08:52	Venus	23:09
Saturn	10:15	Mercury	23:46
Jupiter	11:38	Moon	00:23
Mars	13:01	Saturn	01:01
Sun	14:23	Jupiter	01:38
Venus	15:46	Mars	02:15
Mercury	17:09	Sun	02:53
Moon	18:31	Venus	03:30
Saturn	19:54	Mercury	04:07

Fathers' Day

Aspects

Sun sextile Pallas
Moon square Mars
Mercury sextile Eris
Moon opposite Jupiter
Moon square Juno
Sun sextile Uranus
Mercury opp. Saturn
Sun square Chiron
Moon trine Vesta
Jupiter square Juno
Saturn trine Eris
Uranus conjunct Pallas
Neptune sextile Juno

Planets	**00:00 am**	**Moon**
Sun	27 gem 54	01.00 am - 17 ar 06
Mercury	24 gem 42	03.00 am - 18 ar 16
Venus	12 tau 50	05.00 am - 19 ar 26
Mars	09 can 28	07.00 am - 20 ar 36
Jupiter	13 lib 20	09.00 am - 21 ar 46
Saturn	24 sag 14	11.00 am - 22 ar 57
Uranus	27 ar 42	13.00 pm - 24 ar 08
Neptune	14 pis 15	15.00 pm - 25 ar 18
Pluto	18 cap 38	17.00 pm - 26 ar 29
Oob	Mercury	19.00 pm - 27 ar 41
	Mars	21.00 pm - 28 ar 52
		23.00 pm - 00 tau 04

Monday 19th June

Planetary Directions

Moon into Taurus
21:53

Retrograde Planets

Saturn, Neptune, Pluto, Juno, Haumea, Quaoar

Asteroids		**Dwarf Planets**	
Juno	13 cap 52	Eris	23 ar 47
Vesta	17 leo 20	Haumea	22 lib 41
Pallas	27 ar 31	Makemake	01 lib 51
Ceres	20 gem 58	Salacia	02 ar 14
Chiron	28 pis 47	Orcus	07 vir 14
N Node	26 leo 00	Quaoar	29 sag 45
S Node	26 aq 00	Sedna	26 tau 19

Moon Phase: Balsamic
Sunrise: 04:43 BST
Sunset: 21:20
Moonrise: 02:06
Moonset: 15:17
Voc start: 20:41
Voc end: 22:52

Planetary and Angelic Hours			
Moon	04:44	Venus	21:17
Saturn	06:07	Mercury	21:54
Jupiter	07:30	Moon	22:32
Mars	08:53	Saturn	23:09
Sun	10:15	Jupiter	23:46
Venus	11:38	Mars	00:24
Mercury	13:01	Sun	01:01
Moon	14:23	Venus	01:38
Saturn	15:46	Mercury	02:15
Jupiter	17:09	Moon	02:53
Mars	18:32	Saturn	03:30
Sun	19:54	Jupiter	04:07

Aspects

Moon trine Vesta
Moon square Pluto
Moon sextile Ceres
Moon conjunct Eris
Moon trine Saturn
Moon sextile Mercury
Uranus conjunct Pallas
Moon conjunct Uranus
Moon conjunct Pallas
Sun sextile Moon
Venus trine Juno
Sun square Chiron
Mercury sextile Uranus
Mercury sextile Pallas
Venus sextile Neptune
Jupiter square Juno
Saturn trine Eris

Planets	00:00 am	Moon
Sun	28 gem 52	01.00 am - 01 tau 16
Mercury	26 gem 53	03.00 am - 02 tau 28
Venus	13 tau 53	05.00 am - 03 tau 40
Mars	10 can 07	07.00 am - 04 tau 52
Jupiter	13 lib 22	09.00 am - 06 tau 05
Saturn	24 sag 10	11.00 am - 07 tau 17
Uranus	27 ar 44	13.00 pm - 08 tau 30
Neptune	14 pis 15	15.00 pm - 09 tau 43
Pluto	18 cap 36	17.00 pm - 10 tau 56
Oob	Mercury	19.00 pm - 12 tau 10
	Mars	21.00 pm - 13 tau 23
		23.00 pm - 14 tau 37

Tuesday 20th June

Retrograde Planets

Saturn, Neptune, Pluto, Juno, Haumea, Quaoar

Asteroids		Dwarf Planets	
Juno	13 cap 40	Eris	23 ar 47
Vesta	17 leo 45	Haumea	22 lib 41
Pallas	27 ar 50	Makemake	01 lib 51
Ceres	21 gem 23	Salacia	02 ar 15
Chiron	28 pis 48	Orcus	07 vir 15
N Node	25 leo 56	Quaoar	29 sag 44
S Node	25 aq 56	Sedna	26 tau 20

Moon Phase: Balsamic
Sunrise: 04:43 BST
Sunset: 21:21
Moonrise: 02:34
Moonset: 16:36
Voc start:
Voc end:

Planetary and Angelic Hours			
Mars	04:45	Saturn	21:17
Sun	06:07	Jupiter	21:55
Venus	07:30	Mars	22:32
Mercury	08:53	Sun	23:09
Moon	10:15	Venus	23:47
Saturn	11:38	Mercury	00:24
Jupiter	13:01	Moon	01:01
Mars	14:24	Saturn	01:38
Sun	15:46	Jupiter	02:16
Venus	17:09	Mars	02:53
Mercury	18:32	Sun	03:30
Moon	19:55	Venus	04:07

Aspects

Venus sextile Neptune
Mercury sextile Uranus
Mercury sextile Pallas
Moon sextile Mars
Moon trine Juno
Mercury square Chiron
Moon sextile Neptune
Moon conjunct Venus
Sun conjunct Mercury
Jupiter square Juno
Saturn trine Eris
Uranus conjunct Pallas
Neptune sextile Juno

Planets	00:00 am	Moon
Sun	29 gem 49	01.00 am - 15 tau 51
Mercury	29 gem 05	03.00 am - 17 tau 05
Venus	14 tau 56	05.00 am - 18 tau 19
Mars	10 can 47	07.00 am - 19 tau 33
Jupiter	13 lib 24	09.00 am - 20 tau 47
Saturn	24 sag 05	11.00 am - 22 tau 02
Uranus	27 ar 47	13.00 pm - 23 tau 17
Neptune	14 pis 15	15.00 pm - 24 tau 31
Pluto	18 cap 35	17.00 pm - 25 tau 46
Oob	Mercury	19.00 pm - 27 tau 01
	Mars	21.00 pm - 28 tau 16
		23.00 pm - 29 tau 32

Wednesday 21st June

Planetary Directions

Sun into Cancer 05:24
Mercury into Can at 10:58
Moon into Gem 23:45

Retrograde Planets

Saturn, Neptune, Pluto, Juno, Haumea, Quaoar

Asteroids		Dwarf Planets	
Juno	13 cap 27	Eris	23 ar 47
Vesta	18 leo 10	Haumea	22 lib 40
Pallas	28 ar 08	Makemake	01 lib 51
Ceres	21 gem 48	Salacia	02 ar 15
Chiron	28 pis 49	Orcus	07 vir 16
N Node	25 leo 51	Quaoar	29 sag 43
S Node	25 aq 51	Sedna	26 tau 21

Moon Phase: Balsamic
Sunrise: 04:43 BST
Sunset: 21:21
Moonrise: 03:05
Moonset: 17:55
Voc start: 05:25
Voc end: 23:44

Planetary and Angelic Hours			
Mercury	04:45	Sun	21:18
Moon	06:07	Venus	21:55
Saturn	07:30	Mercury	22:32
Jupiter	08:53	Moon	23:09
Mars	10:16	Saturn	23:47
Sun	11:38	Jupiter	00:24
Venus	13:01	Mars	01:01
Mercury	14:24	Sun	01:39
Moon	15:47	Venus	02:16
Saturn	17:09	Mercury	02:53
Jupiter	18:32	Moon	03:30
Mars	19:55	Saturn	04:08

Summer Solstice 05:24

Aspects

Moon square Vesta
Moon trine Pluto
Jupiter square Juno
Sun conjunct Mercury
Moon conjunct Sedna
Moon sextile Chiron
Saturn trine Eris
Uranus conjunct Pallas

Planets	00:00 am	Moon
Sun	00 can 46	01.00 am - 00 gem 47
Mercury	01 can 17	03.00 am - 02 gem 03
Venus	15 tau 59	05.00 am - 03 gem 18
Mars	11 can 26	07.00 am - 04 gem 34
Jupiter	13 lib 26	09.00 am - 05 gem 49
Saturn	24 sag 01	11.00 am - 07 gem 05
Uranus	27 ar 48	13.00 pm - 08 gem 21
Neptune	14 pis 15	15.00 pm - 09 gem 37
Pluto	18 cap 33	17.00 pm - 10 gem 53
Oob	Mercury	19.00 pm - 12 gem 09
	Mars	21.00 pm - 13 gem 25
		23.00 pm - 14 gem 41

Thursday 22nd June

Retrograde Planets

Saturn, Neptune, Pluto, Juno, Haumea, Quaoar

Asteroids		Dwarf Planets	
Juno	13 cap 14	Eris	23 ar 48
Vesta	18 leo 35	Haumea	22 lib 40
Pallas	28 ar 27	Makemake	01 lib 51
Ceres	22 gem 13	Salacia	02 ar 15
Chiron	28 pis 49	Orcus	07 vir 16
N Node	25 leo 43	Quaoar	29 sag 42
S Node	25 aq 43	Sedna	26 tau 21

Moon Phase: Balsamic
Sunrise: 04:43 BST
Sunset: 21:12
Moonrise: 03:43
Moonset: 19:13
Voc start:
Voc end:

Planetary and Angelic Hours			
Jupiter	04:45	Moon	21:18
Mars	06:08	Saturn	21:55
Sun	07:30	Jupiter	22:32
Venus	08:53	Mars	23:10
Mercury	10:16	Sun	23:47
Moon	11:39	Venus	00:24
Saturn	13:01	Mercury	01:02
Jupiter	14:24	Moon	01:39
Mars	15:47	Saturn	02:16
Sun	17:10	Jupiter	02:53
Venus	18:32	Mars	03:31
Mercury	19:55	Sun	04:08

Aspects

Moon trine Jupiter
Moon square Neptune
Mars opposite Juno
Jupiter square Juno
Saturn trine Eris
Uranus conjunct Pallas

Planets	00:00 am	Moon
Sun	01 can 44	01.00 am - 15 gem 57
Mercury	03 can 28	03.00 am - 17 gem 14
Venus	17 tau 03	05.00 am - 18 gem 30
Mars	12 can 06	07.00 am - 19 gem 46
Jupiter	13 lib 28	09.00 am - 21 gem 02
Saturn	23 sag 56	11.00 am - 22 gem 18
Uranus	27 ar 50	13.00 pm - 23 gem 35
Neptune	14 pis 15	15.00 pm - 24 gem 51
Pluto	18 cap 32	17.00 pm - 25 gem 07
Oob	Mercury	19.00 pm - 27 gem 23
	Mars	21.00 pm - 28 gem 39
		23.00 pm - 29 gem 55

Friday 23rd June

Planetary Directions

Moon into Cancer
23:07

Retrograde Planets

Saturn, Neptune, Pluto, Juno, Haumea, Quaoar

Asteroids		Dwarf Planets	
Juno	13 cap 01	Eris	23 ar 48
Vesta	19 leo 01	Haumea	22 lib 40
Pallas	28 ar 45	Makemake	01 lib 52
Ceres	22 gem 39	Salacia	02 ar 15
Chiron	28 pis 50	Orcus	07 vir 17
N Node	25 leo 35	Quaoar	29 sag 41
S Node	25 aq 35	Sedna	26 tau 22

Moon Phase: Balsamic
Sunrise: 04:44 BST
Sunset: 21:21
Moonrise: 04:28
Moonset: 20:26
Voc start: 19:45
Voc end: 23:06

Planetary and Angelic Hours			
Venus	04:45	Mars	21:18
Mercury	06:08	Sun	21:55
Moon	07:31	Venus	22:33
Saturn	08:53	Mercury	23:10
Jupiter	10:16	Moon	23:47
Mars	11:39	Saturn	00:24
Sun	13:02	Jupiter	01:02
Venus	14:24	Mars	01:39
Mercury	15:47	Sun	02:16
Moon	17:10	Venus	02:54
Saturn	18:33	Mercury	03:31
Jupiter	19:55	Moon	04:08

Aspects

Moon sextile Vesta
Moon conjunct Ceres
Moon sextile Eris
Moon opposite Saturn
Moon sextile Uranus
Moon square Chiron
Moon sextile Pallas
Venus trine Pluto
Mars square Jupiter
Mars opposite Juno
Jupiter square Juno
Saturn opposite Ceres
Saturn trine Eris
Ceres sextile Eris

Planets	00:00 am	Moon
Sun	02 can 41	01.00 am - 01 can 11
Mercury	05 can 39	03.00 am - 02 can 27
Venus	18 tau 06	05.00 am - 03 can 43
Mars	12 can 45	07.00 am - 04 can 59
Jupiter	13 lib 31	09.00 am - 06 can 15
Saturn	23 sag 52	11.00 am - 07 can 31
Uranus	27 ar 52	13.00 pm - 08 can 46
Neptune	14 pis 14	15.00 pm - 10 can 02
Pluto	18 cap 31	17.00 pm - 12 can 17
Oob	Mercury	19.00 pm - 12 can 33
	Mars	21.00 pm - 13 can 48
		23.00 pm - 15 can 03

Saturday 24th June

Retrograde Planets

Saturn, Neptune, Pluto, Juno, Haumea, Quaoar

Asteroids		Dwarf Planets	
Juno	12 cap 48	Eris	23 ar 48
Vesta	19 leo 26	Haumea	22 lib 39
Pallas	29 ar 03	Makemake	01 lib 52
Ceres	23 gem 04	Salacia	02 ar 16
Chiron	28 pis 50	Orcus	07 vir 18
N Node	25 leo 28	Quaoar	29 sag 40
S Node	25 aq 28	Sedna	26 tau 23

New Moon: 03:32
Sunrise: 04:44 BST
Sunset: 21:21
Moonrise: 05:23
Moonset: 21:31
Voc start:
Voc end:

Planetary and Angelic Hours			
Saturn	04:46	Mercury	21L18
Jupiter	06:08	Moon	21:55
Mars	07:31	Saturn	22:33
Sun	08:54	Jupiter	23:10
Venus	10:16	Mars	23:47
Mercury	11:39	Sun	00:25
Moon	13:02	Venus	01:02
Saturn	14:24	Mercury	01:39
Jupiter	15:47	Moon	02:17
Mars	17:10	Saturn	02:54
Sun	18:33	Jupiter	03:31
Venus	19:55	Mars	04:09

Super Moon

Aspects

Mars opposite Juno
Sun conjunct Moon
Moon conj. Mercury
Venus trine Pluto
Moon opposite Juno
Moon conjunct Mars
Moon square Jupiter
Moon trine Neptune
Saturn trine Eris
Venus square Vesta
Mars square Jupiter
Mars trine Neptune
Jupiter square Juno
Saturn opposite Ceres
Ceres sextile Eris

Planets	**00:00 am**	**Moon**
Sun	03 can 38	01.00 am - 16 can 18
Mercury	07 can 49	03.00 am - 17 can 33
Venus	19 tau 10	05.00 am - 18 can 48
Mars	13 can 24	07.00 am - 20 can 03
Jupiter	13 lib 34	09.00 am - 21 can 18
Saturn	23 sag 48	11.00 am - 22 can 32
Uranus	27 ar 54	13.00 pm - 23 can 46
Neptune	14 pis 14	15.00 pm - 25 can 00
Pluto	18 cap 29	17.00 pm - 26 can 14
Oob	Mercury	19.00 pm - 27 can 28
	Mars	21.00 pm - 28 can 42
		23.00 pm - 29 can 56

Sunday 25th June

Planetary Directions

Moon into Leo 23:07

Retrograde Planets

Saturn, Neptune, Pluto, Juno, Haumea, Quaoar

Asteroids		**Dwarf Planets**	
Juno	12 cap 34	Eris	23 ar 48
Vesta	19 leo 52	Haumea	22 lib 39
Pallas	29 ar 22	Makemake	01 lib 52
Ceres	23 gem 29	Salacia	02 ar 16
Chiron	28 pis 50	Orcus	07 vir 18
N Node	25 leo 21	Quaoar	29 sag 38
S Node	25 aq 21	Sedna	26 tau 23

Moon Phase: Crescent
Sunrise: 04:44 BST
Sunset: 21:21
Moonrise: 06:28
Moonset: 22:24
Voc start: 19:44
Voc end: 23:06

Planetary and Angelic Hours			
Sun	04:46	Jupiter	21:18
Venus	06:09	Mars	21:55
Mercury	07:31	Sun	22:33
Moon	08:54	Venus	23:10
Saturn	10:17	Mercury	23:47
Jupiter	11:39	Moon	00:25
Mars	13:02	Saturn	01:02
Sun	14:25	Jupiter	01:40
Venus	15:47	Mars	02:17
Mercury	17:10	Sun	02:54
Moon	18:33	Venus	03:32
Saturn	19:55	Mercury	04:09

Aspects

Moon opposite Pluto
Moon sextile Venus
Mars square Jupiter
Moon square Eris
Saturn opposite Ceres
Moon sextile Sedna
Ceres sextile Eris
Moon square Uranus
Moon trine Chiron
Moon square Pallas
Venus square Vesta
Mars trine Neptune
Saturn trine Eris

Monday 26th June

Planets	00:00 am	Moon
Sun	04 can 35	01.00 am - 01 leo 09
Mercury	09 can 57	03.00 am - 02 leo 22
Venus	20 tau 14	05.00 am - 03 leo 35
Mars	14 can 14	07.00 am - 04 leo 48
Jupiter	13 lib 36	09.00 am - 06 leo 01
Saturn	23 sag 43	11.00 am - 07 leo 13
Uranus	27 ar 56	13.00 pm - 08 leo 26
Neptune	14 pis 14	15.00 pm - 09 leo 38
Pluto	18 cap 28	17.00 pm - 10 leo 50
Oob	Mercury	19.00 pm - 12 leo 02
	Mars	21.00 pm - 13 leo 13
		23.00 pm - 14 leo 25

Retrograde Planets

Saturn, Neptune, Pluto, Juno, Haumea, Quaoar

Asteroids		Dwarf Planets	
Juno	12 cap 21	Eris	23 ar 49
Vesta	20 leo 17	Haumea	22 lib 39
Pallas	29 ar 40	Makemake	01 lib 52
Ceres	23 gem 54	Salacia	02 ar 16
Chiron	28 pis 51	Orcus	07 vir 19
N Node	25 leo 17	Quaoar	29 sag 37
S Node	25 aq 17	Sedna	26 tau 24

Moon Phase: Crescent
Sunrise: 04:45 BST
Sunset: 21:21
Moonrise: 07:39
Moonset: 23:07
Voc start:
Voc end:

Planetary and Angelic Hours			
Moon	04:46	Venus	21:18
Saturn	06:09	Mercury	21:55
Jupiter	07:32	Moon	22:33
Mars	08:54	Saturn	23:10
Sun	10:17	Jupiter	23:48
Venus	11:40	Mars	00:25
Mercury	13:02	Sun	01:02
Moon	14:25	Venus	01:40
Saturn	15:47	Mercury	02:17
Jupiter	17:10	Moon	02:55
Mars	18:33	Saturn	03:32
Sun	19:55	Jupiter	04:09

Aspects

Venus square Vesta
Mars trine Neptune
Moon sextile Jupiter
Mercury opposite Juno
Saturn opposite Ceres
Saturn trine Eris
Ceres sextile Eris

Planets	**00:00 am**	**Moon**
Sun	05 can 33	01.00 am - 15 leo 36
Mercury	12 can 05	03.00 am - 16 leo 47
Venus	21 tau 18	05.00 am - 17 leo 58
Mars	14 can 43	07.00 am - 19 leo 09
Jupiter	13 lib 39	09.00 am - 20 leo 19
Saturn	23 sag 39	11.00 am - 21 leo 29
Uranus	27 ar 58	13.00 pm - 22 leo 39
Neptune	14 pis 14	15.00 pm - 23 leo 49
Pluto	18 cap 26	17.00 pm - 24 leo 59
Oob	Mercury	19.00 pm - 26 leo 09
	Mars	21.00 pm - 27 leo 18
		23.00 pm - 28 leo 27

Tuesday 27th June

Planetary Directions

Pallas into Taurus
03:31

Retrograde Planets

Saturn, Neptune, Pluto, Juno, Haumea, Quaoar

Asteroids		**Dwarf Planets**	
Juno	12 cap 07	Eris	23 ar 49
Vesta	20 leo 43	Haumea	22 lib 39
Pallas	29 ar 58	Makemake	01 lib 52
Ceres	24 gem 20	Salacia	02 ar 16
Chiron	28 pis 51	Orcus	07 vir 20
N Node	25 leo 15	Quaoar	29 sag 36
S Node	25 aq 15	Sedna	26 tau 25

Moon Phase: Crescent
Sunrise: 04:45 BST
Sunset: 21:21
Moonrise: 08:53
Moonset: 23:42
Voc start: 22:11
Voc end:

Planetary and Angelic Hours			
Mars	04:47	Saturn	21:18
Sun	06:09	Jupiter	21:55
Venus	07:32	Mars	22:33
Mercury	08:55	Sun	23:10
Moon	10:17	Venus	23:48
Saturn	11:40	Mercury	00:25
Jupiter	13:02	Moon	01:03
Mars	14:25	Saturn	01:40
Sun	15:48	Jupiter	02:18
Venus	17:10	Mars	02:55
Mercury	18:33	Sun	03:32
Moon	19:55	Venus	04:10

Aspects

Mercury opposite Juno
Moon conjunct Vesta
Moon square Venus
Moon trine Saturn
Moon trine Eris
Moon sextile Ceres
Mercury square Jupiter
Moon square Sedna
Moon trine Uranus
Moon trine Pallas
Mercury trine Neptune
Saturn trine Eris
Ceres sextile Eris

Planets	00:00 am	Moon
Sun	06 can 30	01.00 am - 29 leo 36
Mercury	14 can 11	03.00 am - 00 vir 45
Venus	22 tau 23	05.00 am - 01 vir 53
Mars	15 can 22	07.00 am - 03 vir 01
Jupiter	13 lib 42	09.00 am - 04 vir 10
Saturn	23 sag 35	11.00 am - 05 vir 18
Uranus	27 ar 59	13.00 pm - 06 vir 25
Neptune	14 pis 13	15.00 pm - 07 vir 33
Pluto	18 cap 25	17.00 pm - 08 vir 40
Oob	Mercury	19.00 pm - 09 vir 47
	Mars	21.00 pm - 10 vir 54
		23.00 pm - 12 vir 01

Wednesday 28th June

Planetary Directions

Moon into Virgo 01:42

Retrograde Planets

Saturn, Neptune, Pluto, Juno, Haumea, Quaoar

Asteroids		Dwarf Planets	
Juno	11 cap 53	Eris	23 ar 49
Vesta	21 leo 09	Haumea	22 lib 38
Pallas	00 tau 16	Makemake	01 lib 53
Ceres	24 gem 45	Salacia	02 ar 16
Chiron	28 pis 51	Orcus	07 vir 20
N Node	25 leo 15	Quaoar	29 sag 35
S Node	25 aq 15	Sedna	26 tau 25

Moon Phase: Crescent
Sunrise: 04:46 BST
Sunset: 21:21
Moonrise: 10:08
Moonset: None
Voc start:
Voc end: 01:41

Planetary and Angelic Hours			
Mercury	04:47	Sun	21:18
Moon	06:10	Venus	21:55
Saturn	07:32	Mercury	22:33
Jupiter	08:55	Moon	23:10
Mars	10:17	Saturn	23:48
Sun	11:40	Jupiter	00:25
Venus	13:03	Mars	01:03
Mercury	14:25	Sun	01:40
Moon	15:48	Venus	02:18
Saturn	17:10	Mercury	02:55
Jupiter	18:33	Moon	03:33
Mars	19:55	Saturn	04:10

Aspects

Mercury trine Neptune
Moon trine Pallas
Sun sextile Moon
Mercury conjunct Mars
Moon trine Juno
Saturn trine Eris

Planets	00:00 am	Moon
Sun	07 can 27	01:00 am - 13 vir 08
Mercury	16 can 16	03.00 am - 14 vir 14
Venus	23 tau 27	05.00 am - 15 vir 21
Mars	16 can 01	07.00 am - 16 vir 27
Jupiter	13 lib 46	09.00 am - 17 vir 33
Saturn	23 sag 31	11.00 am - 18 vir 38
Uranus	28 ar 01	13.00 pm - 19 vir 44
Neptune	14 pis 13	15.00 pm - 20 vir 49
Pluto	18 cap 24	17.00 pm - 21 vir 54
Oob	Mercury	19.00 pm - 23 vir 00
	Mars	21.00 pm - 24 vir 04
		23.00 pm - 25 vir 09

Thursday 29th June

Retrograde Planets

Saturn, Neptune, Pluto, Juno, Haumea, Quaoar

Asteroids		Dwarf Planets	
Juno	11 cap 40	Eris	23 ar 49
Vesta	21 leo 35	Haumea	22 lib 38
Pallas	00 tau 33	Makemake	01 lib 53
Ceres	25 gem 10	Salacia	02 ar 16
Chiron	28 pis 51	Orcus	07 vir 21
N Node	25 leo 16	Quaoar	29 sag 34
S Node	25 aq 16	Sedna	26 tau 26

Moon Phase: Crescent
Sunrise: 04:47 BST
Sunset: 21:21
Moonrise: 11:20
Moonset: 00:11
Voc start: 21:34
Voc end:

Planetary and Angelic Hours			
Jupiter	04:48	Moon	21:18
Mars	06:10	Saturn	21:55
Sun	07:33	Jupiter	22:33
Venus	08:55	Mars	23:10
Mercury	10:18	Sun	23:48
Moon	11:40	Venus	00:26
Saturn	13:03	Mercury	01:03
Jupiter	14:25	Moon	01:41
Mars	15:48	Saturn	02:18
Sun	17:10	Jupiter	02:56
Venus	18:33	Mars	03:33
Mercury	19:55	Sun	04:11

Aspects

Moon opp. Neptune
Moon sextile Mars
Moon sextile Mercury
Moon trine Pluto
Moon square Saturn
Moon trine Venus
Moon square Ceres
Moon trine Sedna
Mercury opposite Pluto
Saturn trine Eris

Planets	00:00 am	Moon
Sun	08 can 24	01.00 am - 26 vir 14
Mercury	18 can 19	03.00 am - 27 vir 18
Venus	24 tau 32	05.00 am - 28 vir 22
Mars	16 can 40	07.00 am - 29 vir 26
Jupiter	13 lib 49	09.00 am - 00 lib 30
Saturn	23 sag 26	11.00 am - 01 lib 34
Uranus	28 ar 03	13.00 pm - 02 lib 38
Neptune	14 pis 12	15.00 pm - 03 lib 41
Pluto	18 cap 22	17.00 pm - 04 lib 45
		19.00 pm - 05 lib 48
Oob	Mercury	21.00 pm - 06 lib 51
		23.00 pm - 07 lib 54

Friday 30th June

Planetary Directions

Moon into Libra 08:02

Retrograde Planets

Saturn, Neptune, Pluto, Juno, Haumea, Quaoar

Asteroids		Dwarf Planets	
Juno	11 cap 26	Eris	23 ar 50
Vesta	22 leo 00	Haumea	22 lib 38
Pallas	00 tau 51	Makemake	01 lib 53
Ceres	25 gem 35	Salacia	02 ar 17
Chiron	28 pis 51	Orcus	07 vir 22
N Node	25 leo 17	Quaoar	29 sag 32
S Node	25 aq 17	Sedna	26 tau 27

Moon Phase: Crescent
Sunrise: 04:47 BST
Sunset: 21:21
Moonrise: 12:29
Moonset: 00:37
Voc start:
Voc end: 08:01

Planetary and Angelic Hours			
Venus	04:48	Mars	21:18
Mercury	06:11	Sun	21:55
Moon	07:33	Venus	22:33
Saturn	08:56	Mercury	23:10
Jupiter	10:18	Moon	23:48
Mars	11:41	Saturn	00:26
Sun	13:03	Jupiter	01:03
Venus	14:25	Mars	01:41
Mercury	15:48	Sun	02:19
Moon	17:10	Venus	02:56
Saturn	18:33	Mercury	03:34
Jupiter	19:55	Moon	04:11

Aspects

Moon trine Sedna
Mercury opposite Pluto
Moon opposite Chiron
Sun square Moon
Venus conjunct Sedna
Saturn trine Vesta
Saturn trine Eris

Planets	00:00 am	Moon
Sun	09 can 21	01.00 am - 08 lib 57
Mercury	20 can 20	03.00 am - 09 lib 59
Venus	25 tau 37	05.00 am - 11 lib 02
Mars	17 can 20	07.00 am - 12 lib 04
Jupiter	13 lib 53	09.00 am - 13 lib 07
Saturn	23 sag 22	11.00 am - 14 lib 09
Uranus	28 ar 04	13.00 pm - 15 lib 11
Neptune	14 pis 12	15.00 pm - 16 lib 13
Pluto	18 cap 21	17.00 pm - 17 lib 15
		19.00 pm - 18 lib 17
Oob	Mercury	21.00 pm - 19 lib 18
		23.00 pm - 20 lib 20

Saturday 1st July

Planetary Directions

Chiron retrograde
28 pis 51 at 08:10

Retrograde Planets

Saturn, Neptune, Pluto, Juno, Haumea, Quaoar

Asteroids		Dwarf Planets	
Juno	11 cap 12	Eris	23 ar 50
Vesta	22 leo 27	Haumea	22 lib 38
Pallas	01 tau 09	Makemake	01 lib 53
Ceres	26 gem 01	Salacia	02 ar 17
Chiron	28 pis 51	Orcus	07 vir 23
N Node	25 leo 17	Quaoar	29 sag 31
S Node	25 aq 17	Sedna	26 tau 27

First Quarter: 01:51
Sunrise: 04:48 BST
Sunset: 21:21
Moonrise: 13:37
Moonset: 01:00
Voc start:
Voc end:

Planetary and Angelic Hours			
Saturn	04:49	Mercury	21:17
Jupiter	06:11	Moon	21:55
Mars	07:34	Saturn	22:33
Sun	08:56	Jupiter	23:10
Venus	10:18	Mars	23:48
Mercury	11:41	Sun	00:26
Moon	13:03	Venus	01:03
Saturn	14:25	Mercury	01:41
Jupiter	15:48	Moon	02:19
Mars	17:10	Saturn	02:57
Sun	18:33	Jupiter	03:34
Venus	19:55	Mars	04:12

Aspects

Sun square Moon
Moon square Juno
Moon conjunct Jupiter
Moon square Mars
Moon square Pluto
Venus conjunct Sedna
Sun opposite Juno
Moon square Mercury
Mars opposite Pluto
Saturn trine Vesta
Saturn trine Eris
Vesta trine Eris

Planets	**00:00 am**	**Moon**
Sun	10 can 19	01.00 am - 21 lib 21
Mercury	22 can 20	03.00 am - 22 lib 23
Venus	26 tau 42	05.00 am - 23 lib 24
Mars	17 can 59	07.00 am - 24 lib 25
Jupiter	13 lib 57	09.00 am - 25 lib 26
Saturn	23 sag 18	11.00 am - 26 lib 27
Uranus	28 ar 06	13.00 pm - 27 lib 28
Neptune	14 pis 12	15.00 pm - 28 lib 29
Pluto	18 cap 19	17:00 pm - 29 lib 30
		19.00 pm - 00 sco 30
		21.00 pm - 01 sco 31
Oob		23.00 pm - 02 sco 31

Sunday 2nd July

Planetary Directions

Moon into Scorpio
18:00
Salacia retrograde
02 ar 17 at 18:10

Retrograde Planets

Saturn, Neptune, Pluto, Juno, Chiron, Haumea, Quaoar

Asteroids		**Dwarf Planets**	
Juno	10 cap 58	Eris	23 ar 50
Vesta	22 leo 53	Haumea	22 lib 38
Pallas	01 tau 26	Makemake	01 lib 54
Ceres	26 gem 26	Salacia	02 ar 17
Chiron	28 pis 51	Orcus	07 vir 24
N Node	25 leo 17	Quaoar	29 sag 30
S Node	25 aq 17	Sedna	26 tau 28

Moon Phase: Gibbous
Sunrise: 04:49 BST
Sunset: 21:20
Moonrise: 14:43
Moonset: 01:23
Voc start: 14:16
Voc end: 17:59

Planetary and Angelic Hours

Sun	04:50	Jupiter	21:17
Venus	06:12	Mars	21:55
Mercury	07:34	Sun	22:33
Moon	08:57	Venus	23:10
Saturn	10:19	Mercury	23:48
Jupiter	11:41	Moon	00:26
Mars	13:03	Saturn	01:04
Sun	14:26	Jupiter	01:41
Venus	15:48	Mars	02:19
Mercury	17:10	Sun	02:57
Moon	18:32	Venus	03:35
Saturn	19:55	Mercury	04:13

Aspects

Moon square Mercury
Moon sextile Vesta
Moon sextile Saturn
Moon opposite Eris
Moon trine Ceres
Mars opposite Pluto
Sun opposite Juno
Moon opposite Uranus
Mercury square Eris
Saturn trine Vesta
Moon opposite Pallas
Saturn trine Eris
Vesta trine Eris

Planets	00:00 am	Moon
Sun	11 can 16	01.00 am - 03 sco 32
Mercury	24 can 17	03.00 am - 04 sco 32
Venus	27 tau 48	05.00 am - 05 sco 32
Mars	18 can 38	07.00 am - 06 sco 33
Jupiter	14 lib 01	09.00 am - 07 sco 33
Saturn	23 sag 14	11.00 am - 08 sco 33
Uranus	28 ar 07	13.00 pm - 09 sco 33
Neptune	14 pis 11	15.00 pm - 10 sco 33
Pluto	18 cap 18	17.00 pm - 11 sco 33
		19.00 pm - 12 sco 33
Oob		21.00 pm - 13 sco 33
		23.00 pm - 14 sco 33

Monday 3rd July

Retrograde Planets

Saturn, Neptune, Pluto, Juno, Chiron, Haumea, Salacia, Quaoar

Asteroids		Dwarf Planets	
Juno	10 cap 44	Eris	23 ar 50
Vesta	23 leo 19	Haumea	22 lib 38
Pallas	01 tau 43	Makemake	01 lib 54
Ceres	26 gem 51	Salacia	02 ar 17
Chiron	28 pis 51	Orcus	07 vir 25
N Node	25 leo 14	Quaoar	29 sag 29
S Node	25 aq 14	Sedna	26 tau 28

Moon Phase: Gibbous
Sunrise: 04:49 BST
Sunset: 21:19
Moonrise: 15:46
Moonset: 01:46
Voc start:
Voc end:

Planetary and Angelic Hours			
Moon	04:50	Venus	21:17
Saturn	06:13	Mercury	21:54
Jupiter	07:35	Moon	22:32
Mars	08:57	Saturn	23:10
Sun	10:19	Jupiter	23:48
Venus	11:41	Mars	00:26
Mercury	13:03	Sun	01:04
Moon	14:26	Venus	01:42
Saturn	15:48	Mercury	02:20
Jupiter	17:10	Moon	02:58
Mars	18:32	Saturn	03:35
Sun	19:54	Jupiter	04:13

Aspects

Moon sextile Juno
Sun trine Moon
Moon trine Neptune
Venus sextile Chiron
Mercury sextile Sedna
Saturn trine Vesta
Saturn trine Eris
Uranus sextile Ceres
Vesta trine Eris

Planets	00:00 am	Moon
Sun	12 can 13	01.00 am - 15 sco 32
Mercury	26 can 13	03.00 am - 16 sco 32
Venus	28 tau 53	05.00 am - 17 sco 32
Mars	19 can 17	07.00 am - 18 sco 32
Jupiter	14 lib 05	09.00 am - 19 sco 31
Saturn	23 sag 10	11.00 am - 20 sco 31
Uranus	28 ar 09	13.00 pm - 21 sco 30
Neptune	14 pis 10	15.00 pm - 22 sco 30
Pluto	18 cap 16	17.00 pm - 23 sco 29
		19.00 pm - 24 sco 29
Oob		21.00 pm - 25 sco 28
		23.00 pm - 26 sco 28

Tuesday 4th July

Retrograde Planets

Saturn, Neptune, Pluto, Juno, Chiron, Haumea, Salacia, Quaoar

Asteroids		Dwarf Planets	
Juno	10 cap 30	Eris	23 ar 50
Vesta	23 leo 45	Haumea	22 lib 38
Pallas	02 tau 01	Makemake	01 lib 55
Ceres	27 gem 16	Salacia	02 ar 17
Chiron	28 pis 51	Orcus	07 vir 25
N Node	25 leo 10	Quaoar	29 sag 28
S Node	25 aq 10	Sedna	26 tau 29

Moon Phase: Gibbous
Sunrise: 04:50 BST
Sunset: 21:19
Moonrise: 16:49
Moonset: 02:11
Voc start:
Voc end:

Planetary and Angelic Hours			
Mars	04:51	Saturn	21:16
Sun	06:13	Jupiter	21:54
Venus	07:35	Mars	22:32
Mercury	08:57	Sun	23:10
Moon	10:19	Venus	23:48
Saturn	11:42	Mercury	00:26
Jupiter	13:04	Moon	01:04
Mars	14:26	Saturn	01:42
Sun	15:48	Jupiter	02:20
Venus	17:10	Mars	02:58
Mercury	18:32	Sun	03:36
Moon	19:54	Venus	04:14

Aspects

Mercury sextile Sedna
Vesta trine Eris
Moon sextile Pluto
Moon trine Mars
Moon square Vesta
Moon opposite Sedna
Sun square Jupiter
Sun trine Neptune
Moon trine Mercury
Mercury square Uranus
Mercury trine Chiron
Saturn trine Eris
Uranus sextile Ceres

Planets	00:00 am	Moon
Sun	13 can 10	01.00 am - 27 sco 27
Mercury	28 can 06	03.00 am - 28 sco 27
Venus	29 tau 59	05.00 am - 29 sco 26
Mars	19 can 56	07.00 am - 00 sag 25
Jupiter	14 lib 09	09.00 am - 01 sag 25
Saturn	23 sag 06	11.00 am - 02 sag 24
Uranus	28 ar 10	13.00 pm - 03 sag 23
Neptune	14 pis 10	15.00 pm - 04 sag 23
Pluto	18 cap 15	17.00 pm - 05 sag 22
		19.00 pm - 06 sag 21
Oob		21.00 pm - 07 sag 21
		23.00 pm - 08 sag 20

Wednesday 5th July

Planetary Directions

Venus into Gemini 01:12
Moon into Sag 06:08

Retrograde Planets

Saturn, Neptune, Pluto, Juno, Chiron, Haumea, Salacia, Quaoar

Asteroids		Dwarf Planets	
Juno	10 cap 16	Eris	23 ar 50
Vesta	24 leo 11	Haumea	22 lib 38
Pallas	02 tau 18	Makemake	01 lib 55
Ceres	27 gem 41	Salacia	02 ar 17
Chiron	28 pis 51	Orcus	07 vir 25
N Node	25 leo 04	Quaoar	29 sag 28
S Node	25 aq 04	Sedna	26 tau 29

Moon Phase: Gibbous
Sunrise: 04:51 BST
Sunset: 21:18
Moonrise: 17:50
Moonset: 02:39
Voc start: 02:34
Voc end: 06:07

Planetary and Angelic Hours			
Mercury	04:52	Sun	21:16
Moon	06:14	Venus	21:54
Saturn	07:36	Mercury	22:32
Jupiter	08:58	Moon	23:10
Mars	10:20	Saturn	23:48
Sun	11:42	Jupiter	00:26
Venus	13:04	Mars	01:04
Mercury	14:26	Sun	01:42
Moon	15:48	Venus	02:20
Saturn	17:10	Mercury	02:59
Jupiter	18:32	Moon	03:37
Mars	19:54	Saturn	04:15

Aspects

Mercury square Uranus
Moon trine Mercury
Moon trine Chiron
Moon opposite Venus
Mercury trine Chiron
Sun square Jupiter
Sun trine Neptune
Saturn trine Eris
Uranus sextile Ceres
Chiron square Ceres
Vesta trine Eris

Planets	00:00 am	Moon
Sun	14 can 17	01.00 am - 09 sag 19
Mercury	29 can 58	03.00 am - 10 sag 19
Venus	01 gem 05	05.00 am - 11 sag 18
Mars	20 can 35	07.00 am - 12 sag 17
Jupiter	14 lib 13	09.00 am - 13 sag 17
Saturn	23 sag 02	11.00 am - 14 sag 16
Uranus	28 ar 12	13.00 pm - 15 sag 15
Neptune	14 pis 09	15.00 pm - 16 sag 15
Pluto	18 cap 13	17.00 pm - 17 sag 14
		19.00 pm - 18 sag 13
Oob		21.00 pm - 19 sag 13
		23.00 pm - 20 sag 12

Thursday 6th July

Planetary Directions

Mercury into Leo at 01:20

Retrograde Planets

Saturn, Neptune, Pluto, Juno, Chiron, Haumea, Salacia, Quaoar

Asteroids		Dwarf Planets	
Juno	10 cap 02	Eris	23 ar 51
Vesta	24 leo 38	Haumea	22 lib 38
Pallas	02 tau 35	Makemake	01 lib 55
Ceres	28 gem 07	Salacia	02 ar 16
Chiron	28 pis 51	Orcus	07 vir 27
N Node	24 leo 57	Quaoar	29 sag 26
S Node	24 aq 57	Sedna	26 tau 30

Moon Phase: Gibbous
Sunrise: 04:52 BST
Sunset: 21:18
Moonrise: 18:48
Moonset: 03:10
Voc start:
Voc end:

Planetary and Angelic Hours			
Jupiter	04:53	Moon	21:15
Mars	06:15	Saturn	21:53
Sun	07:37	Jupiter	22:32
Venus	08:58	Mars	23:10
Mercury	10:20	Sun	23:48
Moon	11:42	Venus	00:26
Saturn	13:04	Mercury	01:04
Jupiter	14:26	Moon	01:43
Mars	15:48	Saturn	02:21
Sun	17:10	Jupiter	02:59
Venus	18:31	Mars	03:37
Mercury	19:53	Sun	04:15

Aspects

Sun trine Neptune
Sun square Jupiter
Uranus sextile Ceres
Moon square Neptune
Moon sextile Jupiter
Mercury sextile Venus
Saturn trine Eris
Chiron square Ceres

Planets	00:00 am	Moon
Sun	15 can 05	01.00 am - 21 sag 12
Mercury	01 leo 48	03.00 am - 22 sag 11
Venus	02 gem 11	05.00 am - 23 sag 10
Mars	22 can 14	07.00 am - 24 sag 10
Jupiter	14 lib 18	09.00 am - 25 sag 09
Saturn	22 sag 58	11.00 am - 26 sag 09
Uranus	28 ar 13	13.00 pm - 27 sag 08
Neptune	14 pis 09	15.00 pm - 28 sag 08
Pluto	18 cap 22	17.00 pm - 29 cap 08
		19.00 pm - 00 cap 07
Oob		21.00 pm - 01 cap 07
		23.00 pm - 02 cap 06

Friday 7th July

Planetary Directions

Haumea direct
22 lib 37 at 05:36
Moon into Cap 18:45

Retrograde Planets

Saturn, Neptune, Pluto, Juno, Chiron, Haumea, Salacia, Quaoar

Asteroids		Dwarf Planets	
Juno	09 cap 48	Eris	23 ar 51
Vesta	25 leo 04	Haumea	22 lib 37
Pallas	02 tau 52	Makemake	01 lib 56
Ceres	28 gem 32	Salacia	02 ar 16
Chiron	28 pis 51	Orcus	07 vir 28
N Node	24 leo 50	Quaoar	29 sag 24
S Node	24 aq 50	Sedna	26 tau 31

Moon Phase: Gibbous
Sunrise: 04:53 BST
Sunset: 21:17
Moonrise: 19:42
Moonset: 03:47
Voc start: 15:11
Voc end: 18:44

Planetary and Angelic Hours			
Venus	04:54	Mars	21:15
Mercury	06:15	Sun	21:53
Moon	07:37	Venus	22:31
Saturn	08:59	Mercury	23:10
Jupiter	10:21	Moon	23:48
Mars	11:42	Saturn	00:26
Sun	13:04	Jupiter	01:05
Venus	14:26	Mars	01:43
Mercury	15:48	Sun	02:21
Moon	17:09	Venus	03:00
Saturn	18:31	Mercury	03:38
Jupiter	19:53	Moon	04:16

Aspects

Moon conjunct Saturn
Moon trine Eris
Moon trine Vesta
Mercury sextile Venus
Moon trine Uranus
Moon opposite Ceres
Moon square Chiron
Mercury square Pallas
Chiron square Ceres
Moon trine Pallas
Saturn trine Eris
Uranus sextile Ceres

Planets	00:00 am	Moon
Sun	16 can 02	01.00 am - 03 cap 06
Mercury	03 leo 35	03.00 am - 04 cap 06
Venus	03 gem 17	05.00 am - 05 cap 06
Mars	21 can 53	07.00 am - 06 cap 05
Jupiter	14 lib 23	09.00 am - 07 Cao 05
Saturn	22 sag 54	11.00 am - 08 cap 05
Uranus	28 ar 14	13.00 pm - 09 cap 05
Neptune	14 pis 08	15.00 pm - 10 cap 05
Pluto	18 cap 10	17.00 pm - 11 cap 05
		19.00 pm - 12 cap 05
Oob		21.00 pm - 13 cap 05
		23.00 pm - 14 cap 05

Saturday 8th July

Retrograde Planets

Saturn, Neptune, Pluto, Juno, Chiron, Salacia, Quaoar

Asteroids		Dwarf Planets	
Juno	09 cap 34	Eris	23 ar 51
Vesta	25 leo 31	Haumea	22 lib 38
Pallas	03 tau 09	Makemake	01 lib 56
Ceres	28 gem 57	Salacia	02 ar 16
Chiron	28 pis 50	Orcus	07 vir 29
N Node	24 leo 43	Quaoar	29 sag 23
S Node	24 aq 43	Sedna	26 tau 31

Moon Phase: Gibbous
Sunrise: 04:53 BST
Sunset: 21:17
Moonrise: 20:32
Moonset: 04:30
Voc start:
Voc end:

Planetary and Angelic Hours			
Saturn	04:55	Mercury	21:14
Jupiter	06:16	Moon	21:52
Mars	07:38	Saturn	22:31
Sun	08:59	Jupiter	23:09
Venus	10:21	Mars	23:48
Mercury	11:43	Sun	00:26
Moon	13:04	Venus	01:05
Saturn	14:26	Mercury	01:43
Jupiter	15:48	Moon	02:22
Mars	17:09	Saturn	03:00
Sun	18:31	Jupiter	03:39
Venus	19:52	Mars	04:17

Aspects

Moon trine Pallas
Moon conjunct Juno
Moon sextile Neptune
Moon square Jupiter
Mercury sextile Venus
Chiron square Ceres
Vesta square Sedna

Planets	00:00 am	Moon
Sun	16 can 59	01.00 am - 15 cap 05
Mercury	05 leo 21	03.00 am - 16 cap 05
Venus	04 gem 23	05.00 am - 17 cap 06
Mars	22 can 32	07.00 am - 18 cap 06
Jupiter	14 lib 28	09.00 am - 19 cap 06
Saturn	22 sag 50	11.00 am - 20 cap 06
Uranus	28 ar 16	13.00 pm - 21 cap 07
Neptune	14 pis 07	15.00 pm - 22 cap 07
Pluto	18 cap 09	17.00 pm - 23 cap 08
		19.00 pm - 24 cap 08
Oob		21.00 pm - 25 cap 09
		23.00 pm - 26 cap 09

Sunday 9th July

Retrograde Planets

Saturn, Neptune, Pluto, Juno, Chiron, Salacia, Quaoar

Asteroids		Dwarf Planets	
Juno	09 cap 20	Eris	23 ar 51
Vesta	25 leo 58	Haumea	22 lib 38
Pallas	03 tau 25	Makemake	01 lib 57
Ceres	29 gem 22	Salacia	02 ar 16
Chiron	28 pis 50	Orcus	07 vir 30
N Node	24 leo 37	Quaoar	29 sag 22
S Node	24 aq 37	Sedna	26 tau 32

Full Moon: 05:08
Sunrise: 04:54 BST
Sunset: 21:16
Moonrise: 21:16
Moonset: 05:20
Voc start:
Voc end:

Planetary and Angelic Hours			
Sun	04:56	Jupiter	21:13
Venus	06:17	Mars	21:52
Mercury	07:38	Sun	22:31
Moon	09:00	Venus	23:09
Saturn	10:21	Mercury	23:48
Jupiter	11:43	Moon	00:26
Mars	13:04	Saturn	01:05
Sun	14:26	Jupiter	01:44
Venus	15:47	Mars	02:22
Mercury	17:09	Sun	03:01
Moon	18:30	Venus	03:39
Saturn	19:52	Mercury	04:18

Aspects

Sun opposite Moon
Moon conjunct Pluto
Moon opposite Mars
Moon square Eris
Moon trine Sedna
Sun opposite Pluto
Mars square Eris
Chiron square Ceres
Vesta square Sedna

Planets	00:00 am	Moon
Sun	17 can 56	01.00 am - 27 cap 10
Mercury	07 leo 04	03.00 am - 28 cap 11
Venus	05 gem 30	05.00 am - 29 cap 11
Mars	23 can 11	07.00 am - 00 aq 12
Jupiter	14 lib 33	09.00 am - 01 aq 13
Saturn	22 sag 46	11.00 am - 02 aq 14
Uranus	28 ar 17	13.00 pm - 03 aq 15
Neptune	14 pis 07	15.00 pm - 04 aq 16
Pluto	18 cap 07	17.00 pm - 05 aq 17
		19.00 pm - 06 aq 18
Oob		21.00 pm - 07 aq 20
		23.00 pm - 08 aq 21

Monday 10th July

Planetary Directions

Moon into Aquarius
06:35
Ceres into Cancer
12:45

Retrograde Planets

Saturn, Neptune, Pluto, Juno, Chiron, Salacia, Quaoar

Asteroids		Dwarf Planets	
Juno	09 cap 06	Eris	23 ar 51
Vesta	26 leo 24	Haumea	22 lib 38
Pallas	03 tau 42	Makemake	01 lib 57
Ceres	29 gem 47	Salacia	02 ar 16
Chiron	28 pis 49	Orcus	07 vir 31
N Node	24 leo 32	Quaoar	29 sag 21
S Node	24 aq 32	Sedna	26 tau 32

Phase: Disseminating
Sunrise: 04:55 BST
Sunset: 21:15
Moonrise: 21:54
Moonset: 06:16
Voc start: 03:12
Voc end: 06:34

Planetary and Angelic Hours

Moon	04:56	Venus	21:13
Saturn	06:18	Mercury	21:51
Jupiter	07:39	Moon	22:30
Mars	09:01	Saturn	23:09
Sun	10:22	Jupiter	23:48
Venus	11:43	Mars	00:26
Mercury	13:05	Sun	01:05
Moon	14:26	Venus	01:44
Saturn	15:47	Mercury	02:23
Jupiter	17:09	Moon	03:01
Mars	18:30	Saturn	03:40
Sun	19:51	Jupiter	04:19

Aspects

Moon square Uranus
Moon sextile Chiron
Sun opposite Pluto
Vesta square Sedna
Moon square Pallas
Moon trine Venus
Moon opp. Mercury
Mars square Eris

Planets	00:00 am	Moon
Sun	18 can 53	01.00 am - 09 aq 22
Mercury	08 leo 46	03.00 am - 10 aq 24
Venus	06 gem 36	05.00 am - 11 aq 25
Mars	23 can 50	07.00 am - 12 aq 27
Jupiter	14 lib 38	09.00 am - 13 aq 28
Saturn	22 sag 43	11.00 am - 14 aq 30
Uranus	28 ar 18	13.00 pm - 15 aq 32
Neptune	14 pis 06	15.00 pm - 16 aq 34
Pluto	18 cap 06	17.00 pm - 17 aq 35
		19.00 pm - 18 aq 37
Oob		21.00 pm - 19 aq 39
		23.00 pm - 20 aq 42

Tuesday 11th July

Retrograde Planets

Saturn, Neptune, Pluto, Juno, Chiron, Salacia, Quaoar

Asteroids		Dwarf Planets	
Juno	08 cap 52	Eris	23 ar 51
Vesta	26 leo 51	Haumea	22 lib 38
Pallas	03 tau 58	Makemake	01 lib 58
Ceres	00 can 12	Salacia	02 ar 16
Chiron	28 pis 49	Orcus	07 vir 32
N Node	24 leo 29	Quaoar	29 sag 20
S Node	24 aq 29	Sedna	26 tau 33

Phase: Disseminating
Sunrise: 04:56 BST
Sunset: 21:14
Moonrise: 22:26
Moonset: 07:17
Voc start:
Voc end:

Planetary and Angelic Hours			
Mars	04:58	Saturn	21:12
Sun	06:19	Jupiter	21:51
Venus	07:40	Mars	22:30
Mercury	09:01	Sun	23:09
Moon	10:22	Venus	23:47
Saturn	11:43	Mercury	00:26
Jupiter	13:05	Moon	01:05
Mars	14:26	Saturn	01:44
Sun	15:47	Jupiter	02:23
Venus	17:08	Mars	03:02
Mercury	18:29	Sun	03:41
Moon	19:51	Venus	04:20

Aspects

Mars square Eris
Moon trine Jupiter
Moon sextile Saturn
Vesta square Sedna

Planets	**00:00 am**	**Moon**
		01.00 am - 21 aq 44
Sun	19 can 51	03.00 am - 22 aq 46
Mercury	10 leo 25	05.00 am - 23 aq 48
Venus	07 gem 43	07.00 am - 24 aq 51
Mars	24 can 29	09.00 am - 25 aq 53
Jupiter	14 lib 43	11.00 am - 26 aq 56
Saturn	22 sag 39	13.00 pm - 27 aq 58
Uranus	28 ar 19	15.00 pm - 29 aq 01
Neptune	14 pis 05	17.00 pm - 00 pis 04
Pluto	18 cap 04	19.00 pm - 01 pis 07
		21.00 pm - 02 pis 10
Oob		23.00 pm - 03 pis 13

Wednesday 12th July

Planetary Directions

Moon into Pisces 16:52

Retrograde Planets

Saturn, Neptune, Pluto, Juno, Chiron, Salacia, Quaoar

Asteroids		**Dwarf Planets**	
Juno	08 cap 39	Eris	23 ar 51
Vesta	27 leo 18	Haumea	22 lib 38
Pallas	04 tau 15	Makemake	01 lib 58
Ceres	00 can 37	Salacia	02 ar 16
Chiron	28 pis 48	Orcus	07 vir 33
N Node	24 leo 28	Quaoar	29 sag 19
S Node	24 aq 28	Sedna	26 tau 33

Phase: Disseminating
Sunrise: 04:58 BST
Sunset: 21:13
Moonrise: 22:55
Moonset: 08:22
Voc start: 13:40
Voc end: 16:51

Planetary and Angelic Hours			
Mercury	04:59	Sun	21:11
Moon	06:20	Venus	21:50
Saturn	07:41	Mercury	22:29
Jupiter	09:02	Moon	23:08
Mars	10:23	Saturn	23:47
Sun	11:44	Jupiter	00:26
Venus	13:05	Mars	01:05
Mercury	14:26	Sun	01:44
Moon	15:47	Venus	02:23
Saturn	17:08	Mercury	03:02
Jupiter	18:29	Moon	03:42
Mars	19:50	Saturn	04:21

Aspects

Moon sextile Saturn
Moon sextile Eris
Moon square Sedna
Moon opposite Vesta
Moon sextile Uranus
Moon trine Ceres
Moon sextile Pallas
Uranus trine Vesta

Planets	**00:00 am**	**Moon**
Sun	20 can 48	01.00 am - 04 pis 16
Mercury	12 leo 03	03.00 am - 05 pis 20
Venus	08 gem 50	05.00 am - 06 pis 23
Mars	25 can 08	07.00 am - 07 pis 26
Jupiter	14 lib 49	09.00 am - 08 pis 30
Saturn	22 sag 35	11.00 am - 09 pis 34
Uranus	28 ar 20	13.00 pm - 10 pis 37
Neptune	14 pis 04	15.00 pm - 11 pis 41
Pluto	18 cap 30	17.00 pm - 12 pis 45
		19.00 pm - 13 pis 49
Oob		21.00 pm - 14 pis 53
		23.00 pm - 15 pis 58

Thursday 13th July

Retrograde Planets

Saturn, Neptune, Pluto, Juno, Chiron, Salacia, Quaoar

Asteroids		**Dwarf Planets**	
Juno	08 cap 25	Eris	23 ar 51
Vesta	27 leo 45	Haumea	22 lib 38
Pallas	04 tau 31	Makemake	01 lib 59
Ceres	01 can 03	Salacia	02 ar 15
Chiron	28 pis 48	Orcus	07 vir 34
N Node	24 leo 29	Quaoar	29 sag 18
S Node	24 aq 29	Sedna	26 tau 34

Phase: Disseminating
Sunrise: 04:59 BST
Sunset: 21:13
Moonrise: 23:21
Moonset: 09:29
Voc start:
Voc end:

Planetary and Angelic Hours			
Jupiter	05:00	Moon	21:10
Mars	06:21	Saturn	21:49
Sun	07:41	Jupiter	22:29
Venus	09:02	Mars	23:08
Mercury	10:23	Sun	23:47
Moon	11:44	Venus	00:26
Saturn	13:05	Mercury	01:05
Jupiter	14:26	Moon	01:45
Mars	15:47	Saturn	02:24
Sun	17:0	Jupiter	03:03
Venus	18:28	Mars	03:42
Mercury	19:49	Sun	04:22

Aspects

Moon sextile Pallas
Moon sextile Juno
Moon square Venus
Moon conj. Neptune
Moon sextile Pluto
Mars sextile Sedna
Uranus trine Vesta

Planets	**00:00 am**	**Moon**
Sun	21 can 45	01.00 am - 17 pis 02
Mercury	13 leo 38	03.00 am - 18 pis 07
Venus	09 gem 57	05.00 am - 19 pis 11
Mars	25 can 47	07.00 am - 20 pis 16
Jupiter	14 lib 54	09.00 am - 21 pis 21
Saturn	22 sag 32	11.00 am - 22 pis 26
Uranus	28 ar 21	13.00 pm - 23 pis 31
Neptune	14 pis 03	15.00 pm - 24 pis 36
Pluto	18 cap 02	17.00 pm - 25 pis 41
		19.00 pm - 26 pis 47
Oob		21.00 pm - 27 pis 52
		23.00 pm - 28 pis 58

Friday 14th July

Retrograde Planets

Saturn, Neptune, Pluto, Juno, Chiron, Salacia, Quaoar

Asteroids		**Dwarf Planets**	
Juno	08 cap 12	Eris	23 ar 51
Vesta	28 leo 12	Haumea	22 lib 38
Pallas	04 tau 47	Makemake	01 lib 59
Ceres	01 can 28	Salacia	02 ar 15
Chiron	28 pis 47	Orcus	07 vir 35
N Node	24 leo 30	Quaoar	29 sag 17
S Node	24 aq 30	Sedna	26 tau 34

Phase: Disseminating
Sunrise: 05:00 BST
Sunset: 21:12
Moonrise: 23:46
Moonset: 10:39
Voc start: 18:00
Voc end:

Planetary and Angelic Hours

Venus	05:01	Mars	21:09
Mercury	06:21	Sun	21:49
Moon	07:42	Venus	22:28
Saturn	09:03	Mercury	23:07
Jupiter	10:24	Moon	23:47
Mars	11:44	Saturn	00:26
Sun	13:05	Jupiter	01:06
Venus	14:26	Mars	01:45
Mercury	15:46	Sun	02:24
Moon	17:07	Venus	03:04
Saturn	18:28	Mercury	03:43
Jupiter	19:49	Moon	04:22

Aspects

Moon sextile Pluto
Uranus trine Vesta
Sun trine Moon
Moon square Saturn
Moon trine Mars
Moon sextile Sedna
Mercury sextile Jupiter
Moon conjunct Chiron
Mars sextile Sedna

Planets	00:00 am	Moon
Sun	22 can 42	01.00 am - 00 ar 04
Mercury	15 leo 12	03.00 am - 01 ar 10
Venus	11 gem 04	05.00 am - 02 ar 16
Mars	26 can 26	07.00 am - 03 ar 22
Jupiter	15 lib 00	09.00 am - 04 ar 28
Saturn	22 sag 28	11.00 am - 05 ar 35
Uranus	28 ar 22	13.00 pm - 06 ar 41
Neptune	14 pis 03	15.00 pm - 07 ar 48
Pluto	18 cap 00	17.00 pm - 08 ar 55
		19.00 pm - 10 ar 02
Oob		21.00 pm - 11 ar 09
		23.00 pm - 12 ar 16

Saturday 15th July

Planetary Directions

Moon into Aries 00:53

Retrograde Planets

Saturn, Neptune, Pluto, Juno, Chiron, Salacia, Quaoar

Asteroids		Dwarf Planets	
Juno	07 cap 58	Eris	23 ar 52
Vesta	28 leo 39	Haumea	22 lib 38
Pallas	05 tau 03	Makemake	02 lib 00
Ceres	01 can 53	Salacia	02 ar 15
Chiron	28 pis 47	Orcus	07 vir 36
N Node	24 leo 31	Quaoar	29 sag 16
S Node	24 aq 31	Sedna	26 tau 35

Phase: Disseminating
Sunrise: 05:01 BST
Sunset: 21:11
Moonrise: None
Moonset: 11:49
Voc start:
Voc end: 00:52

Planetary and Angelic Hours			
Saturn	05:02	Mercury	21:08
Jupiter	06:22	Moon	21:48
Mars	07:43	Saturn	22:27
Sun	09:03	Jupiter	23:07
Venus	10:24	Mars	23:47
Mercury	11:45	Sun	00:26
Moon	13:05	Venus	01:06
Saturn	14:26	Mercury	01:45
Jupiter	15:46	Moon	02:25
Mars	17:07	Saturn	03:04
Sun	18:27	Jupiter	03:44
Venus	19:48	Mars	04:23

Aspects

Moon square Ceres
Mars sextile Sedna
Moon square Juno
Moon sextile Venus
Sun square Eris
Uranus trine Vesta

Planets	00:00 am	Moon
Sun	23 can 39	01.00 am - 13 ar 24
Mercury	16 leo 43	03.00 am - 14 ar 31
Venus	12 gem 12	05.00 am - 15 ar 39
Mars	27 can 04	07.00 am - 16 ar 47
Jupiter	15 lib 06	09.00 am - 17 ar 55
Saturn	22 sag 25	11.00 am - 19 ar 03
Uranus	28 ar 23	13.00 pm - 20 ar 11
Neptune	14 pis 02	15.00 pm - 21 ar 19
Pluto	17 cap 59	17.00 pm - 22 ar 28
		19.00 pm - 23 ar 37
Oob		21.00 pm - 24 ar 46
		23.00 pm - 25 ar 54

Sunday 16th July

Retrograde Planets

Saturn, Neptune, Pluto, Juno, Chiron, Salacia, Quaoar

Asteroids		Dwarf Planets	
Juno	07 cap 45	Eris	23 ar 52
Vesta	29 leo 06	Haumea	22 lib 38
Pallas	05 tau 19	Makemake	02 lib 01
Ceres	02 can 18	Salacia	02 ar 15
Chiron	28 pis 46	Orcus	07 vir 37
N Node	24 leo 33	Quaoar	29 sag 15
S Node	24 aq 33	Sedna	26 tau 35

Last Quarter: 20:27
Sunrise: 05:02 BST
Sunset: 21:10
Moonrise: 00:11
Moonset: 13:02
Voc start:
Voc end:

Planetary and Angelic Hours			
Sun	05:03	Jupiter	21:07
Venus	06:23	Mars	21:47
Mercury	07:44	Sun	22:27
Moon	09:04	Venus	23:07
Saturn	10:24	Mercury	23:46
Jupiter	11:45	Moon	00:26
Mars	13:05	Saturn	01:06
Sun	14:26	Jupiter	01:46
Venus	15:46	Mars	02:25
Mercury	17:06	Sun	03:05
Moon	18:27	Venus	03:45
Saturn	19:47	Mercury	04:24

Aspects

Moon opposite Jupiter
Sun square Eris
Moon trine Mercury
Moon square Pluto
Moon trine Saturn
Moon conjunct Eris
Sun square Moon
Moon square Mars
Venus square Neptune
Mars square Uranus

Planets	00:00 am	Moon
Sun	24 can 37	01.00 am - 27 ar 04
Mercury	18 leo 13	03.00 am - 28 ar 13
Venus	13 gem 19	05.00 am - 29 ar 22
Mars	27 can 43	07.00 am - 00 tau 32
Jupiter	15 lib 12	09.00 am - 01 tau 42
Saturn	22 sag 21	11.00 am - 02 tau 51
Uranus	28 ar 24	13.00 pm - 04 tau 01
Neptune	14 pis 01	15.00 pm - 05 tau 12
Pluto	17 cap 57	17.00 pm - 06 tau 22
		19.00 pm - 07 tau 32
Oob		21.00 pm - 08 tau 43
		23.00 pm - 09 tau 54

Monday 17th July

Planetary Directions

Moon into Taurus
06:05

Retrograde Planets

Saturn, Neptune, Pluto, Juno, Chiron, Salacia, Quaoar

Asteroids		Dwarf Planets	
Juno	07 cap 32	Eris	23 ar 52
Vesta	29 leo 33	Haumea	22 lib 39
Pallas	05 tau 34	Makemake	02 lib 01
Ceres	02 can 43	Salacia	02 ar 14
Chiron	28 pis 45	Orcus	07 vir 38
N Node	24 leo 33	Quaoar	29 sag 14
S Node	24 aq 33	Sedna	26 tau 36

Moon Phase: Balsamic
Sunrise: 05:03 BST
Sunset: 21:09
Moonrise: 00:36
Moonset: 14:17
Voc start: 03:18
Voc end: 06:04

Planetary and Angelic Hours			
Moon	05:04	Venus	21:06
Saturn	06:24	Mercury	21:46
Jupiter	07:45	Moon	22:26
Mars	09:05	Saturn	23:06
Sun	10:25	Jupiter	23:46
Venus	11:45	Mars	00:26
Mercury	13:05	Sun	01:06
Moon	14:25	Venus	01:46
Saturn	15:46	Mercury	02:26
Jupiter	17:06	Moon	03:06
Mars	18:26	Saturn	03:46
Sun	19:46	Jupiter	04:26

Aspects

Moon square Mars
Moon conjunct Uranus
Moon trine Vesta
Moon sextile Ceres
Venus square Neptune
Moon conjunct Pallas
Moon trine Juno
Venus trine Jupiter
Mars square Uranus
Mars trine Chiron

Planets	00:00 am	Moon
Sun	25 can 34	01.00 am - 11 tau 05
Mercury	19 leo 40	03.00 am - 12 tau 16
Venus	14 gem 27	05.00 am - 13 tau 27
Mars	28 can 22	07.00 am - 14 tau 38
Jupiter	15 lib 18	09.00 am - 15 tau 49
Saturn	22 sag 18	11.00 am - 17 tau 01
Uranus	28 ar 25	13.00 pm - 18 tau 13
Neptune	14 pis 00	15.00 pm - 19 tau 25
Pluto	17 cap 56	17.00 pm - 20 tau 37
		19.00 pm - 21 tau 49
Oob		21.00 pm - 23 tau 01
		23.00 pm - 24 tau 13

Tuesday 18th July

Planetary Directions

Vesta into Virgo 00:13

Retrograde Planets

Saturn, Neptune, Pluto, Juno, Chiron, Salacia, Quaoar

Asteroids		Dwarf Planets	
Juno	07 cap 19	Eris	23 ar 52
Vesta	00 vir 00	Haumea	22 lib 39
Pallas	05 tau 50	Makemake	02 lib 02
Ceres	03 can 08	Salacia	02 ar 14
Chiron	28 pis 44	Orcus	07 vir 39
N Node	24 leo 32	Quaoar	29 sag 13
S Node	24 aq 32	Sedna	26 tau 36

Moon Phase: Balsamic
Sunrise: 05:05 BST
Sunset: 21:07
Moonrise: 01:05
Moonset: 15:33
Voc start:
Voc end:

Planetary and Angelic Hours			
Mars	05:05	Saturn	21:05
Sun	06:25	Jupiter	21:45
Venus	07:45	Mars	22:26
Mercury	09:05	Sun	23:06
Moon	10:25	Venus	23:46
Saturn	11:45	Mercury	00:26
Jupiter	13:05	Moon	01:06
Mars	14:25	Saturn	01:46
Sun	15:45	Jupiter	02:26
Venus	17:05	Mars	03:06
Mercury	18:25	Sun	03:46
Moon	19:45	Venus	04:27

Aspects

Mars square Uranus
Moon sextile Neptune
Moon trine Pluto
Mars trine Chiron
Moon square Mercury
Venus trine Jupiter
Sun sextile Sedna

Planets	**00:00 am**	**Moon**
Sun	26 can 31	01.00 am - 25 tau 26
Mercury	21 leo 05	03.00 am - 26 tau 38
Venus	15 gem 35	05.00 am - 27 tau 51
Mars	29 can 01	07.00 am - 29 tau 04
Jupiter	15 lib 25	09.00 am - 00 gem 17
Saturn	22 sag 15	11.00 am - 01 gem 30
Uranus	28 ar 25	13.00 pm - 02 gem 43
Neptune	13 pis 59	15.00 pm - 03 gem 56
Pluto	17 cap 54	17.00 pm - 05 gem 10
		19.00 pm - 06 gem 23
Oob		21.00 pm - 07 gem 37
		23.00 pm - 08 gem 51

Wednesday 19th July

Planetary Directions

Moon into Gemini
08:32

Retrograde Planets

Saturn, Neptune, Pluto, Juno, Chiron, Salacia, Quaoar

Asteroids		**Dwarf Planets**	
Juno	07 cap 07	Eris	23 ar 52
Vesta	00 vir 28	Haumea	22 lib 39
Pallas	06 tau 05	Makemake	02 lib 02
Ceres	03 can 33	Salacia	02 ar 14
Chiron	28 pis 43	Orcus	07 vir 41
N Node	24 leo 30	Quaoar	29 sag 11
S Node	24 aq 30	Sedna	26 tau 37

Moon Phase: Balsamic
Sunrise: 05:06 BST
Sunset: 21:06
Moonrise: 01:38
Moonset: 16:50
Voc start: 07:11
Voc end: 08:31

Planetary and Angelic Hours

Mercury	05:07	Sun	21:04
Moon	06:26	Venus	21:45
Saturn	07:46	Mercury	22:25
Jupiter	09:06	Moon	23:05
Mars	10:26	Saturn	23:45
Sun	11:46	Jupiter	00:26
Venus	13:05	Mars	01:06
Mercury	14:25	Sun	01:46
Moon	15:45	Venus	02:27
Saturn	17:05	Mercury	03:07
Jupiter	18:25	Moon	03:47
Mars	19:44	Saturn	04:28

Aspects

Sun sextile Moon
Moon conjunct Sedna
Sun sextile Sedna
Moon sextile Chiron
Moon sextile Mars
Moon square Vesta
Mercury trine Saturn
Sun square Uranus
Mars trine Chiron
Pallas trine Juno

Planets	**00:00 am**	**Moon**
Sun	27 can 28	01.00 am - 10 gem 04
Mercury	22 leo 28	03.00 am - 11 gem 18
Venus	16 gem 42	05.00 am - 12 gem 32
Mars	29 can 40	07.00 am - 13 gem 46
Jupiter	15 lib 31	09.00 am - 15 gem 00
Saturn	22 sag 12	11.00 am - 16 gem 14
Uranus	28 ar 26	13.00 pm - 17 gem 29
Neptune	13 pis 58	15.00 pm - 18 gem 43
Pluto	17 cap 53	17.00 pm - 19 gem 57
		19.00 pm - 21 gem 12
Oob		21.00 pm - 22 gem 25
		23.00 pm - 23 gem 41

Thursday 20th July

Planetary Directions

Eris retrograde
23 ar 52 at 09:53
Mars into Leo 13:20

Retrograde Planets

Saturn, Neptune, Pluto, Juno, Chiron, Salacia, Quaoar

Asteroids		**Dwarf Planets**	
Juno	06 cap 54	Eris	23 ar 52
Vesta	00 vir 55	Haumea	22 lib 39
Pallas	06 tau 21	Makemake	02 lib 03
Ceres	03 can 58	Salacia	02 ar 13
Chiron	28 pis 42	Orcus	07 vir 42
N Node	24 leo 27	Quaoar	29 sag 10
S Node	24 aq 27	Sedna	26 tau 37

Moon Phase: Balsamic
Sunrise: 05:07 BST
Sunset: 21:05
Moonrise: 02:18
Moonset: 18:04
Voc start:
Voc end:

Planetary and Angelic Hours

Jupiter	05:08	Moon	21:03
Mars	06:28	Saturn	21:44
Sun	07:47	Jupiter	22:24
Venus	09:07	Mars	23:05
Mercury	10:26	Sun	23:45
Moon	11:46	Venus	00:26
Saturn	13:05	Mercury	01:06
Jupiter	14:25	Moon	01:47
Mars	15:45	Saturn	02:27
Sun	17:04	Jupiter	03:08
Venus	18:24	Mars	03:48
Mercury	19:43	Sun	04:29

Aspects

Moon square Neptune
Moon trine Jupiter
Moon conjunct Venus
Moon opposite Saturn
Moon sextile Mercury
Moon sextile Eris
Sun square Uranus
Sun trine Chiron
Mercury trine Eris
Pallas trine Juno

Planets	**00:00 am**	**Moon**
Sun	28 can 26	01.00 am - 24 gem 55
Mercury	23 leo 49	03.00 am - 26 gem 10
Venus	17 gem 50	05.00 am - 27 gem 24
Mars	00 leo 18	07.00 am - 28 gem 39
Jupiter	15 lib 38	09.00 am - 29 gem 54
Saturn	22 sag 08	11.00 am - 01 can 08
Uranus	28 ar 27	13.00 pm - 02 can 23
Neptune	13 pis 57	15.00 pm - 03 can 38
Pluto	17 cap 51	17.00 pm - 04 can 52
		19.00 pm - 06 can 07
Oob		21.00 pm - 07 can 22
		23.00 pm - 08 can 36

Friday 21st July

Planetary Directions

Moon into Cancer
09:10

Retrograde Planets

Saturn, Neptune, Pluto, Juno, Chiron, Eris, Salacia, Quaoar

Asteroids		**Dwarf Planets**	
Juno	06 cap 42	Eris	23 ar 52
Vesta	01 vir 23	Haumea	22 lib 40
Pallas	06 tau 36	Makemake	02 lib 04
Ceres	04 can 23	Salacia	02 ar 13
Chiron	28 pis 41	Orcus	07 vir 43
N Node	24 leo 24	Quaoar	29 sag 09
S Node	24 aq 24	Sedna	26 tau 38

Moon Phase: Balsamic
Sunrise: 05:09 BST
Sunset: 21:04
Moonrise: 03:07
Moonset: 19:12
Voc start: 06:40
Voc end: 09:09

Planetary and Angelic Hours

Venus	05:09	Mars	21:02
Mercury	06:29	Sun	21:43
Moon	07:48	Venus	22:23
Saturn	09:07	Mercury	23:04
Jupiter	10:27	Moon	23:45
Mars	11:46	Saturn	00:25
Sun	13:06	Jupiter	01:06
Venus	14:25	Mars	01:47
Mercury	15:44	Sun	02:28
Moon	17:04	Venus	03:08
Saturn	18:23	Mercury	03:49
Jupiter	19:42	Moon	04:30

Aspects

Sun square Uranus
Mercury trine Eris
Moon sextile Uranus
Pallas trine Juno
Moon square Chiron
Sun trine Chiron
Moon sextile Vesta
Moon conjunct Ceres
Moon opposite Juno
Moon sextile Pallas

Planets	00:00 am	Moon
Sun	29 can 23	01.00 am - 09 can 51
Mercury	25 leo 08	03:00 am - 11 can 06
Venus	18 gem 59	05.00 am - 12 can 20
Mars	00 leo 57	07.00 am - 13 can 45
Jupiter	15 leo 45	09.00 am - 14 can 49
Saturn	22 sag 05	11.00 am - 16 can 04
Uranus	28 ar 27	13.00 pm - 17 can 18
Neptune	13 pis 56	15.00 pm - 18 can 33
Pluto	17 cap 50	17.00 pm - 19 can 47
		19.00 pm - 21 can 01
Oob		21.00 pm - 22 can 15
		23.00 pm - 23 can 30

Saturday 22nd July

Planetary Directions

Sun into Leo 16:16

Retrograde Planets

Saturn, Neptune, Pluto, Juno, Chiron, Eris, Salacia, Quaoar

Asteroids		Dwarf Planets	
Juno	06 cap 30	Eris	23 ar 52
Vesta	01 vir 50	Haumea	22 lib 40
Pallas	06 tau 51	Makemake	02 lib 05
Ceres	04 can 48	Salacia	02 ar 12
Chiron	28 pis 40	Orcus	07 vir 44
N Node	24 leo 20	Quaoar	29 sag 08
S Node	24 aq 20	Sedna	26 tau 38

Moon Phase: Balsamic
Sunrise: 05:10 BST
Sunset: 21:03
Moonrise: 04:06
Moonset: 20:10
Voc start:
Voc end:

Planetary and Angelic Hours			
Saturn	05:11	Mercury	21:01
Jupiter	06:30	Moon	21:42
Mars	07:49	Saturn	22:22
Sun	09:08	Jupiter	23:03
Venus	10:27	Mars	23:44
Mercury	11:46	Sun	00:25
Moon	13:06	Venus	01:06
Saturn	14:25	Mercury	01:47
Jupiter	15:44	Moon	02:28
Mars	17:03	Saturn	03:09
Sun	18:22	Jupiter	03:50
Venus	19:41	Mars	04:31

Aspects

Moon trine Neptune
Moon square Jupiter
Moon opposite Pluto
Moon square Eris
Mercury square Sedna
Pallas trine Juno

Planets	00:00 am	Moon
Sun	00 leo 20	01.00 am - 24 can 44
Mercury	26 leo 25	03.00 am - 25 can 58
Venus	20 gem 07	05.00 am - 27 can 11
Mars	01 leo 36	07.00 am - 28 can 25
Jupiter	15 lib 52	09.00 am - 29 can 39
Saturn	22 sag 02	11.00 am - 00 leo 53
Uranus	28 ar 28	13.00 pm - 02 leo 06
Neptune	13 pis 55	15.00 pm - 03 leo 19
Pluto	17 cap 48	17.00 pm - 04 leo 33
		19.00 pm - 05 leo 46
Oob		21.00 pm - 06 leo 59
		23.00 pm - 08 leo 12

Sunday 23rd July

Planetary Directions

Moon into Leo 09:34

Retrograde Planets

Saturn, Neptune, Pluto, Juno, Chiron, Eris, Salacia, Quaoar

Asteroids		Dwarf Planets	
Juno	06 cap 18	Eris	23 ar 52
Vesta	02 vir 18	Haumea	22 lib 40
Pallas	07 tau 05	Makemake	02 lib 05
Ceres	05 can 13	Salacia	02 ar 12
Chiron	28 pis 39	Orcus	07 vir 45
N Node	24 leo 18	Quaoar	29 sag 07
S Node	24 aq 18	Sedna	26 tau 39

New Moon: 10:47
Sunrise: 05:11 BST
Sunset: 21:01
Moonrise: 05:14
Moonset: 20:58
Voc start: 07:04
Voc end: 09:33

Planetary and Angelic Hours			
Sun	05:12	Jupiter	20:59
Venus	06:31	Mars	21:40
Mercury	07:50	Sun	22:22
Moon	09:09	Venus	23:03
Saturn	10:28	Mercury	23:44
Jupiter	11:47	Moon	00:25
Mars	13:06	Saturn	01:06
Sun	14:25	Jupiter	01:47
Venus	15:44	Mars	02:29
Mercury	17:02	Sun	03:10
Moon	18:21	Venus	03:51
Saturn	19:40	Mercury	04:32

Aspects

Moon sextile Sedna
Mercury square Sedna
Moon square Uranus
Moon trine Chiron
Sun conjunct Moon
Moon conjunct Mars
Moon square Pallas
Sun conjunct Mars
Mercury trine Uranus
Venus opposite Saturn
Ceres opposite Juno

Planets	00:00 am	Moon
Sun	01 leo 18	01.00 am - 09 leo 25
Mercury	27 leo 39	03.00 am - 10 leo 37
Venus	21 gem 15	05.00 am - 11 leo 50
Mars	02 leo 14	07.00 am - 13 leo 02
Jupiter	15 lib 59	09.00 am - 14 leo 15
Saturn	21 sag 59	11.00 am - 15 leo 27
Uranus	28 ar 29	13.00 pm - 16 leo 39
Neptune	13 pis 54	15.00 pm - 17 leo 51
Pluto	17 cap 47	17.00 pm - 19 leo 02
		19.00 pm - 20 leo 14
Oob		21.00 pm - 21 leo 25
		23.00 pm - 22 leo 37

Monday 24th July

Retrograde Planets

Saturn, Neptune, Pluto, Juno, Chiron, Eris, Salacia, Quaoar

Asteroids		Dwarf Planets	
Juno	06 cap 07	Eris	23 ar 52
Vesta	02 vir 45	Haumea	22 lib 41
Pallas	07 tau 20	Makemake	02 lib 06
Ceres	05 can 37	Salacia	02 ar 11
Chiron	28 pis 38	Orcus	07 vir 46
N Node	24 leo 16	Quaoar	29 sag 07
S Node	14 aq 16	Sedna	26 tau 39

Moon Phase: Crescent
Sunrise: 05:13 BST
Sunset: 21:00
Moonrise: 06:28
Moonset: 21:38
Voc start:
Voc end:

Planetary and Angelic Hours			
Moon	05:13	Venus	20:58
Saturn	06:32	Mercury	21:39
Jupiter	07:51	Moon	22:21
Mars	09:09	Saturn	23:02
Sun	10:28	Jupiter	23:44
Venus	11:47	Mars	00:25
Mercury	13:06	Sun	01:06
Moon	14:24	Venus	01:48
Saturn	15:43	Mercury	02:29
Jupiter	17:02	Moon	03:10
Mars	18:21	Saturn	03:52
Sun	19:39	Jupiter	04:33

Aspects

Moon sextile Sedna
Mercury square Sedna
Moon square Uranus
Moon trine Chiron
Sun conjunct Moon
Moon conjunct Mars
Moon square Pallas
Sun conjunct Mars
Mercury trine Uranus
Venus opposite Saturn
Ceres opposite Juno

Planets	**00:00 am**	**Moon**
Sun	02 leo 15	01.00 am - 23 leo 48
Mercury	28 leo 51	03.00 am - 24 leo 59
Venus	22 gem 24	05.00 am - 26 leo 09
Mars	02 leo 53	07.00 am - 27 leo 20
Jupiter	16 lib 06	09.00 am - 28 leo 30
Saturn	21 sag 57	11.00 am - 29 leo 41
Uranus	28 ar 29	13.00 pm - 00 vir 51
Neptune	13 pis 53	15.00 pm - 02 vir 01
Pluto	17 cap 46	17.00 pm - 03 vir 10
		19.00 pm - 04 vir 20
Oob		21.00 pm - 05 vir 29
		23.00 pm - 06 vir 39

Tuesday 25th July

Planetary Directions

Moon into Virgo 11:33

Retrograde Planets

Saturn, Neptune, Pluto, Juno, Chiron, Eris, Salacia, Quaoar

Asteroids		**Dwarf Planets**	
Juno	05 cap 55	Eris	23 ar 52
Vesta	03 vir 13	Haumea	22 lib 41
Pallas	07 tau 34	Makemake	02 lib 07
Ceres	06 can 02	Salacia	02 ar 11
Chiron	28 pis 37	Orcus	07 vir 47
N Node	24 leo 15	Quaoar	29 sag 06
S Node	24 aq 15	Sedna	26 tau 39

Moon Phase: Crescent
Sunrise: 05:14 BST
Sunset: 20:58
Moonrise: 07:43
Moonset: 22:10
Voc start: 10:21
Voc end: 11:32

Planetary and Angelic Hours

Mars	05:15	Saturn	20:57
Sun	06:33	Jupiter	21:38
Venus	07:52	Mars	22:20
Mercury	09:10	Sun	23:02
Moon	10:29	Venus	23:43
Saturn	11:47	Mercury	00:25
Jupiter	13:06	Moon	01:06
Mars	14:24	Saturn	01:48
Sun	15:43	Jupiter	02:30
Venus	17:01	Mars	03:11
Mercury	18:20	Sun	03:53
Moon	19:38	Venus	04:34

Aspects

Moon trine Eris
Moon square Sedna
Moon trine Uranus
Moon conj. Mercury
Moon conjunct Vesta
Moon trine Juno
Moon sextile Ceres
Sun conjunct Mars
Moon trine Pallas
Venus sextile Eris
Ceres opposite Juno

Planets	00:00 am	Moon
Sun	03 leo 12	01.00 am - 07 vir 48
Mercury	00 vir 00	03.00 am - 08 vir 57
Venus	23 gem 32	05.00 am - 10 vir 05
Mars	03 leo 32	07.00 am - 11 vir 14
Jupiter	16 lib 13	09.00 am - 12 vir 22
Saturn	21 sag 54	11.00 am - 13 vir 30
Uranus	28 ar 29	13.00 pm - 14 vir 38
Neptune	13 pis 52	15.00 pm - 15 vir 46
Pluto	17 cap 44	17.00 pm - 16 vir 54
		19.00 pm - 18 vir 01
Oob		21.00 pm - 19 vir 09
		23.00 pm - 20 vir 16

Wednesday 26th July

Planetary Directions

Mercury into Virgo at 00:41

Retrograde Planets

Saturn, Neptune, Pluto, Juno, Chiron, Eris, Salacia, Quaoar

Asteroids		Dwarf Planets	
Juno	05 cap 44	Eris	23 ar 52
Vesta	03 vir 41	Haumea	22 lib 41
Pallas	07 tau 48	Makemake	02 lib 08
Ceres	06 can 27	Salacia	02 ar 10
Chiron	28 pis 36	Orcus	07 vir 49
N Node	24 leo 16	Quaoar	29 sag 05
S Node	24 aq 16	Sedna	26 tau 40

Moon Phase: Crescent
Sunrise: 05:15 BST
Sunset: 20:57
Moonrise: 08:58
Moonset: 22:38
Voc start:
Voc end:

Planetary and Angelic Hours			
Mercury	05:16	Sun	20:55
Moon	06:34	Venus	21:37
Saturn	07:52	Mercury	22:19
Jupiter	09:11	Moon	23:01
Mars	10:29	Saturn	23:43
Sun	11:47	Jupiter	00:24
Venus	13:06	Mars	01:06
Mercury	14:24	Sun	01:48
Moon	15:42	Venus	02:30
Saturn	17:00	Mercury	03:12
Jupiter	18:19	Moon	03:54
Mars	19:37	Saturn	04:35

Aspects

Moon trine Pallas
Venus sextile Eris
Moon opp. Neptune
Moon trine Pluto
Sun conjunct Mars
Moon opposite Saturn

Planets	**00:00 am**	**Moon**
Sun	04 leo 10	01.00 am - 21 vir 23
Mercury	01 vir 07	03.00 am - 22 vir 29
Venus	24 gem 41	05.00 am - 23 vir 36
Mars	04 leo 10	07.00 am - 24 vir 42
Jupiter	16 lib 20	09.00 am - 25 vir 49
Saturn	21 sag 51	11.00 am - 26 vir 55
Uranus	28 ar 30	13.00 pm - 28 vir 01
Neptune	13 pis 50	15.00 pm - 29 vir 07
Pluto	17 cap 43	17.00 pm - 00 lib 12
		19.00 pm - 01 lib 18
Oob		21.00 pm - 02 lib 23
		23.00 pm - 03 lib 28

Thursday 27th July

Planetary Directions

Moon into Libra 16:37

Retrograde Planets

Saturn, Neptune, Pluto, Juno, Chiron, Eris, Salacia, Quaoar

Asteroids		**Dwarf Planets**	
Juno	05 cap 33	Eris	23 ar 51
Vesta	04 vir 09	Haumea	22 lib 42
Pallas	08 tau 02	Makemake	02 lib 09
Ceres	06 can 52	Salacia	02 ar 10
Chiron	28 pis 34	Orcus	07 vir 50
N Node	24 leo 17	Quaoar	29 sag 04
S Node	24 aq 17	Sedna	26 tau 40

Moon Phase: Crescent
Sunrise: 05:17 BST
Sunset: 20:56
Moonrise: 10:11
Moonset: 23:03
Voc start: 07:30
Voc end: 16:36

Planetary and Angelic Hours			
Jupiter	05:17	Moon	20:54
Mars	06:35	Saturn	21:36
Sun	07:53	Jupiter	22:18
Venus	09:11	Mars	23:00
Mercury	10:30	Sun	23:42
Moon	11:48	Venus	00:24
Saturn	13:06	Mercury	01:06
Jupiter	14:24	Moon	01:48
Mars	15:42	Saturn	02:30
Sun	17:00	Jupiter	03:13
Venus	18:18	Mars	03:55
Mercury	19:36	Sun	04:37

Aspects

Moon square Saturn
Sun conjunct Mars
Moon square Venus
Moon trine Sedna
Moon opposite Chiron
Sun sextile Moon
Moon sextile Mars
Moon square Juno
Ceres sextile Pallas
Juno trine Vesta

Planets	00:00 am	Moon
Sun	05 leo 07	01.00 am - 04 lib 33
Mercury	02 vir 12	03.00 am - 05 lib 38
Venus	25 gem 50	05.00 am - 06 lib 42
Mars	04 leo 49	07.00 am - 07 lib 47
Jupiter	16 lib 28	09.00 am - 08 lib 51
Saturn	21 sag 48	11.00 am - 09 lib 55
Uranus	28 ar 30	13.00 pm - 10 lib 59
Neptune	13 pis 49	15.00 pm - 12 lib 03
Pluto	17 cap 41	17.00 pm - 13 lib 07
		19.00 pm - 14 lib 10
Oob		21.00 pm - 15 lib 14
		23.00 pm - 16 lib 17

Friday 28th July

Retrograde Planets

Saturn, Neptune, Pluto, Juno, Chiron, Eris, Salacia, Quaoar

Asteroids		Dwarf Planets	
Juno	05 cap 23	Eris	23 ar 51
Vesta	04 vir 36	Haumea	22 lib 42
Pallas	08 tau 16	Makemake	02 lib 09
Ceres	07 can 17	Salacia	02 ar 09
Chiron	28 pis 33	Orcus	07 vir 51
N Node	24 leo 18	Quaoar	29 sag 03
S Node	14 aq 18	Sedna	26 tau 40

Moon Phase: Crescent
Sunrise: 05:18 BST
Sunset: 20:54
Moonrise: 11:21
Moonset: 23:27
Voc start:
Voc end:

Planetary and Angelic Hours

Venus	05:19	Mars	20:52
Mercury	06:37	Sun	21:35
Moon	07:54	Venus	22:17
Saturn	09:12	Mercury	22:59
Jupiter	10:30	Moon	23:42
Mars	11:48	Saturn	00:24
Sun	13:06	Jupiter	01:06
Venus	14:23	Mars	01:49
Mercury	15:41	Sun	02:31
Moon	16:59	Venus	03:13
Saturn	18:17	Mercury	03:56
Jupiter	19:35	Moon	04:38

Aspects

Moon sextile Mars
Sun sextile Moon
Moon square Juno
Moon square Ceres
Moon conjunct Jupiter
Sun conjunct Mars
Moon square Pluto
Ceres sextile Pallas
Juno trine Vesta

Planets	00:00 am	Moon
Sun	06 leo 04	01.00 am - 17 lib 20
Mercury	03 vir 13	03.00 am - 18 lib 23
Venus	26 gem 59	05.00 am - 19 lib 26
Mars	05 leo 28	07.00 am - 20 lib 29
Jupiter	16 leo 36	09.00 am - 21 lib 31
Saturn	21 sag 46	11.00 am - 22 lib 34
Uranus	28 ar 30	13.00 pm - 23 lib 36
Neptune	13 pis 48	15.00 pm - 24 lib 38
Pluto	17 cap 40	17.00 pm - 25 lib 40
		19.00 pm - 26 lib 42
Oob		21.00 pm - 27 lib 44
		23.00 pm - 28 lib 46

Saturday 29th July

Retrograde Planets

Saturn, Neptune, Pluto, Juno, Chiron, Eris, Salacia, Quaoar

Asteroids		Dwarf Planets	
Juno	05 cap 13	Eris	23 ar 51
Vesta	05 vir 04	Haumea	22 lib 43
Pallas	08 tau 30	Makemake	02 lib 10
Ceres	07 can 41	Salacia	02 ar 09
Chiron	28 pis 32	Orcus	07 vir 52
N Node	24 leo 20	Quaoar	29 sag 02
S Node	24 aq 20	Sedna	26 tau 41

Moon Phase: Crescent
Sunrise: 05:20 BST
Sunset: 20:53
Moonrise: 12:29
Moonset: 23:50
Voc start: 22:29
Voc end:

Planetary and Angelic Hours			
Saturn	05:20	Mercury	20:51
Jupiter	06:38	Moon	21:34
Mars	07:55	Saturn	22:16
Sun	09:13	Jupiter	22:59
Venus	10:30	Mars	23:41
Mercury	11:48	Sun	00:24
Moon	13:06	Venus	01:06
Saturn	14:23	Mercury	01:49
Jupiter	15:41	Moon	02:31
Mars	16:58	Saturn	03:14
Sun	18:16	Jupiter	03:56
Venus	19:33	Mars	04:39

Aspects

Moon square Pluto
Juno trine Vesta
Moon sextile Saturn
Moon opposite Eris
Moon trine Venus
Moon opposite Uranus
Sun conjunct Mars
Mercury trine Juno
Venus sextile Uranus
Venus square Chiron
Jupiter square Pluto
Ceres sextile Pallas

Planets	**00:00 am**	**Moon**
Sun	07 leo 02	01.00 am - 29 lib 48
Mercury	04 vir 12	03.00 am - 00 sco 49
Venus	28 gem 07	05.00 am - 01 sco 51
Mars	06 leo 06	07.00 am - 02 sco 52
Jupiter	16 lib 43	09.00 am - 03 sco 53
Saturn	21 sag 43	11.00 am - 04 sco 54
Uranus	28 ar 31	13.00 pm - 05 sco 55
Neptune	13 pis 47	15.00 pm - 06 sco 56
Pluto	17 cap 39	17.00 pm - 07 sco 57
		19.00 pm - 08 sco 58
Oob		21.00 pm - 09 sco 59
		23.00 pm - 10 sco 59

Sunday 30th July

Planetary Directions

Moon into Scorpio
01:23

Retrograde Planets

Saturn, Neptune, Pluto, Juno, Chiron, Eris, Salacia, Quaoar

Asteroids		**Dwarf Planets**	
Juno	05 cap 03	Eris	23 ar 51
Vesta	05 vir 32	Haumea	22 lib 43
Pallas	08 tau 43	Makemake	02 lib 11
Ceres	08 can 06	Salacia	02 ar 08
Chiron	28 pis 30	Orcus	07 vir 54
N Node	24 leo 20	Quaoar	29 sag 01
S Node	24 aq 20	Sedna	26 tau 41

First Quarter: 16:23
Sunrise: 05:21 BST
Sunset: 20:51
Moonrise: 13:34
Moonset: None
Voc start:
Voc end: 01:22

Planetary and Angelic Hours			
Sun	05:22	Jupiter	20:49
Venus	06:39	Mars	21:32
Mercury	07:56	Sun	22:15
Moon	09:14	Venus	22:58
Saturn	10:31	Mercury	23:41
Jupiter	11:48	Moon	00:23
Mars	13:06	Saturn	01:06
Sun	14:23	Jupiter	01:49
Venus	15:40	Mars	02:32
Mercury	16:57	Sun	03:15
Moon	18:15	Venus	03:57
Saturn	19:32	Mercury	04:40

Aspects

Venus square Chiron
Venus sextile Uranus
Moon sextile Mercury
Moon sextile Juno
Moon sextile Vesta
Moon square Mars
Sun square Moon
Moon trine Ceres
Moon opposite Pallas
Mercury trine Juno
Sun square Pallas
Mercury conjunct Vesta
Jupiter square Pluto
Ceres sextile Pallas

Planets	00:00 am	Moon
Sun	07 leo 59	01.00 am - 12 sco 00
Mercury	05 vir 08	03.00 am - 13 sco 00
Venus	29 gem 17	05.00 am - 14 sco 01
Mars	06 leo 45	07.00 am - 15 sco 01
Jupiter	16 lib 51	09.00 am - 16 sco 01
Saturn	21 sag 41	11.00 am - 17 sco 01
Uranus	28 ar 31	13.00 pm - 18 sco 02
Neptune	13 pis 45	15.00 pm - 19 sco 02
Pluto	17 cap 37	17.00 pm - 20 sco 02
		19.00 pm - 21 sco 02
Oob		21.00 pm - 22 sco 01
		23.00 pm - 23 sco 01

Monday 31st July

Planetary Directions

Venus into Cancer 15:54

Retrograde Planets

Saturn, Neptune, Pluto, Juno, Chiron, Eris, Salacia, Quaoar

Asteroids		Dwarf Planets	
Juno	05 cap 53	Eris	23 ar 51
Vesta	06 vir 00	Haumea	22 lib 44
Pallas	08 tau 57	Makemake	02 lib 12
Ceres	08 can 31	Salacia	02 ar 07
Chiron	28 pis 29	Orcus	07 vir 55
N Node	24 leo 20	Quaoar	29 sag 00
S Node	24 aq 20	Sedna	26 tau 42

Moon Phase: Gibbous
Sunrise: 05:23 BST
Sunset: 20:49
Moonrise: 14:38
Moonset: 00:15
Voc start: 12:10
Voc end:

Planetary and Angelic Hours			
Moon	05:23	Venus	20:48
Saturn	06:40	Mercury	21:31
Jupiter	07:57	Moon	22:14
Mars	09:14	Saturn	22:57
Sun	10:31	Jupiter	23:40
Venus	11:48	Mars	00:23
Mercury	13:05	Sun	01:06
Moon	14:23	Venus	01:49
Saturn	15:40	Mercury	02:32
Jupiter	16:57	Moon	03:15
Mars	18:14	Saturn	03:58
Sun	19:31	Jupiter	04:41

Aspects

Moon trine Neptune
Moon sextile Pluto
Sun square Pallas
Mercury conjunct Vesta
Jupiter square Pluto
Ceres sextile Pallas

Planets	00:00 am	Moon
Sun	08 leo 57	01.00 am - 24 sco 01
Mercury	06 vir 01	03.00 am - 25 sco 01
Venus	00 can 26	05.00 am - 26 sco 00
Mars	07 leo 23	07.00 am - 27 sco 00
Jupiter	16 lib 59	09.00 am - 28 sco 00
Saturn	21 sag 39	11.00 am - 28 sco 59
Uranus	28 ar 31	13.00 pm - 29 sco 59
Neptune	13 pis 44	15.00 pm - 00 sag 58
Pluto	17 cap 36	17.00 pm - 01 sag 58
		19.00 pm - 02 sag 57
Oob		21.00 pm - 03 sag 57
		23.00 pm - 04 sag 56

Tuesday 1st August

Planetary Directions

Moon into Sagittarius 13:02

Retrograde Planets

Saturn, Neptune, Pluto, Juno, Chiron, Eris, Salacia, Quaoar

Asteroids		Dwarf Planets	
Juno	04 cap 44	Eris	23 ar 51
Vesta	06 vir 29	Haumea	22 lib 44
Pallas	09 tau 10	Makemake	02 lib 13
Ceres	08 can 56	Salacia	02 ar 07
Chiron	28 pis 27	Orcus	07 vir 56
N Node	24 leo 20	Quaoar	28 sag 59
S Node	24 aq 20	Sedna	26 tau 42

Moon Phase: Gibbous
Sunrise: 05:24 BST
Sunset: 20:48
Moonrise: 15:40
Moonset: 00:41
Voc start:
Voc end: 13:01

Planetary and Angelic Hours

Mars	05:24	Saturn	20:46
Sun	06:41	Jupiter	21:30
Venus	07:58	Mars	22:13
Mercury	09:15	Sun	22:56
Moon	10:32	Venus	23:40
Saturn	11:49	Mercury	00:23
Jupiter	13:05	Moon	01:06
Mars	14:22	Saturn	01:49
Sun	15:39	Jupiter	02:33
Venus	16:56	Mars	03:16
Mercury	18:13	Sun	03:59
Moon	19:30	Venus	04:43

Lughnasadh

Aspects

Moon opposite Sedna
Sun square Pallas
Moon trine Chiron
Moon square Mercury
Mercury conjunct Vesta
Jupiter square Pluto
Ceres sextile Pallas

Planets	00:00 am	Moon
Sun	09 leo 54	01.00 am - 05 sag 56
Mercury	06 vir 51	03.00 am - 06 sag 55
Venus	01 can 35	05.00 am - 07 sag 54
Mars	08 leo 02	07.00 am - 08 sag 54
Jupiter	17 lib 08	09.00 am - 09 sag 53
Saturn	21 sag 37	11.00 am - 10 sag 52
Uranus	28 ar 31	13.00 pm - 11 sag 52
Neptune	13 pis 43	15.00 pm - 12 sag 51
Pluto	17 cap 35	17.00 pm - 13 sag 50
		19.00 pm - 14 sag 50
Oob		21.00 pm - 15 sag 49
		23.00 pm - 16 sag 48

Wednesday 2nd August

Retrograde Planets

Saturn, Neptune, Pluto, Juno, Chiron, Eris, Salacia, Quaoar

Asteroids		Dwarf Planets	
Juno	04 cap 35	Eris	23 ar 51
Vesta	06 vir 57	Haumea	22 lib 45
Pallas	09 tau 23	Makemake	02 lib 14
Ceres	09 can 20	Salacia	02 ar 06
Chiron	28 pis 26	Orcus	07 vir 57
N Node	24 leo 19	Quaoar	28 sag 58
S Node	24 aq 19	Sedna	26 tau 42

Moon Phase: Gibbous
Sunrise: 05:26 BST
Sunset: 20:46
Moonrise: 16:39
Moonset: 01:12
Voc start:
Voc end:

Planetary and Angelic Hours			
Mercury	05:26	Sun	20:45
Moon	06:43	Venus	21:28
Saturn	07:59	Mercury	22:12
Jupiter	09:16	Moon	22:55
Mars	10:32	Saturn	23:39
Sun	11:49	Jupiter	00:23
Venus	13:05	Mars	01:06
Mercury	14:22	Sun	01:50
Moon	15:38	Venus	02:33
Saturn	16:55	Mercury	03:17
Jupiter	18:12	Moon	04:00
Mars	19:28	Saturn	04:44

Aspects

Moon square Mercury
Moon square Vesta
Moon trine Mars
Ceres sextile Pallas
Mercury conjunct Vesta
Sun trine Moon
Moon square Neptune
Moon sextile Jupiter
Mars square Pallas
Jupiter square Pluto

Planets	**00:00 am**	**Moon**
Sun	10 leo 51	01.00 am - 17 sag 48
Mercury	07 vir 37	03.00 am - 18 sag 47
Venus	02 can 44	05.00 am - 19 sag 46
Mars	08 leo 40	07.00 am - 20 sag 45
Jupiter	17 lib 16	09.00 am - 21 sag 45
Saturn	21 sag 34	11.00 am - 22 sag 44
Uranus	28 ar 31	13.00 pm - 23 sag 44
Neptune	13 pis 42	15.00 pm - 24 sag 43
Pluto	17 cap 33	17.00 pm - 25 sag 43
		19.00 pm - 26 sag 43
Oob		21.00 pm - 27 sag 42
		23.00 pm - 28 sag 42

Thursday 3rd August

Planetary Directions

Uranus retrograde
28 ar 31 at 06:31

Retrograde Planets

Saturn, Neptune, Pluto, Juno, Chiron, Eris, Salacia, Quaoar

Asteroids		**Dwarf Planets**	
Juno	04 cap 26	Eris	23 ar 51
Vesta	07 vir 25	Haumea	22 lib 45
Pallas	09 tau 35	Makemake	02 lib 15
Ceres	09 can 45	Salacia	02 ar 05
Chiron	28 pis 24	Orcus	07 vir 59
N Node	24 leo 17	Quaoar	28 sag 58
S Node	24 aq 17	Sedna	26 tau 42

Moon Phase: Gibbous
Sunrise: 05:27 BST
Sunset: 20:44
Moonrise: 17:35
Moonset: 01:46
Voc start: 22:38
Voc end:

Planetary and Angelic Hours			
Jupiter	05:27	Moon	20:43
Mars	06:44	Saturn	21:27
Sun	08:00	Jupiter	22:11
Venus	09:16	Mars	22:55
Mercury	10:33	Sun	23:38
Moon	11:49	Venus	00:22
Saturn	13:05	Mercury	01:06
Jupiter	14:22	Moon	01:50
Mars	15:38	Saturn	02:34
Sun	16:54	Jupiter	03:17
Venus	18:10	Mars	04:01
Mercury	19:27	Sun	04:45

Aspects

Moon conjunct Saturn
Moon trine Eris
Moon square Chiron
Moon trine Uranus
Mercury conjunct Vesta
Venus opposite Juno
Mars square Pallas
Jupiter square Pluto
Ceres sextile Pallas

Planets	00:00 am	Moon
		01.00 am - 29 sag 41
Sun	11 leo 49	03.00 am - 00 cap 41
Mercury	08 vir 20	05.00 am - 01 cap 41
Venus	03 can 54	07.00 am - 02 cap 40
Mars	09 leo 19	09.00 am - 03 cap 40
Jupiter	17 lib 24	11.00 am - 04 cap 40
Saturn	21 sag 32	13.00 pm - 05 cap 40
Uranus	28 ar 31	15.00 pm - 06 cap 40
Neptune	13 pis 40	17.00 pm - 07 cap 39
Pluto	17 cap 32	19.00 pm - 08 cap 39
		21.00 pm - 09 cap 39
Oob		23.00 pm - 10 cap 39

Friday 4th August

Planetary Directions

Moon into Capricorn 01:37

Retrograde Planets

Saturn, Uranus, Neptune, Pluto, Juno, Chiron, Eris, Salacia, Quaoar

Asteroids		Dwarf Planets	
Juno	04 cap 18	Eris	23 ar 51
Vesta	07 vir 53	Haumea	22 lib 46
Pallas	09 tau 48	Makemake	02 lib 16
Ceres	10 can 09	Salacia	02 ar 05
Chiron	28 pis 23	Orcus	08 vir 00
N Node	24 leo 15	Quaoar	28 sag 57
S Node	24 aq 15	Sedna	26 tau 43

Moon Phase: Gibbous
Sunrise: 05:29 BST
Sunset: 20:43
Moonrise: 18:27
Moonset: 02:27
Voc start:
Voc end: 01:36

Planetary and Angelic Hours			
Venus	05:29	Mars	20:41
Mercury	06:45	Sun	21:25
Moon	08:01	Venus	22:10
Saturn	09:17	Mercury	22:54
Jupiter	10:33	Moon	23:38
Mars	11:49	Saturn	00:22
Sun	13:05	Jupiter	01:06
Venus	14:21	Mars	01:50
Mercury	15:37	Sun	02:34
Moon	16:53	Venus	03:18
Saturn	18:09	Mercury	04:02
Jupiter	19:25	Moon	04:46

Aspects

Venus opposite Juno
Moon conjunct Juno
Moon opposite Venus
Moon trine Vesta
Moon trine Mercury
Jupiter square Pluto
Moon trine Pallas
Moon opposite Ceres
Mercury conjunct Vesta
Mars square Pallas
Ceres sextile Pallas

Planets	00:00 am	Moon
Sun	12 leo 46	01.00 am - 11 cap 40
Mercury	08 vir 59	03.00 am - 12 cap 40
Venus	05 can 03	05.00 am - 13 cap 40
Mars	09 leo 57	07.00 am - 14 cap 40
Jupiter	17 lib 33	09.00 am - 15 cap 41
Saturn	21 sag 30	11.00 am - 16 cap 41
Uranus	28 ar 31	13.00 pm - 17 cap 41
Neptune	13 pis 39	15.00 pm - 18 cap 42
Pluto	17 cap 31	17.00 pm - 19 cap 42
		19.00 pm - 20 cap 43
Oob		21.00 pm - 21 cap 44
		23.00 pm - 22 cap 44

Saturday 5th August

Retrograde Planets

Saturn, Uranus, Neptune, Pluto, Juno, Chiron, Eris, Salacia, Quaoar

Asteroids		Dwarf Planets	
Juno	04 cap 09	Eris	23 ar 50
Vesta	08 vir 21	Haumea	22 lib 46
Pallas	10 tau 00	Makemake	02 lib 17
Ceres	10 can 34	Salacia	02 ar 04
Chiron	28 pis 21	Orcus	08 vir 01
N Node	24 leo 13	Quaoar	28 sag 56
S Node	24 aq 13	Sedna	26 tau 43

Moon Phase: Gibbous
Sunrise: 05:30 BST
Sunset: 20:41
Moonrise: 19:13
Moonset: 03:14
Voc start:
Voc end:

Planetary and Angelic Hours			
Saturn	05:30	Mercury	20:40
Jupiter	06:46	Moon	21:24
Mars	08:02	Saturn	22:08
Sun	09:18	Jupiter	22:53
Venus	10:34	Mars	23:37
Mercury	11:49	Sun	00:21
Moon	13:05	Venus	01:06
Saturn	14:21	Mercury	01:50
Jupiter	15:37	Moon	02:35
Mars	16:52	Saturn	03:19
Sun	18:08	Jupiter	04:03
Venus	19:24	Mars	04:48

Aspects

Mars square Pallas
Moon sextile Neptune
Moon conjunct Pluto
Moon square Jupiter
Moon square Eris
Mercury trine Pallas
Mercury conjunct Vesta
Jupiter square Pluto
Ceres sextile Pallas

Planets	00:00 am	Moon
Sun	13 leo 44	01.00 am - 23 cap 45
Mercury	09 vir 35	03.00 am - 24 cap 46
Venus	06 can 13	04.00 am - 25 cap 47
Mars	10 leo 36	07.00 am - 26 cap 48
Jupiter	17 lib 41	09.00 am - 27 cap 49
Saturn	21 sag 29	11.00 am - 28 cap 50
Uranus	28 ar 31	13.00 pm - 29 cap 52
Neptune	13 pis 38	15.00 pm - 00 aq 53
Pluto	17 cap 29	17.00 pm - 01 aq 54
		19.00 pm - 02 aq 56
Oob		21.00 pm - 03 aq 57
		23.00 pm - 04 aq 59

Sunday 6th August

Planetary Directions

Moon into Aquarius
13:16

Retrograde Planets

Saturn, Uranus, Neptune, Pluto, Juno, Chiron, Eris, Salacia, Quaoar

Asteroids		Dwarf Planets	
Juno	04 cap 02	Eris	23 ar 50
Vesta	08 vir 50	Haumea	22 lib 47
Pallas	10 tau 12	Makemake	02 lib 18
Ceres	10 can 58	Salacia	02 ar 03
Chiron	28 pis 19	Orcus	08 vir 03
N Node	24 leo 12	Quaoar	28 sag 55
S Node	24 aq 12	Sedna	26 tau 43

Moon Phase: Gibbous
Sunrise: 05:32 BST
Sunset: 20:39
Moonrise: 19:53
Moonset: 04:08
Voc start: 10:21
Voc end: 13:15

Planetary and Angelic Hours			
Sun	05:32	Jupiter	20:38
Venus	06:47	Mars	21:23
Mercury	08:03	Sun	22:07
Moon	09:18	Venus	22:52
Saturn	10:34	Mercury	23:36
Jupiter	11:49	Moon	00:21
Mars	13:05	Saturn	01:06
Sun	14:20	Jupiter	01:50
Venus	15:36	Mars	02:35
Mercury	16:51	Sun	03:20
Moon	18:07	Venus	04:04
Saturn	19:22	Mercury	04:49

Aspects

Mars square Pallas
Moon sextile Neptune
Moon conjunct Pluto
Moon square Jupiter
Moon square Eris
Mercury trine Pallas
Mercury conjunct Vesta
Jupiter square Pluto
Ceres sextile Pallas

Planets	**00:00 am**	**Moon**
Sun	14 leo 41	01.00 am - 06 aq 01
Mercury	10 vir 06	03.00 am - 07 aq 02
Venus	07 can 23	05.00 am - 08 aq 04
Mars	11 leo 14	07.00 am - 09 aq 06
Jupiter	17 lib 50	09.00 am - 10 aq 08
Saturn	21 sag 27	11.00 am - 11 aq 10
Uranus	28 ar 31	13.00 pm - 12 aq 12
Neptune	13 pis 36	15.00 pm - 13 aq 14
Pluto	17 cap 28	17.00 pm - 14 aq 17
		19.00 pm - 15 aq 19
Oob		21.00 pm - 16 aq 22
		23.00 pm - 17 aq 24

Monday 7th August

Retrograde Planets

Saturn, Uranus, Neptune, Pluto, Juno, Chiron, Eris, Salacia, Quaoar

Asteroids		**Dwarf Planets**	
Juno	03 cap 54	Eris	23 ar 50
Vesta	09 vir 18	Haumea	22 lib 48
Pallas	10 tau 24	Makemake	02 lib 19
Ceres	11 can 23	Salacia	02 ar 02
Chiron	28 pis 17	Orcus	08 vir 04
N Node	24 leo 11	Quaoar	28 sag 54
S Node	24 aq 11	Sedna	26 tau 44

Full Moon: 19:12
Sunrise: 05:33 BST
Sunset: 20:37
Moonrise: 20:28
Moonset: 05:08
Voc start:
Voc end:

Planetary and Angelic Hours			
Moon	05:33	Venus	20:36
Saturn	06:49	Mercury	21:21
Jupiter	08:04	Moon	22:06
Mars	09:19	Saturn	22:51
Sun	10:34	Jupiter	23:36
Venus	11:50	Mars	00:21
Mercury	13:05	Sun	01:06
Moon	14:20	Venus	01:50
Saturn	15:35	Mercury	02:35
Jupiter	16:51	Moon	03:20
Mars	18:06	Saturn	04:05
Sun	19:21	Jupiter	04:50

Penumbral Lunar Eclipse at 19:20

Aspects

Moon square Pallas
Moon opposite Mars
Sun opposite Moon
Moon trine Jupiter
Mercury trine Pallas
Mercury conjunct Vesta
Jupiter square Pluto
Pallas trine Vesta

Planets	**00:00 am**	**Moon**
Sun	15 leo 39	01.00 am - 18 aq 27
Mercury	10 vir 33	03.00 am - 19 aq 30
Venus	08 can 33	05.00 am - 20 aq 32
Mars	11 leo 53	07.00 am - 21 aq 35
Jupiter	17 lib 59	09.00 am - 22 aq 38
Saturn	21 sag 25	11.00 am - 23 aq 41
Uranus	28 ar 30	13.00 pm - 24 aq 45
Neptune	13 pis 35	15.00 pm - 25 aq 48
Pluto	17 cap 27	17.00 pm - 26 aq 51
		19.00 pm - 27 aq 55
Oob		21.00 pm - 28 aq 58
		23.00 pm - 00 pis 02

Tuesday 8th August

Planetary Directions

Moon into Pisces 22:56

Retrograde Planets

Saturn, Uranus, Neptune, Pluto, Juno, Chiron, Eris, Salacia, Quaoar

Asteroids		**Dwarf Planets**	
Juno	03 cap 47	Eris	23 ar 50
Vesta	09 vir 47	Haumea	22 lib 48
Pallas	10 tau 36	Makemake	02 lib 20
Ceres	11 can 47	Salacia	02 ar 02
Chiron	28 pis 16	Orcus	08 vir 05
N Node	24 leo 11	Quaoar	28 sag 54
S Node	24 aq 11	Sedna	26 tau 44

Phase: Disseminating
Sunrise: 05:35 BST
Sunset: 20:36
Moonrise: 20:59
Moonset: 06:12
Voc start: 20:07
Voc end: 22:55

Planetary and Angelic Hours			
Mars	05:35	Saturn	20:34
Sun	06:50	Jupiter	21:20
Venus	08:05	Mars	22:05
Mercury	09:20	Sun	22:50
Moon	10:35	Venus	23:35
Saturn	11:50	Mercury	00:20
Jupiter	13:05	Moon	01:05
Mars	14:20	Saturn	01:51
Sun	15:35	Jupiter	02:36
Venus	16:50	Mars	03:21
Mercury	18:05	Sun	04:06
Moon	19:20	Venus	04:51

Aspects

Moon square Pallas
Moon opposite Mars
Moon trine Jupiter
Mercury trine Pallas
Mercury conjunct Vesta
Jupiter square Pluto
Pallas trine Vesta

Planets	00:00 am	Moon
		01.00 am - 01 pis 05
Sun	16 leo 36	03.00 am - 02 pis 09
Mercury	10 vir 56	05.00 am - 03 pis 13
Venus	09 can 43	07.00 am - 04 pis 17
Mars	12 leo 31	09.00 am - 05 pis 21
Jupiter	18 lib 08	11.00 am - 06 pis 25
Saturn	21 sag 23	13.00 pm - 07 pis 30
Uranus	28 ar 30	15.00 pm - 08 pis 34
Neptune	13 pis 33	17.00 pm - 09 pis 38
Pluto	17 cap 25	19.00 pm - 19 pis 43
		21.00 pm - 11 pis 47
Oob		23.00 pm - 12 pis 52

Wednesday 9th August

Retrograde Planets

Saturn, Uranus, Neptune, Pluto, Juno, Chiron, Eris, Salacia, Quaoar

Asteroids		Dwarf Planets	
Juno	03 cap 41	Eris	23 ar 50
Vesta	10 vir 15	Haumea	22 lib 49
Pallas	10 tau 47	Makemake	02 lib 21
Ceres	12 can 12	Salacia	02 ar 01
Chiron	28 pis 14	Orcus	08 vir 06
N Node	24 leo 11	Quaoar	28 sag 53
S Node	24 aq 11	Sedna	26 tau 44

Phase: Disseminating
Sunrise: 05:37 BST
Sunset: 20:34
Moonrise: 21:26
Moonset: 07:20
Voc start:
Voc end:

Planetary and Angelic Hours			
Mercury	05:36	Sun	20:33
Moon	06:51	Venus	21:18
Saturn	08:06	Mercury	22:04
Jupiter	09:21	Moon	22:49
Mars	10:35	Saturn	23:34
Sun	11:50	Jupiter	00:20
Venus	13:05	Mars	01:05
Mercury	14:19	Sun	01:51
Moon	15:34	Venus	02:36
Saturn	16:49	Mercury	03:22
Jupiter	18:03	Moon	04:07
Mars	19:18	Saturn	04:53

Aspects

Moon sextile Juno
Moon trine Venus
Moon opposite Vesta
Moon sextile Pallas
Venus sextile Vesta
Moon opp. Mercury
Moon trine Ceres
Moon conj. Neptune
Sun sextile Jupiter
Mercury sextile Venus
Mercury trine Pallas
Mercury conjunct Vesta
Venus sextile Pallas
Jupiter square Pluto
Neptune trine Ceres
Pallas trine Vesta

Planets	00:00 am	Moon
Sun	17 leo 34	01.00 am - 13 pis 57
Mercury	11 vir 14	03.00 am - 15 pis 02
Venus	10 can 53	05.00 am - 16 pis 07
Mars	13 leo 10	07.00 am - 17 pis 12
Jupiter	18 lib 17	09.00 am - 18 pis 17
Saturn	21 sag 22	11.00 am - 19 pis 22
Uranus	28 ar 30	13.00 pm - 20 pis 28
Neptune	13 pis 32	15.00 pm - 21 pis 33
Pluto	17 cap 24	17.00 pm - 22 pis 39
		19.00 pm - 23 pis 45
Oob		21.00 pm - 24 pis 50
		23.00 pm - 25 pis 56

Thursday 10th August

Retrograde Planets

Saturn, Uranus, Neptune, Pluto, Juno, Chiron, Eris, Salacia, Quaoar

Asteroids		Dwarf Planets	
Juno	03 cap 34	Eris	23 ar 49
Vesta	10 vir 44	Haumea	22 lib 50
Pallas	10 tau 58	Makemake	02 lib 22
Ceres	12 can 36	Salacia	02 ar 00
Chiron	28 pis 12	Orcus	08 vir 08
N Node	24 leo 11	Quaoar	28 sag 52
S Node	24 aq 11	Sedna	26 tau 44

Phase: Disseminating
Sunrise: 05:38 BST
Sunset: 20:32
Moonrise: 21:52
Moonset: 08:29
Voc start: 14:37
Voc end:

Planetary and Angelic Hours			
Jupiter	05:38	Moon	20:31
Mars	06:52	Saturn	21:17
Sun	08:07	Jupiter	22:02
Venus	09:21	Mars	22:48
Mercury	10:36	Sun	23:34
Moon	11:50	Venus	00:19
Saturn	13:04	Mercury	01:05
Jupiter	14:19	Moon	01:51
Mars	15:33	Saturn	02:37
Sun	16:48	Jupiter	03:22
Venus	18:02	Mars	04:08
Mercury	19:16	Sun	04:54

Aspects

Venus sextile Pallas
Moon sextile Pluto
Mercury sextile Venus
Moon square Saturn
Pallas trine Vesta
Sun sextile Jupiter
Moon sextile Sedna
Mercury trine Pallas
Mercury conjunct Vesta
Venus conjunct Ceres
Venus sextile Vesta
Neptune trine Ceres

Planets	**00:00 am**	**Moon**
Sun	18 leo 31	01.00 am - 27 pis 02
Mercury	11 vir 27	03.00 am - 28 pis 08
Venus	12 can 03	05.00 am - 29 pis 14
Mars	13 leo 48	07.00 am - 00 ar 21
Jupiter	18 lib 26	09.00 am - 01 ar 27
Saturn	21 sag 21	11.00 am - 02 ar 33
Uranus	28 ar 30	13.00 pm - 03 ar 40
Neptune	13 pis 31	15.00 pm - 04 ar 46
Pluto	17 cap 23	17.00 pm - 05 ar 53
		19.00 pm - 07 ar 00
Oob		21.00 pm - 08 ar 07
		23.00 pm - 09 ar 14

Friday 11th August

Planetary Directions

Moon into Aries 06:22

Retrograde Planets

Saturn, Uranus, Neptune, Pluto, Juno, Chiron, Eris, Salacia, Quaoar

Asteroids		**Dwarf Planets**	
Juno	03 cap 28	Eris	23 ar 49
Vesta	11 vir 12	Haumea	22 lib 51
Pallas	11 tau 09	Makemake	02 lib 23
Ceres	13 can 00	Salacia	01 ar 59
Chiron	28 pis 10	Orcus	08 vir 09
N Node	24 leo 11	Quaoar	28 sag 52
S Node	24 aq 11	Sedna	26 tau 44

Phase: Disseminating
Sunrise: 05:40 BST
Sunset: 20:30
Moonrise: 22:16
Moonset: 09:40
Voc start:
Voc end: 06:21

Planetary and Angelic Hours

Venus	05:40	Mars	20:29
Mercury	06:54	Sun	21:15
Moon	08:08	Venus	22:01
Saturn	09:22	Mercury	22:47
Jupiter	10:36	Moon	23:33
Mars	11:50	Saturn	00:19
Sun	13:04	Jupiter	01:05
Venus	14:18	Mars	01:51
Mercury	15:33	Sun	02:37
Moon	16:47	Venus	03:23
Saturn	18:01	Mercury	04:09
Jupiter	19:15	Moon	04:55

Aspects

Moon conjunct Chiron
Moon square Juno
Mercury conjunct Vesta
Sun sextile Jupiter
Mercury trine Pallas
Venus trine Neptune
Venus conjunct Ceres
Neptune trine Ceres
Pallas trine Vesta

Saturday 12th August

Planets	00:00 am
Sun	19 leo 29
Mercury	11 vir 35
Venus	13 can 13
Mars	14 leo 26
Jupiter	18 lib 35
Saturn	21 sag 19
Uranus	28 ar 29
Neptune	13 pis 29
Pluto	17 cap 22
Oob	

Moon

01.00 am - 10 ar 21
03.00 am - 11 ar 28
05.00 am - 12 ar 36
07.00 am - 13 ar 43
09.00 am - 14 ar 50
11.00 am - 15 ar 58
13.00 pm - 17 ar 06
15.00 pm - 18 ar 14
17.00 pm - 19 ar 21
19.00 pm - 20 ar 29
21.00 pm - 21 ar 37
23.00 pm - 22 ar 46

Retrograde Planets

Saturn, Uranus, Neptune, Pluto, Juno, Chiron, Eris, Salacia, Quaoar

Asteroids		Dwarf Planets	
Juno	03 cap 23	Eris	23 ar 49
Vesta	11 vir 41	Haumea	22 lib 51
Pallas	11 tau 20	Makemake	02 lib 24
Ceres	13 can 25	Salacia	01 ar 58
Chiron	28 pis 08	Orcus	08 vir 11
N Node	24 leo 12	Quaoar	28 sag 51
S Node	24 aq 12	Sedna	26 tau 45

Phase: Disseminating
Sunrise: 05:41 BST
Sunset: 20:28
Moonrise: 22:42
Moonset: 10:53
Voc start:
Voc end:

Planetary and Angelic Hours			
Saturn	05:41	Mercury	20:27
Jupiter	06:55	Moon	21:13
Mars	08:09	Saturn	22:00
Sun	09:23	Jupiter	22:46
Venus	10:36	Mars	23:32
Mercury	11:50	Sun	00:19
Moon	13:04	Venus	01:05
Saturn	14:18	Mercury	01:51
Jupiter	15:32	Moon	02:37
Mars	16:46	Saturn	03:24
Sun	17:59	Jupiter	04:10
Venus	19:13	Mars	04:56

Aspects

Neptune trine Ceres
Venus trine Neptune
Moon square Venus
Moon square Ceres
Venus conjunct Ceres
Moon trine Mars
Moon square Pluto
Moon opposite Jupiter
Moon trine Saturn
Moon conjunct Eris
Sun trine Saturn
Mercury trine Pallas
Mercury conjunct Vesta
Pallas trine Vesta

Planets	**00:00 am**	**Moon**
Sun	20 leo 26	01.00 am - 23 ar 54
Mercury	11 vir 38	03.00 am - 25 ar 02
Venus	14 can 24	05.00 am - 26 ar 11
Mars	15 leo 05	07.00 am - 27 ar 19
Jupiter	18 lib 45	09.00 am - 28 ar 28
Saturn	21 sag 18	11.00 am - 29 ar 37
Uranus	28 ar 29	13.00 pm - 00 tau 46
Neptune	13 pis 28	15.00 pm - 01 tau 55
Pluto	17 cap 21	17.00 pm - 03 tau 04
		19.00 pm - 04 tau 13
		21.00 pm - 05 tau 22
Oob		23.00 pm - 06 tau 31

Sunday 13th August

Planetary Directions

Mercury retrograde
11 vir 38 at 02:01
Moon into Taurus 11:40

Retrograde Planets

Mercury, Saturn,
Uranus, Neptune, Pluto,
Juno, Chiron, Eris,
Salacia, Quaoar

Asteroids		**Dwarf Planets**	
Juno	03 cap 23	Eris	23 ar 49
Vesta	11 vir 41	Haumea	22 lib 52
Pallas	11 tau 20	Makemake	02 lib 25
Ceres	13 can 25	Salacia	01 ar 57
Chiron	28 pis 08	Orcus	08 vir 12
N Node	24 leo 12	Quaoar	28 sag 51
S Node	24 aq 12	Sedna	26 tau 45

Phase: Disseminating
Sunrise: 05:43 BST
Sunset: 20:26
Moonrise: 23:09
Moonset: 12:06
Voc start: 09:00
Voc end: 11:39

Planetary and Angelic Hours			
Sun	05:43	Jupiter	20:25
Venus	06:56	Mars	21:12
Mercury	08:10	Sun	21:58
Moon	09:23	Venus	22:45
Saturn	10:37	Mercury	23:32
Jupiter	11:50	Moon	00:18
Mars	13:04	Saturn	01:05
Sun	14:17	Jupiter	01:51
Venus	15:31	Mars	02:38
Mercury	16:45	Sun	03:24
Moon	17:58	Venus	04:11
Saturn	19:12	Mercury	04:58

Aspects

Moon conjunct Uranus
Mercury trine Pallas
Moon trine Juno
Sun trine Saturn
Neptune trine Ceres
Neptune opposite Vesta
Pallas trine Vesta

Planets	**00:00 am**	**Moon**
Sun	21 leo 24	01.00 am - 07 tau 41
Mercury	11 vir 35	03.00 am - 08 tau 50
Venus	15 can 34	05.00 am - 10 tau 00
Mars	15 leo 43	07.00 am - 11 tau 09
Jupiter	18 lib 54	09.00 am - 12 tau 19
Saturn	21 sag 17	11.00 am - 13 tau 29
Uranus	28 ar 28	13.00 pm - 14 tau 39
Neptune	13 pis 26	15.00 pm - 15 tau 49
Pluto	17 cap 19	17.00 pm - 16 tau 59
		19.00 pm - 18 tau 09
Oob		21.00 pm - 19 tau 20
		23.00 pm - 20 tau 30

Monday 14th August

Retrograde Planets

Mercury, Saturn, Uranus, Neptune, Pluto, Juno, Chiron, Eris, Salacia, Quaoar

Asteroids		**Dwarf Planets**	
Juno	03 cap 13	Eris	23 ar 49
Vesta	12 vir 38	Haumea	22 lib 53
Pallas	11 tau 40	Makemake	02 lib 26
Ceres	14 can 13	Salacia	01 ar 57
Chiron	28 pis 04	Orcus	08 vir 13
N Node	24 leo 13	Quaoar	28 sag 50
S Node	24 aq 13	Sedna	26 tau 45

Phase: Disseminating
Sunrise: 05:44 BST
Sunset: 20:24
Moonrise: 23:39
Moonset: 13:21
Voc start:
Voc end:

Planetary and Angelic Hours			
Moon	05:44	Venus	20:23
Saturn	06:57	Mercury	21:10
Jupiter	08:11	Moon	21:57
Mars	09:24	Saturn	22:44
Sun	10:37	Jupiter	23:31
Venus	11:50	Mars	00:18
Mercury	13:04	Sun	01:05
Moon	14:17	Venus	01:51
Saturn	15:30	Mercury	02:38
Jupiter	16:44	Moon	03:25
Mars	17:57	Saturn	04:12
Sun	19:10	Jupiter	04:59

Aspects

Moon trine Mercury
Moon conjunct Pallas
Moon trine Vesta
Moon sextile Neptune
Moon sextile Ceres
Moon square Mars
Moon sextile Venus
Moon trine Pluto
Sun square Moon
Mercury trine Pallas
Venus opposite Pluto
Neptune opposite Vesta

Planets	**00:00 am**	**Moon**
		01.00 am - 21 tau 40
Sun	22 leo 22	03.00 am - 22 tau 51
Mercury	11 vir 27	05.00 am - 24 tau 02
Venus	16 can 45	07.00 am - 25 tau 12
Mars	16 leo 21	09.00 am - 26 tau 23
Jupiter	19 lib 03	11.00 am - 27 tau 34
Saturn	21 sag 16	13.00 pm - 28 tau 45
Uranus	28 ar 28	15.00 pm - 29 tau 56
Neptune	13 pis 25	17.00 pm - 01 gem 07
Pluto	17 cap 18	19.00 pm - 02 gem 18
		21.00 pm - 03 gem 29
Oob		23.00 pm - 04 gem 41

Tuesday 15th August

Planetary Directions

Moon into Gemini
15:06

Retrograde Planets

Mercury, Saturn, Uranus, Neptune, Pluto, Juno, Chiron, Eris, Salacia, Quaoar

Asteroids		**Dwarf Planets**	
Juno	03 cap 08	Eris	23 ar 48
Vesta	13 vir 07	Haumea	22 lib 54
Pallas	11 tau 50	Makemake	02 lib 27
Ceres	14 can 37	Salacia	01 ar 56
Chiron	28 pis 02	Orcus	08 vir 15
N Node	24 leo 13	Quaoar	28 sag 49
S Node	24 aq 13	Sedna	26 tau 45

Last Quarter: 02:16
Sunrise: 05:46 BST
Sunset: 20:22
Moonrise: None
Moonset: 14:35
Voc start: 02:14
Voc end: 15:05

Planetary and Angelic Hours			
Mars	05:46	Saturn	20:21
Sun	06:59	Jupiter	21:09
Venus	08:12	Mars	21:56
Mercury	09:25	Sun	22:43
Moon	10:38	Venus	23:30
Saturn	11:51	Mercury	00:17
Jupiter	13:04	Moon	01:04
Mars	14:17	Saturn	01:51
Sun	15:29	Jupiter	02:39
Venus	16:42	Mars	03:26
Mercury	17:55	Sun	04:13
Moon	19:08	Venus	05:00

Aspects

Sun square Moon
Moon conjunct Sedna
Moon sextile Chiron
Venus opposite Pluto
Neptune opposite Vesta
Sun trine Eris
Mercury trine Pallas

Planets	00:00 am	Moon
Sun	23 leo 19	01.00 am - 05 gem 52
Mercury	11 vir 14	03.00 am - 07 gem 04
Venus	17 can 55	05.00 am - 08 gem 15
Mars	17 leo 00	07.00 am - 09 gem 27
Jupiter	19 lib 13	09.00 am - 10 gem 38
Saturn	21 sag 15	11.00 am - 11 gem 50
Uranus	28 ar 27	13.00 pm - 13 gem 02
Neptune	13 pis 23	15.00 pm - 14 gem 14
Pluto	17 cap 17	17.00 pm - 15 gem 26
		19.00 pm - 16 gem 37
Oob		21.00 pm - 17 gem 49
		23.00 pm - 19 gem 01

Wednesday 16th August

Retrograde Planets

Mercury, Saturn, Uranus, Neptune, Pluto, Juno, Chiron, Eris, Salacia, Quaoar

Asteroids		Dwarf Planets	
Juno	03 cap 04	Eris	23 ar 48
Vesta	13 vir 36	Haumea	22 lib 54
Pallas	12 tau 00	Makemake	02 lib 28
Ceres	15 can 01	Salacia	01 ar 55
Chiron	28 pis 00	Orcus	08 vir 16
N Node	24 leo 13	Quaoar	28 sag 48
S Node	24 aq 13	Sedna	26 tau 45

Moon Phase: Balsamic
Sunrise: 05:48 BST
Sunset: 20:20
Moonrise: 00:16
Moonset: 15:48
Voc start:
Voc end:

Planetary and Angelic Hours			
Mercury	05:47	Sun	20:19
Moon	07:00	Venus	21:07
Saturn	08:13	Mercury	21:54
Jupiter	09:25	Moon	22:42
Mars	10:38	Saturn	23:29
Sun	11:51	Jupiter	00:17
Venus	13:03	Mars	01:04
Mercury	14:16	Sun	01:52
Moon	15:29	Venus	02:39
Saturn	16:41	Mercury	03:26
Jupiter	17:54	Moon	04:14
Mars	19:07	Saturn	05:01

Aspects

Moon square Mercury
Sun trine Eris
Moon square Neptune
Moon square Vesta
Moon sextile Mars
Moon trine Jupiter
Venus square Jupiter
Neptune opposite Vesta

Planets	**00:00 am**	**Moon**
Sun	24 leo 17	01.00 am - 20 gem 14
Mercury	10 vir 55	03.00 am - 21 gem 26
Venus	19 can 06	05.00 am - 22 gem 38
Mars	17 leo 38	07.00 am - 23 gem 50
Jupiter	19 lib 23	09.00 am - 25 gem 02
Saturn	21 sag 14	11.00 am - 26 gem 15
Uranus	28 ar 26	13.00 pm - 27 gem 27
Neptune	13 pis 22	15.00 pm - 28 gem 39
Pluto	17 cap 16	17.00 pm - 29 gem 52
		19.00 pm - 01 can 04
Oob		21.00 pm - 02 can 17
		23.00 pm - 03 can 29

Thursday 17th August

Planetary Directions

Moon into Cancer
17:13

Retrograde Planets

Mercury, Saturn, Uranus, Neptune, Pluto, Juno, Chiron, Eris, Salacia, Quaoar

Asteroids		**Dwarf Planets**	
Juno	03 cap 00	Eris	23 ar 48
Vesta	14 vir 05	Haumea	22 lib 55
Pallas	12 tau 09	Makemake	02 lib 29
Ceres	15 can 26	Salacia	01 ar 54
Chiron	27 pis 58	Orcus	08 vir 17
N Node	24 leo 13	Quaoar	28 sag 48
S Node	24 aq 13	Sedna	26 tau 45

Moon Phase: Balsamic
Sunrise: 05:49 BST
Sunset: 20:18
Moonrise: 00:59
Moonset: 16:57
Voc start: 14:37
Voc end: 17:12

Planetary and Angelic Hours			
Jupiter	05:49	Moon	20:17
Mars	07:01	Saturn	21:05
Sun	08:14	Jupiter	21:53
Venus	09:26	Mars	22:41
Mercury	10:38	Sun	23:28
Moon	11:51	Venus	00:16
Saturn	13:03	Mercury	01:04
Jupiter	14:16	Moon	01:52
Mars	15:28	Saturn	02:39
Sun	16:40	Jupiter	03:27
Venus	17:53	Mars	04:15
Mercury	19:05	Sun	05:03

Aspects

Moon opposite Saturn
Moon sextile Eris
Venus square Jupiter
Sun sextile Moon
Moon square Chiron
Moon sextile Uranus
Moon opposite Juno

Planets	**00:00 am**	**Moon**
Sun	25 leo 15	01.00 am - 04 can 41
Mercury	10 vir 30	03.00 am - 05 can 54
Venus	20 can 17	05.00 am - 07 can 06
Mars	18 leo 16	07.00 am - 08 can 19
Jupiter	19 lib 33	09.00 am - 09 can 32
Saturn	21 sag 13	11.00 am - 10 can 44
Uranus	28 ar 26	13.00 pm - 11 can 57
Neptune	13 pis 20	15.00 pm - 13 can 09
Pluto	17 cap 15	17.00 pm - 14 can 22
		19.00 pm - 15 can 34
Oob		21.00 pm - 16 can 47
		23.00 pm - 17 can 59

Friday 18th August

Retrograde Planet

Mercury, Saturn, Uranus, Neptune, Pluto, Juno, Chiron, Eris, Salacia, Quaoar

Asteroids		**Dwarf Planets**	
Juno	02 cap 57	Eris	23 ar 47
Vesta	14 vir 34	Haumea	22 lib 56
Pallas	12 tau 18	Makemake	02 lib 30
Ceres	15 can 50	Salacia	01 ar 53
Chiron	27 pis 55	Orcus	08 vir 19
N Node	24 leo 13	Quaoar	28 sag 47
S Node	24 aq 13	Sedna	26 tau 46

Moon Phase: Balsamic
Sunrise: 05:51 BST
Sunset: 20:16
Moonrise: 01:52
Moonset: 17:58
Voc start:
Voc end:

Planetary and Angelic Hours			
Venus	05:50	Mars	20:15
Mercury	07:02	Sun	21:03
Moon	08:15	Venus	21:52
Saturn	09:27	Mercury	22:40
Jupiter	10:39	Moon	23:28
Mars	11:51	Saturn	00:16
Sun	13:03	Jupiter	01:04
Venus	14:15	Mars	01:52
Mercury	15:27	Sun	02:40
Moon	16:39	Venus	03:28
Saturn	17:51	Mercury	04:16
Jupiter	19:03	Moon	05:04

Aspects

Moon sextile Mercury
Moon sextile Pallas
Moon trine Neptune
Moon sextile Vesta
Moon conjunct Ceres
Moon opposite Pluto
Sun square Sedna
Moon square Jupiter
Mars sextile Jupiter
Neptune sextile Pallas

Planets	**00:00 am**	**Moon**
Sun	26 leo 12	01.00 am - 19 can 12
Mercury	10 vir 00	03.00 am - 20 can 24
Venus	21 can 28	05.00 am - 21 can 37
Mars	18 leo 55	07.00 am - 22 can 49
Jupiter	19 lib 43	09.00 am - 24 can 01
Saturn	21 sag 12	11.00 am - 25 can 14
Uranus	28 ar 25	13.00 pm - 26 can 26
Neptune	13 pis 18	15.00 pm - 27 can 38
Pluto	17 cap 14	17.00 pm - 28 can 51
		19.00 pm - 00 leo 03
Oob		21.00 pm - 01 leo 15
		23.00 pm - 02 leo 27

Saturday 19th August

Planetary Directions

Moon into Leo 18:55

Retrograde Planets

Mercury, Saturn, Uranus, Neptune, Pluto, Juno, Chiron, Eris, Salacia, Quaoar

Asteroids		**Dwarf Planets**	
Juno	02 cap 54	Eris	23 ar 47
Vesta	15 vir 03	Haumea	22 lib 57
Pallas	12 tau 27	Makemake	02 lib 32
Ceres	16 can 14	Salacia	01 ar 52
Chiron	27 pis 53	Orcus	08 vir 20
N Node	24 leo 13	Quaoar	28 sag 47
S Node	24 aq 13	Sedna	26 tau 46

Moon Phase: Balsamic
Sunrise: 05:52 BST
Sunset: 20:14
Moonrise: 02:54
Moonset: 18:49
Voc start: 16:16
Voc end: 18:54

Planetary and Angelic Hours			
Saturn	05:52	Mercury	20:13
Jupiter	07:04	Moon	21:02
Mars	08:16	Saturn	21:50
Sun	09:27	Jupiter	22:38
Venus	10:39	Mars	23:27
Mercury	11:51	Sun	00:15
Moon	13:03	Venus	01:03
Saturn	14:14	Mercury	01:52
Jupiter	15:26	Moon	02:40
Mars	16:38	Saturn	03:28
Sun	17:50	Jupiter	04:17
Venus	19:02	Mars	05:05

Aspects

Moon square Jupiter
Moon conjunct Venus
Moon square Eris
Moon sextile Sedna
Sun square Sedna
Moon trine Chiron
Moon square Uranus
Mars sextile Jupiter
Neptune sextile Pallas
Pluto opposite Ceres

Planets	00:00 am	Moon
Sun	27 leo 10	01.00 am - 03 leo 39
Mercury	09 vir 25	03.00 am - 04 leo 51
Venus	22 can 39	05.00 am - 06 leo 03
Mars	19 leo 33	07.00 am - 07 leo 15
Jupiter	19 lib 53	09.00 am - 08 leo 27
Saturn	21 sag 12	11.00 am - 09 leo 38
Uranus	28 ar 24	13.00 pm - 10 leo 50
Neptune	13 pis 17	15.00 pm - 12 leo 02
Pluto	17 cap 13	17.00 pm - 13 leo 13
		19.00 pm - 14 leo 25
Oob		21.00 pm - 15 leo 36
		23.00 pm - 16 leo 47

Sunday 20th August

Retrograde Planets

Mercury, Saturn, Uranus, Neptune, Pluto, Juno, Chiron, Eris, Salacia, Quaoar

Asteroids		Dwarf Planets	
Juno	02 cap 51	Eris	23 ar 47
Vesta	15 vir 32	Haumea	22 lib 58
Pallas	12 tau 35	Makemake	02 lib 33
Ceres	16 can 38	Salacia	01 ar 51
Chiron	27 pis 51	Orcus	08 vir 22
N Node	24 leo 13	Quaoar	28 sag 46
S Node	24 aq 13	Sedna	26 tau 46

Moon Phase: Balsamic
Sunrise: 05:54 BST
Sunset: 20:12
Moonrise: 04:04
Moonset: 19:32
Voc start:
Voc end:

Planetary and Angelic Hours			
Sun	05:53	Jupiter	20:11
Venus	07:05	Mars	21:00
Mercury	08:16	Sun	21:49
Moon	09:28	Venus	22:37
Saturn	10:39	Mercury	23:26
Jupiter	11:51	Moon	00:15
Mars	13:02	Saturn	01:03
Sun	14:14	Jupiter	01:52
Venus	15:25	Mars	02:41
Mercury	16:37	Sun	03:29
Moon	17:48	Venus	04:18
Saturn	19:00	Mercury	05:06

Aspects

Moon square Pallas
Mars sextile Jupiter
Venus square Eris
Sun trine Uranus
Neptune sextile Pallas
Pluto opposite Ceres

Planets	**00:00 am**	**Moon**
Sun	28 leo 08	01.00 am - 17 leo 58
Mercury	08 vir 45	03.00 am - 19 leo 10
Venus	23 can 50	05.00 am - 20 leo 21
Mars	20 leo 11	07.00 am - 21 leo 32
Jupiter	20 lib 03	09.00 am - 22 leo 42
Saturn	21 sag 11	11.00 am - 23 leo 53
Uranus	28 ar 23	13.00 pm - 25 leo 04
Neptune	13 pis 15	15.00 pm - 26 leo 14
Pluto	17 cap 12	17.00 pm - 27 leo 25
		19.00 pm - 28 leo 35
Oob		21.00 pm - 29 leo 45
		23.00 pm - 00 vir 55

Monday 21st August

Planetary Directions

Moon into Virgo 21:25

Retrograde Planets

Mercury, Saturn, Uranus, Neptune, Pluto, Juno, Chiron, Eris, Salacia, Quaoar

Asteroids		**Dwarf Planets**	
Juno	02 cap 49	Eris	23 ar 47
Vesta	16 vir 01	Haumea	22 lib 59
Pallas	12 tau 44	Makemake	02 lib 34
Ceres	17 can 01	Salacia	01 ar 50
Chiron	27 pis 49	Orcus	08 vir 23
N Node	24 leo 13	Quaoar	28 sag 46
S Node	24 aq 13	Sedna	26 tau 46

New Moon: 19:31
Sunrise: 05:55 BST
Sunset: 20:10
Moonrise: 05:19
Moonset: 20:07
Voc start: 19:30
Voc end: 21:24

Planetary and Angelic Hours

Moon	05:55	Venus	20:09
Saturn	07:06	Mercury	20:58
Jupiter	08:17	Moon	21:47
Mars	09:29	Saturn	22:36
Sun	10:40	Jupiter	23:25
Venus	11:51	Mars	00:14
Mercury	13:02	Sun	01:03
Moon	14:13	Venus	01:52
Saturn	15:25	Mercury	02:41
Jupiter	16:36	Moon	03:30
Mars	17:47	Saturn	04:19
Sun	18:58	Jupiter	05:08

Black Moon
Solar Eclipse 14:30
28 Leo 53

Aspects

Moon sextile Jupiter
Moon conjunct Mars
Moon trine Saturn
Sun trine Uranus
Moon trine Eris
Pluto opposite Ceres
Moon square Sedna
Moon trine Uranus
Sun conjunct Moon
Moon trine Juno
Mars sextile Jupiter
Mars trine Saturn
Pluto trine Vesta

Planets	00:00 am	Moon
Sun	29 leo 06	01.00 am - 02 vir 05
Mercury	08 vir 00	03.00 am - 03 vir 15
Venus	25 can 01	05.00 am - 04 vir 24
Mars	20 leo 50	07.00 am - 05 vir 34
Jupiter	20 lib 13	09.00 am - 06 vir 43
Saturn	21 sag 11	11.00 am - 07 vir 53
Uranus	28 ar 23	13.00 pm - 09 vir 02
Neptune	13 pis 14	15.00 pm - 10 vir 11
Pluto	17 cap 11	17.00 pm - 11 vir 20
		19.00 pm - 12 vir 29
Oob		21.00 pm - 13 vir 37
		23.00 pm - 14 vir 46

Tuesday 22nd August

Planetary Directions

Sun into Virgo 23:21

Retrograde Planets

Mercury, Saturn, Uranus, Neptune, Pluto, Juno, Chiron, Eris, Salacia, Quaoar

Asteroids		Dwarf Planets	
Juno	02 cap 47	Eris	23 ar 47
Vesta	16 vi 30	Haumea	23 lib 00
Pallas	12 tau 51	Makemake	02 lib 35
Ceres	17 can 25	Salacia	01 ar 49
Chiron	27 pis 46	Orcus	08 vir 24
N Node	24 leo 13	Quaoar	28 sag 45
S Node	24 aq 13	Sedna	26 tau 46

Moon Phase: Crescent
Sunrise: 05:57 BST
Sunset: 20:08
Moonrise: 06:34
Moonset: 20:37
Voc start:
Voc end:

Planetary and Angelic Hours			
Mars	05:57	Saturn	20:07
Sun	07:08	Jupiter	20:57
Venus	08:18	Mars	21:46
Mercury	09:29	Sun	22:35
Moon	10:40	Venus	23:24
Saturn	11:51	Mercury	00:14
Jupiter	13:02	Moon	01:03
Mars	14:13	Saturn	01:52
Sun	15:24	Jupiter	02:41
Venus	16:35	Mars	03:30
Mercury	17:46	Sun	04:20
Moon	18:56	Venus	05:09

Aspects

Moon trine Juno
Moon conj. Mercury
Mars trine Saturn
Moon trine Pallas
Moon opp. Neptune
Venus sextile Sedna
Jupiter sextile Saturn
Neptune sextile Pallas
Pluto opposite Ceres
Pluto trine Vesta
Chiron sextile Sedna
Ceres sextile Vesta

Planets	**00:00 am**	**Moon**
Sun	00 vir 04	01.00 am - 15 vir 54
Mercury	07 vir 12	03.00 am - 17 vir 02
Venus	26 can 12	05.00 am - 18 vir 11
Mars	21 leo 28	07.00 am - 19 vir 19
Jupiter	20 lib 23	09.00 am - 20 vir 26
Saturn	21 sag 11	11.00 am - 21 vir 34
Uranus	28 ar 22	13.00 pm - 22 vir 42
Neptune	13 pis 12	15.00 pm - 23 vir 49
Pluto	17 cap 10	17.00 pm - 24 vir 56
		19.00 pm - 26 vir 03
Oob		21.00 pm - 27 vir 10
		23.00 pm - 28 vir 17

Wednesday 23rd August

Retrograde Planets

Mercury, Saturn, Uranus, Neptune, Pluto, Juno, Chiron, Eris, Salacia, Quaoar

Asteroids		**Dwarf Planets**	
Juno	02 cap 45	Eris	23 ar 46
Vesta	16 vir 59	Haumea	23 lib 01
Pallas	12 tau 59	Makemake	02 lib 36
Ceres	17 can 49	Salacia	01 ar 48
Chiron	27 pis 44	Orcus	08 vir 24
N Node	24 leo 13	Quaoar	28 sag 45
S Node	24 aq 13	Sedna	26 tau 46

Moon Phase: Crescent
Sunrise: 05:59 BST
Sunset: 20:06
Moonrise: 07:49
Moonset: 21:04
Voc start: 21:02
Voc end:

Planetary and Angelic Hours			
Mercury	05:58	Sun	20:05
Moon	07:09	Venus	20:55
Saturn	08:19	Mercury	21:44
Jupiter	09:30	Moon	22:34
Mars	10:41	Saturn	23:23
Sun	11:51	Jupiter	00:13
Venus	13:02	Mars	01:02
Mercury	14:12	Sun	01:52
Moon	15:23	Venus	02:42
Saturn	16:33	Mercury	03:31
Jupiter	17:44	Moon	04:21
Mars	18:55	Saturn	05:10

Aspects

Moon conjunct Vesta
Moon trine Pluto
Moon sextile Ceres
Pluto trine Vesta
Moon square Saturn
Venus sextile Sedna
Moon trine Sedna
Moon sextile Venus
Moon opposite Chiron
Venus square Uranus
Venus trine Chiron
Mars trine Saturn
Jupiter sextile Saturn
Neptune sextile Pallas
Chiron sextile Sedna
Ceres sextile Vesta

Planets	**00:00 am**	**Moon**
Sun	01 vir 01	01.00 am - 29 vir 24
Mercury	06 vir 21	03.00 am - 00 lib 30
Venus	27 can 23	05.00 am - 01 lib 37
Mars	22 leo 06	07.00 am - 02 lib 43
Jupiter	20 lib 34	09.00 am - 03 lib 49
Saturn	21 sag 11	11.00 am - 04 lib 55
Uranus	28 ar 21	13.00 pm - 06 lib 01
Neptune	13 pis 11	15.00 pm - 07 lib 06
Pluto	17 cap 09	16.00 pm - 08 lib 12
		19.00 pm - 09 lib 17
Oob		21.00 pm - 10 lib 22
		23.00 pm - 11 lib 27

Thursday 24th August

Planetary Directions

Moon into Libra 02:05

Retrograde Planets

Mercury, Saturn, Uranus, Neptune, Pluto, Juno, Chiron, Eris, Salacia, Quaoar

Asteroids		**Dwarf Planets**	
Juno	02 cap 44	Eris	23 ar 46
Vesta	17 vir 28	Haumea	23 lib 01
Pallas	13 tau 06	Makemake	02 lib 38
Ceres	18 can 13	Salacia	01 ar 47
Chiron	27 pis 42	Orcus	08 vir 27
N Node	24 leo 12	Quaoar	28 sag 44
S Node	24 aq 12	Sedna	26 tau 46

Moon Phase: Crescent
Sunrise: 06:00 BST
Sunset: 20:04
Moonrise: 09:01
Moonset: 21:28
Voc start:
Voc end: 02:04

Planetary and Angelic Hours			
Jupiter	06:00	Moon	20:03
Mars	07:10	Saturn	20:53
Sun	08:20	Jupiter	21:43
Venus	09:31	Mars	22:33
Mercury	10:41	Sun	23:23
Moon	11:51	Venus	00:12
Saturn	13:01	Mercury	01:02
Jupiter	14:12	Moon	01:52
Mars	15:22	Saturn	02:42
Sun	16:32	Jupiter	03:32
Venus	17:43	Mars	04:22
Mercury	18:53	Sun	05:11

Aspects

Venus trine Chiron
Moon square Juno
Neptune sextile Pallas
Venus square Uranus
Sun trine Juno
Jupiter sextile Saturn
Pluto trine Vesta
Chiron sextile Sedna
Ceres sextile Vesta

Planets	**00:00 am**	**Moon**
Sun	01 vir 59	01.00 am - 12 lib 32
Mercury	05 vir 28	03.00 am - 13 lib 37
Venus	28 can 35	05.00 am - 14 lib 42
Mars	22 leo 44	07.00 am - 15 lib 46
Jupiter	20 lib 44	09.00 am - 16 lib 50
Saturn	21 sag 10	11.00 am - 17 lib 55
Uranus	28 ar 20	13.00 pm - 18 lib 59
Neptune	13 pis 09	15.00 pm - 20 lib 03
Pluto	17 cap 08	17.00 pm - 21 lib 06
		19.00 pm - 22 lib 10
Oob		21.00 pm - 23 lib 14
		23.00 pm - 24 lib 17

Friday 25th August

Planetary Directions

Saturn direct
21 sag 10 at 13:09

Retrograde Planets

Mercury, Saturn, Uranus, Neptune, Pluto, Juno, Chiron, Eris, Salacia, Quaoar

Asteroids		**Dwarf Planets**	
Juno	02 cap 43	Eris	23 ar 45
Vesta	17 vir 58	Haumea	23 lib 03
Pallas	13 tau 13	Makemake	02 lib 39
Ceres	18 can 36	Salacia	01 ar 46
Chiron	27 pis 39	Orcus	08 vir 29
N Node	24 leo 11	Quaoar	28 sag 44
S Node	24 aq 11	Sedna	26 tau 46

Moon Phase: Crescent
Sunrise: 06:02 BST
Sunset: 20:01
Moonrise: 10:11
Moonset: 21:52
Voc start:
Voc end:

Planetary and Angelic Hours			
Venus	06:01	Mars	20:01
Mercury	07:11	Sun	20:51
Moon	08:21	Venus	21:41
Saturn	09:31	Mercury	22:31
Jupiter	10:41	Moon	23:22
Mars	11:51	Saturn	00:12
Sun	13:01	Jupiter	01:02
Venus	14:11	Mars	01:52
Mercury	15:21	Sun	02:42
Moon	16:31	Venus	03:32
Saturn	17:41	Mercury	04:23
Jupiter	18:51	Moon	05:13

Aspects

Moon square Pluto
Moon square Ceres
Moon conjunct Jupiter
Moon sextile Saturn
Sun trine Juno
Moon sextile Mars
Moon opposite Eris
Mars trine Eris
Jupiter sextile Saturn
Neptune sextile Pallas
Chiron sextile Sedna
Ceres sextile Vesta

Planets	00:00 am	Moon
Sun	02 vir 57	01.00 am - 25 lib 20
Mercury	04 vir 34	03.00 am - 26 lib 23
Venus	29 can 46	05.00 am - 27 lib 26
Mars	23 leo 23	07.00 am - 28 lib 29
Jupiter	20 lib 55	09.00 am - 29 lib 32
Saturn	21 sag 10	11.00 am - 00 sco 35
Uranus	28 ar 19	13.00 pm - 01 sco 37
Neptune	13 pis 07	15.00 pm - 02 sco 39
Pluto	17 cap 07	17.00 pm - 03 sco 42
		19.00 pm - 04 sco 44
Oob		21.00 pm - 05 sco 46
		23.00 pm - 06 sco 48

Saturday 26th August

Planetary Directions

Venus in Leo 05:30
Moon into Scorpio 09:53
Juno direct at 18:14

Retrograde Planets

\Mercury, Uranus, Neptune, Pluto, Juno, Chiron, Eris, Salacia, Quaoar

Asteroids		Dwarf Planets	
Juno	02 cap 43	Eris	23 ar 45
Vesta	18 vir 47	Haumea	23 lib 04
Pallas	13 tau 20	Makemake	02 lib 40
Ceres	19 can 00	Salacia	01 ar 45
Chiron	27 pis 37	Orcus	08 vir 30
N Node	24 leo 10	Quaoar	28 sag 44
S Node	24 aq 10	Sedna	26 tau 46

Moon Phase: Crescent
Sunrise: 06:03 BST
Sunset: 19:59
Moonrise: 11:19
Moonset: 22:16
Voc start: 06:39
Voc end: 09:52

Planetary and Angelic Hours

Saturn	06:03	Mercury	19:59
Jupiter	07:13	Moon	20:49
Mars	08:22	Saturn	21:40
Sun	09:32	Jupiter	22:30
Venus	10:42	Mars	23:21
Mercury	11:51	Sun	00:11
Moon	13:01	Venus	01:02
Saturn	14:11	Mercury	01:52
Jupiter	15:20	Moon	02:43
Mars	16:30	Saturn	03:33
Sun	17:40	Jupiter	04:23
Venus	18:49	Mars	05:14

Aspects

Moon opposite Uranus
Moon square Venus
Mars trine Eris
Moon sextile Juno
Sun sextile Moon
Moon sextile Mercury
Sun conjunct Mercury
Mercury trine Juno
Jupiter sextile Saturn
Neptune sextile Pallas
Chiron sextile Sedna
Ceres sextile Vesta

Planets	**00:00 am**	**Moon**
Sun	03 vir 55	01.00 am - 07 sco 50
Mercury	03 vir 40	03.00 am - 08 sco 51
Venus	00 leo 58	05.00 am - 09 sco 53
Mars	24 leo 01	07.00 am - 10 sco 54
Jupiter	21 lib 05	09.00 am - 11 sco 56
Saturn	21 sag 11	11.00 am - 12 sco 57
Uranus	28 ar 17	13.00 pm - 13 sco 58
Neptune	13 pis 06	15.00 pm - 14 sco 59
Pluto	17 cap 06	17.00 pm - 16 sco 00
		19.00 pm - 17 sco 01
Oob		21.00 pm - 18 sco 02
		23.00 pm - 19 sco 03

Sunday 27th August

Planetary Directions

Sedna retrograde
26 tau 46 at 19:41

Retrograde Planets

Mercury, Uranus, Neptune, Pluto, Chiron, Eris, Salacia, Quaoar

Asteroids		**Dwarf Planets**	
Juno	02 cap 43	Eris	23 ar 44
Vesta	18 vir 56	Haumea	23 lib 05
Pallas	13 tau 26	Makemake	02 lib 41
Ceres	19 can 24	Salacia	01 ar 44
Chiron	27 pis 34	Orcus	08 vir 31
N Node	24 leo 09	Quaoar	28 sag 43
S Node	24 aq 09	Sedna	26 tau 46

Moon Phase: Crescent
Sunrise: 06:05 BST
Sunset: 19:57
Moonrise: 12:24
Moonset: 22:42
Voc start:
Voc end:

Planetary and Angelic Hours			
Sun	06:04	Jupiter	19:57
Venus	07:14	Mars	20:48
Mercury	08:23	Sun	21:38
Moon	09:33	Venus	22:29
Saturn	10:42	Mercury	23:20
Jupiter	11:51	Moon	00:11
Mars	13:01	Saturn	01:01
Sun	14:10	Jupiter	01:52
Venus	15:19	Mars	02:43
Mercury	16:29	Sun	03:34
Moon	17:38	Venus	04:24
Saturn	18:47	Mercury	05:15

Aspects

Sun conjunct Mercury
Moon trine Neptune
Moon opposite Pallas
Jupiter sextile Saturn
Moon sextile Pluto
Moon sextile Vesta
Moon trine Ceres
Mercury trine Juno
Mars trine Eris
Neptune sextile Pallas
Chiron sextile Sedna
Ceres sextile Vesta

Planets	00:00 am	Moon
Sun	04 vir 53	01.00 am - 20 sco 03
Mercury	02 vir 46	03.00 am - 21 sco 04
Venus	02 leo 09	05.00 am - 22 sco 04
Mars	24 leo 39	07.00 am - 23 sco 05
Jupiter	21 lib 16	09.00 am - 24 sco 05
Saturn	21 sag 11	11.00 am - 25 sco 05
Uranus	28 ar 16	13.00 pm - 26 sco 06
Neptune	13 pis 04	15.00 pm - 27 sco 06
Pluto	17 cap 05	17.00 pm - 28 sco 06
		19.00 pm - 29 sco 06
Oob		21.00 pm - 00 sag 06
		23.00 pm - 01 sag 06

Monday 28th August

Planetary Directions

Moon into Sagittarius 20:48

Retrograde Planets

Mercury, Uranus, Neptune, Pluto, Chiron, Eris, Salacia, Quaoar, Sedna

Asteroids		Dwarf Planets	
Juno	02 cap 43	Eris	23 ar 44
Vesta	19 vir 25	Haumea	23 lib 06
Pallas	13 tau 32	Makemake	02 lib 43
Ceres	19 can 47	Salacia	01 ar 43
Chiron	27 pis 32	Orcus	08 vir 33
N Node	24 leo 08	Quaoar	28 sag 43
S Node	24 aq 08	Sedna	26 tau 46

Moon Phase: Crescent
Sunrise: 06:07 BST
Sunset: 19:55
Moonrise: 13:28
Moonset: 23:11
Voc start: 10:37
Voc end: 20:47

Planetary and Angelic Hours

Moon	06:06	Venus	19:55
Saturn	07:15	Mercury	20:46
Jupiter	08:24	Moon	21:37
Mars	09:33	Saturn	22:28
Sun	10:42	Jupiter	23:19
Venus	11:51	Mars	00:10
Mercury	13:00	Sun	01:01
Moon	14:09	Venus	01:52
Saturn	15:18	Mercury	02:43
Jupiter	16:27	Moon	03:34
Mars	17:37	Saturn	04:25
Sun	18:46	Jupiter	05:16

Summer Bank Holiday

Aspects

Mercury trine Juno
Moon square Mars
Moon opposite Sedna
Moon trine Chiron
Moon square Mercury
Jupiter sextile Saturn
Neptune sextile Pallas
Chiron sextile Sedna
Ceres sextile Vesta

Planets	00:00 am	Moon
Sun	05 vir 51	01.00 am - 02 sag 05
Mercury	01 vir 55	03.00 am - 03 sag 05
Venus	03 leo 21	05.00 am - 04 sag 05
Mars	25 leo 17	07.00 am - 05 sag 05
Jupiter	21 lib 27	09.00 am - 06 sag 04
Saturn	21 sag 11	11.00 am - 07 sag 04
Uranus	28 ar 15	13.00 pm - 08 sag 04
Neptune	13 pis 02	15.00 pm - 09 sag 03
Pluto	17 cap 04	17.00 pm - 10 sag 03
		19.00 pm - 11 sag 02
Oob		21.00 pm - 12 sag 02
		23.00 pm - 13 sag 01

Tuesday 29th August

Retrograde Planets

Mercury, Uranus, Neptune, Pluto, Chiron, Eris, Salacia, Quaoar, Sedna

Asteroids		Dwarf Planets	
Juno	02 cap 44	Eris	23 ar 44
Vesta	18 vir 55	Haumea	23 lib 07
Pallas	13 tau 38	Makemake	02 lib 44
Ceres	20 can 11	Salacia	01 ar 41
Chiron	27 pis 30	Orcus	08 vir 34
N Node	24 leo 08	Quaoar	28 sag 43
S Node	24 aq 08	Sedna	26 tau 46

First Quarter: 09:14
Sunrise: 06:08 BST
Sunset: 19:53
Moonrise: 14:29
Moonset: 23:44
Voc start:
Voc end:

Planetary and Angelic Hours

Mars	06:08	Saturn	19:53
Sun	07:16	Jupiter	20:44
Venus	08:25	Mars	21:35
Mercury	09:34	Sun	22:27
Moon	10:43	Venus	23:18
Saturn	11:51	Mercury	00:09
Jupiter	13:00	Moon	01:01
Mars	14:09	Saturn	01:52
Sun	15:18	Jupiter	02:44
Venus	16:26	Mars	03:35
Mercury	17:35	Sun	04:26
Moon	18:44	Venus	05:18

Aspects

Moon trine Venus
Sun square Moon
Moon square Neptune
Mars square Sedna
Jupiter sextile Saturn
Saturn square Vesta
Neptune sextile Pallas
Chiron sextile Sedna
Ceres sextile Vesta

Planets	00:00 am	Moon
Sun	06 vir 49	01.00 am - 14 sag 00
Mercury	01 vir 08	03.00 am - 15 sag 00
Venus	04 leo 33	05.00 am - 15 sag 59
Mars	25 leo 55	07.00 am - 16 sag 59
Jupiter	21 lib 38	09.00 am - 17 sag 58
Saturn	21 sag 11	11.00 am - 18 sag 57
Uranus	28 ar 14	13.00 pm - 19 sag 57
Neptune	13 pis 01	15.00 pm - 20 sag 56
Pluto	17 cap 03	17.00 pm - 21 sag 55
		19.00 pm - 22 sag 55
Oob		21.00 pm - 23 sag 54
		23.00 pm - 24 sag 53

Wednesday 30th August

Retrograde Planets

Mercury, Uranus, Neptune, Pluto, Chiron, Eris, Salacia, Quaoar, Sedna

Asteroids		Dwarf Planets	
Juno	02 cap 45	Eris	23 ar 43
Vesta	20 vir 24	Haumea	23 lib 08
Pallas	13 tau 43	Makemake	02 lib 45
Ceres	20 can 34	Salacia	01 ar 40
Chiron	27 pis 27	Orcus	08 vir 36
N Node	24 leo 08	Quaoar	28 sag 42
S Node	24 aq 08	Sedna	26 tau 46

Moon Phase: Gibbous
Sunrise: 06:10 BST
Sunset: 19:51
Moonrise: 15:26
Moonset: None
Voc start:
Voc end:

Planetary and Angelic Hours

Mercury	06:09	Sun	19:50
Moon	07:18	Venus	20:42
Saturn	08:26	Mercury	21:34
Jupiter	09\:34	Moon	22:25
Mars	10:43	Saturn	23:17
Sun	11:51	Jupiter	00:09
Venus	13:00	Mars	01:00
Mercury	14:08	Sun	01:52
Moon	15:17	Venus	02:44
Saturn	16:25	Mercury	03:36
Jupiter	17:33	Moon	04:27
Mars	18:42	Saturn	05:19

Aspects

Moon square Vesta
Moon conjunct Saturn
Moon sextile Jupiter
Moon trine Eris
Moon trine Mars
Mars square Sedna
Jupiter sextile Saturn
Jupiter square Ceres
Saturn square Vesta
Neptune sextile Pallas
Chiron sextile Sedna
Ceres sextile Vesta

Planets	00:00 am	Moon
Sun	07 vir 47	01.00 am - 25 sag 53
Mercury	00 vir 25	03.00 am - 26 sag 52
Venus	05 leo 44	05.00 am - 27 sag 52
Mars	26 leo 34	07.00 am - 28 sag 51
Jupiter	21 lib 48	09.00 am - 29 sag 50
Saturn	21 sag 12	11.00 am - 00 cap 50
Uranus	28 ar 13	13.00 pm - 01 cap 49
Neptune	12 pis 59	15.00 pm - 02 cap 49
Pluto	17 cap 03	17.00 pm - 03 cap 48
		19.00 pm - 04 cap 48
		21.00 pm - 05 cap 48
Oob		23.00 pm - 06 cap 47

Thursday 31st August

Planetary Directions

Moon into Capicorn 09:19

Mercury rx -enters Leo at 16:28

Retrograde Planets

Mercury, Uranus, Neptune, Pluto, Chiron, Eris, Salacia, Quaoar, Sedna

Asteroids		Dwarf Planets	
Juno	02 cap 46	Eris	23 ar 43
Vesta	20 vir 54	Haumea	23 lib 09
Pallas	13 tau 48	Makemake	02 lib 46
Ceres	20 can 57	Salacia	01 ar 39
Chiron	27 pis 25	Orcus	08 vir 37
N Node	24 leo 09	Quaoar	28 sag 42
S Node	24 aq 09	Sedna	26 tau 46

Moon Phase: Gibbous
Sunrise: 06:11 BST
Sunset: 19:48
Moonrise: 16:19
Moonset: 00:23
Voc start: 05:42
Voc end: 09:18

Planetary and Angelic Hours			
Jupiter	06:11	Moon	19:48
Mars	07:19	Saturn	20:40
Sun	08:27	Jupiter	21:32
Venus	09:35	Mars	22:24
Mercury	10:43	Sun	23:16
Moon	11:51	Venus	00:08
Saturn	12:59	Mercury	01:00
Jupiter	14:08	Moon	01:52
Mars	15:16	Saturn	02:44
Sun	16:24	Jupiter	03:36
Venus	17:32	Mars	04:28
Mercury	18:40	Sun	05:20

Aspects

Moon trine Mars
Moon square Chiron
Moon trine Uranus
Mars square Sedna
Moon trine Mercury
Ceres sextile Vesta
Moon conjunct Juno
Saturn square Vesta
Sun trine Moon
Mars trine Uranus
Jupiter sextile Saturn
Jupiter square Ceres
Neptune sextile Pallas
Chiron sextile Sedna

Planets	00:00 am	Moon
Sun	08 vir 45	01.00 am - 07 cap 47
Mercury	29 leo 47	03.00 am - 08 cap 47
Venus	06 leo 56	05.00 am - 09 cap 47
Mars	27 leo 12	07.00 am - 10 cap 47
Jupiter	21 leo 59	09.00 am - 11 cap 46
Saturn	21 sag 13	11.00 am - 12 cap 46
Uranus	28 ar 11	13.00 pm - 13 cap 46
Neptune	12 pis 58	15.00 pm - 14 cap 47
Pluto	17 cap 02	17.00 pm - 15 cap 47
		19.00 pm - 16 cap 47
Oob		21.00 pm - 17 cap 47
		23.00 pm - 18 cap 47

Friday 1st September

Retrograde Planets

Mercury, Uranus, Neptune, Pluto, Chiron, Eris, Salacia, Quaoar, Sedna

Asteroids		Dwarf Planets	
Juno	02 cap 48	Eris	23 ar 44
Vesta	21 vir 23	Haumea	23 lib 10
Pallas	13 tau 52	Makemake	02 lib 48
Ceres	21 can 21	Salacia	01 ar 38
Chiron	27 pis 22	Orcus	08 vir 39
N Node	24 leo 10	Quaoar	28 sag 42
S Node	24 aq 10	Sedna	26 tau 46

Moon Phase: Gibbous
Sunrise: 06:13 BST
Sunset: 19:46
Moonrise: 17:07
Moonset: 01:07
Voc start:
Voc end:

Planetary and Angelic Hours			
Venus	06:12	Mars	19:46
Mercury	07:20	Sun	20:38
Moon	08:28	Venus	21:31
Saturn	09:36	Mercury	22:23
Jupiter	10:43	Moon	23:15
Mars	11:51	Saturn	00:08
Sun	12:59	Jupiter	01:00
Venus	14:07	Mars	01:52
Mercury	15:15	Sun	02:44
Moon	16:23	Venus	03:37
Saturn	17:30	Mercury	04:29
Jupiter	18.38	Moon	05:21

Aspects

Sun trine Moon
Moon sextile Neptune
Moon trine Pallas
Moon conjunct Pluto
Mars trine Uranus
Jupiter sextile Saturn
Jupiter square Ceres
Saturn square Vesta
Chiron sextile Sedna
Ceres sextile Vesta

Planets	00:00 am	Moon
Sun	09 vir 43	01.00 am - 19 cap 48
Mercury	29 leo 15	03.00 am - 20 cap 48
Venus	08 leo 08	05.00 am - 21 cap 49
Mars	27 leo 50	07.00 am - 22 cap 50
Jupiter	22 lib 11	09.00 am - 23 cap 50
Saturn	21 sag 13	11.00 am - 24 cap 41
Uranus	28 ar 10	13.00 pm - 25 cap 52
Neptune	12 pis 56	15.00 pm - 26 cap 53
Pluto	17 cap 01	17.00 pm - 27 cap 54
		19.00 pm - 28 cap 55
Oob		21.00 pm - 29 cap 56
		23.00 pm - 00 aq 58

Saturday 2nd September

Planetary Directions

Moon into Aquarius 21:07

Retrograde Planets

Mercury, Uranus, Neptune, Pluto, Chiron, Eris, Salacia, Quaoar, Sedna

Asteroids		Dwarf Planets	
Juno	02 cap 50	Eris	23 ar 42
Vesta	21 vir 53	Haumea	23 lib 11
Pallas	13 tau 56	Makemake	02 lib 49
Ceres	21 can 44	Salacia	01 ar 37
Chiron	27 pis 19	Orcus	08 vir 40
N Node	24 leo 11	Quaoar	28 sag 42
S Node	24 aq 11	Sedna	26 tau 46

Moon Phase: Gibbous
Sunrise: 06:15 BST
Sunset: 19:44
Moonrise: 17:50
Moonset: 01:58
Voc start: 17:29
Voc end: 21:06

Planetary and Angelic Hours			
Saturn	06:14	Mercury	19:44
Jupiter	07:21	Moon	20:36
Mars	08:29	Saturn	21:29
Sun	09:36	Jupiter	22:22
Venus	10:44	Mars	23:14
Mercury	11:51	Sun	00:07
Moon	12:59	Venus	01:00
Saturn	14:06	Mercury	01:52
Jupiter	15:14	Moon	02:45
Mars	16:21	Saturn	03:37
Sun	17:29	Jupiter	04:30
Venus	18:36	Mars	05:23

Aspects

Moon opposite Ceres
Moon trine Vesta
Moon square Jupiter
Moon square Eris
Mars trine Uranus
Moon trine Sedna
Moon sextile Chiron
Moon square Uranus
Mercury conjunct Mars
Mercury trine Uranus
Jupiter square Ceres
Chiron sextile Sedna
Ceres sextile Vesta

Planets	00:00 am	Moon
Sun	10 vir 41	01.00 am - 01 aq 59
Mercury	28 leo 51	03.00 am - 03 aq 00
Venus	09 leo 20	05.00 am - 04 aq 02
Mars	28 leo 28	07.00 am - 05 aq 04
Jupiter	22 lib 22	09.00 am - 06 aq 06
Saturn	21 sag 14	11.00 am - 07 aq 07
Uranus	28 ar 09	13.00 pm - 08 aq 09
Neptune	12 pis 54	15.00 pm - 09 aq 11
Pluto	17 cap 00	17.00 pm - 10 aq 14
		19.00 pm - 11 aq 16
Oob		21.00 pm - 12 aq 18
		23.00 pm - 13 aq 21

Sunday 3rd September

Retrograde Planets

Mercury, Uranus, Neptune, Pluto, Chiron, Eris, Salacia, Quaoar, Sedna

Asteroids		Dwarf Planets	
Juno	02 cap 52	Eris	23 ar 42
Vesta	22 vir 22	Haumea	23 lib 12
Pallas	14 tau 00	Makemake	02 lib 50
Ceres	22 can 07	Salacia	01 ar 36
Chiron	27 pis 17	Orcus	08 vir 41
N Node	24 leo 12	Quaoar	28 sag 41
S Node	24 aq 12	Sedna	26 tau 46

Moon Phase: Gibbous
Sunrise: 06:16 BST
Sunset: 19:42
Moonrise: 18:27
Moonset: 02:56
Voc start:
Voc end:

Planetary and Angelic Hours			
Sun	06:15	Jupiter	19:42
Venus	07:23	Mars	20:35
Mercury	08:30	Sun	21:27
Moon	09:37	Venus	22:20
Saturn	10:44	Mercury	23:13
Jupiter	11:51	Moon	00:06
Mars	12:58	Saturn	00:59
Sun	14:06	Jupiter	01:52
Venus	15:13	Mars	02:45
Mercury	16:20	Sun	03:38
Moon	17:27	Venus	04:31
Saturn	18:34	Mercury	05:24

Aspects

Mercury conjunct Mars
Moon opposite Venus
Moon square Pallas
Mercury trine Uranus
Mars trine Uranus
Jupiter square Ceres
Chiron sextile Sedna
Ceres sextile Vesta

Planets	00:00 am	Moon
Sun	11 vir 39	01.00 am - 14 aq 24
Mercury	28 leo 34	03.00 am - 15 aq 26
Venus	10 leo 32	05.00 am - 16 aq 29
Mars	29 leo 06	07.00 am - 17 aq 32
Jupiter	22 lib 33	09.00 am - 18 aq 35
Saturn	21 sag 15	11.00 am - 19 aq 38
Uranus	28 ar 07	13.00 pm - 20 aq 42
Neptune	12 pis 53	15.00 pm - 21 aq 45
Pluto	17 cap 00	17.00 pm - 22 aq 49
		19.00 pm - 23 aq 52
Oob		21.00 pm - 24 aq 56
		23.00 pm - 26 aq 00

Monday 4th September

Retrograde Planets

Mercury, Uranus, Neptune, Pluto, Chiron, Eris, Salacia, Quaoar, Sedna

Asteroids		Dwarf Planets	
Juno	02 cap 55	Eris	23 ar 41
Vesta	22 vir 52	Haumea	23 lib 13
Pallas	14 tau 03	Makemake	02 lib 52
Ceres	22 can 30	Salacia	01 ar 35
Chiron	27 pis 14	Orcus	08 vir 43
N Node	24 leo 13	Quaoar	28 sag 41
S Node	24 aq 13	Sedna	26 tau 46

Moon Phase: Gibbous
Sunrise: 06:18 BST
Sunset: 19:39
Moonrise: 18:59
Moonset: 03:58
Voc start:
Voc end:

Planetary and Angelic Hours			
Moon	06:17	Venus	19:39
Saturn	07:24	Mercury	20:33
Jupiter	08:31	Moon	21:26
Mars	09:37	Saturn	22:19
Sun	10:44	Jupiter	23:12
Venus	11:51	Mars	00:06
Mercury	12:58	Sun	00:59
Moon	14:05	Venus	01:52
Saturn	15:12	Mercury	02:45
Jupiter	16:19	Moon	03:39
Mars	17:26	Saturn	04:32
Sun	18:32	Jupiter	05:25

Aspects

Jupiter square Ceres
Moon sextile Saturn
Moon trine Jupiter
Moon sextile Eris
Moon square Sedna
Sun opposite Neptune
Mercury trine Uranus
Jupiter opposite Eris
Chiron sextile Sedna
Ceres sextile Vesta
Ceres square Eris

Planets	**00:00 am**	**Moon**
Sun	12 vir 37	01.00 am - 27 aq 04
Mercury	28 leo 26	03.00 am - 28 aq 08
Venus	11 leo 45	05.00 am - 29 aq 12
Mars	29 leo 44	07.00 am - 00 pis 17
Jupiter	22 lib 44	09.00 am - 01 pis 21
Saturn	21 sag 16	11.00 am - 02 pis 26
Uranus	28 ar 06	13.00 pm - 03 pis 30
Neptune	12 pis 51	15.00 pm - 04 pis 35
Pluto	16 cap 59	17.00 pm - 05 pis 40
		19.00 pm - 06 pis 45
Oob		21.00 pm - 07 pis 50
		23.00 pm - 08 pis 56

Tuesday 5th September

Planetary Directions

Moon into Pisces 06:29
Mars into Virgo 10:35
Mercury direct
28 leo 25 at 12:30

Retrograde Planets

Mercury, Uranus, Neptune, Pluto, Chiron, Eris, Salacia, Quaoar, Sedna

Asteroids		**Dwarf Planets**	
Juno	02 cap 58	Eris	23 ar 41
Vesta	23 vir 22	Haumea	23 lib 14
Pallas	14 tau 06	Makemake	02 lib 53
Ceres	22 can 53	Salacia	01 ar 33
Chiron	27 pis 12	Orcus	08 vir 44
N Node	24 leo 14	Quaoar	28 sag 41
S Node	24 aq 12	Sedna	26 tau 46

Moon Phase: Gibbous
Sunrise: 06:19 BST
Sunset: 19:37
Moonrise: 19:28
Moonset: 05:05
Voc start: 06:15
Voc end: 06:28

Planetary and Angelic Hours

Mars	06:18	Saturn	19:37
Sun	07:25	Jupiter	20:31
Venus	08:32	Mars	21:24
Mercury	09:38	Sun	22:18
Moon	10:45	Venus	23:11
Saturn	11:51	Mercury	00:05
Jupiter	12:58	Moon	00:59
Mars	14:04	Saturn	01:52
Sun	15:11	Jupiter	02:46
Venus	16:17	Mars	03:39
Mercury	17:24	Sun	04:33
Moon	18:31	Venus	05:26

Aspects

Moon sextile Uranus
Moon opp. Mercury
Moon opposite Mars
Sun opposite Neptune
Moon sextile Juno
Sun trine Pallas
Mercury trine Uranus
Jupiter square Ceres
Jupiter opposite Eris
Chiron sextile Sedna
Ceres sextile Vesta
Ceres square Eris

Wednesday 6th September

Planets	00:00 am	Moon
Sun	13 vir 36	01.00 am - 10 pis 01
Mercury	28 leo 26	03.00 am - 11 pis 07
Venus	12 leo 57	05.00 am - 12 pis 12
Mars	00 vir 22	07.00 am - 13 pis 18
Jupiter	22 lib 55	09.00 am - 14 pis 24
Saturn	21 sag 17	11.00 am - 15 pis 30
Uranus	28 ar 04	13.00 pm - 16 pis 36
Neptune	12 pis 49	15.00 pm - 17 pis 42
Pluto	16 cap 58	17.00 pm - 18 pis 49
		19.00 pm - 19 pis 55
Oob		21.00 pm - 21 pis 02
		23.00 pm - 22 pis 09

Retrograde Planets

Uranus, Neptune, Pluto, Chiron, Eris, Salacia, Quaoar, Sedna

Asteroids		Dwarf Planets	
Juno	03 cap 02	Eris	23 ar 40
Vesta	23 vir 51	Haumea	23 lib 16
Pallas	14 tau 09	Makemake	02 lib 54
Ceres	23 can 16	Salacia	01 ar 32
Chiron	27 pis 09	Orcus	08 vir 46
N Node	24 leo 13	Quaoar	28 sag 41
S Node	24 aq 13	Sedna	26 tau 46

Full Moon: 08:04
Sunrise: 06:21 BST
Sunset: 19:35
Moonrise: 19:55
Moonset: 06:15
Voc start: 21:28
Voc end:

Planetary and Angelic Hours			
Mercury	06:20	Sun	19:35
Moon	07:26	Venus	20:29
Saturn	08:32	Mercury	21:23
Jupiter	09:39	Moon	22:17
Mars	10:45	Saturn	23:10
Sun	11:51	Jupiter	00:04
Venus	12:57	Mars	00:58
Mercury	14:04	Sun	01:52
Moon	15:10	Venus	02:46
Saturn	16:16	Mercury	03:40
Jupiter	17:22	Moon	04:34
Mars	18:29	Saturn	05:28

Aspects

Moon conj. Neptune
Sun trine Moon
Moon sextile Pallas
Moon sextile Pluto
Sun trine Pallas
Moon square Saturn
Moon trine Ceres
Mercury trine Uranus
Venus square Pallas
Jupiter square Ceres
Jupiter opposite Eris
Chiron sextile Sedna
Ceres sextile Vesta
Ceres square Eris

Planets	00:00 am	Moon
Sun	14 vir 34	01.00 am - 23 pis 15
Mercury	28 leo 35	03.00 am - 24 pis 22
Venus	14 leo 09	05.00 am - 25 pis 29
Mars	01 vir 01	07.00 am - 26 pis 37
Jupiter	23 lib 07	09.00 am - 27 pis 44
Saturn	21 sag 18	11.00 am - 28 pis 51
Uranus	28 ar 03	13.00 pm - 29 pis 59
Neptune	12 pis 48	15.00 pm - 01 ar 06
Pluto	16 cap 58	17.00 pm - 02 ar 14
		19.00 pm - 03 ar 22
Oob		21.00 pm - 04 ar 30
		23.00 pm - 05 ar 38

Thursday 7th September

Planetary Directions

Moon into Aries 13:02

Retrograde Planets

Uranus, Neptune, Pluto, Chiron, Eris, Salacia, Quaoar, Sedna

Asteroids		Dwarf Planets	
Juno	03 cap 05	Eris	23 ar 40
Vesta	24 vir 21	Haumea	23 lib 17
Pallas	14 tau 11	Makemake	02 lib 54
Ceres	23 can 39	Salacia	01 ar 31
Chiron	27 pis 06	Orcus	08 vir 47
N Node	24 leo 11	Quaoar	28 sag 41
S Node	24 aq 11	Sedna	26 tau 45

Phase: Disseminating
Sunrise: 06:23 BST
Sunset: 19:33
Moonrise: 20:20
Moonset: 07:27
Voc start:
Voc end: 13:01

Planetary and Angelic Hours			
Jupiter	06:22	Moon	19:33
Mars	07:27	Saturn	20:27
Sun	08:33	Jupiter	21:21
Venus	09:39	Mars	22:15
Mercury	10:45	Sun	23:09
Moon	11:51	Venus	00:04
Saturn	12:57	Mercury	00:58
Jupiter	14:03	Moon	01:52
Mars	15:09	Saturn	02:46
Sun	16:15	Jupiter	03:40
Venus	17:21	Mars	04:35
Mercury	18:27	Sun	05:29

Aspects

Venus square Pallas
Moon trine Ceres
Ceres square Eris
Moon opposite Vesta
Moon sextile Sedna
Moon conjunct Chiron
Moon square Juno
Mercury trine Uranus
Jupiter square Ceres
Jupiter opposite Eris
Chiron sextile Sedna
Ceres sextile Vesta

Planets	00:00 am	Moon
Sun	15 vir 32	01.00 am - 06 ar 46
Mercury	28 leo 53	03.00 am - 07 ar 54
Venus	15 leo 22	05.00 am - 09 ar 02
Mars	01 vir 39	07.00 am - 10 ar 11
Jupiter	23 lib 18	09.00 am - 11 ar 19
Saturn	21 sag 19	11.00 am - 12 ar 28
Uranus	28 ar 01	13.00 pm - 13 ar 36
Neptune	12 pis 46	15.00 pm - 14 ar 45
Pluto	16 cap 57	17.00 pm - 15 ar 54
		19.00 pm - 17 ar 03
Oob		21.00 pm - 18 ar 12
		23.00 pm - 19 ar 21

Friday 8th September

Retrograde Planets

Uranus, Neptune, Pluto, Chiron, Eris, Salacia, Quaoar, Sedna

Asteroids		Dwarf Planets	
Juno	03 cap 10	Eris	23 ar 39
Vesta	24 vir 51	Haumea	23 lib 18
Pallas	14 tau 13	Makemake	02 lib 57
Ceres	24 can 01	Salacia	01 ar 30
Chiron	27 pis 04	Orcus	08 vir 49
N Node	24 leo 09	Quaoar	28 sag 41
S Node	24 aq 09	Sedna	26 tau 45

Phase: Disseminating
Sunrise: 06:24 BST
Sunset: 19:30
Moonrise: 20:45
Moonset: 08:41
Voc start:
Voc end:

Planetary and Angelic Hours			
Venus	06:23	Mars	19:30
Mercury	07:29	Sun	20:25
Moon	08:34	Venus	21:19
Saturn	09:40	Mercury	22:14
Jupiter	10:46	Moon	23:09
Mars	11:51	Saturn	00:03
Sun	12:57	Jupiter	00:58
Venus	14:02	Mars	01:52
Mercury	15:08	Sun	02:47
Moon	16:14	Venus	03:41
Saturn	17:19	Mercury	04:36
Jupiter	18:25	Moon	05:30

Aspects

Moon trine Vesta
Moon square Pluto
Sun trine Pluto
Moon trine Saturn
Mars trine Juno
Jupiter square Ceres
Jupiter opposite Eris
Chiron sextile Sedna
Ceres sextile Vesta
Ceres square Eris

Planets	00:00 am	Moon
Sun	16 vir 30	01.00 am - 20 ar 30
Mercury	29 leo 20	03.00 am - 21 ar 40
Venus	16 leo 34	05.00 am - 22 ar 49
Mars	02 vir 17	07.00 am - 23 ar 58
Jupiter	23 lib 30	09.00 am - 25 ar 08
Saturn	21 sag 21	11.00 am - 26 ar 17
Uranus	27 ar 59	13.00 pm - 27 ar 27
Neptune	12 pis 44	15.00 pm - 28 ar 37
Pluto	16 cap 57	17.00 pm - 29 ar 46
		19.00 pm - 00 tau 56
Oob		21.00 pm - 02 tau 06
		23.00 pm - 03 tau 16

Saturday 9th September

Planetary Directions

Moon into Taurus
17:23

Retrograde Planets

Uranus, Neptune, Pluto, Chiron, Eris, Salacia, Quaoar, Sedna

Asteroids		Dwarf Planets	
Juno	03 cap 14	Eris	23 ar 39
Vesta	25 vir 20	Haumea	23 lib 19
Pallas	14 tau 14	Makemake	02 lib 58
Ceres	24 can 24	Salacia	01 ar 29
Chiron	27 pis 01	Orcus	08 vir 50
N Node	24 leo 06	Quaoar	28 sag 41
S Node	24 aq 06	Sedna	26 tau 45

Phase: Disseminating
Sunrise: 06:26 BST
Sunset: 19:28
Moonrise: 21:12
Moonset: 09:56
Voc start: 16:52
Voc end: 17:22

Planetary and Angelic Hours			
Saturn	06:25	Mercury	19:28
Jupiter	07:30	Moon	20:23
Mars	08:35	Saturn	21:18
Sun	09:41	Jupiter	22:13
Venus	10:46	Mars	23:08
Mercury	11:51	Sun	00:02
Moon	12:56	Venus	00:57
Saturn	14:02	Mercury	01:52
Jupiter	15:07	Moon	02:47
Mars	16:12	Saturn	03:42
Sun	17:18	Jupiter	04:37
Venus	18:23	Mars	05:31

Aspects

Moon trine Saturn
Moon opposite Jupiter
Moon conjunct Eris
Moon square Ceres
Sun trine Pluto
Moon conjunct Uranus
Moon trine Mercury
Jupiter opposite Eris
Moon trine Mars
Moon trine Juno
Mars trine Juno
Chiron sextile Sedna
Vesta trine Sedna

Planets	00:00 am	Moon
		01.00 am - 04 tau 26
Sun	17 vir 28	03.00 am - 05 tau36
Mercury	29 leo 55	05.00 am - 06 tau 46
Venus	17 leo 47	07.00 am - 07 tau 56
Mars	02 vir 55	09.00 am - 09 tau 07
Jupiter	23 lib 42	11.00 am - 10 tau 17
Saturn	21 sag 22	13.00 pm - 11 tau 27
Uranus	27 ar 58	15.00 pm - 12 tau 38
Neptune	12 pis 43	17.00 pm - 13 tau 38
Pluto	16 cap 56	19.00 pm - 14 tau 58
		21.00 pm - 16 tau 09
Oob		23.00 pm - 17 tau 20

Sunday 10th September

Planetary Directions

Mercury re enters Virgo at 03:52

Retrograde Planets

Uranus, Neptune, Pluto, Chiron, Eris, Salacia, Quaoar, Sedna

Asteroids		Dwarf Planets	
Juno	03 cap 19	Eris	23 ar 39
Vesta	25 vir 50	Haumea	23 lib 20
Pallas	14 tau 15	Makemake	03 lib 00
Ceres	24 can 47	Salacia	01 ar 27
Chiron	26 pis 58	Orcus	08 vir 51
N Node	24 leo 02	Quaoar	28 sag 41
S Node	24 aq 02	Sedna	26 tau 45

Phase: Disseminating
Sunrise: 06:27 BST
Sunset: 19:26
Moonrise: 21:42
Moonset: 11:11
Voc start:
Voc end:

Planetary and Angelic Hours

Sun	06:26	Jupiter	19:26
Venus	07:31	Mars	20:21
Mercury	08:36	Sun	21:16
Moon	09:41	Venus	22:11
Saturn	10:46	Mercury	23:07
Jupiter	11:51	Moon	00:02
Mars	12:56	Saturn	00:57
Sun	14:01	Jupiter	01:52
Venus	15:06	Mars	02:47
Mercury	16:11	Sun	03:42
Moon	17:16	Venus	04:37
Saturn	18:21	Mercury	05:33

Aspects

Moon sextile Neptune
Moon conjunct Pallas
Mars trine Juno
Moon trine Pluto
Sun trine Moon
Moon square Venus
Jupiter opposite Eris
Chiron opposite Vesta
Chiron sextile Sedna
Vesta trine Sedna

Planets	00:00 am	Moon
Sun	18 vir 27	01.00 am - 18 tau 30
Mercury	00 vir 38	03.00 am - 19 tau 41
Venus	18 leo 59	05.00 am - 20 tau 51
Mars	03 vir 33	07.00 am - 22 tau 02
Jupiter	23 lib 53	09.00 am - 23 tau 13
Saturn	21 sag 24	11.00 am - 24 tau 24
Uranus	27 ar 56	13.00 pm - 25 tau 34
Neptune	12 pis 41	15.00 pm - 26 tau 45
Pluto	16 cap 55	17.00 pm - 27 tau 56
		19.00 pm - 29 tau 07
Oob		21.00 pm - 00 gem 18
		23.00 pm - 01 gem 29

Monday 11th September

Planetary Directions

Quaoar direct
28 sag 40 at 16:35
Pallas retrograde
14 tau 16 at 18:49
Moon in Gemini 20:30

Retrograde Planets

Uranus, Neptune, Pluto, Chiron, Eris, Salacia, Quaoar, Sedna

Asteroids		Dwarf Planets	
Juno	03 cap 24	Eris	23 ar 38
Vesta	26 vir 20	Haumea	23 lib 22
Pallas	14 tau 16	Makemake	03 lib 01
Ceres	25 can 09	Salacia	01 ar 26
Chiron	26 pis 56	Orcus	08 vir 53
N Node	24 leo 00	Quaoar	28 sag 40
S Node	24 aq 00	Sedna	26 tau 45

Phase: Disseminating
Sunrise: 06:29 BST
Sunset: 19:24
Moonrise: 22:16
Moonset: 12:26
Voc start: 01:53
Voc end: 20:29

Planetary and Angelic Hours			
Moon	06:28	Venus	19:24
Saturn	07:32	Mercury	20:19
Jupiter	08:37	Moon	21:15
Mars	09:42	Saturn	22:10
Sun	10:46	Jupiter	23:06
Venus	11:51	Mars	00:01
Mercury	12:56	Sun	00:57
Moon	14:00	Venus	01:52
Saturn	15:05	Mercury	02:47
Jupiter	16:10	Moon	03:43
Mars	17:14	Saturn	04:38
Sun	18:19	Jupiter	05:34

Aspects

Moon square Venus
Moon sextile Ceres
Moon trine Vesta
Moon conjunct Sedna
Moon sextile Chiron
Vesta trine Sedna
Moon square Mercury
Mars trine Juno
Jupiter opposite Eris
Chiron opposite Vesta
Chiron sextile Sedna

Planets	00:00 am	Moon
Sun	19 vir 25	01.00 am - 02 gem 39
Mercury	01 vir 30	03.00 am - 03 gem 50
Venus	20 leo 12	05.00 am - 05 gem 01
Mars	04 vir 11	07.00 am - 06 gem 12
Jupiter	24 lib 05	09.00 am - 07 gem 23
Saturn	21 sag 25	11.00 am - 08 gem 34
Uranus	27 ar 54	13.00 pm - 09 gem 45
Neptune	12 pis 39	15.00 pm - 10 gem 56
Pluto	16 cap 55	17.00 pm - 12 gem 07
		19.00 pm - 13 gem 18
Oob		21.00 pm - 14 gem 29
		23.00 pm - 15 gem 40

Tuesday 12th September

Retrograde Planets

Uranus, Neptune, Pluto, Pallas, Chiron, Eris, Salacia, Sedna

Asteroids		Dwarf Planets	
Juno	03 cap 30	Eris	23 ar 38
Vesta	26 vir 50	Haumea	23 lib 23
Pallas	14 tau 16	Makemake	03 lib 02
Ceres	25 can 32	Salacia	01 ar 25
Chiron	26 pis 53	Orcus	08 vir 54
N Node	23 leo 57	Quaoar	28 sag 40
S Node	23 aq 57	Sedna	26 tau 45

Phase: Disseminating
Sunrise: 06:30 BST
Sunset: 19:21
Moonrise: 22:57
Moonset: 13:40
Voc start:
Voc end:

Planetary and Angelic Hours			
Mars	06:29	Saturn	19:21
Sun	07:34	Jupiter	20:17
Venus	08:38	Mars	21:13
Mercury	09:42	Sun	22:09
Moon	10:47	Venus	23:05
Saturn	11:51	Mercury	00:00
Jupiter	12:55	Moon	00:56
Mars	14:00	Saturn	01:52
Sun	15:04	Jupiter	02:48
Venus	16:08	Mars	03:44
Mercury	17:13	Sun	04:39
Moon	18:17	Venus	05:35

Aspects

Chiron opposite Vesta
Moon square Mars
Moon square Neptune
Venus trine Saturn
Jupiter opposite Eris
Chiron trine Ceres
Chiron sextile Sedna
Ceres sextile Sedna
Vesta trine Sedna

Planets	00:00 am	Moon
Sun	20 vir 23	01.00 am - 16 gem 51
Mercury	02 vir 29	03.00 am - 18 gem 02
Venus	21 leo 25	05.00 am - 19 gem 13
Mars	04 vir 49	07.00 am - 20 gem 24
Jupiter	24 lib 17	09.00 am - 21 gem 35
Saturn	21 sag 27	11.00 am - 22 gem 46
Uranus	27 ar 53	13.00 pm - 23 gem 57
Neptune	12 pis 38	15.00 pm - 25 gem 08
Pluto	16 cap 54	17.00 pm - 26 gem 19
		19.00 pm - 27 gem 30
Oob		21.00 pm - 28 gem 41
		23.00 pm - 29 gem 52

Wed 13th September

Planetary Directions

Moon into Cancer
23:13

Retrograde Planets

Uranus, Neptune, Pluto, Pallas, Chiron, Eris, Salacia, Sedna

Asteroids		Dwarf Planets	
Juno	03 cap 36	Eris	23 ar 37
Vesta	27 vir 20	Haumea	23 lib 24
Pallas	14 tau 16	Makemake	03 lib 04
Ceres	25 can 54	Salacia	01 ar 24
Chiron	26 pis 50	Orcus	08 vir 56
N Node	23 leo 57	Quaoar	28 sag 41
S Node	23 aq 57	Sedna	26 tau 45

Last Quarter: 07:26
Sunrise: 06:32 BST
Sunset: 19:19
Moonrise: 23:46
Moonset: 14:49
Voc start: 19:35
Voc end: 23:12

Planetary and Angelic Hours			
Mercury	06:31	Sun	19:19
Moon	07:35	Venus	20:15
Saturn	08:39	Mercury	21:11
Jupiter	09:43	Moon	22:07
Mars	10:47	Saturn	23:04
Sun	11:51	Jupiter	00:00
Venus	12:55	Mars	00:56
Mercury	13:59	Sun	01:52
Moon	15:03	Venus	02:48
Saturn	16:07	Mercury	03:44
Jupiter	17:11	Moon	04:40
Mars	18:15	Saturn	05:36

Aspects

Venus trine Saturn
Sun square Moon
Moon opposite Saturn
Moon sextile Venus
Moon sextile Eris
Moon trine Jupiter
Moon square Chiron
Moon square Vesta
Moon sextile Uranus
Sun square Saturn
Mercury trine Juno
Venus trine Eris
Jupiter opposite Eris
Chiron trine Ceres
Chiron sextile Sedna
Ceres sextile Sedna

Planets	00:00 am	Moon
Sun	21 vir 22	01.00 am - 01 can 03
Mercury	03 vir 35	03.00 am - 02 can 14
Venus	22 leo 37	05.00 am - 03 can 25
Mars	05 vir 27	07.00 am - 04 can 36
Jupiter	24 lib 29	09.00 am - 05 can 47
Saturn	21 sag 29	11.00 am - 06 can 58
Uranus	27 ar 51	13.00 pm - 08 can 08
Neptune	12 pis 36	15.00 pm - 09 can 19
Pluto	16 cap 54	17.00 pm - 10 can 30
		19.00 pm - 11 can 41
Oob		21.00 pm - 12 can 52
		23.00 pm - 14 can 02

Thursday 14th September

Retrograde Planets

Uranus, Neptune, Pluto, Pallas, Chiron, Eris, Salacia, Sedna

Asteroids		Dwarf Planets	
Juno	03 cap 42	Eris	23 ar 37
Vesta	27 vir 50	Haumea	23 lib 25
Pallas	14 tau 15	Makemake	03 lib 05
Ceres	26 can 16	Salacia	01 ar 23
Chiron	26 pis 47	Orcus	08 vir 57
N Node	23 leo 57	Quaoar	28 sag 41
S Node	23 aq 57	Sedna	26 tau 44

Moon Phase: Balsamic
Sunrise: 06:34 BST
Sunset: 19:17
Moonrise: None
Moonset: 15:51
Voc start:
Voc end:

Planetary and Angelic Hours			
Jupiter	06:32	Moon	19:17
Mars	07:36	Saturn	20:13
Sun	08:40	Jupiter	21:10
Venus	09:44	Mars	22:06
Mercury	10:47	Sun	23:03
Moon	11:51	Venus	23:59
Saturn	12:55	Mercury	00:55
Jupiter	13:58	Moon	01:52
Mars	15:02	Saturn	02:48
Sun	16:06	Jupiter	03:45
Venus	17:09	Mars	04:41
Mercury	18:13	Sun	05:38

Aspects

Mercury trine Juno
Sun square Saturn
Moon opposite Juno
Moon sextile Mercury
Moon sextile Mars
Venus trine Eris
Moon trine Neptune
Moon sextile Pallas
Venus sextile Jupiter
Chiron trine Ceres
Chiron sextile Sedna
Ceres sextile Sedna

Planets	00:00 am	Moon
Sun	22 vir 20	01.00 am - 15 can 13
Mercury	04 vir 48	03.00 am - 16 can 24
Venus	23 leo 50	05.00 am - 17 can 34
Mars	06 vir 05	07.00 am - 18 can 45
Jupiter	24 lib 40	09.00 am - 19 can 56
Saturn	21 sag 31	11.00 am - 21 can 06
Uranus	27 ar 49	13.00 pm - 22 can 17
Neptune	12 pis 35	15.00 pm - 23 can 27
Pluto	16 cap 54	17.00 pm - 24 can 38
		19.00 pm - 25 can 48
Oob		21.00 pm - 26 can 59
		23.00 pm - 28 can 09

Friday 15th September

Retrograde Planets

Uranus, Neptune, Pluto, Pallas, Chiron, Eris, Salacia, Sedna

Asteroids		Dwarf Planets	
Juno	03 cap 48	Eris	23 ar 36
Vesta	28 vir 20	Haumea	23 lib 27
Pallas	14 tau 14	Makemake	03 lib 07
Ceres	26 can 39	Salacia	01 ar 21
Chiron	26 pis 45	Orcus	08 vir 58
N Node	23 leo 58	Quaoar	28 sag 41
S Node	23 aq 58	Sedna	26 tau 44

Moon Phase: Balsamic
Sunrise: 06:35 BST
Sunset: 19:14
Moonrise: 00:44
Moonset: 16:44
Voc start: 22:23
Voc end:

Planetary and Angelic Hours			
Venus	06:34	Mars	19:15
Mercury	07:37	Sun	20:11
Moon	08:41	Venus	21:08
Saturn	09:44	Mercury	22:05
Jupiter	10:48	Moon	23:02
Mars	11:51	Saturn	23:58
Sun	12:54	Jupiter	00:55
Venus	13:58	Mars	01:52
Mercury	15:01	Sun	02:49
Moon	16:04	Venus	03:45
Saturn	17:08	Mercury	04:42
Jupiter	18:11	Moon	05:39

Aspects

Moon opposite Pluto
Chiron sextile Sedna
Chiron trine Ceres
Ceres sextile Sedna
Sun sextile Moon
Moon square Eris
Moon square Jupiter
Moon trine Chiron
Moon sextile Sedna
Venus sextile Jupiter
Moon conjunct Ceres
Moon square Uranus
Moon sextile Vesta
Mercury conjunct Mars
Uranus square Ceres

Planets	00:00 am	Moon
Sun	23 vir 19	01.00 am - 29 can 29
Mercury	06 vir 07	03.00 am - 00 leo 29
Venus	25 leo 03	05.00 am - 01 leo 40
Mars	06 vir 43	07.00 am - 02 leo 50
Jupiter	24 lib 52	09.00 am - 04 leo 00
Saturn	21 sag 33	11.00 am - 05 leo 10
Uranus	27 ar 47	13.00 pm - 06 leo 20
Neptune	12 pis 33	15.00 pm - 07 leo 30
Pluto	16 cap 53	17.00 pm - 08 leo 40
		19.00 pm - 09 leo 50
Oob		21.00 pm - 11 leo 00
		23.00 pm - 12 leo 10

Saturday 16th September

Planetary Directions

Moon into Leo 02:09

Retrograde Planets

Uranus, Neptune, Pluto, Pallas, Chiron, Eris, Salacia, Sedna

Asteroids		Dwarf Planets	
Juno	03 cap 55	Eris	23 ar 36
Vesta	28 vir 50	Haumea	23 lib 28
Pallas	14 tau 12	Makemake	03 lib 08
Ceres	27 can 01	Salacia	01 ar 20
Chiron	26 pis 42	Orcus	09 vir 00
N Node	23 leo 59	Quaoar	28 sag 41
S Node	23 aq 59	Sedna	26 tau 44

Moon Phase: Balsamic
Sunrise: 06:37 BST
Sunset: 19:12
Moonrise: 01:49
Moonset: 17:29
Voc start:
Voc end: 02:08

Planetary and Angelic Hours			
Saturn	06:36	Mercury	19:12
Jupiter	07:39	Moon	20:09
Mars	08:42	Saturn	21:06
Sun	09:45	Jupiter	22:04
Venus	10:48	Mars	23:01
Mercury	11:51	Sun	23:58
Moon	12:54	Venus	00:55
Saturn	13:57	Mercury	01:52
Jupiter	15:00	Moon	02:49
Mars	16:03	Saturn	03:46
Sun	17:06	Jupiter	04:43
Venus	18:09	Mars	05:40

Aspects

Mercury conjunct Mars
Moon square Pallas
Venus square Sedna
Uranus square Ceres
Chiron trine Ceres
Chiron sextile Sedna
Ceres sextile Sedna

Planets	00:00 am	Moon
Sun	24 vir 17	01.00 am - 13 leo 19
Mercury	07 vir 31	03.00 am - 14 leo 29
Venus	26 leo 16	05.00 am - 15 leo 39
Mars	07 vir 21	07.00 am - 16 leo 48
Jupiter	25 lib 04	09.00 am - 17 leo 58
Saturn	21 sag 35	11.00 am - 19 leo 07
Uranus	27 ar 45	13.00 pm - 20 leo 17
Neptune	12 pis 31	15.00 pm - 21 leo 26
Pluto	16 cap 53	17.00 pm - 22 leo 35
		19.00 pm - 23 leo 45
Oob		21.00 pm - 24 leo 54
		23.00 pm - 26 leo 03

Sunday 17th September

Retrograde Planets

Uranus, Neptune, Pluto, Pallas, Chiron, Eris, Salacia, Sedna

Asteroids		Dwarf Planets	
Juno	04 cap 02	Eris	23 ar 35
Vesta	29 vir 20	Haumea	23 lib 29
Pallas	14 tau 10	Makemake	03 lib 09
Ceres	27 can 23	Salacia	01 ar 19
Chiron	26 pis 39	Orcus	09 vir 01
N Node	24 leo 01	Quaoar	28 sag 41
S Node	24 aq 01	Sedna	26 tau 44

Moon Phase: Balsamic
Sunrise: 06:38 BST
Sunset: 19:10
Moonrise: 03:00
Moonset: 18:06
Voc start:
Voc end:

Planetary and Angelic Hours			
Sun	06:37	Jupiter	19:10
Venus	07:40	Mars	20:07
Mercury	08:43	Sun	21:05
Moon	09:45	Venus	22:02
Saturn	10:48	Mercury	23:00
Jupiter	11:51	Moon	23:57
Mars	12:54	Saturn	00:54
Sun	13:56	Jupiter	01:52
Venus	14:59	Mars	02:49
Mercury	16:02	Sun	03:47
Moon	17:05	Venus	04:44
Saturn	18:07	Mercury	05:41

Aspects

Moon square Pallas
Venus square Sedna
Moon trine Saturn
Moon trine Eris
Moon sextile Jupiter
Uranus square Ceres
Moon square Sedna
Moon conjunct Venus
Moon trine Uranus
Venus trine Uranus
Chiron trine Sedna

Planets	**00:00 am**	**Moon**
Sun	25 vir 16	01.00 am - 27 leo 12
Mercury	09 vir 00	03.00 am - 28 leo 21
Venus	27 leo 29	05.00 am - 29 leo 30
Mars	07 vir 59	07.00 am - 00 vir 38
Jupiter	25 lib 16	09.00 am - 01 vir 47
Saturn	21 sag 37	11.00 am - 02 vir 56
Uranus	27 ar 43	13.00 pm - 04 vir 04
Neptune	12 pis 30	15.00 pm - 05 vir 13
Pluto	16 cap 52	17.00 pm - 06 vir 21
		19.00 pm - 07 vir 29
Oob		21.00 pm - 08 vir 38
		23.00 pm - 09 vir 46

Monday 18th September

Planetary Directions

Moon into Virgo 05:53
Vesta into Libra 08:48

Retrograde Planets

Uranus, Neptune, Pluto, Pallas, Chiron, Eris, Salacia, Sedna

Asteroids		**Dwarf Planets**	
Juno	04 cap 09	Eris	23 ar 35
Vesta	29 vir 50	Haumea	23 lib 31
Pallas	14 tau 07	Makemake	03 lib 11
Ceres	27 can 45	Salacia	01 ar 18
Chiron	26 pis 37	Orcus	09 vir 03
N Node	24 leo 01	Quaoar	28 sag 41
S Node	24 aq 01	Sedna	26 tau 43

Moon Phase: Balsamic
Sunrise: 06:40 BST
Sunset: 19:07
Moonrise: 04:14
Moonset: 18:37
Voc start: 01:54
Voc end: 05:52

Planetary and Angelic Hours

Moon	06:39	Venus	19:08
Saturn	07:41	Mercury	20:06
Jupiter	08:44	Moon	21:03
Mars	09:46	Saturn	22:01
Sun	10:48	Jupiter	22:59
Venus	11:51	Mars	23:56
Mercury	12:53	Sun	00:54
Moon	13:56	Venus	01:52
Saturn	14:58	Mercury	02:49
Jupiter	16:01	Moon	03:47
Mars	17:03	Saturn	04:45
Sun	18:05	Jupiter	05:43

Aspects

Moon conjunct Venus
Moon trine Uranus
Venus trine Uranus
Moon trine Juno
Moon conjunct Mars
Moon conj. Mercury
Sun opposite Chiron
Sun trine Sedna
Uranus square Ceres
Chiron sexile Sedna

Planets	00:00 am	Moon
Sun	26 vir 15	01.00 am - 10 vir 54
Mercury	10 vir 34	03.00 am - 12 vir 02
Venus	28 lib 42	05.00 am - 13 vir 10
Mars	08 vir 37	07.00 am - 14 vir 17
Jupiter	25 lib 29	09.00 am - 15 vir 25
Saturn	21 sag 39	11.00 am - 16 vir 33
Uranus	27 ar 41	13.00 pm - 17 vir 40
Neptune	12 pis 28	15.00 pm - 18 vir 48
Pluto	16 cap 52	17.00 pm - 19 vir 55
		19.00 pm - 21 vir 02
Oob		21.00 pm - 22 vir 09
		23.00 pm - 23 vir 16

Tuesday 19th September

Retrograde Planets

Uranus, Neptune, Pluto, Pallas, Chiron, Eris, Salacia, Sedna

Asteroids		Dwarf Planets	
Juno	04 cap 17	Eris	23 ar 34
Vesta	00 lib 20	Haumea	23 lib 32
Pallas	14 tau 04	Makemake	03 lib 12
Ceres	28 can 07	Salacia	01 ar 16
Chiron	26 pis 34	Orcus	09 vir 04
N Node	24 leo 00	Quaoar	28 sag 41
S Node	24 aq 00	Sedna	26 tau 43

Moon Phase: Balsamic
Sunrise: 06:42 BST
Sunset: 19:05
Moonrise: 05:28
Moonset: 19:04
Voc start:
Voc end:

Planetary and Angelic Hours			
Mars	06:40	Saturn	19:06
Sun	07:42	Jupiter	20:04
Venus	08:44	Mars	21:02
Mercury	09:47	Sun	22:00
Moon	10:49	Venus	22:58
Saturn	11:51	Mercury	23:56
Jupiter	12:53	Moon	00:54
Mars	13:55	Saturn	01:52
Sun	14:57	Jupiter	02:50
Venus	15:59	Mars	03:48
Mercury	17:01	Sun	04:46
Moon	18:03	Venus	05:44

Aspects

Moon opp. Neptune
Moon trine Pallas
Sun opposite Chiron
Moon trine Pluto
Sun trine Sedna
Moon square Saturn
Mercury opp. Neptune
Uranus square Ceres
Chiron sextile Sedna

Planets	00:00 am	Moon
Sun	27 vir 13	01.00 am - 24 vir 23
Mercury	12 vir 11	03.00 am - 25 vir 30
Venus	29 leo 56	05.00 am - 26 vir 37
Mars	09 vir 15	07.00 am - 27 vir 43
Jupiter	25 lib 41	09.00 am - 28 vir 50
Saturn	21 sag 42	11.00 am - 29 vir 56
Uranus	27 ar 39	13.00 pm - 01 lib 02
Neptune	12 pis 27	15.00 pm - 02 lib 09
Pluto	16 cap 52	17.00 pm - 03 lib 15
		19.00 pm - 04 lib 21
		21.00 pm - 05 lib 27
Oob		23.00 pm - 06 lib 32

Wednesday 20th September

Planetary Directions

Venus into Virgo 02:16
Moon into Libra 11:06

Retrograde Planets

Uranus, Neptune, Pluto, Pallas, Chiron, Eris, Salacia, Sedna

Asteroids		Dwarf Planets	
Juno	04 cap 25	Eris	23 ar 34
Vesta	00 lib 50	Haumea	23 lib 33
Pallas	14 tau 01	Makemake	03 lib 14
Ceres	28 can 28	Salacia	01 ar 15
Chiron	26 pis 31	Orcus	09 vir 05
N Node	23 leo 57	Quaoar	28 sag 41
S Node	23 aq 57	Sedna	26 tau 43

New Moon: 06:30
Sunrise: 06:43 BST
Sunset: 19:03
Moonrise: 06:41
Moonset: 19:29
Voc start: 06:29
Voc end: 11:05

Planetary and Angelic Hours

Mercury	06:42	Sun	19:03
Moon	07:44	Venus	20:02
Saturn	08:45	Mercury	21:00
Jupiter	09:47	Moon	21:58
Mars	10:49	Saturn	22:57
Sun	11:51	Jupiter	23:55
Venus	12:53	Mars	00:53
Mercury	13:54	Sun	01:52
Moon	14:56	Venus	02:50
Saturn	15:58	Mercury	03:48
Jupiter	17:00	Moon	04:47
Mars	18:01	Saturn	05:45

Aspects

Moon opposite Chiron
Mercury opp. Neptune
Moon trine Sedna
Sun conjunct Moon
Moon sextile Ceres
Moon conjunct Vesta
Moon square Juno
Moon trine Pallas
Chiron sextile Sedna

Thursday 21st September

Planets	**00:00 am**	**Moon**
Sun	28 vir 12	01.00 am - 07 lib 38
Mercury	13 vir 50	03.00 am - 08 lib 43
Venus	01 vir 09	05.00 am - 09 lib 49
Mars	09 vir 54	07.00 am - 10 lib 54
Jupiter	25 lib 53	09.00 am - 11 lib 59
Saturn	21 sag 44	11.00 am - 13 lib 04
Uranus	27 ar 37	13.00 pm - 14 lib 09
Neptune	12 pis 25	15.00 pm - 15 lib 14
Pluto	16 cap 52	17.00 pm - 16 lib 19
		19.00 pm - 17 lib 24
Oob		21.00 pm - 18 lib 28
		23.00 pm - 19 lib 33

Retrograde Planets

Uranus, Neptune, Pluto, Pallas, Chiron, Eris, Salacia, Sedna

Asteroids		**Dwarf Planets**	
Juno	04 cap 33	Eris	23 ar 33
Vesta	01 lib 20	Haumea	23 lib 35
Pallas	13 tau 56	Makemake	03 lib 15
Ceres	28 can 50	Salacia	01 ar 14
Chiron	26 pis 28	Orcus	09 vir 07
N Node	23 leo 53	Quaoar	28 sag 42
S Node	23 aq 53	Sedna	26 tau 43

Moon Phase: Crescent
Sunrise: 06:45 BST
Sunset: 19:01
Moonrise: 07:52
Moonset: 19:53
Voc start:
Voc end:

Planetary and Angelic Hours

Jupiter	06:43	Moon	19:01
Mars	07:45	Saturn	20:00
Sun	08:46	Jupiter	20:58
Venus	09:48	Mars	21:57
Mercury	10:49	Sun	22:56
Moon	11:51	Venus	23:54
Saturn	12:52	Mercury	00:53
Jupiter	13:54	Moon	01:52
Mars	14:55	Saturn	02:50
Sun	15:57	Jupiter	03:49
Venus	16:58	Mars	04:48
Mercury	18:00	Sun	05:46

Aspects

Mercury trine Pallas
Moon square Pluto
Sun sextile Ceres
Chiron sextile Sedna

Planets	**00:00 am**	**Moon**
Sun	29 vir 10	01.00 am - 20 lib 37
Mercury	15 vir 33	03.00 am - 21 lib 41
Venus	02 vir 22	05.00 am - 22 lib 45
Mars	10 vir 32	07.00 am - 23 lib 49
Jupiter	26 lib 05	09.00 am - 24 lib 53
Saturn	21 sag 47	11.00 am - 25 lib 56
Uranus	27 ar 35	13.00 pm - 27 lib 00
Neptune	12 pis 23	15.00 pm - 28 lib 03
Pluto	16 cap 51	17.00 pm - 29 lib 07
		19.00 pm - 00 sco 10
Oob		21.00 pm - 01 sco 13
		23.00 pm - 02 sco 16

Friday 22nd September

Planetary Directions

Moon into Scorpio 18:40
Sun into Libra at 21:02

Retrograde Planets

Uranus, Neptune, Pluto, Pallas, Chiron, Eris, Salacia, Sedna

Asteroids		**Dwarf Planets**	
Juno	04 cap 42	Eris	23 ar 32
Vesta	01 lib 50	Haumea	23 lib 36
Pallas	13 tau 52	Makemake	03 lib 16
Ceres	29 can 12	Salacia	01 ar 13
Chiron	26 pis 26	Orcus	09 vir 08
N Node	23 leo 47	Quaoar	28 sag 42
S Node	23 aq 47	Sedna	26 tau 42

Moon Phase: Crescent
Sunrise: 06:46 BST
Sunset: 18:58
Moonrise: 09:01
Moonset: 20:17
Voc start: 14:04
Voc end: 18:39

Planetary and Angelic Hours			
Venus	06:45	Mars	18:59
Mercury	07:46	Sun	19:58
Moon	08:47	Venus	20:57
Saturn	09:48	Mercury	21:56
Jupiter	10:50	Moon	22:55
Mars	11:51	Saturn	23:54
Sun	12:52	Jupiter	00:53
Venus	13:53	Mars	01:52
Mercury	14:54	Sun	02:51
Moon	15:55	Venus	03:50
Saturn	16:56	Mercury	04:49
Jupiter	17:58	Moon	05:48

Mabon
Autumn Equinox
21:02

Aspects

Sun sexile Ceres
Moon sextile Saturn
Moon opposite Eris
Moon conjunct Jupiter
Moon opposite Uranus
Moon square Ceres
Mercury trine Pluto
Moon sextile Venus
Chiron sextile Sedna

Planets	00:00 am	Moon
Sun	00 lib 09	01.00 am - 03 sco 19
Mercury	17 vir 18	03.00 am - 04 sco 22
Venus	03 vir 36	05.00 am - 05 sco 25
Mars	11 vir 10	07.00 am - 06 sco 27
Jupiter	26 lib 18	09.00 am - 07 sco 30
Saturn	21 sag 50	11.00 am - 08 sco 32
Uranus	27 ar 33	13.00 pm - 09 sco 34
Neptune	12 pis 22	15.00 pm - 10 sco 36
Pluto	16 cap 51	17.00 pm - 11 sco 38
		19.00 pm - 12 sco 40
Oob		21.00 pm - 13 sco 42
		23.00 pm - 14 sco 44

Saturday 23rd September

Retrograde Planets

Uranus, Neptune, Pluto, Pallas, Chiron, Eris, Salacia, Sedna

Asteroids		Dwarf Planets	
Juno	04 cap 51	Eris	23 ar 32
Vesta	02 lib 20	Haumea	23 lib 37
Pallas	13 tau 47	Makemake	03 lib 18
Ceres	29 can 33	Salacia	01 ar 11
Chiron	26 pis 23	Orcus	09 vir 09
N Node	23 leo 41	Quaoar	28 sag 42
S Node	23 aq 41	Sedna	26 tau 42

Moon Phase: Crescent
Sunrise: 06:48 BST
Sunset: 18:56
Moonrise: 10:09
Moonset: 20:42
Voc start:
Voc end:

Planetary and Angelic Hours			
Saturn	06:47	Mercury	18:56
Jupiter	07:47	Moon	19:56
Mars	08:48	Saturn	20:55
Sun	09:49	Jupiter	21:54
Venus	10:50	Mars	22:54
Mercury	11:51	Sun	23:53
Moon	12:51	Venus	00:52
Saturn	13:52	Mercury	01:52
Jupiter	14:53	Moon	02:51
Mars	15:54	Saturn	03:50
Sun	16:55	Jupiter	04:49
Venus	17:56	Mars	05:49

Aspects

Moon sextile Venus
Moon sextile Juno
Moon sextile Mars
Moon trine Neptune
Moon opposite Pallas
Venus trine Juno
Mars opposite Neptune
Chiron sextile Sedna

Planets	00:00 am	Moon
Sun	01 lib 08	01.00 am - 15 sco 46
Mercury	19 vir 04	03.00 am - 16 sco 47
Venus	04 vir 49	05.00 am - 17 sco 49
Mars	11 vir 48	07.00 am - 18 sco 50
Jupiter	26 lib 30	09.00 am - 19 sco 51
Saturn	21 sag 52	11.00 am - 20 sco 52
Uranus	27 ar 31	13.00 pm - 21 sco 53
Neptune	12 pis 20	15.00 pm - 22 sco 54
Pluto	16 cap 51	17.00 pm - 23 sco 55
		19.00 pm - 24 sco 56
Oob		21.00 pm - 25 sco 57
		23.00 pm - 26 sco 58

Sunday 24th September

Planetary Directions

Ceres into Leo 06:42

Retrograde Planets

Uranus, Neptune, Pluto, Pallas, Chiron, Eris, Salacia, Sedna

Asteroids		Dwarf Planets	
Juno	05 cap 00	Eris	23 ar 31
Vesta	02 lib 51	Haumea	23 lib 39
Pallas	13 tau 41	Makemake	03 lib 19
Ceres	29 can 54	Salacia	01 ar 10
Chiron	26 pis 20	Orcus	09 vir 11
N Node	23 leo 34	Quaoar	28 sag 42
S Node	23 aq 34	Sedna	26 tau 42

Moon Phase: Crescent
Sunrise: 06:50 BST
Sunset: 18:54
Moonrise: 11:14
Moonset: 21:10
Voc start: 08:32
Voc end:

Planetary and Angelic Hours			
Sun	06:48	Jupiter	18:54
Venus	07:49	Mars	19:54
Mercury	08:49	Sun	20:53
Moon	09:50	Venus	21:53
Saturn	10:50	Mercury	22:53
Jupiter	11:51	Moon	23:52
Mars	12:51	Saturn	00:52
Sun	13:52	Jupiter	01:52
Venus	14:52	Mars	02:51
Mercury	15:53	Sun	03:51
Moon	16:53	Venus	04:50
Saturn	17:54	Mercury	05:50

Aspects

Moon sextile Pluto
Venus trine Juno
Moon sextile Mercury
Mars opposite Neptune
Moon trine Chiron
Moon opposite Sedna
Jupiter opposite Uranus
Chiron sextile Sedna

Planets	**00:00 am**	**Moon**
Sun	02 lib 07	01.00 am - 27 sco 58
Mercury	20 vir 51	03.00 am - 28 sco 59
Venus	06 vir 02	05.00 am - 29 sco 59
Mars	12 vir 26	07.00 am - 00 sag 59
Jupiter	26 vir 42	09.00 am - 02 sag 00
Saturn	21 sag 55	11.00 am - 03 sag 00
Uranus	27 ar 29	13.00 pm - 04 sag 00
Neptune	12 pis 19	15.00 pm - 05 sag 00
Pluto	16 cap 51	17.00 pm - 06 sag 00
		19.00 pm - 07 sag 00
Oob		21.00 pm - 08 sag 00
		23.00 pm - 09 sag 00

Monday 25th September

Planetary Directions

Moon into Sagittarius
05:01

Retrograde Planets

Uranus, Neptune, Pluto, Pallas, Chiron, Eris, Salacia, Sedna

Asteroids		**Dwarf Planets**	
Juno	05 cap 10	Eris	23 ar 31
Vesta	03 lib 21	Haumea	23 lib 40
Pallas	13 tau 35	Makemake	03 lib 21
Ceres	00 leo 16	Salacia	01 ar 09
Chiron	26 pis 17	Orcus	09 vir 12
N Node	23 leo 29	Quaoar	28 sag 44
S Node	23 aq 29	Sedna	26 tau 41

Moon Phase: Crescent
Sunrise: 06:51 BST
Sunset: 18:51
Moonrise: 12:17
Moonset: 21:41
Voc start:
Voc end: 05:00

Planetary and Angelic Hours			
Moon	06:50	Venus	18:52
Saturn	07:50	Mercury	19:52
Jupiter	08:50	Moon	20:52
Mars	09:50	Saturn	21:52
Sun	10:50	Jupiter	22:52
Venus	11:51	Mars	23:52
Mercury	12:51	Sun	00:52
Moon	13:51	Venus	01:52
Saturn	14:51	Mercury	02:51
Jupiter	15:51	Moon	03:51
Mars	16:52	Saturn	04:51
Sun	17:52	Jupiter	05:51

Aspects

Moon trine Ceres
Sun sextile Moon
Moon sextile Vesta
Mercury square Saturn
Moon square Venus
Sun conjunct Vesta
Mars opposite Neptune
Mars trine Pallas
Jupiter opposite Uranus
Chiron sextile Sedna

Planets	00:00 am	Moon
Sun	03 lib 06	01.00 am - 10 sag 00
Mercury	22 vir 39	03.00 am - 10 sag 59
Venus	07 vir 16	05.00 am - 11 sag 59
Mars	13 vir 04	07.00 am - 12 sag 59
Jupiter	26 lib 55	09.00 am - 13 sag 58
Saturn	21 sag 58	11.00 am - 14 sag 58
Uranus	27 ar 27	13.00 pm - 15 sag 57
Neptune	12 pis 17	15.00 pm - 16 sag 57
Pluto	16 cap 51	17.00 pm - 17 sag 56
		19.00 pm - 18 sag 55
Oob		21.00 pm - 19 sag 55
		23.00 pm - 20 sag 54

Tuesday 26th September

Retrograde Planets

Uranus, Neptune, Pluto, Pallas, Chiron, Eris, Salacia, Sedna

Asteroids		Dwarf Planets	
Juno	05 cap 19	Eris	23 ar 30
Vesta	03 lib 51	Haumea	23 lib 41
Pallas	13 tau 29	Makemake	03 lib 22
Ceres	00 leo 37	Salacia	01 ar 08
Chiron	26 pis 15	Orcus	09 vir 13
N Node	23 leo 25	Quaoar	28 sag 43
S Node	23 aq 25	Sedna	26 tau 41

Moon Phase: Crescent
Sunrise: 06:53 BST
Sunset: 18:49
Moonrise: 13:16
Moonset: 22:17
Voc start:
Voc end:

Planetary and Angelic Hours			
Mars	06:51	Saturn	18:50
Sun	07:51	Jupiter	19:50
Venus	08:51	Mars	20:50
Mercury	09:51	Sun	21:50
Moon	10:51	Venus	22:51
Saturn	11:51	Mercury	23:51
Jupiter	12:50	Moon	00:51
Mars	13:50	Saturn	01:52
Sun	14:50	Jupiter	02:52
Venus	15:50	Mars	03:52
Mercury	16:50	Sun	04:52
Moon	17:50	Venus	05:53

Aspects

Moon square Neptune
Moon square Mars
Mars trine Pallas
Sun conjunct Vesta
Moon conjunct Saturn
Jupiter opposite Uranus
Chiron sextile Sedna

Planets	**00:00 am**	**Moon**
Sun	04 lib 04	01.00 am - 21 sag 54
Mercury	24 vir 28	03.00 am - 22 sag 53
Venus	08 vir 30	05.00 am - 23 sag 52
Mars	13 vir 42	07.00 am - 24 sag 51
Jupiter	27 lib 07	09.00 am - 25 sag 51
Saturn	22 sag 01	11.00 am - 26 sag 50
Uranus	27 ar 25	13.00 pm - 27 sag 49
Neptune	12 pis 16	15.00 pm - 28 sag 48
Pluto	16 cap 51	17.00 pm - 29 sag 48
		19.00 pm - 00 cap 47
Oob		21.00 pm - 01 cap 46
		23.00 pm - 02 cap 45

Wednesday 27th September

Planetary Directions

Moon into Capricorn
17:24

Retrograde Planets

Uranus, Neptune, Pluto, Pallas, Chiron, Eris, Salacia, Sedna

Asteroids		**Dwarf Planets**	
Juno	05 cap 30	Eris	23 ar 30
Vesta	04 lib 21	Haumea	23 lib 43
Pallas	13 tau 22	Makemake	03 lib 23
Ceres	00 leo 58	Salacia	01 ar 06
Chiron	26 pis 12	Orcus	09 vir 15
N Node	23 leo 22	Quaoar	28 sag 43
S Node	23 aq 22	Sedna	26 tau 41

Moon Phase: Crescent
Sunrise: 06:54 BST
Sunset: 18:47
Moonrise: 14:11
Moonset: 22:59
Voc start: 12:08
Voc end: 17:23

Planetary and Angelic Hours			
Mercury	06:53	Sun	18:47
Moon	07:52	Venus	19:48
Saturn	08:52	Mercury	20:49
Jupiter	09:51	Moon	21:49
Mars	10:51	Saturn	22:50
Sun	11:51	Jupiter	23:50
Venus	12:50	Mars	00:51
Mercury	13:50	Sun	01:51
Moon	14:49	Venus	02:52
Saturn	15:49	Mercury	03:53
Jupiter	16:48	Moon	04:53
Mars	17:48	Saturn	05:54

Aspects

Moon conjunct Saturn
Moon trine Eris
Moon square Mercury
Moon square Chiron
Moon sextile Jupiter
Moon trine Uranus
Sun conjunct Vesta
Mercury opp. Chiron
Sun square Juno
Mercury trine Sedna
Jupiter opposite Uranus
Chiron sextile Sedna
Juno square Vesta

Planets	00:00 am	Moon
Sun	05 lib 03	01.00 am - 03 cap 45
Mercury	26 vir 18	03.00 am - 04 cap 44
Venus	09 vir 43	05.00 am - 05 cap 43
Mars	14 vir 20	07.00 am - 06 cap 43
Jupiter	27 lib 20	09.00 am - 07 cap 42
Saturn	22 sag 04	11.00 am - 08 cap 41
Uranus	27 ar 22	13.00 pm - 09 cap 41
Neptune	12 pis 14	15.00 pm - 10 cap 40
Pluto	16 cap 51	17.00 pm - 11 cap 40
		19.00 pm - 12 cap 39
Oob		21.00 pm - 13 cap 39
		23.00 pm - 14 cap 38

Thursday 28th September

Planetary Directions

Pluto direct
16 cap 51 at 20:36

Retrograde Planets

Uranus, Neptune, Pluto, Pallas, Chiron, Eris, Salacia, Sedna

Asteroids		Dwarf Planets	
Juno	05 cap 40	Eris	23 ar 29
Vesta	04 lib 52	Haumea	23 lib 44
Pallas	13 tau 14	Makemake	03 lib 25
Ceres	01 leo 19	Salacia	01 ar 05
Chiron	26 pis 09	Orcus	09 vir 16
N Node	23 leo 21	Quaoar	28 sag 44
S Node	23 aq 21	Sedna	26 tau 41

First Quarter: 03:55
Sunrise: 06:56 BST
Sunset: 18:44
Moonrise: 15:01
Moonset: 23:47
Voc start:
Voc end:

Planetary and Angelic Hours			
Jupiter	06:54	Moon	18:45
Mars	07:54	Saturn	19:46
Sun	08:53	Jupiter	20:47
Venus	09:52	Mars	21:48
Mercury	10:51	Sun	22:49
Moon	11:51	Venus	23:50
Saturn	12:50	Mercury	00:51
Jupiter	13:49	Moon	01:51
Mars	14:48	Saturn	02:52
Sun	15:47	Jupiter	03:53
Venus	16:47	Mars	04:54
Mercury	17:46	Sun	05:55

Aspects

Moon square Vesta
Sun square Moon
Moon conjunct Juno
Jupiter opposite Uranus
Mercury trine Sedna
Moon trine Venus
Moon sextile Neptune
Sun square Juno
Moon trine Pallas
Moon trine Mars
Sun conjunct Vesta
Neptune sextile Pallas
Chiron sextile Sedna
Juno square Vesta

Planets	00:00 am	Moon
Sun	06 lib 02	01.00 am - 15 cap 38
Mercury	28 vir 07	03.00 am - 16 cap 37
Venus	10 vir 57	05.00 am - 17 cap 37
Mars	14 vir 58	07.00 am - 18 cap 37
Jupiter	27 lib 32	09.00 am - 19 cap 37
Saturn	22 sag 07	11.00 am - 20 cap 37
Uranus	27 ar 20	13.00 pm - 21 cap 37
Neptune	12 pis 13	15.00 pm - 22 cap 37
Pluto	16 cap 51	17.00 pm - 23 cap 37
		19.00 pm - 24 cap 37
Oob		21.00 pm - 25 cap 37
		23.00 pm - 26 cap 38

Friday 29th September

Retrograde Planets

Uranus, Neptune, Pallas, Chiron, Eris, Salacia, Sedna

Asteroids		Dwarf Planets	
Juno	05 cap 50	Eris	23 ar 29
Vesta	05 lib 22	Haumea	23 lib 46
Pallas	13 tau 06	Makemake	03 lib 26
Ceres	01 leo 40	Salacia	01 ar 04
Chiron	26 pis 07	Orcus	09 vir 17
N Node	23 leo 22	Quaoar	28 sag 44
S Node	23 aq 22	Sedna	26 tau 40

Moon Phase: Gibbous
Sunrise: 06:58 BST
Sunset: 18:42
Moonrise: 15:45
Moonset: None
Voc start:
Voc end:

Planetary and Angelic Hours			
Venus	06:56	Mars	18:43
Mercury	07:55	Sun	19:44
Moon	08:54	Venus	20:45
Saturn	09:53	Mercury	21:47
Jupiter	10:52	Moon	22:48
Mars	11:51	Saturn	23:49
Sun	12:49	Jupiter	00:50
Venus	13:48	Mars	01:51
Mercury	14:47	Sun	02:53
Moon	15:46	Venus	03:54
Saturn	16:45	Mercury	04:55
Jupiter	17:44	Moon	05:56

Aspects

Moon conjunct Pluto
Moon square Eris
Moon sextile Chiron
Moon trine Sedna
Moon square Uranus
Sun square Juno
Moon square Jupiter
Venus opp. Neptune
Venus trine Pallas
Jupiter opposite Uranus
Neptune sextile Pallas
Chiron sextile Sedna
Juno square Vesta

Planets	00:00 am	Moon
Sun	07 lib 01	01.00 am - 27 cap 38
Mercury	29 vir 56	03.00 am - 28 cap 39
Venus	12 vir 11	05.00 am - 29 cap 39
Mars	15 vir 36	07.00 am - 00 aq 40
Jupiter	27 lib 45	09.00 am - 01 aq 41
Saturn	22 sag 11	11.00 am - 02 aq 42
Uranus	27 ar 18	13.00 pm - 03 aq 42
Neptune	12 pis 11	15.00 pm - 04 aq 44
Pluto	16 cap 51	17.00 pm - 05 aq 45
		19.00 pm - 06 aq 46
Oob		21.00 pm - 07 aq 47
		23.00 pm - 08 aq 49

Saturday 30th September

Planetary Directions

Mercury into Libra at 01:43

Moon into Aquarius 05:41

Retrograde Planets

Uranus, Neptune, Pallas, Chiron, Eris,Salacia, Sedna

Asteroids		Dwarf Planets	
Juno	06 cap 01	Eris	23 ar 28
Vesta	05 lib 52	Haumea	23 lib 47
Pallas	12 tau 58	Makemake	03 lib 28
Ceres	02 leo 00	Salacia	01 ar 03
Chiron	26 pis 04	Orcus	09 vir 19
N Node	23 leo 23	Quaoar	28 sag 44
S Node	23 aq 23	Sedna	26 tau 40

Moon Phase: Gibbous
Sunrise: 06:59 BST
Sunset: 18:40
Moonrise: 16:24
Moonset: 00:42
Voc start: 01:13
Voc end: 05:40

Planetary and Angelic Hours			
Saturn	06:58	Mercury	18:41
Jupiter	07:56	Moon	19:42
Mars	08:55	Saturn	20:44
Sun	09:53	Jupiter	21:45
Venus	10:52	Mars	22:47
Mercury	11:51	Sun	23:48
Moon	12:49	Venus	00:50
Saturn	13:48	Mercury	01:51
Jupiter	14:46	Moon	02:53
Mars	15:45	Saturn	03:55
Sun	16:43	Jupiter	04:56
Venus	17:42	Mars	05:58

Aspects

Venus opp. Neptune
Moon square Jupiter
Moon trine Mercury
Moon opposite Ceres
Juno square Vesta
Venus trine Pallas
Moon trine Vesta
Sun trine Moon
Mercury sextile Ceres
Mars trine Pluto
Jupiter opposite Uranus
Neptune sextile Pallas
Chiron sextile Sedna

Planets	00:00 am	Moon
Sun	08 lib 00	01.00 am - 09 aq 50
Mercury	01 lib 45	03.00 am - 10 aq 52
Venus	13 vir 24	05.00 am - 11 aq 54
Mars	16 vir 14	07.00 am - 12 aq 56
Jupiter	27 lib 57	09.00 am - 13 aq 58
Saturn	22 sag 14	11.00 am - 15 aq 00
Uranus	27 ar 16	13.00 pm - 16 aq 03
Neptune	12 pis 10	15.00 pm - 17 aq 05
Pluto	16 cap 51	17.00 pm - 18 aq 08
		19.00 pm - 19 aq 10
Oob		21.00 pm - 20 aq 13
		23.00 pm - 21 aq 16

Sunday 1st October

Retrograde Planets

Uranus, Neptune, Pallas, Chiron, Eris, Salacia, Sedna

Asteroids		Dwarf Planets	
Juno	06 cap 12	Eris	23 ar 27
Vesta	06 lib 23	Haumea	23 lib 48
Pallas	12 tau 49	Makemake	03 lib 29
Ceres	02 leo 21	Salacia	01 ar 01
Chiron	26 pis 01	Orcus	09 vir 20
N Node	23 leo 24	Quaoar	28 sag 45
S Node	23 aq 24	Sedna	26 tau 39

Moon Phase: Gibbous
Sunrise: 07:01 BST
Sunset: 18:38
Moonrise: 16:58
Moonset: 01:42
Voc start:
Voc end:

Planetary and Angelic Hours			
Sun	06:59	Jupiter	18:38
Venus	07:57	Mars	19:40
Mercury	08:56	Sun	20:42
Moon	09:54	Venus	21:44
Saturn	10:52	Mercury	22:46
Jupiter	11:51	Moon	23:48
Mars	12:49	Saturn	00:50
Sun	13:47	Jupiter	01:51
Venus	14:45	Mars	02:53
Mercury	15:44	Sun	03:55
Moon	16:42	Venus	04:57
Saturn	17:40	Mercury	05:59

Aspects

Moon square Pallas
Mercury sextile Ceres
Mars trine Pluto
Moon sextile Saturn
Jupiter opposite Uranus
Neptune sextile Pallas
Chiron sextile Sedna
Juno square Vesta

Planets	**00:00 am**	**Moon**
Sun	08 lib 59	01.00 am - 22 aq 19
Mercury	03 lib 34	03.00 am - 23 aq 23
Venus	14 vir 38	05.00 am - 24 aq 26
Mars	16 vir 52	07.00 am - 25 aq 30
Jupiter	28 lib 10	09.00 am - 26 aq 33
Saturn	22 sag 18	11.00 am - 27 aq 37
Uranus	27 ar 13	13.00 pm - 28 aq 41
Neptune	12 pis 08	15.00 pm - 29 aq 45
Pluto	16 cap 51	17.00 pm - 00 pis 50
		19.00 pm - 01 pis 54
Oob		21.00 pm - 02 pis 59
		23.00 pm - 04 pis 04

Monday 2nd October

Planetary Directions

Moon into Pisces 15:27

Retrograde Planets

Uranus, Neptune, Pallas, Chiron, Eris, Salacia, Sedna

Asteroids		**Dwarf Planets**	
Juno	06 cap 24	Eris	23 ar 27
Vesta	06 lib 53	Haumea	23 lib 50
Pallas	12 tau 39	Makemake	03 lib 30
Ceres	02 leo 41	Salacia	01 ar 00
Chiron	25 pis 59	Orcus	09 vir 21
N Node	23 leo 25	Quaoar	28 sag 45
S Node	23 aq 25	Sedna	26 tau 39

Moon Phase: Gibbous
Sunrise: 07:03 BST
Sunset: 18:35
Moonrise: 17:28
Moonset: 02:47
Voc start: 12:12
Voc end: 15:26

Planetary and Angelic Hours

Moon	07:01	Venus	18:36
Saturn	07:59	Mercury	19:38
Jupiter	08:57	Moon	20:40
Mars	09:55	Saturn	21:43
Sun	10:53	Jupiter	22:45
Venus	11:51	Mars	23:47
Mercury	12:48	Sun	00:49
Moon	13:46	Venus	01:51
Saturn	14:44	Mercury	02:54
Jupiter	15:42	Moon	03:56
Mars	16:40	Saturn	04:58
Sun	17:38	Jupiter	06:00

Aspects

Moon sextile Eris
Moon square Sedna
Moon sextile Uranus
Moon trine Jupiter
Venus trine Pluto
Mars trine Pluto
Neptune sextile Pallas
Chiron sextile Sedna
Juno square Vesta

Planets	**00:00 am**	**Moon**
		01.00 am - 05 pis 09
Sun	09 lib 58	03.00 am - 06 pis 14
Mercury	05 lib 22	05.00 am - 07 pis 19
Venus	15 vir 52	07.00 am - 08 pis 24
Mars	17 vir 29	09.00 am - 09 pis 30
Jupiter	28 lib 23	11.00 am - 10 pis 36
Saturn	22 sag 21	13.00 pm - 11 pis 41
Uranus	27 ar 11	15.00 pm - 12 pis 47
Neptune	12 pis 07	17.00 pm - 13 pis 54
Pluto	16 cap 51	19.00 pm - 15 pis 00
		21.00 pm - 16 pis 06
Oob		23.00 pm - 17 pis 13

Tuesday 3rd October

Retrograde Planets

Uranus, Neptune, Pallas, Chiron, Eris, Salacia, Sedna

Asteroids		**Dwarf Planets**	
Juno	06 cap 36	Eris	23 ar 26
Vesta	07 lib 24	Haumea	23 lib 51
Pallas	12 tau 30	Makemake	03 lib 32
Ceres	03 leo 02	Salacia	00 ar 59
Chiron	25 pis 56	Orcus	09 vir 22
N Node	23 leo 24	Quaoar	28 sag 46
S Node	23 aq 24	Sedna	26 tau 39

Moon Phase: Gibbous
Sunrise: 07:04 BST
Sunset: 18:33
Moonrise: 17:55
Moonset: 03:56
Voc start:
Voc end:

Planetary and Angelic Hours			
Mars	07:02	Saturn	18:34
Sun	08:00	Jupiter	19:36
Venus	08:58	Mars	20:39
Mercury	09:55	Sun	21:41
Moon	10:53	Venus	22:44
Saturn	11:51	Mercury	23:46
Jupiter	12:48	Moon	00:49
Mars	13:46	Saturn	01:51
Sun	14:43	Jupiter	02:54
Venus	15:41	Mars	03:56
Mercury	16:39	Sun	04:59
Moon	17:36	Venus	06:02

Aspects

Moon sextile Juno
Moon conj. Neptune
Moon sextile Pallas
Mercury square Juno
Venus trine Pluto
Moon sextile Pluto
Moon opposite Venus
Moon opposite Mars
Mercury conjunct Vesta
Neptune sextile Pallas
Chiron sextile Sedna

Planets	00:00 am	Moon
Sun	10 lib 57	01.00 am - 18 pis 20
Mercury	07 lib 10	03.00 am - 19 pis 27
Venus	17 vir 06	05.00 am - 20 pis 34
Mars	18 vir 07	07.00 am - 21 pis 41
Jupiter	28 lib 35	09.00 am -`22 pis 49
Saturn	22 sag 25	11.00 am - 23 pis 56
Uranus	27 ar 09	13.00 pm - 25 pis 04
Neptune	12 pis 06	15.00 pm - 26 pis 12
Pluto	16 cap 51	17.00 pm - 27 pis 20
		19.00 pm - 28 pis 29
Oob		21.00 pm - 29 pis 37
		23.00 pm - 00 ar 45

Wednesday 4th October

Planetary Directions

Moon into Aries 21:40

Retrograde Planets

Uranus, Neptune, Pallas, Chiron, Eris, Salacia, Sedna

Asteroids		Dwarf Planets	
Juno	06 cap 47	Eris	23 ar 26
Vesta	07 lib 54	Haumea	23 lib 53
Pallas	12 tau 19	Makemake	03 lib 33
Ceres	03 leo 22	Salacia	00 ar 58
Chiron	25 pis 53	Orcus	09 vir 24
N Node	23 leo 22	Quaoar	28 sag 46
S Node	23 aq 22	Sedna	26 tau 38

Moon Phase: Gibbous
Sunrise: 07:06 BST
Sunset: 18:31
Moonrise: 18:21
Moonset: 05:07
Voc start: 08:18
Voc end: 21:39

Planetary and Angelic Hours			
Mercury	07:04	Sun	18:32
Moon	08:01	Venus	19:34
Saturn	08:59	Mercury	20:37
Jupiter	09:56	Moon	21:40
Mars	10:53	Saturn	22:43
Sun	11:51	Jupiter	23:46
Venus	12:48	Mars	00:49
Mercury	13:45	Sun	01:51
Moon	14:42	Venus	02:54
Saturn	15:40	Mercury	03:57
Jupiter	16:37	Moon	05:00
Mars	17:34	Saturn	06:03

Aspects

Moon square Saturn
Moon conjunct Chiron
Mercury conjunct Vesta
Moon sextile Sedna
Venus conjunct Mars
Saturn trine Eris
Neptune sextile Pallas
Chiron sextile Sedna

Planets	00:00 am	Moon
Sun	11 lib 57	01.00 am - 01 ar 54
Mercury	08 lib 57	03.00 am - 03 ar 03
Venus	18 vir 20	05.00 am - 04 ar 12
Mars	18 vir 45	07.00 am - 05 ar 21
Jupiter	28 lib 48	09.00 am - 06 ar 30
Saturn	22 sag 28	11.00 am - 07 ar 40
Uranus	27 ar 06	13.00 pm - 08 ar 49
Neptune	12 pis 04	15.00 pm - 09 ar 59
Pluto	16 cap 51	17.00 pm - 11 ar 09
		19.00 pm - 12 ar 19
Oob		21.00 pm - 13 ar 29
		23.00 pm - 14 ar 39

Thursday 5th October

Retrograde Planets

Uranus, Neptune, Pallas, Chiron, Eris, Salacia, Sedna

Asteroids		Dwarf Planets	
Juno	07 cap 00	Eris	23 ar 25
Vesta	08 lib 24	Haumea	23 lib 54
Pallas	12 tau 08	Makemake	03 lib 35
Ceres	03 leo 42	Salacia	00 ar 56
Chiron	25 pis 51	Orcus	09 vir 25
N Node	23 leo 17	Quaoar	28 sag 47
S Node	23 aq 17	Sedna	26 tau 38

Full Moon: 19:41
Sunrise: 07:08 BST
Sunset: 18:29
Moonrise: 18:47
Moonset: 06:21
Voc start:
Voc end:

Planetary and Angelic Hours			
Jupiter	07:06	Moon	18:29
Mars	08:03	Saturn	19:33
Sun	09:00	Jupiter	20:36
Venus	09:57	Mars	21:39
Mercury	10:54	Sun	22:42
Moon	11:51	Venus	23:45
Saturn	12:48	Mercury	00:48
Jupiter	13:45	Moon	01:51
Mars	14:41	Saturn	02:55
Sun	15:38	Jupiter	03:58
Venus	16:35	Mars	05:01
Mercury	17:32	Sun	06:04

Aspects

Moon trine Ceres
Moon square Juno
Neptune sextile Pallas
Moon opposite Vesta
Venus conjunct Mars
Sun opposite Moon
Saturn trine Eris
Chiron sextile Sedna

Planets	00:00 am	Moon
Sun	12 lib 55	01.00 am - 15 ar 49
Mercury	10 lib 44	03.00 am - 17 ar 00
Venus	19 vir 34	05.00 am - 18 ar 10
Mars	19 vir 23	07.00 am - 19 ar 21
Jupiter	29 lib 01	09.00 am - 20 ar 32
Saturn	22 sag 32	11.00 am - 21 ar 43
Uranus	27 ar 04	13.00 pm - 22 ar 54
Neptune	12 pis 03	15.00 pm - 24 ar 05
Pluto	16 cap 52	17.00 pm - 25 ar 16
		19.00 pm - 26 ar 27
Oob		21.00 pm - 27 ar 39
		23.00 pm - 28 ar 58

Friday 6th October

Retrograde Planets

Uranus, Neptune, Pallas, Chiron, Eris, Salacia, Sedna

Asteroids		Dwarf Planets	
Juno	07 cap 12	Eris	23 ar 24
Vesta	08 lib 55	Haumea	23 lib 56
Pallas	11 tau 57	Makemake	03 lib 36
Ceres	04 leo 02	Salacia	00 ar 55
Chiron	25 pis 48	Orcus	09 vir 26
N Node	23 leo 10	Quaoar	28 sag 47
S Node	23 aq 10	Sedna	26 tau 37

Phase: Disseminating
Sunrise: 07:09 BST
Sunset: 18:26
Moonrise: 19:13
Moonset: 07:37
Voc start: 23:37
Voc end:

Planetary and Angelic Hours			
Venus	07:07	Mars	18:27
Mercury	08:04	Sun	19:31
Moon	09:01	Venus	20:34
Saturn	09:57	Mercury	21:38
Jupiter	10:54	Moon	22:41
Mars	11:51	Saturn	23:45
Sun	12:47	Jupiter	00:48
Venus	13:44	Mars	01:52
Mercury	14:41	Sun	02:55
Moon	15:37	Venus	03:58
Saturn	16:34	Mercury	05:02
Jupiter	17:31	Moon	06:05

Aspects

Moon square Pluto
Moon trine Saturn
Moon conjunct Eris
Moon conjunct Uranus
Moon opposite Jupiter
Venus conjunct Mars
Saturn trine Eris
Neptune sextile Pallas
Chiron sextile Sedna

Planets	**00:00 am**	**Moon**
Sun	13 lib 54	01.00 am - 00 tau 02
Mercury	12 lib 29	03.00 am - 01 tau 14
Venus	20 vir 48	05.00 am - 02 tau 25
Mars	20 vir 01	07.00 am - 03 tau 37
Jupiter	29 lib 14	09.00 am - 04 tau 49
Saturn	22 sag 36	11.00 am - 06 tau 01
Uranus	27 ar 02	13.00 pm - 07 tau 13
Neptune	12 pis 01	15.00 pm - 08 tau 25
Pluto	16 cap 52	17.00 pm - 09 tau 37
		19.00 pm - 10 tau 50
Oob		21.00 pm - 12 tau 02
		23.00 pm - 13 tau 14

Saturday 7th October

Planetary Directions

Moon into Taurus
00:56

Retrograde Planets

Uranus, Neptune, Pallas, Chiron, Eris, Salacia, Sedna

Asteroids		**Dwarf Planets**	
Juno	07 cap 25	Eris	23 ar 24
Vesta	09 lib 25	Haumea	23 lib 57
Pallas	11 tau 45	Makemake	03 lib 37
Ceres	04 leo 21	Salacia	00 ar 54
Chiron	25 pis 46	Orcus	09 vir 27
N Node	23 leo 02	Quaoar	28 sag 48
S Node	23 aq 02	Sedna	26 tau 37

Phase: Disseminating
Sunrise: 07:11 BST
Sunset: 18:24
Moonrise: 19:42
Moonset: 08:55
Voc start:
Voc end: 00:55

Planetary and Angelic Hours

Saturn	07:09	Mercury	18:25
Jupiter	08:05	Moon	19:29
Mars	09:02	Saturn	20:33
Sun	09:58	Jupiter	21:36
Venus	10:54	Mars	22:40
Mercury	11:51	Sun	23:44
Moon	12:47	Venus	00:48
Saturn	13:43	Mercury	01:52
Jupiter	14:40	Moon	02:55
Mars	15:36	Saturn	03:59
Sun	16:32	Jupiter	05:03
Venus	17:29	Mars	06:07

Aspects

Moon square Ceres
Moon trine Juno
Moon conjunct Pallas
Moon sextile Neptune
Sun conjunct Mercury
Venus square Saturn
Saturn trine Eris
Neptune sextile Pallas
Chiron sextile Sedna

Sunday 8th October

Planets	00:00 am	Moon
Sun	14 lib 54	01.00 am - 14 tau 26
Mercury	14 lib 14	03.00 am - 15 tau 39
Venus	22 vir 02	05.00 am - 16 tau 51
Mars	20 vir 39	07.00 am - 18 tau 04
Jupiter	29 lib 27	09.00 am - 19 tau 16
Saturn	22 sag 40	11.00 am - 20 tau 29
Uranus	26 ar 59	13.00 pm - 21 tau 41
Neptune	12 pis 00	15.00 pm - 22 tau 54
Pluto	16 cap 52	17.00 pm - 24 tau 06
		19.00 pm - 25 tau 19
Oob		21.00 pm - 26 tau 31
		23.00 pm - 27 tau 44

Retrograde Planets

Uranus, Neptune, Pallas, Chiron, Eris, Salacia, Sedna

Asteroids		Dwarf Planets	
Juno	07 cap 37	Eris	23 ar 23
Vesta	09 lib 56	Haumea	23 lib 58
Pallas	11 tau 33	Makemake	03 lib 39
Ceres	04 leo 41	Salacia	00 ar 53
Chiron	25 pis 43	Orcus	09 vir 29
N Node	22 leo 54	Quaoar	28 sag 49
S Node	22 aq 54	Sedna	26 tau 37

Phase: Disseminating
Sunrise: 07:12 BST
Sunset: 18:22
Moonrise: 20:16
Moonset: 10:13
Voc start: 14:45
Voc end:

Planetary and Angelic Hours

Sun	07:11	Jupiter	18:23
Venus	08:07	Mars	19:27
Mercury	09:03	Sun	20:31
Moon	09:59	Venus	21:35
Saturn	10:55	Mercury	22:39
Jupiter	11:51	Moon	23:43
Mars	12:47	Saturn	00:47
Sun	13:43	Jupiter	01:52
Venus	14:39	Mars	02:56
Mercury	15:35	Sun	04:00
Moon	16:31	Venus	05:04
Saturn	17:27	Mercury	06:08

Aspects

Moon trine Pluto
Moon trine Mars
Venus square Saturn
Moon trine Venus
Moon sextile Chiron
Moon conjunct Sedna
Sun conjunct Mercury
Sun square Pluto
Mercury square Pluto
Saturn trine Eris
Neptune sextile Pallas
Chiron sextile Sedna

Planets	00:00 am	Moon
Sun	15 lib 53	01.00 am - 28 tau 56
Mercury	15 lib 59	03.00 am - 00 gem 09
Venus	23 vir 16	05.00 am - 01 gem 21
Mars	21 vir 17	07.00 am - 02 gem 34
Jupiter	29 lib 39	09.00 am - 03 gem 47
Saturn	22 sag 44	11.00 am - 04 gem 59
Uranus	26 ar 57	13.00 pm - 06 gem 11
Neptune	11 pis 59	15.00 pm - 07 gem 24
Pluto	16 cap 52	17.00 pm - 08 gem 36
		19.00 pm - 09 gem 49
Oob		21.00 pm - 11 gem 01
		23.00 pm - 12 gem 13

Monday 9th October

Planetary Directions

Moon into Gemini
02:45

Retrograde Planets

Uranus, Neptune, Pallas, Chiron, Eris, Salacia, Sedna

Asteroids		Dwarf Planets	
Juno	07 cap 51	Eris	23 ar 23
Vesta	10 lib 26	Haumea	24 lib 00
Pallas	11 tau 20	Makemake	03 lib 40
Ceres	05 leo 01	Salacia	00 ar 51
Chiron	25 pis 40	Orcus	09 vir 30
N Node	22 leo 46	Quaoar	28 sag 49
S Node	22 aq 46	Sedna	26 tau 36

Phase: Disseminating
Sunrise: 07:14 BST
Sunset: 18:20
Moonrise: 20:55
Moonset: 11:29
Voc start:
Voc end: 02:44

Planetary and Angelic Hours			
Moon	07:12	Venus	18:21
Saturn	08:08	Mercury	19:25
Jupiter	09:04	Moon	20:29
Mars	09:59	Saturn	21:34
Sun	10:55	Jupiter	22:38
Venus	11:51	Mars	23:43
Mercury	12:46	Sun	00:47
Moon	13:42	Venus	01:52
Saturn	14:38	Mercury	02:56
Jupiter	15:34	Moon	04:00
Mars	16:29	Saturn	05:05
Sun	17:25	Jupiter	06:09

Aspects

Moon sextile Ceres
Mercury square Pluto
Moon trine Vesta
Moon square Neptune
Sun conjunct Mercury
Sun square Pluto
Mars square Saturn
Saturn trine Eris
Neptune sextile Pallas
Chiron sextile Sedna

Planets	00:00 am	Moon
Sun	16 lib 52	01.00 am - 13 gem 26
Mercury	17 lib 42	03.00 am - 14 gem 38
Venus	24 vir 31	05.00 am - 15 gem 50
Mars	21 vir 55	07.00 am - 17 gem 02
Jupiter	29 lib 52	09.00 am - 18 gem 14
Saturn	22 sag 48	11.00 am - 19 gem 27
Uranus	26 ar 55	13.00 pm - 20 gem 39
Neptune	11 pis 58	15.00 pm - 21 gem 50
Pluto	16 cap 53	17.00 pm - 23 gem 02
		19.00 pm - 24 gem 14
Oob		21.00 pm - 25 gem 26
		23.00 pm - 26 gem 38

Tuesday 10th October

Planetary Directions

Jupiter into Scorpio
14:21

Retrograde Planets

Uranus, Neptune,
Pallas, Chiron, Eris,
Salacia, Sedna

Asteroids		Dwarf Planets	
Juno	08 cap 04	Eris	23 ar 22
Vesta	10 lib 57	Haumea	24 lib 01
Pallas	11 tau 06	Makemake	03 lib 42
Ceres	05 leo 20	Salacia	00 ar 50
Chiron	25 pis 38	Orcus	09 vir 31
N Node	22 leo 40	Quaoar	28 sag 50
S Node	22 aq 40	Sedna	26 tau 36

Phase: Disseminating
Sunrise: 07:16 BST
Sunset: 18:18
Moonrise: 21:42
Moonset: 12:42
Voc start: 23:24
Voc end:

Planetary and Angelic Hours			
Mars	07:14	Saturn	18:18
Sun	08:09	Jupiter	19:23
Venus	09:05	Mars	20:28
Mercury	10:00	Sun	21:33
Moon	10:55	Venus	22:37
Saturn	11:51	Mercury	23:42
Jupiter	12:46	Moon	00:47
Mars	13:42	Saturn	01:52
Sun	14:37	Jupiter	02:56
Venus	15:32	Mars	04:01
Mercury	16:28	Sun	05:06
Moon	17:23	Venus	06:11

Aspects

Sun square Pluto
Sun trine Moon
Moon trine Mercury
Moon square Mars
Moon opposite Saturn
Moon sextile Eris
Moon square Venus
Moon square Chiron
Venus opposite Chiron
Moon sextile Uranus
Venus trine Sedna
Mars square Sedna
Saturn trine Eris
Chiron sextile Sedna

Wednesday 11th October

Planets	00:00 am	Moon
Sun	17 lib 51	01.00 am - 27 gem 49
Mercury	19 lib 25	03.00 am - 29 gem 01
Venus	25 vir 45	05.00 am - 00 can 12
Mars	22 vir 33	07.00 am - 01 can 24
Jupiter	00 sco 05	09.00 am - 02 can 35
Saturn	22 sag 52	11.00 am - 03 can 47
Uranus	26 ar 52	13.00 pm - 04 can 58
Neptune	11 pis 56	15.00 pm - 06 can 09
Pluto	16 cap 53	17.00 pm - 07 can 20
		19.00 pm - 08 can 31
Oob		21.00 pm - 09 can 42
		23.00 pm - 10 can 53

Planetary Directions

Moon into Cancer
04:39

Retrograde Planets

Uranus, Neptune,
Pallas, Chiron, Eris,
Salacia, Sedna

Asteroids		Dwarf Planets	
Juno	08 cap 18	Eris	23 ar 22
Vesta	11 lib 28	Haumea	24 lib 03
Pallas	10 tau 53	Makemake	03 lib 43
Ceres	05 leo 39	Salacia	00 ar 49
Chiron	25 pis 35	Orcus	09 vir 32
N Node	22 leo 36	Quaoar	28 sag 51
S Node	22 aq 36	Sedna	26 tau 35

Phase: Disseminating
Sunrise: 07:17 BST
Sunset: 18:15
Moonrise: 22:37
Moonset: 13:47
Voc start:
Voc end: 04:38

Planetary and Angelic Hours

Mercury	07:15	Sun	18:16
Moon	08:10	Venus	19:21
Saturn	09:06	Mercury	20:26
Jupiter	10:01	Moon	21:31
Mars	10:56	Saturn	22:37
Sun	11:51	Jupiter	23:42
Venus	12:46	Mars	00:47
Mercury	13:41	Sun	01:52
Moon	14:36	Venus	02:57
Saturn	15:31	Mercury	04:02
Jupiter	16:26	Moon	05:07
Mars	17:21	Saturn	06:12

Aspects

Moon trine Jupiter
Mars square Saturn
Venus trine Sedna
Moon opposite Juno
Moon sextile Pallas
Moon trine Neptune
Moon square Vesta
Saturn trine Eris

Planets	00:00 am	Moon
Sun	18 lib 51	01.00 am - 12 can 04
Mercury	21 lib 07	03.00 am - 13 can 04
Venus	26 vir 59	05.00 am - 14 can 25
Mars	23 vir 11	07.00 am - 15 can 35
Jupiter	00 sco 18	09.00 am - 16 can 46
Saturn	22 sag 56	11.00 am - 17 can 58
Uranus	26 ar 50	13.00 pm - 19 can 07
Neptune	11 pis 55	15.00 pm - 20 can 17
Pluto	16 cap 53	17.00 pm - 21 can 27
		19.00 pm - 22 can 37
Oob		21.00 pm - 23 can 47
		23.00 pm - 24 can 57

Thursday 12th October

Retrograde Planets

Uranus, Neptune, Pallas, Chiron, Eris, Salacia, Sedna

Asteroids		Dwarf Planets	
Juno	08 cap 31	Eris	23 ar 21
Vesta	11 lib 58	Haumea	24 lib 04
Pallas	10 tau 39	Makemake	03 lib 44
Ceres	05 leo 58	Salacia	00 ar 48
Chiron	25 pis 33	Orcus	09 vir 33
N Node	22 leo 34	Quaoar	28 sag 51
S Node	22 aq 34	Sedna	26 tau 35

Last Quarter: 13:27
Sunrise: 07:19 BST
Sunset: 18:13
Moonrise: 23:41
Moonset: 14:43
Voc start:
Voc end:

Planetary and Angelic Hours			
Jupiter	07:17	Moon	18:14
Mars	08:12	Saturn	19:20
Sun	09:07	Jupiter	20:25
Venus	10:01	Mars	21:30
Mercury	10:56	Sun	22:36
Moon	11:51	Venus	23:41
Saturn	12:46	Mercury	00:46
Jupiter	13:40	Moon	01:52
Mars	14:35	Saturn	02:57
Sun	15:30	Jupiter	04:03
Venus	16:25	Mars	05:08
Mercury	17:19	Sun	06:13

Aspects

Moon opposite Pluto
Sun square Moon
Moon square Mercury
Moon square Eris
Moon sextile Mars
Moon trine Chiron
Moon square Uranus
Moon sextile Sedna
Mercury sextile Saturn
Mercury opposite Eris
Mars square Saturn
Saturn trine Eris

Planets	00:00 am	Moon
Sun	19 lib 50	01.00 am - 26 can 07
Mercury	22 lib 49	03.00 am - 27 can 16
Venus	28 vir 14	05.00 am - 28 can 26
Mars	23 vir 49	07.00 am - 29 can 36
Jupiter	00 sco 31	09.00 am - 00 leo 45
Saturn	23 sag 01	11.00 am - 01 leo 54
Uranus	26 ar 47	13.00 pm - 03 leo 04
Neptune	11 pis 54	15.00 pm - 04 leo 13
Pluto	16 cap 54	17.00 pm - 05 leo 22
		19.00 pm - 06 leo 31
Oob		21.00 pm - 07 leo 40
		23.00 pm - 08 leo 49

Friday 13th October

Planetary Directions

Moon into Leo 07:42

Retrograde Planets

Uranus, Neptune, Pallas, Chiron, Eris, Salacia, Sedna

Asteroids		Dwarf Planets	
Juno	08 cap 45	Eris	23 ar 20
Vesta	12 lib 29	Haumea	24 lib 06
Pallas	10 tau 24	Makemake	03 lib 46
Ceres	06 leo 17	Salacia	00 ar 47
Chiron	25 pis 31	Orcus	09 vir 34
N Node	22 leo 34	Quaoar	28 sag 52
S Node	22 aq 34	Sedna	26 tau 34

Moon Phase: Balsamic
Sunrise: 07:21 BST
Sunset: 18:11
Moonrise: None
Moonset: 15:30
Voc start: 04:59
Voc end: 07:41

Planetary and Angelic Hours			
Venus	07:19	Mars	18:12
Mercury	08:13	Sun	19:18
Moon	09:08	Venus	20:23
Saturn	10:02	Mercury	21:29
Jupiter	10:56	Moon	22:35
Mars	11:51	Saturn	23:40
Sun	12:45	Jupiter	00:46
Venus	13:40	Mars	01:52
Mercury	14:34	Sun	02:58
Moon	15:29	Venus	04:03
Saturn	16:23	Mercury	05:09
Jupiter	17:18	Moon	06:15

Aspects

Moon sextile Sedna
Moon square Uranus
Mercury sextile Saturn
Moon sextile Venus
Mercury opposite Eris
Moon square Jupiter
Moon conjunct Ceres
Moon square Pallas
Saturn trine Eris

Planets	00:00 am	Moon
Sun	20 lib 50	01.00 am - 09 leo 58
Mercury	24 lib 29	03.00 am - 11 leo 06
Venus	29 vir 28	05.00 am - 12 leo 15
Mars	24 vir 27	07.00 am - 13 leo 24
Jupiter	00 sco 44	09.00 am - 14 leo 32
Saturn	23 sag 05	11.00 am - 15 leo 41
Uranus	26 ar 45	13.00 pm - 16 leo 49
Neptune	11 pis 53	15.00 pm - 17 leo 57
Pluto	16 cap 54	17.00 pm - 19 leo 05
		19.00 pm - 20 leo 13
Oob		21.00 pm - 21 leo 21
		23.00 pm - 22 leo 29

Saturday 14th October

Planetary Directions

Venus into Libra
11:12

Retrograde Planets

Uranus, Neptune, Pallas, Chiron, Eris, Salacia, Sedna

Asteroids		Dwarf Planets	
Juno	09 cap 00	Eris	23 ar 20
Vesta	12 lib 59	Haumea	24 lib 07
Pallas	10 tau 09	Makemake	03 lib 47
Ceres	06 leo 36	Salacia	00 ar 45
Chiron	25 pis 28	Orcus	09 vir 36
N Node	22 leo 35	Quaoar	28 sag 53
S Node	22 aq 35	Sedna	26 tau 34

Moon Phase: Balsamic
Sunrise: 07:23 BST
Sunset: 18:09
Moonrise: 00:49
Moonset: 16:08
Voc start:
Voc end:

Planetary and Angelic Hours			
Saturn	07:20	Mercury	18:10
Jupiter	08:15	Moon	19:16
Mars	09:09	Saturn	20:22
Sun	10:03	Jupiter	21:28
Venus	10:57	Mars	22:34
Mercury	11:51	Sun	23:40
Moon	12:45	Venus	00:46
Saturn	13:39	Mercury	01:52
Jupiter	14:33	Moon	02:58
Mars	15:27	Saturn	04:04
Sun	16:22	Jupiter	05:10
Venus	17:16	Mars	06:16

Aspects

Moon square Pallas
Moon sextile Vesta
Sun sextile Moon
Moon trine Saturn
Moon trine Eris
Mercury opp. Uranus
Mars opposite Chiron
Saturn trine Eris
Pallas trine Juno

Planets	**00:00 am**	**Moon**
Sun	21 lib 49	01.00 am - 23 leo 37
Mercury	26 lib 09	03.00 am - 24 leo 45
Venus	00 lib 42	05.00 am - 25 leo 53
Mars	25 vir 05	07.00 am - 27 leo 00
Jupiter	00 sco 57	09.00 am - 28 leo 08
Saturn	23 sag 10	11.00 am - 29 leo 15
Uranus	26 ar 42	13.00 pm - 00 vir 23
Neptune	11 pis 51	15.00 pm - 01 vir 30
Pluto	16 cap 55	17.00 pm - 02 vir 37
		19.00 pm - 03 vir 44
Oob		21.00 pm - 04 vir 51
		23.00 pm - 05 vir 58

Sunday 15th October

Planetary Directions

Moon into Virgo 12:19

Retrograde Planets

Uranus, Neptune, Pallas, Chiron, Eris, Salacia, Sedna

Asteroids		**Dwarf Planets**	
Juno	09 cap 14	Eris	23 ar 19
Vesta	13 lib 30	Haumea	24 lib 09
Pallas	09 tau 53	Makemake	03 lib 48
Ceres	06 leo 55	Salacia	00 ar 44
Chiron	25 pis 26	Orcus	09 vir 37
N Node	22 leo 35	Quaoar	28 sag 53
S Node	22 aq 35	Sedna	26 tau 33

Moon Phase: Balsamic
Sunrise: 07:24 BST
Sunset: 18:07
Moonrise: 02:01
Moonset: 16:40
Voc start: 06:27
Voc end: 12:18

Planetary and Angelic Hours			
Sun	07:22	Jupiter	18:08
Venus	08:16	Mars	19:14
Mercury	09:10	Sun	20:20
Moon	10:03	Venus	21:27
Saturn	10:57	Mercury	22:33
Jupiter	11:51	Moon	23:39
Mars	12:45	Saturn	00:46
Sun	13:39	Jupiter	01:52
Venus	14:33	Mars	02:58
Mercury	15:26	Sun	04:05
Moon	16:20	Venus	05:11
Saturn	17:14	Mercury	06:17

Aspects

Moon sextile Mercury
Moon square Sedna
Moon trine Uranus
Mercury opp. Uranus
Mars opposite Chiron
Moon sextile Jupiter
Sun sextile Saturn
Sun opposite Eris
Mars trine Sedna
Saturn trine Eris
Pallas trine Juno

Planets	00:00 am	Moon
Sun	22 lib 49	01.00 am - 07 vir 05
Mercury	27 lib 48	03.00 am - 08 vir 12
Venus	01 lib 57	05.00 am - 09 vir 19
Mars	25 vir 43	07.00 am - 10 vir 26
Jupiter	01 sco 10	09.00 am - 11 vir 32
Saturn	23 sag 14	11.00 am - 12 vir 39
Uranus	26 ar 40	13.00 pm - 13 vir 45
Neptune	11 pis 50	15.00 pm - 14 vir 52
Pluto	16 cap 55	17.00 pm - 15 vir 58
		19.00 pm - 17 vir 04
Oob		21.00 pm - 18 vir 10
		23.00 pm - 19 vir 16

Monday 16th October

Retrograde Planets

Uranus, Neptune, Pallas, Chiron, Eris, Salacia, Sedna

Asteroids		Dwarf Planets	
Juno	09 cap 29	Eris	23 ar 19
Vesta	14 lib 01	Haumea	24 lib 10
Pallas	09 tau 38	Makemake	03 lib 50
Ceres	07 leo 13	Salacia	00 ar 43
Chiron	25 pis 23	Orcus	09 vir 38
N Node	22 leo 34	Quaoar	28 sag 54
S Node	22 aq 34	Sedna	26 tau 33

Moon Phase: Balsamic
Sunrise: 07:26 BST
Sunset: 18:05
Moonrise: 03:13
Moonset: 17:07
Voc start:
Voc end:

Planetary and Angelic Hours			
Moon	07:24	Venus	18:06
Saturn	08:17	Mercury	19:12
Jupiter	09:11	Moon	20:19
Mars	10:04	Saturn	21:26
Sun	10:58	Jupiter	22:32
Venus	11:51	Mars	23:39
Mercury	12:45	Sun	00:46
Moon	13:38	Venus	01:52
Saturn	14:32	Mercury	02:59
Jupiter	15:25	Moon	04:05
Mars	16:19	Saturn	05:12
Sun	17:12	Jupiter	06:19

Aspects

Moon trine Juno
Moon trine Pallas
Pallas trine Juno
Moon opp. Neptune
Sun sextile Saturn
Sun opposite Eris
Moon trine Pluto
Saturn trine Eris
Mars opposite Chiron
Mars trine Sedna

Planets	**00:00 am**	**Moon**
Sun	23 lib 48	01.00 am - 20 vir 22
Mercury	29 lib 27	03.00 am - 21 vir 28
Venus	03 lib 11	05.00 am - 22 vir 34
Mars	26 vir 21	07.00 am - 23 vir 40
Jupiter	01 sco 23	09.00 am - 24 vir 46
Saturn	23 sag 19	11.00 am - 25 vir 51
Uranus	26 ar 38	13.00 pm - 26 vir 57
Neptune	11 pis 49	15.00 pm - 28 vir 02
Pluto	16 cap 56	17.00 pm - 29 vir 08
		19.00 pm - 00 lib 13
Oob		21.00 pm - 01 lib 18
		23.00 pm - 02 lib 24

Tuesday 17th October

Planetary Directions

Mercury into Scorpio at 08:59
Moon into Libra 18:35

Retrograde Planets

Uranus, Neptune, Pallas, Chiron, Eris, Salacia, Sedna

Asteroids		**Dwarf Planets**	
Juno	09 cap 44	Eris	23 ar 18
Vesta	14 lib 31	Haumea	24 lib 12
Pallas	09 tau 21	Makemake	03 lib 51
Ceres	07 leo 31	Salacia	00 ar 42
Chiron	25 pis 21	Orcus	09 vir 39
N Node	22 leo 31	Quaoar	28 sag 55
S Node	22 aq 31	Sedna	26 tau 32

Moon Phase: Balsamic
Sunrise: 07:28 BST
Sunset: 18:02
Moonrise: 04:25
Moonset: 17:32
Voc start: 12:26
Voc end: 18:34

Planetary and Angelic Hours

Mars	07:25	Saturn	18:04
Sun	08:19	Jupiter	19:11
Venus	09:12	Mars	20:17
Mercury	10:05	Sun	21:24
Moon	10:58	Venus	22:31
Saturn	11:51	Mercury	23:38
Jupiter	12:44	Moon	00:45
Mars	13:38	Saturn	01:52
Sun	14:31	Jupiter	02:59
Venus	15:24	Mars	04:06
Mercury	16:17	Sun	05:13
Moon	17:10	Venus	06:20

Aspects

Moon square Saturn
Mars trine Sedna
Moon opposite Chiron
Moon trine Sedna
Moon conjunct Mars
Moon conjunct Venus
Mercury conj. Jupiter
Saturn trine Eris
Pallas trine Juno

Planets	00:00 am	Moon
Sun	24 lib 48	01.00 am - 03 lib 29
Mercury	01 sco 05	03.00 am - 04 lib 34
Venus	04 lib 26	05.00 am - 05 lib 39
Mars	26 vir 59	07.00 am - 06 lib 43
Jupiter	01 sco 36	09.00 am - 07 lib 48
Saturn	23 sag 23	11.00 am - 08 lib 53
Uranus	26 ar 35	13.00 pm - 09 lib 58
Neptune	11 pis 48	15.00 pm - 11 lib 02
Pluto	16 cap 56	17.00 pm - 12 lib 07
		19.00 pm - 13 lib 11
Oob		21.00 pm - 14 lib 15
		23.00 pm - 15 lib 19

Wednesday 18th October

Retrograde Planets

Uranus, Neptune, Pallas, Chiron, Eris, Salacia, Sedna

Asteroids		Dwarf Planets	
Juno	09 cap 59	Eris	23 ar 17
Vesta	15 lib 02	Haumea	24 lib 13
Pallas	09 tau 05	Makemake	03 lib 52
Ceres	07 leo 49	Salacia	00 ar 41
Chiron	25 pis 19	Orcus	09 vir 40
N Node	22 leo 25	Quaoar	28 sag 56
S Node	22 aq 25	Sedna	26 tau 32

Moon Phase: Balsamic
Sunrise: 07:29 BST
Sunset: 18:00
Moonrise: 05:36
Moonset: 17:56
Voc start:
Voc end:

Planetary and Angelic Hours			
Mercury	07:27	Sun	18:01
Moon	08:20	Venus	19:09
Saturn	09:13	Mercury	20:16
Jupiter	10:06	Moon	21:23
Mars	10:59	Saturn	22:31
Sun	11:51	Jupiter	23:38
Venus	12:44	Mars	00:45
Mercury	13:37	Sun	01:52
Moon	14:30	Venus	03:00
Saturn	15:23	Mercury	04:07
Jupiter	16:16	Moon	05:14
Mars	17:09	Saturn	06:21

Aspects

Moon conjunct Venus
Moon sextile Ceres
Mercury conj. Jupiter
Moon square Juno
Moon conjunct Vesta
Sun opposite Uranus
Moon square Pluto
Saturn trine Eris
Ceres square Pallas

Planets	00:00 am	Moon
Sun	25 lib 47	01.00 am - 16 lib 24
Mercury	02 sco 42	03.00 am - 17 lib 28
Venus	05 lib 40	05.00 am - 18 lib 32
Mars	27 vir 37	07.00 am - 19 lib 35
Jupiter	01 sco 49	09.00 am - 20 lib 39
Saturn	23 sag 28	11.00 am - 21 lib 43
Uranus	26 ar 33	13.00 pm - 22 lib 47
Neptune	11 pis 47	15.00 pm - 23 lib 50
Pluto	16 cap 57	17.00 pm - 24 lib 54
		19.00 pm - 25 lib 57
Oob		21.00 pm - 27 lib 00
		23.00 pm - 28 lib 03

Thursday 19th October

Retrograde Planets

Uranus, Neptune, Pallas, Chiron, Eris, Salacia, Sedna

Asteroids		Dwarf Planets	
Juno	10 cap 14	Eris	23 ar 17
Vesta	15 lib 33	Haumea	24 lib 14
Pallas	08 tau 48	Makemake	03 lib 54
Ceres	08 leo 07	Salacia	00 ar 40
Chiron	25 pis 16	Orcus	09 vir 41
N Node	22 leo 17	Quaoar	28 sag 57
S Node	22 aq 17	Sedna	26 tau 31

New Moon: 20:12
Sunrise: 07:31 BST
Sunset: 17:58
Moonrise: 06:46
Moonset: 18:19
Voc start: 20:11
Voc end:

Planetary and Angelic Hours			
Jupiter	07:29	Moon	17:59
Mars	08:21	Saturn	19:07
Sun	09:14	Jupiter	20:15
Venus	10:06	Mars	21:22
Mercury	10:59	Sun	22:30
Moon	11:52	Venus	23:37
Saturn	12:44	Mercury	00:45
Jupiter	13:37	Moon	01:53
Mars	14:29	Saturn	03:00
Sun	15:22	Jupiter	04:08
Venus	16:14	Mars	05:15
Mercury	17:07	Sun	06:23

Aspects

Moon square Pluto
Moon opposite Eris
Moon sextile Saturn
Sun opposite Uranus
Moon opposite Uranus
Sun conjunct Moon
Saturn trine Eris
Pluto square Vesta
Ceres square Pallas

Planets	**00:00 am**	**Moon**
Sun	26 lib 47	01.00 am - 29 lib 07
Mercury	04 sco 19	03.00 am - 00 sco 10
Venus	06 lib 55	05.00 am - 01 sco 13
Mars	28 vir 14	07.00 am - 02 sco 15
Jupiter	02 sco 02	09.00 am - 03 sco 18
Saturn	23 sag 33	11.00 am - 04 sco 21
Uranus	26 ar 30	13.00 pm - 05 sco 23
Neptune	11 pis 46	15.00 pm - 06 sco 26
Pluto	16 cap 57	17.00 pm - 07 sco 28
		18.00 pm - 08 sco 31
Oob		21.00 pm - 09 sco 33
		23.00 pm - 10 sco 35

Friday 20th October

Planetary Directions

Moon into Scorpio
02:41

Retrograde Planets

Uranus, Neptune, Pallas, Chiron, Eris, Salacia, Sedna

Asteroids		**Dwarf Planets**	
Juno	10 cap 30	Eris	23 ar 16
Vesta	16 lib 03	Haumea	24 lib 16
Pallas	08 tau 31	Makemake	03 lib 55
Ceres	08 leo 25	Salacia	00 ar 39
Chiron	25 pis 14	Orcus	09 vir 42
N Node	22 leo 06	Quaoar	28 sag 58
S Node	22 aq 06	Sedna	26 tau 31

Moon Phase: Crescent
Sunrise: 07:33 BST
Sunset: 17:56
Moonrise: 07:54
Moonset: 18:43
Voc start:
Voc end: 02:40

Planetary and Angelic Hours			
Venus	07:30	Mars	17:57
Mercury	08:23	Sun	19:05
Moon	09:15	Venus	20:13
Saturn	10:07	Mercury	21:21
Jupiter	10:59	Moon	22:29
Mars	11:52	Saturn	23:37
Sun	12:44	Jupiter	00:45
Venus	13:36	Mars	01:53
Mercury	14:28	Sun	03:01
Moon	15:21	Venus	04:08
Saturn	16:13	Mercury	05:16
Jupiter	17:05	Moon	06:24

Aspects

Ceres square Pallas
Moon conjunct Jupiter
Moon conj. Mercury
Moon opposite Pallas
Moon square Ceres
Moon sextile Juno
Moon trine Neptune
Venus sextile Ceres
Saturn trine Eris
Neptune sexile Juno
Pluto square Vesta

Planets	**00:00 am**	**Moon**
Sun	27 lib 47	01.00 am - 11 sco 37
Mercury	05 sco 55	03.00 am - 12 sco 39
Venus	08 lib 10	05.00 am - 13 sco 41
Mars	28 vir 52	07.00 am - 14 sco 43
Jupiter	02 sco 15	09.00 am - 15 sco 45
Saturn	23 sag 38	11.00 am - 16 sco 47
Uranus	26 ar 28	13.00 pm - 17 sco 48
Neptune	11 pis 45	15.00 pm - 18 sco 50
Pluto	16 cap 58	17.00 pm - 19 sco 51
		19.00 pm - 20 sco 53
Oob		21.00 pm - 21 sco 54
		23.00 pm - 22 sco 55

Saturday 21st October

Retrograde Planets

Uranus, Neptune, Pallas, Chiron, Eris, Salacia, Sedna

Asteroids		**Dwarf Planets**	
Juno	10 cap 46	Eris	23 ar 16
Vesta	16 lib 34	Haumea	24 lib 17
Pallas	08 tau 13	Makemake	03 lib 56
Ceres	08 leo 43	Salacia	00 ar 37
Chiron	25 pis 12	Orcus	09 vir 43
N Node	21 leo 53	Quaoar	28 sag 58
S Node	21 aq 53	Sedna	26 tau 30

Moon Phase: Crescent
Sunrise: 07:34 BST
Sunset: 17:54
Moonrise: 09:00
Moonset: 19:10
Voc start:
Voc end:

Planetary and Angelic Hours			
Saturn	07:32	Mercury	17:55
Jupiter	08:24	Moon	19:04
Mars	09:16	Saturn	20:12
Sun	10:08	Jupiter	21:20
Venus	11:00	Mars	22:28
Mercury	11:52	Sun	23:36
Moon	12:44	Venus	00:45
Saturn	13:36	Mercury	01:53
Jupiter	14:28	Moon	03:01
Mars	15:20	Saturn	04:09
Sun	16:11	Jupiter	05:17
Venus	17:03	Mars	06:26

Aspects

Moon trine Neptune
Moon sextile Pluto
Venus sextile Ceres
Pluto square Vesta
Mercury opp. Pallas
Saturn trine Eris
Neptune sextile Juno

Planets	00:00 am	Moon
Sun	28 lib 46	01.00 am - 23 sco 56
Mercury	07 sco 30	03.00 am - 24 sco 57
Venus	09 lib 24	05.00 am - 25 sco 58
Mars	29 vir 30	07.00 am - 26 sco 59
Jupiter	02 sco 28	09.00 am - 28 sco 00
Saturn	23 sag 43	11.00 am - 29 sco 01
Uranus	26 ar 25	13.00 pm - 00 sag 01
Neptune	11 pis 44	15.00 pm - 01 sag 02
Pluto	16 cap 59	17.00 pm - 02 sag 02
		19.00 pm - 03 sag 03
Oob		21.00 pm - 04 sag 03
		23.00 pm - 05 sag 03

Sunday 22nd October

Planetary Directions

Moon into Sagittarius 12:57
Mars into Libra 19:29

Retrograde Planets

Uranus, Neptune, Pallas, Chiron, Eris, Salacia, Sedna

Asteroids		Dwarf Planets	
Juno	11 cap 02	Eris	23 ar 15
Vesta	17 lib 05	Haumea	24 lib 19
Pallas	07 tau 55	Makemake	03 lib 58
Ceres	09 leo 00	Salacia	00 ar 36
Chiron	25 pis 10	Orcus	09 vir 44
N Node	21 leo 41	Quaoar	28 sag 59
S Node	21 aq 41	Sedna	26 tau 30

Moon Phase: Crescent
Sunrise: 07:36 BST
Sunset: 17:52
Moonrise: 10:05
Moonset: 19:40
Voc start: 12:35
Voc end: 12:56

Planetary and Angelic Hours

Sun	07:34	Jupiter	17:53
Venus	08:25	Mars	19:02
Mercury	09:17	Sun	20:10
Moon	10:09	Venus	21:19
Saturn	11:00	Mercury	22:27
Jupiter	11:52	Moon	23:36
Mars	12:44	Saturn	00:44
Sun	13:35	Jupiter	01:53
Venus	14:27	Mars	03:01
Mercury	15:18	Sun	04:10
Moon	16:10	Venus	05:18
Saturn	17:02	Mercury	06:27

Aspects

Moon trine Chiron
Moon opposite Sedna
Mercury opp. Pallas
Moon sextile Mars
Mercury square Ceres
Venus square Juno
Saturn trine Eris
Neptune sextile Juno
Pluto square Vesta

Planets	00:00 am	Moon
Sun	29 lib 46	01.00 am - 06 sag 04
Mercury	09 sco 05	03.00 am - 07 sag 04
Venus	10 lib 39	05.00 am - 08 sag 04
Mars	00 lib 08	07.00 am - 09 sag 04
Jupiter	02 sco 41	09.00 am - 10 sag 04
Saturn	23 sag 48	11.00 am - 11 sag 04
Uranus	26 ar 23	13.00 pm - 12 sag 04
Neptune	11 pis 43	15.00 pm - 13 sag 04
Pluto	16 cap 59	17.00 pm - 14 sag 04
		19.00 pm - 15 sag 04
Oob		21.00 pm - 16 sag 04
		22.00 pm - 17 sag 04

Monday 23rd October

Planetary Directions

Sun into Sco 06:27

Retrograde Planets

Uranus, Neptune, Pallas, Chiron, Eris, Salacia, Sedna

Asteroids		Dwarf Planets	
Juno	11 cap 18	Eris	23 ar 14
Vesta	17 lib 35	Haumea	24 lib 20
Pallas	07 tau 37	Makemake	03 lib 59
Ceres	09 leo 17	Salacia	00 ar 35
Chiron	25 pis 08	Orcus	09 vir 45
N Node	21 leo 29	Quaoar	29 sag 00
S Node	21 aq 29	Sedna	26 tau 29

Moon Phase: Crescent
Sunrise: 07:38 BST
Sunset: 17:50
Moonrise: 11:06
Moonset: 20:13
Voc start:
Voc end:

Planetary and Angelic Hours

Moon	07:36	Venus	17:51
Saturn	08:27	Mercury	19:00
Jupiter	09:18	Moon	20:09
Mars	10:09	Saturn	21:18
Sun	11:01	Jupiter	22:27
Venus	11:52	Mars	23:35
Mercury	12:43	Sun	00:44
Moon	13:35	Venus	01:53
Saturn	14:26	Mercury	03:02
Jupiter	15:17	Moon	04:11
Mars	16:09	Saturn	05:20
Sun	17:00	Jupiter	06:28

Aspects

Mercury square Ceres
Moon trine Ceres
Moon sextile Venus
Moon square Neptune
Venus square Juno
Moon sextile Vesta
Mercury sextile Juno
Saturn trine Eris
Neptune sextile Juno

Planets	00:00 am	Moon
		01.00 am - 18 sag 02
Sun	00 sco 46	03.00 am - 19 sag 01
Mercury	10 sco 39	05.00 am - 20 sag 01
Venus	11 lib 54	07.00 am - 21 sag 00
Mars	00 lib 46	09.00 am - 22 sag 00
Jupiter	02 sco 55	11.00 am - 22 sag 59
Saturn	23 sag 53	13.00 pm - 23 sag 58
Uranus	26 ar 20	15.00 pm - 24 sag 58
Neptune	11 pis 42	17.00 pm - 25 sag 57
Pluto	17 cap 00	19.00 pm - 26 sag 56
		21.00 pm - 27 sag 55
Oob		23.00 pm - 28 sag 54

Tuesday 24th October

Retrograde Planets

Uranus, Neptune, Pallas, Chiron, Eris, Salacia, Sedna

Asteroids		Dwarf Planets	
Juno	11 cap 34	Eris	23 ar 14
Vesta	18 lib 06	Haumea	24 lib 22
Pallas	07 tau 19	Makemake	04 lib 00
Ceres	09 leo 34	Salacia	00 ar 34
Chiron	25 pis 06	Orcus	09 vir 46
N Node	21 leo 20	Quaoar	29 sag 01
S Node	21 aq 20	Sedna	26 tau 29

Moon Phase: Crescent
Sunrise: 07:40 BST
Sunset: 17:48
Moonrise: 12:03
Moonset: 20:53
Voc start: 17:44
Voc end:

Planetary and Angelic Hours			
Mars	07:37	Saturn	17:49
Sun	08:28	Jupiter	18:59
Venus	09:19	Mars	20:08
Mercury	10:10	Sun	21:17
Moon	11:01	Venus	22:26
Saturn	11:52	Mercury	23:35
Jupiter	12:43	Moon	00:44
Mars	13:34	Saturn	01:53
Sun	14:25	Jupiter	03:02
Venus	15:16	Mars	04:12
Mercury	16:07	Sun	05:21
Moon	16:58	Venus	06:30

Aspects

Moon sextile Vesta
Moon trine Eris
Neptune sextile Juno
Moon conjunct Saturn
Moon square Chiron
Mercury trine Neptune
Moon trine Uranus
Mercury sextile Juno
Saturn trine Eris

Planets	**00:00 am**	**Moon**
Sun	01 sco 46	01.00 am - 29 sag 54
Mercury	12 sco 13	03.00 am - 00 cap 53
Venus	13 lib 09	05.00 am - 01 cap 52
Mars	01 lib 24	07.00 am - 02 cap 51
Jupiter	03 sco 08	09.00 am - 03 cap 50
Saturn	23 sag 58	11.00 am - 04 cap 49
Uranus	26 ar 18	13.00 pm - 05 cap 48
Neptune	11 pis 41	15.00 pm - 06 cap 47
Pluto	17 cap 01	17.00 pm - 07 cap 46
		19.00 pm - 08 cap 45
Oob		21.00 pm - 09 cap 44
		23.00 pm - 10 cap 43

Wednesday 25th October

Planetary Directions

Moon into Capricorn
01:13

Retrograde Planets

Uranus, Neptune, Pallas, Chiron, Eris, Salacia, Sedna

Asteroids		**Dwarf Planets**	
Juno	11 cap 51	Eris	23 ar 13
Vesta	18 lib 37	Haumea	24 lib 23
Pallas	07 tau 00	Makemake	04 lib 02
Ceres	09 leo 51	Salacia	00 ar 33
Chiron	25 pis 04	Orcus	09 vir 47
N Node	21 leo 13	Quaoar	29 sag 02
S Node	21 aq 13	Sedna	26 tau 28

Moon Phase: Crescent
Sunrise: 07:41 BST
Sunset: 17:46
Moonrise: 12:55
Moonset: 21:38
Voc start:
Voc end: 01:12

Planetary and Angelic Hours			
Mercury	07:39	Sun	17:47
Moon	08:30	Venus	18:57
Saturn	09:20	Mercury	20:06
Jupiter	10:11	Moon	21:16
Mars	11:02	Saturn	22:25
Sun	11:52	Jupiter	23:35
Venus	12:43	Mars	00:44
Mercury	13:34	Sun	01:53
Moon	14:25	Venus	03:03
Saturn	15:15	Mercury	04:12
Jupiter	16:06	Moon	05:22
Mars	16:57	Saturn	06:31

Aspects

Moon square Mars
Sun sextile Moon
Moon sextile Jupiter
Moon trine Pallas
Moon sextile Neptune
Sun conjunct Jupiter
Moon conjunct Juno
Saturn square Chiron
Saturn trine Eris
Neptune sextile Juno

Planets	00:00 am	Moon
Sun	02 sco 45	01.00 am - 11 cap 42
Mercury	13 sco 46	03.00 am - 12 cap 41
Venus	14 lib 23	05.00 am - 13 cap 40
Mars	02 lib 02	07.00 am - 14 cap 40
Jupiter	03 sco 21	09.00 am - 15 cap 39
Saturn	24 sag 03	11.00 am - 16 cap 38
Uranus	26 ar 16	13.00 pm - 17 cap 37
Neptune	11 pis 40	15.00 pm - 18 cap 36
Pluto	17 cap 02	17.00 pm - 19 cap 35
		19.00 pm - 20 cap 35
Oob		21.00 pm - 21 cap 34
		23.00 pm - 22 cap 33

Thursday 26th October

Retrograde Planets

Uranus, Neptune, Pallas, Chiron, Eris, Salacia, Sedna

Asteroids		Dwarf Planets	
Juno	12 cap 07	Eris	23 ar 13
Vesta	19 lib 08	Haumea	24 lib 25
Pallas	06 tau 41	Makemake	04 lib 03
Ceres	10 leo 08	Salacia	00 ar 32
Chiron	25 pis 02	Orcus	09 vir 48
N Node	21 leo 08	Quaoar	29 sag 03
S Node	21 aq 08	Sedna	26 tau 28

Moon Phase: Crescent
Sunrise: 07:43 BST
Sunset: 17:44
Moonrise: 13:42
Moonset: 22:29
Voc start:
Voc end:

Planetary and Angelic Hours			
Jupiter	07:41	Moon	17:46
Mars	08:31	Saturn	18:55
Sun	09:21	Jupiter	20:05
Venus	10:12	Mars	21:15
Mercury	11:02	Sun	22:24
Moon	11:53	Venus	23:34
Saturn	12:43	Mercury	00:44
Jupiter	13:33	Moon	01:54
Mars	14:24	Saturn	03:03
Sun	15:14	Jupiter	04:13
Venus	16:05	Mars	05:23
Mercury	16:55	Sun	06:33

Aspects

Moon conjunct Juno
Moon sextile Mercury
Moon square Venus
Moon conjunct Pluto
Moon square Vesta
Sun conjunct Jupiter
Moon square Eris
Saturn square Chiron
Saturn trine Eris
Neptune sextile Juno

Planets	00:00 am	Moon
Sun	03 sco 45	01.00 am - 23 cap 33
Mercury	15 sco 18	03.00 am - 24 cap 32
Venus	15 lib 38	05.00 am - 25 cap 32
Mars	02 lib 40	07.00 am - 26 cap 31
Jupiter	03 sco 34	09.00 am - 27 cap 31
Saturn	24 sag 09	11.00 am - 28 cap 31
Uranus	26 ar 13	13.00 pm - 29 cap 30
Neptune	11 pis 39	15.00 pm - 00 aq 30
Pluto	17 cap 03	17.00 pm - 01 aq 30
		19.00 pm - 02 aq 30
Oob		21.00 pm - 03 aq 30
		23.00 pm - 04 aq 30

Friday 27th October

Planetary Directions

Moon into Aquarius
13:59

Retrograde Planets

Uranus, Neptune, Pallas, Chiron, Eris, Salacia, Sedna

Asteroids		Dwarf Planets	
Juno	12 cap 24	Eris	23 ar 12
Vesta	19 lib 38	Haumea	24 lib 26
Pallas	06 tau 22	Makemake	04 lib 04
Ceres	10 leo 24	Salacia	00 ar 31
Chiron	25 pis 00	Orcus	09 vir 49
N Node	21 leo 06	Quaoar	29 sag 04
S Node	21 aq 06	Sedna	26 tau 27

First Quarter: 23:22
Sunrise: 07:45 BST
Sunset: 17:42
Moonrise: 14:22
Moonset: 23:26
Voc start: 06:22
Voc end: 13:58

Planetary and Angelic Hours			
Venus	07:42	Mars	17:44
Mercury	08:32	Sun	18:54
Moon	09:23	Venus	20:04
Saturn	10:13	Mercury	21:14
Jupiter	11:03	Moon	22:24
Mars	11:53	Saturn	23:34
Sun	12:43	Jupiter	00:44
Venus	13:33	Mars	01:54
Mercury	14:23	Sun	03:04
Moon	15:13	Venus	04:14
Saturn	16:03	Mercury	05:24
Jupiter	16:54	Moon	06:34

Aspects

Moon sextile Chiron
Moon square Uranus
Moon trine Sedna
Moon trine Mars
Moon square Jupiter
Sun square Moon
Sun conjunct Jupiter
Moon square Pallas
Mercury sextile Pluto
Venus square Pluto
Saturn square Chiron

Saturday 28th October

Planets	00:00 am	Moon
Sun	04 sco 45	01.00 am - 05 aq 30
Mercury	16 sco 51	03.00 am - 06 aq 30
Venus	16 lib 53	05.00 am - 07 aq 31
Mars	03 lib 18	07.00 am - 08 aq 31
Jupiter	03 sco 47	09.00 am - 09 aq 32
Saturn	24 sag 14	11.00 am - 10 aq 32
Uranus	26 ar 11	13.00 pm - 11 aq 33
Neptune	11 pis 38	15.00 pm - 12 aq 34
Pluto	17 cap 03	17.00 pm - 13 aq 35
		19.00 pm - 14 aq 36
Oob		21.00 pm - 15 aq 37
		23.00 pm - 16 aq 38

Retrograde Planets

Uranus, Neptune, Pallas, Chiron, Eris, Salacia, Sedna

Asteroids		Dwarf Planets	
Juno	12 cap 41	Eris	23 ar 11
Vesta	20 lib 09	Haumea	24 lib 28
Pallas	06 tau 03	Makemake	04 lib 05
Ceres	10 leo 40	Salacia	00 ar 30
Chiron	24 pis 58	Orcus	09 vir 50
N Node	21 leo 05	Quaoar	29 sag 05
S Node	21 aq 05	Sedna	26 tau 26

Moon Phase: Gibbous
Sunrise: 07:47 BST
Sunset: 17:40
Moonrise: 14:57
Moonset: None
Voc start:
Voc end:

Planetary and Angelic Hours			
Saturn	07:44	Mercury	17:42
Jupiter	08:34	Moon	18:52
Mars	09:24	Saturn	20:02
Sun	10:13	Jupiter	21:13
Venus	11:03	Mars	22:23
Mercury	11:53	Sun	23:33
Moon	12:43	Venus	00:44
Saturn	13:33	Mercury	01:54
Jupiter	14:23	Moon	03:04
Mars	15:12	Saturn	04:15
Sun	16:02	Jupiter	05:25
Venus	16:52	Mars	06:35

Aspects

Moon square Pallas
Venus square Pluto
Mercury sextile Pluto
Moon opposite Ceres
Sun opposite Pallas
Moon square Mercury
Moon trine Venus
Saturn square Chiron

Planets	00:00 am	Moon
Sun	05 sco 45	00.00 am - 17 aq 40
Mercury	18 sco 22	02.00 am - 18 aq 41
Venus	18 lib 08	04.00 am - 19 aq 43
Mars	03 lib 56	06.00 am - 20 aq 45
Jupiter	04 sco 00	08.00 am - 21 aq 46
Saturn	24 sag 20	10.00 am - 22 aq 48
Uranus	26 ar 08	12.00 pm - 23 aq 51
Neptune	11 pis 38	14.00 pm - 24 aq 53
Pluto	17 cap 04	16.00 pm - 25 aq 55
		18.00 pm - 26 aq 58
Oob		20.00 pm - 28 aq 01
		22.00 pm - 29 aq 04

Sunday 29th October

Planetary Directions

Moon into Pisces 23:47

Retrograde Planets

Uranus, Neptune, Pallas, Chiron, Eris, Salacia, Sedna

Asteroids		Dwarf Planets	
Juno	12 cap 59	Eris	23 ar 11
Vesta	20 lib 40	Haumea	24 lib 29
Pallas	05 tau 44	Makemake	04 lib 07
Ceres	10 leo 56	Salacia	00 ar 29
Chiron	24 pis 56	Orcus	09 vir 51
N Node	21 leo 06	Quaoar	29 sag 06
S Node	21 aq 06	Sedna	26 tau 26

Moon Phase: Gibbous
Sunrise: 06:48 GMT
Sunset: 16:39 GMT
Moonrise: 14:28 GMT
Moonset: 00:29 BST
Voc start: 16:21
Voc end: 23:46

Planetary and Angelic Hours			
Sun	06:46	Jupiter	16:40
Venus	07:35	Mars	17:51
Mercury	08:25	Sun	19:01
Moon	09:14	Venus	20:12
Saturn	10:04	Mercury	21:22
Jupiter	10:53	Moon	22:33
Mars	11:43	Saturn	23:44
Sun	12:32	Jupiter	00:54
Venus	13:22	Mars	02:05
Mercury	14:11	Sun	03:16
Moon	15:01	Venus	04:26
Saturn	15.50	Mercury	05:37

Aspects

Moon trine Venus
Moon square Mercury
Moon trine Vesta
Moon sextile Eris
Moon sextile Saturn
Moon sextile Uranus
Moon square Sedna
Saturn square Chiron

Planets	**00:00 am**	**Moon**
Sun	06 sco 45	00.00 am - 00 pis 07
Mercury	19 sco 53	02.00 am - 01 pis 10
Venus	19 lib 23	04.00 am - 02 pis 13
Mars	04 lib 33	06.00 am - 03 pis 17
Jupiter	04 sco 13	08.00 am - 04 pis 23
Saturn	24 sag 25	10.00 am - 05 pis 24
Uranus	26 ar 06	12.00 pm - 06 pis 28
Neptune	11 pis 37	14.00 pm - 07 pis 33
Pluto	17 cap 05	16.00 pm - 08 pis 37
		18.00 pm - 09 pis 42
Oob		20.00 pm - 10 pis 46
		22.00 pm - 11 pis 51

Monday 30th October

Retrograde Planets

Uranus, Neptune, Pallas, Chiron, Eris, Salacia, Sedna

Asteroids		**Dwarf Planets**	
Juno	13 cap 16	Eris	23 ar 10
Vesta	21 lib 11	Haumea	24 lib 31
Pallas	05 tau 24	Makemake	04 lib 08
Ceres	11 leo 12	Salacia	00 ar 28
Chiron	24 pis 54	Orcus	09 vir 52
N Node	21 leo 05	Quaoar	29 sag 07
S Node	21 aq 05	Sedna	26 tau 25

Moon Phase: Gibbous
Sunrise: 06:50 GMT
Sunset: 16:37
Moonrise: 14:56
Moonset: 00:35
Voc start:
Voc end:

Planetary and Angelic Hours			
Moon	06:48	Venus	16:38
Saturn	07:37	Mercury	17:49
Jupiter	08:26	Moon	19:00
Mars	09:15	Saturn	20:11
Sun	10:04	Jupiter	21:22
Venus	10:54	Mars	22:33
Mercury	11:43	Sun	23:44
Moon	12:32	Venus	00:55
Saturn	13:21	Mercury	02:06
Jupiter	14:10	Moon	03:16
Mars	15:00	Saturn	04:27
Sun	15:49	Jupiter	05:38

Aspects

Moon trine Jupiter
Moon sextile Pallas
Sun trine Moon
Moon conj. Neptune
Moon sextile Juno
Jupiter opposite Pallas
Saturn square Chiron

Planets	00:00 am	Moon
Sun	07 sco 45	00.00 am - 12 pis 56
Mercury	21 sco 24	02.00 am - 14 pis 02
Venus	20 lib 38	04.00 am - 15 pis 07
Mars	05 lib 11	06.00 am - 16 pis 13
Jupiter	04 sco 26	08.00 am - 17 pis 19
Saturn	24 sag 31	10.00 am - 18 pis 25
Uranus	26 ar 04	12.00 pm - 19 pis 31
Neptune	11 pis 36	14.00 pm - 20 pis 37
Pluto	17 cap 06	16.00 pm - 21 pis 44
		18.00 pm - 22 pis 51
Oob		20.00 pm - 23 pis 58
		22.00 pm - 25 pis 05

Tuesday 31st October

Planetary Directions

Moon into Aries 06:43

Retrograde Planets

Uranus, Neptune, Pallas, Chiron, Eris, Salacia, Sedna

Asteroids		Dwarf Planets	
Juno	13 cap 34	Eris	23 ar 10
Vesta	21 lib 42	Haumea	24 lib 32
Pallas	05 tau 05	Makemake	04 lib 09
Ceres	11 leo 28	Salacia	00 ar 27
Chiron	24 pis 52	Orcus	09 vir 52
N Node	21 leo 04	Quaoar	29 sag 08
S Node	21 aq 04	Sedna	26 tau 25

Moon Phase: Gibbous
Sunrise: 06:52 GMT
Sunset: 16:35
Moonrise: 15:22
Moonset: 01:44
Voc start: 21:07
Voc end:

Planetary and Angelic Hours

Mars	06:49	Saturn	16:36
Sun	07:38	Jupiter	17:47
Venus	08:27	Mars	18:59
Mercury	09:16	Sun	20:10
Moon	10:05	Venus	21:21
Saturn	10:54	Mercury	22:32
Jupiter	11:43	Moon	23:44
Mars	12:32	Saturn	00:55
Sun	13:21	Jupiter	02:06
Venus	14:09	Mars	03:17
Mercury	14:58	Sun	04:29
Moon	15:47	Venus	05:40

Halloween

Aspects

Moon sextile Juno
Moon sextile Pluto
Moon trine Mercury
Moon square Saturn
Moon conjunct Chiron
Moon sextile Sedna
Venus conjunct Vesta
Jupiter opposite Pallas
Saturn square Chiron
Vesta opposite Eris

Planets	00:00 am	Moon
Sun	08 sco 45	00.00 am - 26 pis 12
Mercury	22 sco 54	02.00 am - 27 pis 20
Venus	21 lib 53	04.00 am - 28 pis 27
Mars	05 lib 49	06.00 am - 29 pis 35
Jupiter	04 sco 39	08.00 am - 00 ar 43
Saturn	24 sag 36	10.00 am - 01 ar 52
Uranus	26 ar 01	12.00 pm - 03 ar 00
Neptune	11 pis 35	14.00 pm - 04 ar 09
Pluto	17 cap 07	16.00 pm - 05 ar 18
		18.00 pm - 06 ar 27
Oob		20.00 pm - 07 ar 36
		22.00 pm - 08 ar 46

Wednesday 1st November

Retrograde Planets

Uranus, Neptune, Pallas, Chiron, Eris, Salacia, Sedna

Asteroids		Dwarf Planets	
Juno	13 cap 52	Eris	23 ar 09
Vesta	22 lib 12	Haumea	24 lib 33
Pallas	04 tau 45	Makemake	04 lib 10
Ceres	11 leo 43	Salacia	00 ar 26
Chiron	24 pis 50	Orcus	09 vir 53
N Node	21 leo 00	Quaoar	29 sag 09
S Node	21 aq 00	Sedna	26 tau 24

Moon Phase: Gibbous
Sunrise: 06:54 GMT
Sunset: 16:33
Moonrise: 15:47
Moonset: 02:56
Voc start:
Voc end: 06:42

Planetary and Angelic Hours			
Mercury	06:51	Sun	16:34
Moon	07:40	Venus	17:46
Saturn	08:28	Mercury	18:57
Jupiter	09:17	Moon	20:09
Mars	10:05	Saturn	21:21
Sun	10:54	Jupiter	22:32
Venus	11:43	Mars	23:44
Mercury	12:31	Sun	00:55
Moon	13:20	Venus	02:07
Saturn	14:09	Mercury	03:18
Jupiter	14:57	Moon	04:30
Mars	15:46	Saturn	05:41

Samhain

Aspects

Moon sextile Sedna
Jupiter opposite Pallas
Venus conjunct Vesta
Moon opposite Mars
Mercury trine Chiron
Venus opposite Eris
Saturn square Chiron
Vesta opposite Eris

Planets	00:00 am	Moon
Sun	09 sco 45	00.00 am - 09 ar 56
Mercury	24 sco 23	02.00 am - 11 ar 06
Venus	23 lib 08	04.00 am - 12 ar 16
Mars	06 lib 27	06.00 am - 13 ar 26
Jupiter	04 sco 52	08.00 am - 14 ar 36
Saturn	24 sag 42	10.00 am - 15 ar 47
Uranus	25 ar 59	12.00 pm - 16 ar 58
Neptune	11 pis 35	14.00 pm - 18 ar 09
Pluto	17 cap 08	16.00 pm - 19 ar 20
		18.00 pm - 20 ar 31
Oob		20.00 pm - 21 ar 43
		22.00 pm - 22 ar 55

Thursday 2nd November

Retrograde Planets

Uranus, Neptune, Pallas, Chiron, Eris, Salacia, Sedna

Asteroids		Dwarf Planets	
Juno	14 cap 10	Eris	23 ar 08
Vesta	22 lib 43	Haumea	24 lib 35
Pallas	04 tau 26	Makemake	04 lib 11
Ceres	11 leo 58	Salacia	00 ar 25
Chiron	24 pis 48	Orcus	09 vir 54
N Node	20 leo 53	Quaoar	29 sag 11
S Node	20 aq 53	Sedna	26 tau 23

Moon Phase: Gibbous
Sunrise: 06:55 GMT
Sunset: 16:31
Moonrise: 16:12
Moonset: 04:11
Voc start:
Voc end:

Planetary and Angelic Hours			
Jupiter	06:53	Moon	16:33
Mars	07:41	Saturn	17:44
Sun	08:29	Jupiter	18:56
Venus	09:18	Mars	20:08
Mercury	10:06	Sun	21:20
Moon	10:54	Venus	22:32
Saturn	11:43	Mercury	23:44
Jupiter	12:31	Moon	00:55
Mars	13:19	Saturn	02:07
Sun	14:08	Jupiter	03:19
Venus	14:56	Mars	04:31
Mercury	15:44	Sun	05:43

Aspects

Vesta opposite Eris
Moon trine Ceres
Mercury trine Chiron
Moon square Juno
Moon square Pluto
Vesta opposite Eris
Saturn square Chiron
Moon conjunct Eris
Moon opposite Vesta
Sun square Neptune
Moon opposite Venus
Moon trine Saturn
Mercury opp. Sedna
Venus sextile Saturn
Jupiter opposite Pallas

Planets	00:00 am	Moon
Sun	10 sco 45	00.00 am - 24 ar 06
Mercury	25 sco 52	02.00 am - 25 ar 18
Venus	24 lib 23	04.00 am - 26 ar 31
Mars	07 lib 05	06.00 am - 27 ar 43
Jupiter	05 sco 05	08.00 am - 28 ar 55
Saturn	24 sag 47	10.00 am - 00 tau 08
Uranus	25 ar 56	12.00 pm - 01 tau 21
Neptune	11 pis 34	14.00 pm - 02 tau 34
Pluto	17 cap 09	16.00 pm - 03 tau 47
		18.00 pm - 05 tau 00
		20.00 pm - 06 tau 13
Oob		22.00 pm - 07 tau 26

Friday 3rd November

Planetary Directions

Moon into Taurus
09:47

Retrograde Planets

Uranus, Neptune, Pallas, Chiron, Eris, Salacia, Sedna

Asteroids		Dwarf Planets	
Juno	14 cap 28	Eris	23 ar 08
Vesta	23 lib 14	Haumea	24 lib 36
Pallas	04 tau 06	Makemake	04 lib 13
Ceres	12 leo 13	Salacia	00 ar 24
Chiron	24 pis 47	Orcus	09 vir 55
N Node	20 leo 43	Quaoar	29 sag 12
S Node	20 aq 43	Sedna	26 tau 23

Moon Phase: Gibbous
Sunrise: 06:57 GMT
Sunset: 16:29
Moonrise: 16:40
Moonset: 05:29
Voc start: 03:02
Voc end: 09:46

Planetary and Angelic Hours			
Venus	06:54	Mars	16:31
Mercury	07:42	Sun	17:43
Moon	08:31	Venus	18:55
Saturn	09:19	Mercury	20:07
Jupiter	10:07	Moon	21:19
Mars	10:55	Saturn	22:31
Sun	11:43	Jupiter	23:44
Venus	12:31	Mars	00:56
Mercury	13:19	Sun	02:08
Moon	14:07	Venus	03:20
Saturn	14:55	Mercury	04:32
Jupiter	15:43	Moon	05:44

Aspects

Moon opposite Venus
Moon trine Saturn
Moon conjunct Uranus
Mercury opp. Sedna
Venus sextile Saturn
Moon conjunct Pallas
Moon opposite Jupiter
Sun trine Neptune
Sun square Ceres
Venus opposite Uranus
Saturn square Chiron
Vesta opposite Eris

Planets	00:00 am	Moon
Sun	11 sco 45	00.00 am - 08 tau 40
Mercury	27 sco 21	02.00 am - 09 tau 54
Venus	25 lib 38	04.00 am - 11 tau 04
Mars	07 lib 43	06.00 am - 12 tau 21
Jupiter	05 sco 18	08.00 am - 13 tau 35
Saturn	24 sag 53	10.00 am - 14 tau 49
Uranus	25 ar 54	12.00 pm - 16 tau 03
Neptune	11 pis 33	14.00 pm - 17 tau 18
Pluto	17 cap 10	16.00 pm - 18 tau 32
		18.00 pm - 19 tau 46
Oob		20.00 pm - 21 tau 01
		22.00 pm - 22 tau 15

Saturday 4th November

Retrograde Planets

Uranus, Neptune, Pallas, Chiron, Eris, Salacia, Sedna

Asteroids		Dwarf Planets	
Juno	14 cap 46	Eris	23 ar 07
Vesta	23 lib 45	Haumea	24 lib 38
Pallas	03 tau 46	Makemake	04 lib 14
Ceres	12 leo 28	Salacia	00 ar 23
Chiron	24 pis 45	Orcus	09 vir 56
N Node	20 leo 32	Quaoar	29 sag 13
S Node	20 aq 32	Sedna	26 tau 22

Full Moon: 05:24
Sunrise: 06:59 GMT
Sunset: 16:28
Moonrise: 17:11
Moonset: 06:48
Voc start:
Voc end:

Planetary and Angelic Hours			
Saturn	06:56	Mercury	16:29
Jupiter	07:44	Moon	17:42
Mars	08:32	Saturn	18:54
Sun	09:19	Jupiter	20:06
Venus	10:07	Mars	21:19
Mercury	10:55	Sun	22:31
Moon	11:43	Venus	23:44
Saturn	12:30	Mercury	00:56
Jupiter	13:18	Moon	02:08
Mars	14:06	Saturn	03:21
Sun	14:54	Jupiter	04:33
Venus	15:41	Mars	05:46

Aspects

Moon sextile Neptune
Venus opposite Uranus
Sun opposite Moon
Moon square Ceres
Moon trine Juno
Moon trine Pluto
Sun square Ceres
Saturn trine Uranus
Saturn square Chiron
Saturn sextile Vesta

Planets	**00:00 am**	**Moon**
Sun	12 sco 45	00.00 am - 23 tau 30
Mercury	28 sco 49	02.00 am - 24 tau 44
Venus	26 lib 53	04.00 am - 25 tau 59
Mars	08 lib 21	06.00 am - 27 tau 14
Jupiter	05 sco 32	08.00 am - 28 tau 29
Saturn	24 sag 59	10.00 am - 29 tau 43
Uranus	25 ar 52	12.00 pm - 00 gem 58
Neptune	11 pis 33	14.00 pm - 02 gem 13
Pluto	17 cap 11	16.00 pm - 03 gem 28
		18.00 pm - 04 gem 42
Oob		20.00 pm - 05 gem 57
		22.00 pm - 07 gem 12

Sunday 5th November

Planetary Directions
Moon into Gemni
10:26
Mercury into
Sagittarius at 19:19

Retrograde Planets

Uranus, Neptune,
Pallas, Chiron, Eris,
Salacia, Sedna

Asteroids		**Dwarf Planets**	
Juno	15 cap 05	Eris	23 ar 07
Vesta	24 lib 15	Haumea	24 lib 39
Pallas	03 tau 27	Makemake	04 lib 15
Ceres	12 leo 42	Salacia	00 ar 23
Chiron	24 pis 44	Orcus	09 vir 56
N Node	20 leo 20	Quaoar	29 sag 14
S Node	20 aq 20	Sedna	26 tau 22

Phase: Disseminating
Sunrise: 07:01 GMT
Sunset: 16:26
Moonrise: 17:49
Moonset: 08:08
Voc start: 09:28
Voc end: 10:25

Planetary and Angelic Hours			
Sun	06:58	Jupiter	16:28
Venus	07:45	Mars	17:40
Mercury	08:33	Sun	18:53
Moon	09:20	Venus	20:06
Saturn	10:08	Mercury	21:18
Jupiter	10:55	Moon	22:31
Mars	11:43	Saturn	23:44
Sun	12:30	Jupiter	00:56
Venus	13:18	Mars	02:09
Mercury	14:05	Sun	03:22
Moon	14:53	Venus	04:34
Saturn	15:40	Mercury	05:47

Guy Fawkes Night

Aspects

Moon sextile Chiron
Moon conjunct Sedna
Moon opp. Mercury
Sun square Ceres
Moon trine Mars
Saturn trine Uranus
Saturn square Chiron
Saturn sextile Vesta

Planets	00:00 am	Moon
Sun	13 sco 45	00.00 am - 08 gem 27
Mercury	00 sag 17	02.00 am - 09 gem 42
Venus	28 lib 08	04.00 am - 10 gem 56
Mars	08 lib 58	06.00 am - 12 gem 11
Jupiter	05 sco 45	08.00 am - 13 gem 25
Saturn	25 sag 05	10.00 am - 14 gem 41
Uranus	25 ar 49	12.00 pm - 15 gem 55
Neptune	11 pis 32	14.00 pm - 17 gem 10
Pluto	17 cap 12	16.00 pm - 18 gem 24
		18.00 pm - 19 gem 39
Oob		20.00 pm - 20 gem 53
		22.00 pm - 22 gem 08

Monday 6th November

Retrograde Planets

Uranus, Neptune, Pallas, Chiron, Eris, Salacia, Sedna

Asteroids		Dwarf Planets	
Juno	15 cap 23	Eris	23 ar 06
Vesta	24 lib 46	Haumea	24 lib 40
Pallas	03 tau 07	Makemake	04 lib 16
Ceres	12 leo 56	Salacia	00 ar 22
Chiron	24 pis 42	Orcus	09 vir 57
N Node	20 leo 09	Quaoar	29 sag 15
S Node	20 aq 09	Sedna	26 tau 21

Phase: Disseminating
Sunrise: 07:03 GMT
Sunset: 16:24
Moonrise: 18:34
Moonset: 09:26
Voc start:
Voc end:

Planetary and Angelic Hours			
Moon	07:00	Venus	16:26
Saturn	07:47	Mercury	17:39
Jupiter	08:34	Moon	18:52
Mars	09:21	Saturn	20:05
Sun	10:08	Jupiter	21:18
Venus	10:56	Mars	22:31
Mercury	11:43	Sun	23:44
Moon	12:30	Venus	00:57
Saturn	13:17	Mercury	02:10
Jupiter	14:04	Moon	03:22
Mars	14:51	Saturn	04:35
Sun	15:39	Jupiter	05:48

Aspects

Moon trine Mars
Moon square Neptune
Moon sextile Ceres
Saturn sextile Vesta
Moon sextile Eris
Sun sextile Juno
Saturn trine Uranus
Saturn square Chiron
Uranus opposite Vesta

Planets	00:00 am	Moon
Sun	14 sco 45	00.00 am - 23 gem 22
Mercury	01 sag 43	02.00 am - 24 gem 36
Venus	29 lib 23	04.00 am - 25 gem 50
Mars	09 lib 36	06.00 am - 27 gem 04
Jupiter	05 sco 58	08.00 am - 28 gem 18
Saturn	26 sag 11	10.00 am - 29 gem 32
Uranus	25 ar 47	12.00 pm - 00 can 46
Neptune	11 pis 32	14.00 pm - 02 can 00
Pluto	17 cap 14	16.00 pm - 03 can 13
		18.00 pm - 04 can 27
Oob		20.00 pm - 05 can 40
		22.00 pm - 06 can 53

Tuesday 7th November

Planetary Directions

Moon into Cancer
10:45
Venus into Scorpio
11:39

Retrograde Planets

Uranus, Neptune, Pallas, Chiron, Eris, Salacia, Sedna

Asteroids		Dwarf Planets	
Juno	15 cap 42	Eris	23 ar 06
Vesta	25 lib 17	Haumea	24 lib 42
Pallas	02 tau 48	Makemake	04 lib 17
Ceres	13 leo 10	Salacia	00 ar 21
Chiron	24 pis 40	Orcus	09 vir 58
N Node	20 leo 00	Quaoar	29 sag 16
S Node	20 aq 00	Sedna	26 tau 20

Phase: Disseminating
Sunrise: 07:04 GMT
Sunset: 16:23
Moonrise: 19:28
Moonset: 10:37
Voc start:10:39
Voc end: 10:44

Planetary and Angelic Hours			
Mars	07:01	Saturn	16:24
Sun	07:48	Jupiter	17:37
Venus	08:35	Mars	18:51
Mercury	09:22	Sun	20:04
Moon	10:09	Venus	21:17
Saturn	10:56	Mercury	22:30
Jupiter	11:43	Moon	23:44
Mars	12:30	Saturn	00:57
Sun	13:17	Jupiter	02:10
Venus	14:04	Mars	03:23
Mercury	14:50	Sun	04:37
Moon	15:37	Venus	05:50

Aspects

Moon square Chiron
Moon opposite Saturn
Moon trine Vesta
Moon sextile Uranus
Moon trine Venus
Moon sextile Pallas
Moon trine Jupiter
Uranus opposite Vesta
Sun sextile Juno
Saturn trine Uranus
Saturn square Chiron
Saturn sextile Vesta

Planets	00:00 am	Moon
Sun	15 sco 46	00.00 am - 08 can 07
Mercury	03 sag 10	02.00 am - 09 can 20
Venus	00 sco 38	04.00 am - 10 can 33
Mars	10 lib 14	06.00 am - 11 can 45
Jupiter	06 sco 11	08.00 am - 12 can 58
Saturn	25 sag 17	10.00 am - 14 can 11
Uranus	25 ar 45	12.00 pm - 15 can 23
Neptune	11 pis 31	14.00 pm - 16 can 35
Pluto	17 cap 15	16.00 pm - 17 can 48
		18.00 pm - 19 can 00
Oob		20.00 pm - 20 can 12
		22.00 pm - 21 can 23

Wednesday 8th November

Retrograde Planets

Uranus, Neptune, Pallas, Chiron, Eris, Salacia, Sedna

Asteroids		Dwarf Planets	
Juno	16 cap 01	Eris	23 ar 05
Vesta	25 lib 48	Haumea	24 lib 43
Pallas	02 tau 29	Makemake	04 lib 18
Ceres	13 leo 24	Salacia	00 ar 20
Chiron	24 pis 39	Orcus	09 vir 59
N Node	19 leo 54	Quaoar	29 sag 18
S Node	08 can 07	Sedna	26 tau 20

Phase: Disseminating
Sunrise: 07:06 GMT
Sunset: 16:21
Moonrise: 20:30
Moonset: 11:39
Voc start:
Voc end:

Planetary and Angelic Hours			
Mercury	07:03	Sun	16:23
Moon	07:50	Venus	17:36
Saturn	08:36	Mercury	18:50
Jupiter	09:23	Moon	20:03
Mars	10:10	Saturn	21:17
Sun	10:56	Jupiter	22:30
Venus	11:43	Mars	23:44
Mercury	12:29	Sun	00:57
Moon	13:16	Venus	02:11
Saturn	14:03	Mercury	03:24
Jupiter	14:49	Moon	04:38
Mars	15:36	Saturn	05:51

Aspects

Moon square Mars
Moon trine Neptune
Sun sextile Juno
Moon opposite Juno
Sun trine Moon
Moon opposite Pluto
Sun sextile Pluto
Moon square Eris
Venus opposite Pallas
Saturn trine Uranus
Saturn square Chiron
Saturn sextile Vesta
Uranus opposite Vesta
Pluto conjunct Juno

Planets	00:00 am	Moon
Sun	16 sco 46	00.00 am - 22 can 35
Mercury	04 sag 36	02.00 am - 23 can 47
Venus	01 sco 53	04.00 am - 24 can 58
Mars	10 lib 52	06.00 am - 26 can 09
Jupiter	06 sco 24	08.00 am - 27 can 21
Saturn	25 sag 23	10.00 am - 28 can 31
Uranus	25 ar 43	12.00 pm - 29 can 42
Neptune	11 pis 31	14.00 pm - 00 leo 53
Pluto	17 cap 16	16.00 pm - 02 leo 04
		18.00 pm - 03 leo 14
Oob	Mercury	20.00 pm - 04 leo 24
		22.00 pm - 05 leo 35

Thursday 9th November

Planetary Directions

Moon into Leo 12:30

Retrograde Planets

Uranus, Neptune, Pallas, Chiron, Eris, Salacia, Sedna

Asteroids		Dwarf Planets	
Juno	16 cap 20	Eris	23 ar 05
Vesta	26 lib 19	Haumea	24 lib 45
Pallas	02 tau 10	Makemake	04 lib 19
Ceres	13 leo 38	Salacia	00 ar 19
Chiron	24 pis 38	Orcus	09 vir 59
N Node	19 leo 50	Quaoar	29 sag 19
S Node	19 aq 50	Sedna	26 tau 19

Phase: Disseminating
Sunrise: 07:08 GMT
Sunset: 16:20
Moonrise: 21:39
Moonset: 12:30
Voc start: 05:14
Voc end: 12:29

Planetary and Angelic Hours

Jupiter	07:05	Moon	16:21
Mars	07:51	Saturn	17:35
Sun	08:38	Jupiter	18:49
Venus	09:24	Mars	20:02
Mercury	10:10	Sun	21:16
Moon	10:57	Venus	22:30
Saturn	11:43	Mercury	23:44
Jupiter	12:29	Moon	00:58
Mars	13:16	Saturn	02:11
Sun	14:02	Jupiter	03:25
Venus	14:48	Mars	04:39
Mercury	15:35	Sun	05:53

Aspects

Moon square Eris
Moon trine Chiron
Venus opposite Pallas
Moon square Uranus
Moon sextile Sedna
Moon square Vesta
Sun sextile Pluto
Moon square Pallas
Moon square Venus
Moon trine Mercury
Moon square Jupiter
Saturn trine Uranus
Saturn square Chiron
Pluto conjunct Juno

Planets	00:00 am	Moon
Sun	17 sco 46	00.00 am - 06 leo 45
Mercury	06 sag 01	02.00 am - 07 leo 54
Venus	03 sco 08	04.00 am - 09 leo 04
Mars	11 lib 30	06.00 am - 10 leo 14
Jupiter	06 sco 37	08.00 am - 11 leo 23
Saturn	25 sag 29	10.00 am - 12 leo 33
Uranus	25 ar 40	12.00 pm - 13 leo 42
Neptune	11 pis 30	14.00 pm - 14 leo 51
Pluto	17 cap 17	16.00 pm - 16 leo 00
		18.00 pm - 17 leo 08
Oob	Mercury	20.00 pm - 18 leo 17
		22.00 pm - 19 leo 26

Friday 10th November

Retrograde Planets

Uranus, Neptune, Pallas, Chiron, Eris, Salacia, Sedna

Asteroids		Dwarf Planets	
Juno	16 cap 39	Eris	23 ar 04
Vesta	26 lib 49	Haumea	24 lib 46
Pallas	01 tau 51	Makemake	04 lib 20
Ceres	13 leo 51	Salacia	00 ar 18
Chiron	24 pis 36	Orcus	10 vir 00
N Node	19 leo 49	Quaoar	29 sag 20
S Node	19 aq 49	Sedna	26 tau 19

Last Quarter: 20:38
Sunrise: 07:10 GMT
Sunset: 16:18
Moonrise: 22:51
Moonset: 13:12
Voc start:
Voc end:

Planetary and Angelic Hours			
Venus	07:07	Mars	16:20
Mercury	07:53	Sun	17:34
Moon	08:39	Venus	18:48
Saturn	09:25	Mercury	20:02
Jupiter	10:11	Moon	21:16
Mars	10:57	Saturn	22:30
Sun	11:43	Jupiter	23:44
Venus	12:29	Mars	00:58
Mercury	13:15	Sun	02:12
Moon	14:01	Venus	03:26
Saturn	14:47	Mercury	04:40
Jupiter	15:33	Moon	05:54

Aspects

Moon sextile Mars
Moon conjunct Ceres
Sun square Moon
Saturn trine Uranus
Pluto conjunct Juno

Planets	00:00 am	Moon
Sun	18 sco 46	00.00 am - 20 leo 34
Mercury	07 sag 25	02.00 am - 21 leo 42
Venus	04 sco 24	04.00 am - 22 leo 50
Mars	12 lib 08	06.00 am - 23 leo 58
Jupiter	06 sco 50	08.00 am - 25 leo 06
Saturn	25 sag 35	10.00 am - 26 leo 14
Uranus	25 ar 38	12.00 pm - 27 leo 22
Neptune	11 pis 30	14.00 pm - 28 leo 29
Pluto	17 cap 18	16.00 pm - 29 leo 35
		18.00 pm - 00 vir 44
Oob	Mercury	20.00 pm - 01 vir 51
		22.00 pm - 02 vir 58

Saturday 11th November

Planetary Directions

Moon into Virgo 16:42

Retrograde Planets

Uranus, Neptune, Pallas, Chiron, Eris, Salacia, Sedna

Asteroids		Dwarf Planets	
Juno	16 cap 59	Eris	23 ar 03
Vesta	27 lib 20	Haumea	24 lib 47
Pallas	01 tau 32	Makemake	04 lib 22
Ceres	14 leo 04	Salacia	00 ar 18
Chiron	24 pis 35	Orcus	10 vir 01
N Node	19 leo 49	Quaoar	29 sag 21
S Node	19 aq 49	Sedna	26 tau 18

Moon Phase: Balsamic
Sunrise: 07:11 GMT
Sunset: 16:16
Moonrise: None
Moonset: 13:45
Voc start: 08:55
Voc end: 16:41

Planetary and Angelic Hours			
Saturn	07:08	Mercury	16:18
Jupiter	07:54	Moon	17:32
Mars	08:40	Saturn	18:47
Sun	09:26	Jupiter	20:01
Venus	10:12	Mars	21:15
Mercury	10:57	Sun	22:30
Moon	11:43	Venus	23:44
Saturn	12:29	Mercury	00:58
Jupiter	13:15	Moon	02:13
Mars	14:01	Saturn	03:27
Sun	14:46	Jupiter	04:41
Venus	15:32	Mars	05:56

Aspects

Moon trine Eris
Moon trine Saturn
Moon trine Uranus
Saturn trine Uranus
Moon square Sedna
Moon sextile Vesta
Moon trine Pallas
Pluto conjunct Juno

Planets	00:00 am	Moon
Sun	19 sco 47	00.00 am - 04 vir 05
Mercury	08 sag 48	02.00 am - 05 vir 11
Venus	05 sco 39	04.00 am - 06 vir 18
Mars	12 lib 46	06.00 am - 07 vir 24
Jupiter	07 sco 03	08.00 am - 08 vir 31
Saturn	25 sag 41	10.00 am - 09 vir 37
Uranus	25 ar 36	12.00 pm - 10 vir 43
Neptune	11 pis 29	14.00 pm - 11 vir 49
Pluto	17 cap 20	16.00 pm - 12 vir 55
		18.00 pm - 14 vir 01
Oob	Mercury	20.00 pm - 15 vir 07
		22.00 pm - 16 vir 13

Sunday 12th November

Retrograde Planets

Uranus, Neptune, Pallas, Chiron, Eris, Salacia, Sedna

Asteroids		Dwarf Planets	
Juno	17 cap 18	Eris	23 ar 03
Vesta	27 lib 51	Haumea	24 lib 49
Pallas	01 tau 13	Makemake	04 lib 23
Ceres	14 leo 16	Salacia	00 ar 17
Chiron	24 pis 34	Orcus	10 vir 01
N Node	19 leo 48	Quaoar	29 sag 23
S Node	19 aq 48	Sedna	26 tau 17

Moon Phase: Balsamic
Sunrise: 07:13 GMT
Sunset: 16:15
Moonrise: 00:04
Moonset: 14:14
Voc start:
Voc end:

Planetary and Angelic Hours			
Sun	07:10	Jupiter	16:17
Venus	07:56	Mars	17:31
Mercury	08:41	Sun	18:46
Moon	09:27	Venus	20:00
Saturn	10:12	Mercury	21:15
Jupiter	10:58	Moon	22:30
Mars	11:43	Saturn	23:44
Sun	12:29	Jupiter	00:59
Venus	13:14	Mars	02:13
Mercury	14:00	Sun	03:28
Moon	14:45	Venus	04:42
Saturn	15:31	Mercury	05:57

Rememberance Sunday

Aspects

Pluto conjunct Juno
Moon sextile Venus
Moon sextile Jupiter
Moon square Mercury
Moon opp. Neptune
Moon trine Pluto
Moon trine Juno
Venus conjunct Jupiter
Saturn trine Uranus

Planets	00:00 am	Moon
Sun	20 sco 47	00.00 am - 17 vir 18
Mercury	10 sag 11	02.00 am - 18 vir 24
Venus	06 sco 54	04.00 am - 19 vir 29
Mars	13 lib 23	06.00 am - 20 vir 34
Jupiter	07 sco 16	08.00 am - 21 vir 40
Saturn	25 sag 47	10.00 am - 22 vir 45
Uranus	25 ar 34	12.00 pm - 23 vir 50
Neptune	11 pis 29	14.00 pm - 24 vir 55
Pluto	17 cap 21	16.00 pm - 25 vir 59
		18.00 pm - 27 vir 04
Oob	Mercury	20.00 pm - 28 vir 09
		22.00 pm - 29 vir 13

Monday 13th November

Planetary Directions

Moon into Libra 23:27

Retrograde Planets

Uranus, Neptune, Pallas, Chiron, Eris, Salacia, Sedna

Asteroids		Dwarf Planets	
Juno	17 cap 38	Eris	23 ar 02
Vesta	28 lib 22	Haumea	24 lib 50
Pallas	00 tau 55	Makemake	04 lib 24
Ceres	14 leo 29	Salacia	00 ar 16
Chiron	24 pis 32	Orcus	10 vir 02
N Node	19 leo 47	Quaoar	29 sag 24
S Node	19 aq 47	Sedna	26 tau 17

Moon Phase: Balsamic
Sunrise: 07:15 GMT
Sunset: 16:14
Moonrise: 01:16
Moonset: 14:38
Voc start: 15:45
Voc end: 23:26

Planetary and Angelic Hours			
Moon	07:12	Venus	16:15
Saturn	07:57	Mercury	17:30
Jupiter	08:42	Moon	18:45
Mars	09:28	Saturn	20:00
Sun	10:13	Jupiter	21:15
Venus	10:58	Mars	22:29
Mercury	11:43	Sun	23:44
Moon	12:29	Venus	00:59
Saturn	13:14	Mercury	02:14
Jupiter	13:59	Moon	03:29
Mars	14:45	Saturn	04:44
Sun	15:30	Jupiter	05:59

Aspects

Moon trine Pluto
Moon trine Juno
Sun sextile Moon
Venus conjunct Jupiter
Moon opposite Chiron
Moon square Saturn
Moon trine Sedna
Mercury sq. Neptune
Mars sextile Ceres
Saturn trine Uranus
Pluto conjunct Juno

Planets	00:00 am
Sun	21 sco 47
Mercury	11 sag 33
Venus	08 sco 09
Mars	14 lib 01
Jupiter	07 sco 28
Saturn	25 sag 53
Uranus	25 ar 32
Neptune	11 pis 29
Pluto	17 cap 22
Oob	Mercury

Moon
00.00 am - 00 lib 18
02.00 am - 01 lib 22
04.00 am - 02 lib 26
06.00 am - 03 lib 30
08.00 am - 04 lib 34
10.00 am - 05 lib 38
12.00 pm - 06 lib 42
14.00 pm - 07 lib 46
16.00 pm - 08 lib 50
18.00 pm - 09 lib 54
20.00 pm - 10 lib 57
22.00 pm - 12 lib 01

Tuesday 14th November

Retrograde Planets

Uranus, Neptune, Pallas, Chiron, Eris, Salacia, Sedna

Asteroids		Dwarf Planets	
Juno	17 cap 58	Eris	23 ar 02
Vesta	28 lib 53	Haumea	24 lib 51
Pallas	00 tau 37	Makemake	04 lib 25
Ceres	14 leo 41	Salacia	00 ar 16
Chiron	24 pis 31	Orcus	10 vir 02
N Node	19 leo 42	Quaoar	29 sag 25
S Node	19 aq 42	Sedna	26 tau 16

Moon Phase: Balsamic
Sunrise: 07:16 GMT
Sunset: 16:12
Moonrise: 02:26
Moonset: 15:01
Voc start:
Voc end:

Planetary and Angelic Hours			
Mars	07:13	Saturn	16:14
Sun	07:58	Jupiter	17:29
Venus	08:43	Mars	18:44
Mercury	09:28	Sun	19:59
Moon	10:13	Venus	21:14
Saturn	10:59	Mercury	22:29
Jupiter	11:44	Moon	23:44
Mars	12:29	Saturn	01:00
Sun	13:14	Jupiter	02:15
Venus	13:59	Mars	03:30
Mercury	14:44	Sun	04:45
Moon	15:29	Venus	06:00

Aspects

Moon sextile Mercury
Mars sextile Ceres
Saturn trine Uranus
Pluto conjunct Juno
Pallas opposite Vesta

Planets	**00:00 am**	**Moon**
		00.00 am - 13 lib 04
Sun	22 sco 48	02.00 am - 14 lib 08
Mercury	12 sag 53	04.00 am - 15 lib 11
Venus	09 sco 25	06.00 am - 16 lib 14
Mars	14 lib 39	08.00 am - 17 lib 17
Jupiter	07 sco 41	10.00 am - 18 lib 20
Saturn	26 sag 00	12.00 pm - 19 lib 23
Uranus	25 ar 30	14.00 pm - 20 lib 26
Neptune	11 pis 28	16.00 pm - 21 lib 29
Pluto	17 cap 23	18.00 pm - 22 lib 32
		20.00 pm - 23 lib 35
Oob	Mercury	22.00 pm - 24 lib 37

Wednesday 15th November

Retrograde Planets

Uranus, Neptune, Pallas, Chiron, Eris, Salacia, Sedna

Asteroids		**Dwarf Planets**	
Juno	18 cap 18	Eris	23 ar 01
Vesta	29 lib 23	Haumea	24 lib 53
Pallas	00 tau 19	Makemake	04 lib 26
Ceres	14 leo 53	Salacia	00 ar 15
Chiron	24 pis 30	Orcus	10 vir 03
N Node	19 leo 35	Quaoar	29 sag 27
S Node	19 aq 35	Sedna	26 tau 16

Moon Phase: Balsamic
Sunrise: 07:18 GMT
Sunset: 16:11
Moonrise: 03:35
Moonset: 15:24
Voc start:
Voc end:

Planetary and Angelic Hours			
Mercury	07:15	Sun	16:12
Moon	08:00	Venus	17:28
Saturn	08:45	Mercury	18:43
Jupiter	09:29	Moon	19:58
Mars	10:14	Saturn	21:14
Sun	10:59	Jupiter	22:29
Venus	11:44	Mars	23:45
Mercury	12:29	Sun	01:00
Moon	13:13	Venus	02:15
Saturn	13:58	Mercury	03:31
Jupiter	14:43	Moon	04:46
Mars	15:28	Saturn	06:01

Aspects

Moon conjunct Mars
Moon sextile Ceres
Moon square Pluto
Moon square Juno
Mars sextile Ceres
Moon opposite Eris
Moon opposite Uranus
Sun trine Chiron
Moon sextile Saturn
Mercury trine Ceres
Venus trine Neptune
Saturn trine Uranus
Pallas opposite Vesta

Thursday 16th November

Planets	00:00 am	Moon
Sun	23 sco 48	00.00 am - 25 lib 40
Mercury	14 sag 13	02.00 am - 26 lib 43
Venus	10 sco 40	04.00 am - 27 lib 45
Mars	15 lib 17	06.00 am - 28 lib 47
Jupiter	07 sco 54	08.00 am - 29 lib 50
Saturn	26 sag 06	10.00 am - 00 sco 52
Uranus	25 ar 28	12.00 pm - 01 sco 54
Neptune	11 pis 28	14.00 pm - 02 sco 56
Pluto	17 cap 25	16.00 pm - 03 sco 58
		18.00 pm - 05 sco 00
Oob	Mercury	20.00 pm - 06 sco 02
		22.00 pm - 07 sco 04

Planetary Directions

Vesta into Sco 04:14
Pallas rx into Aries 03:02
Moon into Scorpio 08:19

Retrograde Planets

Uranus, Neptune, Pallas, Chiron, Eris, Salacia, Sedna

Asteroids		Dwarf Planets	
Juno	18 cap 38	Eris	23 ar 01
Vesta	29 lib 54	Haumea	24 lib 53
Pallas	00 tau 02	Makemake	04 lib 26
Ceres	15 leo 04	Salacia	00 ar 15
Chiron	24 pis 29	Orcus	10 vir 03
N Node	19 leo 25	Quaoar	29 sag 27
S Node	19 aq 25	Sedna	26 tau 16

Moon Phase: Balsamic
Sunrise: 07:20 GMT
Sunset: 16:09
Moonrise: 04:42
Moonset: 15:47
Voc start: 00:50
Voc end: 08:18

Planetary and Angelic Hours

Jupiter	07:17	Moon	16:11
Mars	08:01	Saturn	17:27
Sun	08:46	Jupiter	18:42
Venus	09:30	Mars	19:58
Mercury	10:15	Sun	21:14
Moon	10:59	Venus	22:29
Saturn	11:44	Mercury	23:45
Jupiter	12:28	Moon	01:00
Mars	13:13	Saturn	02:16
Sun	13:57	Jupiter	03:32
Venus	14:42	Mars	04:47
Mercury	15:27	Sun	06:03

Aspects

Moon sextile Saturn
Pallas opposite Vesta
Moon opposite Pallas
Moon conjunct Vesta
Venus trine Neptune
Sun trine Chiron
Mercury trine Ceres
Moon conjunct Jupiter
Mercury sextile Mars
Mars sextile Ceres
Saturn trine Uranus

Planets	**00:00 am**	**Moon**
		00.00 am - 08 sco 06
Sun	24 sco 49	02.00 am - 09 sco 08
Mercury	15 sag 31	04.00 am - 10 sco 09
Venus	11 sco 55	06.00 am - 11 sco 11
Mars	15 lib 55	08.00 am - 12 sco 13
Jupiter	08 sco 07	10.00 am - 13 sco 14
Saturn	26 sag 12	12.00 pm - 14 sco 16
Uranus	25 ar 26	14.00 pm - 15 sco 17
Neptune	11 pis 28	16.00 pm - 16 sco 18
Pluto	17 cap 26	18.00 pm - 17 sco 19
		20.00 pm - 18 sco 21
Oob	Mercury	22.00 pm - 19 sco 22

Friday 17th November

Retrograde Planets

Uranus, Neptune, Pallas, Chiron, Eris, Salacia, Sedna

Asteroids		**Dwarf Planets**	
Juno	18 cap 59	Eris	23 ar 00
Vesta	00 sco 25	Haumea	24 lib 55
Pallas	29 ar 45	Makemake	04 lib 28
Ceres	15 leo 15	Salacia	00 ar 14
Chiron	24 pis 28	Orcus	10 vir 04
N Node	19 leo 12	Quaoar	29 sag 29
S Node	19 aq 12	Sedna	26 tau 14

Moon Phase: Balsamic
Sunrise: 07:22 GMT
Sunset: 16:08
Moonrise: 05:49
Moonset: 16:12
Voc start:
Voc end:

Planetary and Angelic Hours			
Venus	07:18	Mars	16:10
Mercury	08:03	Sun	17:26
Moon	08:47	Venus	18:42
Saturn	09:31	Mercury	19:57
Jupiter	10:16	Moon	21:13
Mars	11:00	Saturn	22:29
Sun	11:44	Jupiter	23:45
Venus	12:28	Mars	01:01
Mercury	13:13	Sun	02:17
Moon	13:57	Venus	03:32
Saturn	14:41	Mercury	04:48
Jupiter	15:26	Moon	06:04

Aspects

Moon conjunct Jupiter
Moon trine Neptune
Moon conjunct Venus
Moon square Ceres
Mercury sextile Mars
Moon sextile Pluto
Moon sextile Juno
Sun opposite Sedna
Mars square Pluto
Saturn trine Uranus

Planets	00:00 am	Moon
		00.00 am - 20 sco 23
Sun	25 sco 49	02.00 am - 21 sco 24
Mercury	16 sag 48	04.00 am - 22 sco 25
Venus	13 sco 11	06.00 am - 23 sco 26
Mars	16 lib 33	08.00 am - 24 sco 26
Jupiter	08 sco 20	10.00 am - 25 sco 27
Saturn	26 sag 19	12.00 pm - 26 sco 28
Uranus	25 ar 24	14.00 pm - 27 sco 29
Neptune	11 pis 28	16.00 pm - 28 sco 29
Pluto	17 cap 28	18.00 pm - 29 sco 30
		20.00 pm - 00 sag 30
Oob	Mercury	22.00 pm - 01 sag 31

Saturday 18th November

Planetary Directions

Moon into Sagittarius 18:59

Retrograde Planets

Uranus, Neptune, Pallas, Chiron, Eris, Salacia, Sedna

Asteroids		Dwarf Planets	
Juno	19 cap 19	Eris	23 ar 00
Vesta	00 sco 56	Haumea	24 lib 57
Pallas	29 ar 28	Makemake	04 lib 29
Ceres	15 leo 26	Salacia	00 ar 13
Chiron	24 pis 27	Orcus	10 vir 04
N Node	18 leo 58	Quaoar	29 sag 31
S Node	18 aq 58	Sedna	26 tau 14

New Moon: 11:42
Sunrise: 07:23 GMT
Sunset: 16:07
Moonrise: 06:54
Moonset: 16:40
Voc start: 11:42
Voc end: 18:58

Planetary and Angelic Hours			
Saturn	07:20	Mercury	16:09
Jupiter	08:04	Moon	17:25
Mars	08:48	Saturn	18:41
Sun	09:32	Jupiter	19:57
Venus	10:16	Mars	21:13
Mercury	11:00	Sun	22:29
Moon	11:44	Venus	23:45
Saturn	12:28	Mercury	01:01
Jupiter	13:12	Moon	02:17
Mars	13:56	Saturn	03:33
Sun	14:40	Jupiter	04:49
Venus	15:25	Mars	06:06

Aspects

Moon trine Chiron
Sun opposite Sedna
Moon opposite Sedna
Mercury sextile Mars
Mars square Pluto

Planets	00:00 am	Moon
Sun	26 sco 50	00.00 am - 02 sag 31
Mercury	18 sag 03	02.00 am - 03 sag 31
Venus	14 sco 56	04.00 am - 04 sag 32
Mars	17 lib 10	06.00 am - 05 sag 32
Jupiter	08 sco 33	08.00 am - 06 sag 32
Saturn	26 sag 25	10.00 am - 07 sag 32
Uranus	25 ar 22	12.00 pm - 08 sag 32
Neptune	11 pis 28	14.00 pm - 09 sag 32
Pluto	17 cap 29	16.00 pm - 10 sag 32
		18.00 pm - 11 sag 32
Oob	Mercury	20.00 pm - 12 sag 32
		22.00 pm - 13 sag 32

Sunday 19th November

Retrograde Planets

Uranus, Neptune, Pallas, Chiron, Eris, Salacia, Sedna

Asteroids		Dwarf Planets	
Juno	19 cap 40	Eris	22 ar 59
Vesta	01 sco 26	Haumea	24 lib 58
Pallas	29 ar 12	Makemake	04 lib 30
Ceres	15 leo 37	Salacia	00 ar 12
Chiron	24 pis 26	Orcus	10 vir 05
N Node	18 leo 43	Quaoar	29 sag 31
S Node	18 aq 43	Sedna	26 tau 13

Moon Phase: Crescent
Sunrise: 07:25 GMT
Sunset: 16:06
Moonrise: 07:57
Moonset: 17:12
Voc start:
Voc end:

Planetary and Angelic Hours			
Sun	07:22	Jupiter	16:07
Venus	08:05	Mars	17:24
Mercury	08:49	Sun	18:40
Moon	09:33	Venus	19:56
Saturn	10:17	Mercury	21:13
Jupiter	11:01	Moon	22:29
Mars	11:45	Saturn	23:45
Sun	12:28	Jupiter	01:02
Venus	13:12	Mars	02:18
Mercury	13:56	Sun	03:34
Moon	14:40	Venus	04:51
Saturn	15:24	Mercury	06:07

Aspects

Mars square Pluto
Moon square Neptune
Venus square Ceres

Monday 20th November

Planets	00:00 am	Moon
Sun	27 sco 51	00.00 am - 14 sag 31
Mercury	19 sag 16	02.00 am - 15 sag 31
Venus	15 sco 41	04.00 am - 16 sag 31
Mars	17 lib 48	06.00 am - 17 sag 30
Jupiter	08 sco 46	08.00 am - 18 sag 30
Saturn	26 sag 32	10.00 am - 19 sag 29
Uranus	25 ar 20	12.00 pm - 20 sag 29
Neptune	11 pis 28	14.00 pm - 21 sag 29
Pluto	17 cap 30	16.00 pm - 22 sag 28
		18.00 pm - 23 sag 27
Oob	Mercury	20.00 pm - 24 sag 27
		22.00 pm - 25 sag 26

Retrograde Planets

Uranus, Neptune, Pallas, Chiron, Eris, Salacia, Sedna

Asteroids		Dwarf Planets	
Juno	20 cap 00	Eris	22 ar 59
Vesta	01 sco 57	Haumea	24 lib 59
Pallas	28 ar 56	Makemake	04 lib 30
Ceres	15 leo 47	Salacia	00 ar 12
Chiron	24 pis 25	Orcus	10 vir 05
N Node	18 leo 29	Quaoar	29 sag 33
S Node	18 aq 29	Sedna	26 tau 12

Moon Phase: Crescent
Sunrise: 07:27 GMT
Sunset: 16:05
Moonrise: 08:56
Moonset: 17:49
Voc start:
Voc end:

Planetary and Angelic Hours			
Moon	07:23	Venus	16:06
Saturn	08:07	Mercury	17:23
Jupiter	08:50	Moon	18:39
Mars	09:34	Saturn	19:56
Sun	10:18	Jupiter	21:12
Venus	11:01	Mars	22:29
Mercury	11:45	Sun	23:46
Moon	12:28	Venus	01:02
Saturn	13:12	Mercury	02:19
Jupiter	13:55	Moon	03:35
Mars	14:39	Saturn	04:52
Sun	15:23	Jupiter	06:08

Aspects

Venus square Ceres
Moon trine Ceres
Moon sextile Mars
Moon conj. Mercury
Moon trine Eris
Moon square Chiron
Moon trine Uranus
Moon conjunct Saturn
Venus sextile Pluto
Mars square Pluto

Planets	00:00 am	Moon
Sun	28 sco 51	00.00 am - 26 sag 25
Mercury	20 sag 27	02.00 am - 27 sag 25
Venus	16 sco 57	04.00 am - 28 sag 24
Mars	18 lib 26	06.00 am - 29 sag 23
Jupiter	08 sco 58	08.00 am - 00 cap 22
Saturn	26 sag 38	10.00 am - 01 cap 21
Uranus	25 ar 18	12.00 pm - 02 cap 20
Neptune	11 pis 27	14.00 pm - 03 cap 19
Pluto	17 cap 32	16.00 pm - 04 cap 19
		18.00 pm - 05 cap 18
		20.00 pm - 06 cap 17
Oob	Mercury	22.00 pm - 07 cap 16

Tuesday 21st November

Planetary Directions

Moon into Capricorn
07:14

Retrograde Planets

Uranus, Neptune,
Pallas, Chiron, Eris,
Salacia, Sedna

Asteroids		Dwarf Planets	
Juno	20 cap 21	Eris	22 ar 58
Vesta	02 sco 28	Haumea	25 lib 01
Pallas	28 ar 40	Makemake	04 lib 31
Ceres	15 leo 57	Salacia	00 ar 11
Chiron	24 pis 24	Orcus	10 vir 06
N Node	18 leo 17	Quaoar	29 sag 35
S Node	18 aq 17	Sedna	26 tau 12

Moon Phase: Crescent
Sunrise: 07:28 GMT
Sunset: 16:03
Moonrise: 09:51
Moonset: 18:32
Voc start: 00:26
Voc end: 07:13

Planetary and Angelic Hours			
Mars	07:25	Saturn	16:05
Sun	08:08	Jupiter	17:22
Venus	08:52	Mars	18:39
Mercury	09:35	Sun	19:55
Moon	10:18	Venus	21:12
Saturn	11:02	Mercury	22:29
Jupiter	11:45	Moon	23:46
Mars	12:28	Saturn	01:03
Sun	13:12	Jupiter	02:19
Venus	13:55	Mars	03:36
Mercury	14:38	Sun	04:53
Moon	15:22	Venus	06:10

Aspects

Moon conjunct Saturn
Moon trine Pallas
Venus sextile Pluto
Moon sextile Vesta
Moon sextile Jupiter

Wednesday 22nd November

Planets	00:00 am	Moon
Sun	29 sco 52	00.00 am - 08 cap 15
Mercury	21 sag 36	02.00 am - 09 cap 14
Venus	18 sco 12	04.00 am - 10 cap 13
Mars	19 lib 04	06.00 am - 11 cap 11
Jupiter	09 sco 11	08.00 am - 12 cap 10
Saturn	26 sag 45	10.00 am - 13 cap 09
Uranus	25 ar 16	12.00 pm - 14 cap 08
Neptune	11 pis 27	14.00 pm - 15 cap 07
Pluto	17 cap 33	16.00 pm - 16 cap 06
		18.00 pm - 17 cap 05
Oob	Mercury	20.00 pm - 18 cap 04
		22.00 pm - 19 cap 03

Planetary Directions

Sun into Sag 03:05
Neptune direct
11 pis 27 at 14:21

Retrograde Planets

Uranus, Neptune, Pallas, Chiron, Eris, Salacia, Sedna

Asteroids		Dwarf Planets	
Juno	20 cap 42	Eris	22 ar 58
Vesta	02 sco 59	Haumea	25 lib 02
Pallas	28 ar 25	Makemake	04 lib 32
Ceres	16 leo 07	Salacia	00 ar 11
Chiron	24 pis 24	Orcus	10 vir 06
N Node	18 leo 08	Quaoar	29 sag 36
S Node	18 aq 08	Sedna	26 tau 11

Moon Phase: Crescent
Sunrise: 07:30 GMT
Sunset: 16:02
Moonrise: 10:39
Moonset: 19:21
Voc start:
Voc end:

Planetary and Angelic Hours			
Mercury	07:27	Sun	16:04
Moon	08:10	Venus	17:21
Saturn	08:53	Mercury	18:38
Jupiter	09:36	Moon	19:55
Mars	10:19	Saturn	21:12
Sun	11:02	Jupiter	22:29
Venus	11:45	Mars	23:46
Mercury	12:28	Sun	01:03
Moon	13:12	Venus	02:20
Saturn	13:55	Mercury	03:37
Jupiter	14:38	Moon	04:54
Mars	15:21	Saturn	06:11

Aspects

Moon sextile Jupiter
Moon sextile Neptune
Moon conjunct Pluto
Moon sextile Venus
Moon square Mars
Mercury trine Eris

Thursday 23rd November

Planets	00:00 am	Moon
		00.00 am - 20 cap 02
Sun	00 sag 52	02.00 am - 21 cap 01
Mercury	22 sag 42	04.00 am - 22 cap 00
Venus	19 sco 27	06.00 am - 22 cap 59
Mars	19 lib 42	08.00 am - 23 cap 58
Jupiter	09 sco 24	10.00 am - 24 cap 57
Saturn	26 sag 51	12.00 pm - 25 cap 56
Uranus	25 ar 14	14.00 pm - 26 cap 55
Neptune	11 pis 27	16.00 pm - 27 cap 54
Pluto	17 cap 35	18.00 pm - 28 cap 53
		20.00 pm - 29 cap 52
Oob	Mercury	22.00 pm - 00 aq 52

Planetary Directions

Moon into Aquarius 20:15

Retrograde Planets

Uranus, Pallas, Chiron, Eris, Salacia, Sedna

Asteroids		Dwarf Planets	
Juno	20 cap 42	Eris	22 ar 58
Vesta	02 sco 59	Haumea	25 lib 03
Pallas	28 ar 25	Makemake	04 lib 33
Ceres	16 leo 07	Salacia	00 ar 10
Chiron	24 pis 24	Orcus	10 vir 07
N Node	18 leo 02	Quaoar	29 sag 38
S Node	18 aq 02	Sedna	26 tau 11

Moon Phase: Crescent
Sunrise: 07:31 GMT
Sunset: 16:01
Moonrise: 11:22
Moonset: 20:15
Voc start: 10:32
Voc end: 20:14

Planetary and Angelic Hours			
Jupiter	07:28	Moon	16:03
Mars	08:11	Saturn	17:20
Sun	08:54	Jupiter	18:37
Venus	09:37	Mars	19:55
Mercury	10:20	Sun	21:12
Moon	11:03	Venus	22:29
Saturn	11:46	Mercury	23:46
Jupiter	12:28	Moon	01:04
Mars	13:11	Saturn	02:21
Sun	13:54	Jupiter	03:38
Venus	14:37	Mars	04:55
Mercury	15:20	Sun	06:12

Aspects

Moon conjunct Juno
Mercury trine Eris
Moon square Eris
Moon sextile Chiron
Moon square Uranus
Moon trine Sedna
Moon square Pallas
Sun sextile Moon
Mercury square Chiron
Venus sextile Juno
Saturn trine Pallas

Planets	00:00 am	Moon
Sun	01 sag 53	00.00 am - 01 aq 51
Mercury	23 sag 45	02.00 am - 02 aq 50
Venus	20 sco 43	04.00 am - 03 aq 50
Mars	20 lib 19	06.00 am - 04 aq 49
Jupiter	09 sco 36	08.00 am - 05 aq 48
Saturn	26 sag 58	10.00 am - 06 aq 48
Uranus	25 ar 12	12.00 pm - 07 aq 47
Neptune	11 pis 27	14.00 pm - 08 aq 47
Pluto	17 cap 36	16.00 pm - 09 aq 47
		18.00 pm - 10 aq 46
Oob	Mercury	20.00 pm - 11 aq 46
		22.00 pm - 12 aq 46

Friday 24th November

Retrograde Planets

Uranus, Pallas, Chiron, Eris, Salacia, Sedna

Asteroids		Dwarf Planets	
Juno	21 cap 25	Eris	22 ar 57
Vesta	04 sco 00	Haumea	25 lib 04
Pallas	27 ar 56	Makemake	04 lib 34
Ceres	16 leo 25	Salacia	00 ar 10
Chiron	24 pis 22	Orcus	10 vir 07
N Node	17 leo 59	Quaoar	29 sag 39
S Node	17 aq 59	Sedna	26 tau 10

Moon Phase: Crescent
Sunrise: 07:33 GMT
Sunset: 16:00
Moonrise: 11:59
Moonset: 21:15
Voc start:
Voc end:

Planetary and Angelic Hours			
Venus	07:30	Mars	16:02
Mercury	08:12	Sun	17:19
Moon	08:55	Venus	18:37
Saturn	09:38	Mercury	19:54
Jupiter	10:20	Moon	21:12
Mars	11:03	Saturn	22:29
Sun	11:46	Jupiter	23:47
Venus	12:29	Mars	01:04
Mercury	13:11	Sun	02:21
Moon	13:54	Venus	03:39
Saturn	14:37	Mercury	04:56
Jupiter	15:19	Moon	06:14

Aspects

Sun sextile Moon
Moon square Vesta
Mercury square Chiron
Moon square Jupiter
Venus sextile Juno
Mercury trine Uranus
Mars square Juno
Saturn trine Pallas

Planets	00:00 am	Moon
Sun	02 sag 54	00.00 am - 13 aq 46
Mercury	24 sag 44	02.00 am - 14 aq 46
Venus	21 sco 58	04.00 am - 15 aq 46
Mars	20 lib 57	06.00 am - 16 aq 46
Jupiter	09 sco 49	08.00 am - 17 aq 47
Saturn	27 sag 05	10.00 am - 18 aq 47
Uranus	25 ar 10	12.00 pm - 19 aq 47
Neptune	11 pis 28	14.00 pm - 20 aq 48
Pluto	17 cap 38	16.00 pm - 21 aq 48
		18.00 pm - 22 aq 49
Oob	Mercury	20.00 pm - 23 aq 50
		22.00 pm - 24 aq 51

Saturday 25th November

Retrograde Planets

Uranus, Pallas, Chiron, Eris, Salacia, Sedna

Asteroids		Dwarf Planets	
Juno	21 cap 46	Eris	22 ar 56
Vesta	04 sco 31	Haumea	25 lib 05
Pallas	27 ar 43	Makemake	04 lib 35
Ceres	16 leo 34	Salacia	00 ar 09
Chiron	24 pis 22	Orcus	10 vir 07
N Node	17 leo 58	Quaoar	29 sag 40
S Node	17 aq 58	Sedna	26 tau 09

Moon Phase: Crescent
Sunrise: 07:35 GMT
Sunset: 15:59
Moonrise: 12:30
Moonset: 22:18
Voc start:
Voc end:

Planetary and Angelic Hours			
Saturn	07:31	Mercury	16:01
Jupiter	08:14	Moon	17:19
Mars	08:56	Saturn	18:36
Sun	09:39	Jupiter	19:54
Venus	10:21	Mars	21:12
Mercury	11:04	Sun	22:29
Moon	11:46	Venus	23:47
Saturn	12:29	Mercury	01:05
Jupiter	13:11	Moon	02:22
Mars	13:54	Saturn	03:40
Sun	14:36	Jupiter	04:57
Venus	15:19	Mars	06:15

Aspects

Moon opposite Ceres
Mercury trine Uranus
Moon trine Mars
Moon square Venus
Moon sextile Eris
Moon sextile Uranus
Moon sextile Mercury
Moon square Sedna
Mars square Juno
Saturn trine Pallas
Juno square Eris

Planets	00:00 am	Moon
Sun	03 sag 54	00.00 am - 25 aq 52
Mercury	25 sag 39	02.00 am - 26 aq 53
Venus	23 sco 13	04.00 am - 27 aq 55
Mars	21 lib 35	06.00 am - 28 aq 56
Jupiter	10 sco 01	08.00 am - 29 aq 57
Saturn	27 sag 11	10.00 am - 00 pis 59
Uranus	25 ar 08	12.00 pm - 02 pis 01
Neptune	11 pis 28	14.00 pm - 03 pis 03
Pluto	17 cap 40	16.00 pm - 04 pis 05
		18.00 pm - 05 pis 07
Oob	Mercury	20.00 pm - 06 pis 09
		22.00 pm - 07 pis 12

Sunday 26th November

Planetary Directions

Moon into Pisces 08:04

Retrograde Planets

Uranus, Pallas, Chiron, Eris, Salacia, Sedna

Asteroids		Dwarf Planets	
Juno	22 cap 07	Eris	22 ar 56
Vesta	05 sco 01	Haumea	25 lib 07
Pallas	27 ar 29	Makemake	04 lib 36
Ceres	16 leo 42	Salacia	00 ar 09
Chiron	24 pis 21	Orcus	10 vir 08
N Node	17 leo 58	Quaoar	29 sag 42
S Node	17 aq 58	Sedna	26 tau 09

First Quarter: 17:03
Sunrise: 07:36 GMT
Sunset: 15:59
Moonrise: 12:58
Moonset: 23:24
Voc start: 02:36
Voc end: 08:03

Planetary and Angelic Hours			
Sun	07:33	Jupiter	16:00
Venus	08:15	Mars	17:18
Mercury	08:57	Sun	18:36
Moon	09:40	Venus	19:54
Saturn	10:22	Mercury	21:12
Jupiter	11:04	Moon	22:29
Mars	11:46	Saturn	23:47
Sun	12:29	Jupiter	01:05
Venus	13:11	Mars	02:23
Mercury	13:53	Sun	03:41
Moon	14:36	Venus	04:59
Saturn	15:18	Mercury	06:16

Aspects

Moon square Sedna
Moon sextile Saturn
Moon sextile Pallas
Sun square Moon
Moon trine Vesta
Venus trine Chiron
Saturn trine Pallas
Mercury conj. Saturn
Mercury trine Pallas
Mars square Juno
Mars opposite Eris
Juno square Eris

Planets	00:00 am	Moon
Sun	04 sag 55	00.00 am - 08 pis 15
Mercury	26 sag 29	02.00 am - 09 pis 17
Venus	24 sco 29	04.00 am - 10 pis 20
Mars	22 lib 13	06.00 am - 11 pis 23
Jupiter	10 sco 14	08.00 am - 12 pis 27
Saturn	27 sag 18	10.00 am - 13 pis 30
Uranus	25 ar 07	12.00 pm - 14 pis 34
Neptune	11 pis 28	14.00 pm - 15 pis 37
Pluto	17 cap 41	16.00 pm - 16 pis 41
		18.00 pm - 17 pis 45
Oob	Mercury	20.00 pm - 18 pis 50
		22.00 pm - 19 pis 54

Monday 27th November

Retrograde Planets

Uranus, Pallas, Chiron, Eris, Salacia, Sedna

Asteroids		Dwarf Planets	
Juno	22 cap 29	Eris	22 ar 56
Vesta	05 sco 32	Haumea	25 lib 08
Pallas	27 ar 17	Makemake	04 lib 36
Ceres	16 leo 50	Salacia	00 ar 08
Chiron	24 pis 20	Orcus	10 vir 08
N Node	17 leo 58	Quaoar	29 sag 43
S Node	17 aq 58	Sedna	26 tau 08

Moon Phase: Gibbous
Sunrise: 07:38 GMT
Sunset: 15:58
Moonrise: 13:24
Moonset: None
Voc start:
Voc end:

Planetary and Angelic Hours			
Moon	07:34	Venus	15:59
Saturn	08:16	Mercury	17:17
Jupiter	08:58	Moon	18:35
Mars	09:41	Saturn	19:53
Sun	10:23	Jupiter	21:11
Venus	11:05	Mars	22:29
Mercury	11:47	Sun	23:48
Moon	12:29	Venus	01:06
Saturn	13:11	Mercury	02:24
Jupiter	13:53	Moon	03:42
Mars	14:35	Saturn	05:00
Sun	15:17	Jupiter	06:18

Aspects

Moon trine Jupiter
Moon conj. Neptune
Moon sextile Pluto
Mercury trine Pallas
Mercury conj. Saturn
Venus opposite Sedna
Mars square Juno
Mars opposite Eris
Saturn trine Pallas
Juno square Eris

Planets	00:00 am	Moon
Sun	05 sag 56	00.00 am - 20 pis 59
Mercury	27 sag 15	02.00 am - 22 pis 04
Venus	25 sco 44	04.00 am - 23 pis 09
Mars	22 lib 50	06.00 am - 24 pis 14
Jupiter	10 sco 26	08.00 am - 25 pis 19
Saturn	27 sag 25	10.00 am - 26 pis 25
Uranus	25 ar 05	12.00 pm - 27 pis 31
Neptune	11 pis 28	14.00 pm - 28 pis 37
Pluto	17 cap 43	16.00 pm - 29 pis 43
		18.00 pm - 00 ar 49
Oob	Mercury	20.00 pm - 01 ar 56
		22.00 pm - 03 ar 03

Tuesday28th November

Planetary Directions

Moon into Aries 16:31

Retrograde Planets

Uranus, Pallas, Chiron, Eris, Salacia, Sedna

Asteroids		Dwarf Planets	
Juno	22 cap 51	Eris	22 ar 55
Vesta	06 sco 03	Haumea	25 lib 09
Pallas	27 ar 05	Makemake	04 lib 37
Ceres	16 leo 58	Salacia	00 ar 08
Chiron	24 pis 20	Orcus	10 vir 08
N Node	17 leo 57	Quaoar	29 sag 45
S Node	17 aq 57	Sedna	26 tau 07

Moon Phase: Gibbous
Sunrise: 07:39 GMT
Sunset: 15:57
Moonrise: 13:48
Moonset: 00:33
Voc start: 12:08
Voc end: 16:30

Planetary and Angelic Hours			
Mars	07:36	Saturn	15:59
Sun	08:18	Jupiter	17:17
Venus	09:00	Mars	18:35
Mercury	09:41	Sun	19:53
Moon	10:23	Venus	21:11
Saturn	11:05	Mercury	22:30
Jupiter	11:47	Moon	23:48
Mars	12:29	Saturn	01:06
Sun	13:11	Jupiter	02:24
Venus	13:53	Mars	03:43
Mercury	14:35	Sun	05:01
Moon	15:17	Venus	06:19

Aspects

Mars square Juno
Mars opposite Eris
Moon sextile Juno
Juno square Eris
Moon conjunct Chiron
Mercury conj. Saturn
Venus opposite Sedna
Moon sextile Sedna
Moon trine Venus
Moon square Saturn
Moon square Mercury
Jupiter trine Neptune
Saturn trine Pallas

Wednesday 29th November

Planets	00:00 am	Moon
Sun	06 sag 57	00.00 am - 04 ar 10
Mercury	27 sag 54	02.00 am - 05 ar 17
Venus	27 sco 00	04.00 am - 06 ar 24
Mars	23 lib 28	06.00 am - 07 ar 32
Jupiter	10 sco 39	08.00 am - 08 ar 40
Saturn	27 sag 32	10.00 am - 09 ar 48
Uranus	25 ar 03	12.00 pm - 10 ar 56
Neptune	11 pis 28	14.00 pm - 12 ar 04
Pluto	17 cap 44	16.00 pm - 13 ar 13
		18.00 pm - 14 ar 22
		20.00 pm - 15 ar 31
Oob	Mercury	22.00 pm - 16 ar 40

Retrograde Planets

Uranus, Pallas, Chiron, Eris, Salacia, Sedna

Asteroids		Dwarf Planets	
Juno	23 cap 13	Eris	22 ar 55
Vesta	06 sco 33	Haumea	25 lib 10
Pallas	26 ar 53	Makemake	04 lib 38
Ceres	17 leo 05	Salacia	00 ar 08
Chiron	24 pis 20	Orcus	10 vir 08
N Node	17 leo 54	Quaoar	29 sag 46
S Node	17 aq 54	Sedna	26 tau 07

Moon Phase: Gibbous
Sunrise: 07:41 GMT
Sunset: 15:56
Moonrise: 14:12
Moonset: 01:45
Voc start:
Voc end:

Planetary and Angelic Hours

Mercury	07:37	Sun	15:58
Moon	08:19	Venus	17:16
Saturn	09:01	Mercury	18:35
Jupiter	09:42	Moon	19:53
Mars	10:24	Saturn	21:11
Sun	11:06	Jupiter	22:30
Venus	11:47	Mars	23:48
Mercury	12:29	Sun	01:07
Moon	13:11	Venus	02:25
Saturn	13:53	Mercury	03:43
Jupiter	14:34	Moon	05:02
Mars	15:16	Saturn	06:20

Aspects

Sun trine Moon
Moon trine Ceres
Moon square Pluto
Mercury conj. Saturn
Mars opposite Uranus
Mars square Juno
Jupiter trine Neptune
Saturn trine Pallas
Chiron sextile Juno
Juno square Eris

Planets	00:00 am	Moon
Sun	07 sag 57	00.00 am - 17 ar 50
Mercury	28 sag 27	02.00 am - 19 ar 00
Venus	28 sco 15	04.00 am - 20 ar 09
Mars	24 lib 06	06.00 am - 21 ar 20
Jupiter	10 sco 51	08.00 am - 22 ar 30
Saturn	27 sag 38	10.00 am - 23 ar 41
Uranus	25 ar 02	12.00 pm - 24 ar 51
Neptune	11 pis 28	14.00 pm - 26 ar 02
Pluto	17 cap 46	16.00 pm - 27 ar 14
		18.00 pm - 28 ar 25
Oob	Mercury	20.00 pm - 29 ar 37
		22.00 pm - 00 tau 48

Thursday 30th November

Planetary Directions

Moon into Taurus
20:39

Retrograde Planets

Uranus, Pallas, Chiron, Eris, Salacia, Sedna

Asteroids		Dwarf Planets	
Juno	23 cap 34	Eris	22 ar 54
Vesta	07 sco 04	Haumea	25 lib 11
Pallas	26 ar 42	Makemake	04 lib 39
Ceres	17 leo 12	Salacia	00 ar 07
Chiron	24 pis 19	Orcus	10 vir 09
N Node	17 leo 48	Quaoar	29 sag 48
S Node	17 aq 48	Sedna	26 tau 06

Moon Phase: Gibbous
Sunrise: 07:42 GMT
Sunset: 15:55
Moonrise: 14:38
Moonset: 03:00
Voc start: 18:37
Voc end: 20:38

Planetary and Angelic Hours			
Jupiter	07:39	Moon	15:57
Mars	08:20	Saturn	17:16
Sun	09:02	Jupiter	18:34
Venus	09:43	Mars	19:53
Mercury	10:25	Sun	21:11
Moon	11:06	Venus	22:30
Saturn	11:48	Mercury	23:49
Jupiter	12:29	Moon	01:07
Mars	13:11	Saturn	02:26
Sun	13:52	Jupiter	03:44
Venus	14:34	Mars	05:03
Mercury	15:16	Sun	06:21

St Andrews' Day

Moon conjunct Eris
Moon square Juno
Moon opposite Mars
Moon conjunct Uranus
Moon conjunct Pallas
Moon trine Saturn
Moon trine Mercury
Mars opposite Uranus
Mars square Juno
Jupiter trine Neptune
Chiron sextile Juno

Planets	00:00 am	Moon
Sun	08 sag 58	00.00 am - 02 tau 01
Mercury	28 sag 52	02.00 am - 03 tau 13
Venus	29 sco 30	04.00 am - 04 tau 25
Mars	24 lib 44	06.00 am - 05 tau 38
Jupiter	11 sco 04	08.00 am - 06 tau 51
Saturn	27 sag 45	10.00 am - 08 tau 03
Uranus	25 ar 00	12.00 pm - 09 tau 17
Neptune	11 pis 29	14.00 pm - 10 tau 30
Pluto	17 cap 48	16.00 pm - 11 tau 44
		18.00 pm - 12 tau 57
Oob	Mercury	20.00 pm - 14 tau 11
		22.00 pm - 15 tau 25

Friday 1st December

Planetary Directions

Venus into Sagittarius 09:15

Retrograde Planets

Uranus, Pallas, Chiron, Eris, Salacia, Sedna

Asteroids		Dwarf Planets	
Juno	23 cap 57	Eris	22 ar 54
Vesta	07 sco 34	Haumea	25 lib 12
Pallas	26 ar 32	Makemake	04 lib 39
Ceres	17 leo 19	Salacia	00 ar 07
Chiron	24 pis 19	Orcus	10 vir 09
N Node	17 leo 40	Quaoar	29 sag 49
S Node	17 aq 40	Sedna	26 tau 06

Moon Phase: Gibbous
Sunrise: 07:43 GMT
Sunset: 15:55
Moonrise: 15:06
Moonset: 04:17
Voc start:
Voc end:

Planetary and Angelic Hours			
Venus	07:40	Mars	15:56
Mercury	08:21	Sun	17:15
Moon	09:03	Venus	18:34
Saturn	09:44	Mercury	19:53
Jupiter	10:25	Moon	21:11
Mars	11:07	Saturn	22:30
Sun	11:48	Jupiter	23:49
Venus	12:30	Mars	01:08
Mercury	13:11	Sun	02:26
Moon	13:52	Venus	03:45
Saturn	14:34	Mercury	05:04
Jupiter	15:15	Moon	06:23

Aspects

Moon opposite Vesta
Mars opposite Uranus
Moon opposite Jupiter
Moon sextile Neptune
Moon square Ceres
Jupiter trine Neptune
Uranus square Juno
Chiron sextile Juno

Saturday 2nd December

Planets	**00:00 am**	**Moon**
Sun	09 sag 59	00.00 am - 16 tau 39
Mercury	29 sag 09	02.00 am - 17 tau 54
Venus	00 sag 46	04.00 am - 19 tau 08
Mars	25 lib 21	06.00 am - 20 tau 23
Jupiter	11 sco 16	08.00 am - 21 tau 37
Saturn	27 sag 52	10.00 am - 22 tau 52
Uranus	24 ar 59	12.00 pm - 24 tau 07
Neptune	11 pis 29	14.00 pm - 25 tau 22
Pluto	17 cap 49	16.00 pm - 26 tau 38
		18.00 pm - 27 tau 53
Oob	Mercury	20.00 pm - 29 tau 09
		22.00 pm - 00 gem 24

Planetary Directions

Moon into Gemini
21:21

Retrograde Planets

Uranus, Pallas, Chiron, Eris, Salacia, Sedna

Asteroids		**Dwarf Planets**	
Juno	24 cap 19	Eris	22 ar 53
Vesta	08 sco 05	Haumea	25 lib 14
Pallas	26 ar 22	Makemake	04 lib 40
Ceres	17 leo 25	Salacia	00 ar 07
Chiron	24 pis 19	Orcus	10 vir 09
N Node	17 leo 31	Quaoar	29 sag 51
S Node	17 aq 31	Sedna	26 tau 05

Moon Phase: Gibbous
Sunrise: 07:45 GMT
Sunset: 15:54
Moonrise: 15:40
Moonset: 05:37
Voc start: 01:53
Voc end: 21:20

Planetary and Angelic Hours			
Saturn	07:41	Mercury	15:56
Jupiter	08:23	Moon	17:15
Mars	09:04	Saturn	18:34
Sun	09:45	Jupiter	19:53
Venus	10:26	Mars	21:11
Mercury	11:07	Sun	22:30
Moon	11:49	Venus	23:49
Saturn	12:30	Mercury	01:08
Jupiter	13:11	Moon	02:27
Mars	13:52	Saturn	03:46
Sun	14:33	Jupiter	05:05
Venus	15:15	Mars	06:24

Aspects

Chiron sextile Juno
Moon square Ceres
Moon trine Pluto
Moon sextile Chiron
Moon trine Juno
Moon conjunct Sedna
Sun square Neptune
Moon opposite Venus
Mars opposite Pallas
Jupiter trine Neptune
Uranus square Juno

Planets	00:00 am	Moon
Sun	11 sag 00	00.00 am - 01 gem 40
Mercury	29 sag 17	02.00 am - 02 gem 56
Venus	02 sag 01	04.00 am - 04 gem 11
Mars	25 lib 59	06.00 am - 05 gem 27
Jupiter	11 sco 28	08.00 am - 06 gem 43
Saturn	27 sag 59	10.00 am - 07 gem 59
Uranus	24 ar 57	12.00 pm - 09 gem 16
Neptune	11 pis 29	14.00 pm - 10 gem 32
Pluto	17 cap 51	16.00 pm - 11 gem 48
		18.00 pm - 13 gem 04
		20.00 pm - 14 gem 21
Oob	Mercury	22.00 pm - 15 gem 37

Sunday 3rd December

Planetary Directions

Mercury retrograde
29 sag 18 at 07:35

Retrograde Planets

Uranus, Pallas, Chiron, Eris, Salacia, Sedna

Asteroids		Dwarf Planets	
Juno	24 cap 41	Eris	22 ar 53
Vesta	08 sco 35	Haumea	25 lib 15
Pallas	26 ar 13	Makemake	04 lib 41
Ceres	17 leo 31	Salacia	00 ar 06
Chiron	24 pis 19	Orcus	10 vir 09
N Node	17 leo 20	Quaoar	29 sag 52
S Node	17 aq 20	Sedna	26 tau 04

Full Moon: 15:48
Sunrise: 07:46 GMT
Sunset: 15:54
Moonrise: 16:21
Moonset: 06:58
Voc start:
Voc end:

Planetary and Angelic Hours			
Sun	07:43	Jupiter	15:55
Venus	08:24	Mars	17:14
Mercury	09:05	Sun	18:33
Moon	09:46	Venus	19:52
Saturn	10:27	Mercury	21:12
Jupiter	11:08	Moon	22:31
Mars	11:49	Saturn	23:50
Sun	12:30	Jupiter	01:09
Venus	13:11	Mars	02:28
Mercury	13:52	Sun	03:47
Moon	14:33	Venus	05:06
Saturn	15:14	Mercury	06:25

Super Full Moon

Aspects

Moon opposite Venus
Jupiter opp. Neptune
Mars opposite Pallas
Sun square Neptune
Moon square Neptune
Sun opposite Moon
Uranus square Juno
Moon sextile Ceres
Chiron sextile Juno

Planets	00:00 am	Moon
Sun	12 sag 01	00.00 am - 16 gem 53
Mercury	29 sag 15	02.00 am - 18 gem 10
Venus	03 sag 17	04.00 am - 19 gem 26
Mars	26 lib 37	06.00 am - 20 gem 42
Jupiter	11 sco 40	08.00 am - 21 gem 59
Saturn	28 sag 06	10.00 am - 23 gem 15
Uranus	24 ar 56	12.00 pm - 24 gem 31
Neptune	11 pis 30	14.00 pm - 25 gem 48
Pluto	17 cap 53	16.00 pm - 27 gem 04
		18.00 pm - 28 gem 20
Oob	Mercury	20.00 pm - 29 gem 36
		22.00 pm - 00 can 52

Monday 4th December

Planetary Directions

Moon into Cancer
20:37

Retrograde Planets

Mercury, Uranus,
Pallas, Chiron, Eris,
Salacia, Sedna

Asteroids		Dwarf Planets	
Juno	25 cap 03	Eris	22 ar 53
Vesta	09 sco 06	Haumea	25 lib 16
Pallas	26 ar 04	Makemake	04 lib 42
Ceres	17 leo 36	Salacia	00 ar 06
Chiron	24 pis 19	Orcus	10 vir 09
N Node	17 leo 10	Quaoar	29 sag 54
S Node	17 aq 10	Sedna	26 tau 04

Phase: Disseminating
Sunrise: 07:47 GMT
Sunset: 15:53
Moonrise: 17:11
Moonset: 08:15
Voc start: 19:12
Voc end: 20:36

Planetary and Angelic Hours			
Moon	07:44	Venus	15:55
Saturn	08:25	Mercury	17:14
Jupiter	09:06	Moon	18:33
Mars	09:47	Saturn	19:52
Sun	10:28	Jupiter	21:12
Venus	11:09	Mars	22:31
Mercury	11:49	Sun	23:50
Moon	12:30	Venus	01:09
Saturn	13:11	Mercury	02:28
Jupiter	13:52	Moon	03:48
Mars	14:33	Saturn	05:07
Sun	15:14	Jupiter	06:26

Aspects

Moon sextile Ceres
Moon sextile Eris
Moon square Chiron
Moon sextile Uranus
Moon sextile Pallas
Moon trine Mars
Moon opposite Saturn
Moon opp. Mercury
Mercury conj. Saturn
Mars sextile Saturn
Jupiter trine Neptune
Uranus square Juno
Pallas square Juno
Juno trine Sedna

Planets	00:00 am	Moon
Sun	13 sag 01	00.00 am - 02 can 08
Mercury	29 sag 03	02.00 am - 03 can 24
Venus	04 sag 32	04.00 am - 04 can 40
Mars	27 lib 15	06.00 am - 05 can 56
Jupiter	11 sco 52	08.00 am - 07 can 12
Saturn	28 sag 13	10.00 am - 08 can 28
Uranus	24 ar 54	12.00 pm - 09 can 43
Neptune	11 pis 30	14.00 pm - 10 can 59
Pluto	17 cap 55	16.00 pm - 12 can 14
		18.00 pm - 13 can 29
Oob	Mercury	20.00 pm - 14 can 45
		22.00 pm - 16 can 00

Tuesday 5th December

Planetary Directions

Chiron direct
24 pis 18 at 09:47

Retrograde Planets

Mercury, Uranus, Pallas, Chiron, Eris, Salacia, Sedna

Asteroids		Dwarf Planets	
Juno	25 cap 26	Eris	22 ar 53
Vesta	09 sco 36	Haumea	25 lib 16
Pallas	25 ar 56	Makemake	04 lib 42
Ceres	17 leo 41	Salacia	00 ar 06
Chiron	24 pis 19	Orcus	10 vir 09
N Node	17 leo 02	Quaoar	29 sag 54
S Node	17 aq 02	Sedna	26 tau 04

Phase: Disseminating
Sunrise: 07:49 GMT
Sunset: 15:53
Moonrise: 18:12
Moonset: 09:24
Voc start:
Voc end:

Planetary and Angelic Hours			
Mars	07:45	Saturn	15:54
Sun	08:26	Jupiter	17:14
Venus	09:07	Mars	18:33
Mercury	09:48	Sun	19:52
Moon	10:28	Venus	21:12
Saturn	11:09	Mercury	22:31
Jupiter	11:50	Moon	23:50
Mars	12:31	Saturn	01:10
Sun	13:11	Jupiter	02:29
Venus	13:52	Mars	03:48
Mercury	14:33	Sun	05:08
Moon	15:14	Venus	06:27

Aspects

Moon trine Vesta
Moon trine Neptune
Moon trine Jupiter
Pallas square Juno
Moon opposite Pluto
Mercury sextile Mars
Mercury conj. Saturn
Mars sextile Saturn
Jupiter trine Neptune
Uranus conjunct Pallas
Uranus square Juno
Juno trine Sedna

Wednesday 6th December

Planets	00:00 am	Moon
Sun	14 sag 02	00.00 am - 17 can 15
Mercury	28 sag 39	02.00 am - 18 can 29
Venus	05 sag 48	04.00 am - 19 can 44
Mars	27 lib 52	06.00 am - 20 can 59
Jupiter	12 sco 05	08.00 am - 22 can 13
Saturn	28 sag 20	10.00 am - 23 can 27
Uranus	24 ar 53	12.00 pm - 24 can 42
Neptune	11 pis 31	14.00 pm - 25 can 56
Pluto	17 cap 56	16.00 pm - 27 can 09
		18.00 pm - 28 can 23
Oob	Mercury	20.00 pm - 29 can 37
		22.00 pm - 00 leo 50

Planetary Directions

Moon into Leo 20:38

Retrograde Planets

Mercury, Uranus, Pallas, Eris, Salacia, Sedna

Asteroids		Dwarf Planets	
Juno	25 cap 49	Eris	22 ar 52
Vesta	10 sco 07	Haumea	25 lib 18
Pallas	25 ar 48	Makemake	04 lib 43
Ceres	17 leo 46	Salacia	00 ar 06
Chiron	24 pis 19	Orcus	10 vir 09
N Node	16 leo 56	Quaoar	29 sag 57
S Node	16 aq 56	Sedna	26 tau 03

Phase: Disseminating
Sunrise: 07:50 GMT
Sunset: 15:52
Moonrise: 19:21
Moonset: 10:23
Voc start: 17:55
Voc end: 20:37

Planetary and Angelic Hours

Mercury	07:47	Sun	15:54
Moon	08:27	Venus	17:13
Saturn	09:08	Mercury	18:33
Jupiter	09:48	Moon	19:52
Mars	10:29	Saturn	21:12
Sun	11:10	Jupiter	22:31
Venus	11:50	Mars	23:51
Mercury	12:31	Sun	01:10
Moon	13:12	Venus	02:30
Saturn	13:52	Mercury	03:49
Jupiter	14:33	Moon	05:09
Mars	15:13	Saturn	06:28

Aspects

Moon opposite Pluto
Moon square Eris
Moon trine Chiron
Mercury conj. Saturn
Moon square Uranus
Moon square Pallas
Moon opposite Juno
Moon sextile Sedna
Juno trine Sedna
Mercury sextile Mars
Moon square Mars
Mars sextile Saturn
Jupiter trine Neptune
Uranus conjunct Pallas
Neptune trine Vesta
Pallas square Juno

Planets	00:00 am	Moon
		00.00 am - 02 leo 03
Sun	15 sag 03	02.00 am - 03 leo 16
Mercury	28 sag 04	04.00 am - 04 leo 29
Venus	07 sag 03	06.00 am - 05 leo 42
Mars	28 lib 30	08.00 am - 06 leo 55
Jupiter	12 sco 17	10.00 am - 08 leo 07
Saturn	28 sag 27	12.00 pm - 09 leo 19
Uranus	24 ar 52	14.00 pm - 10 leo 31
Neptune	11 pis 31	16.00 pm - 11 leo 43
Pluto	17 cap 58	18.00 pm - 12 leo 55
		20.00 pm - 14 leo 06
Oob	Mercury	22.00 pm - 15 leo 18

Thursday 7th December

Planetary Directions

Quaoar re enters Capricorn 15:42

Retrograde Planets

Mercury, Uranus, Pallas, Eris, Salacia, Sedna

Asteroids		Dwarf Planets	
Juno	26 cap 11	Eris	22 ar 52
Vesta	10 sco 37	Haumea	25 lib 19
Pallas	25 ar 41	Makemake	04 lib 43
Ceres	17 leo 51	Salacia	00 ar 05
Chiron	24 pis 19	Orcus	10 vir 10
N Node	16 leo 53	Quaoar	29 sag 58
S Node	16 aq 53	Sedna	26 tau 02

Phase: Disseminating
Sunrise: 07:51 GMT
Sunset: 15:52
Moonrise: 20:35
Moonset: 11:10
Voc start:
Voc end:

Planetary and Angelic Hours

Jupiter	07:48	Moon	15:54
Mars	08:28	Saturn	17:13
Sun	09:09	Jupiter	18:33
Venus	09:49	Mars	19:52
Mercury	10:30	Sun	21:12
Moon	11:10	Venus	22:32
Saturn	11:51	Mercury	23:51
Jupiter	12:31	Moon	01:11
Mars	13:12	Saturn	02:30
Sun	13:52	Jupiter	03:50
Venus	14:33	Mars	05:10
Mercury	15:13	Sun	06:29

Aspects

Moon opposite Pluto
Moon square Eris
Moon trine Chiron
Mercury conj. Saturn
Moon square Uranus
Moon square Pallas
Moon opposite Juno
Moon sextile Sedna
Juno trine Sedna
Mercury sextile Mars
Moon square Mars
Mars sextile Saturn
Jupiter trine Neptune
Uranus conjunct Pallas
Neptune trine Vesta
Pallas square Juno

Planets	00:00 am	Moon
Sun	16 sag 04	00.00 am - 16 leo 29
Mercury	27 sag 18	02.00 am - 17 leo 40
Venus	08 sag 19	04.00 am - 18 leo 51
Mars	29 lib 08	06.00 am - 20 leo 01
Jupiter	12 sco 29	08.00 am - 21 leo 12
Saturn	28 sag 34	10.00 am - 22 leo 22
Uranus	24 ar 50	12.00 pm - 23 leo 32
Neptune	11 pis 32	14.00 pm - 24 leo 42
Pluto	18 cap 00	16.00 pm - 25 leo 52
		18.00 pm - 27 leo 01
Oob		20.00 pm - 28 leo 11
		22.00 pm - 29 leo 20

Friday 8th December

Planetary Directions

Moon into Virgo 23:09

Retrograde Planets

Mercury, Uranus, Pallas, Eris, Salacia, Sedna

Asteroids		Dwarf Planets	
Juno	26 cap 34	Eris	22 ar 51
Vesta	11 sco 08	Haumea	25 lib 20
Pallas	25 ar 35	Makemake	04 lib 44
Ceres	17 leo 54	Salacia	00 ar 05
Chiron	24 pis 19	Orcus	10 vir 10
N Node	16 leo 52	Quaoar	00 cap 00
S Node	16 aq 52	Sedna	26 tau 01

Phase: Disseminating
Sunrise: 07:52 GMT
Sunset: 15:52
Moonrise: 21:51
Moonset: 11:48
Voc start: 22:40
Voc end: 23:08

Planetary and Angelic Hours			
Venus	07:49	Mars	15:53
Mercury	08:29	Sun	17:13
Moon	09:10	Venus	18:33
Saturn	09:50	Mercury	19:53
Jupiter	10:30	Moon	21:12
Mars	11:11	Saturn	22:32
Sun	11:51	Jupiter	23:52
Venus	12:32	Mars	01:11
Mercury	13:12	Sun	02:31
Moon	13:52	Venus	03:51
Saturn	14:33	Mercury	05:11
Jupiter	15:13	Moon	06:30

Aspects

Moon conjunct Ceres
Moon trine Eris
Moon trine Uranus
Moon trine Pallas
Moon square Sedna
Moon trine Mercury
Neptune trine Vesta
Moon trine Saturn
Moon sextile Mars
Sun trine Ceres
Mercury trine Pallas
Uranus conjunct Pallas
Juno trine Sedna

Planets	00:00 am	Moon
Sun	17 sag 05	00.00 am - 00 vir 29
Mercury	26 sag 22	02.00 am - 01 vir 38
Venus	09 sag 34	04.00 am - 02 vir 47
Mars	29 lib 45	06.00 am - 03 vir 55
Jupiter	12 sco 41	08.00 am - 05 vir 04
Saturn	28 sag 41	10.00 am - 06 vir 12
Uranus	24 ar 59	12.00 pm - 07 vir 20
Neptune	11 pis 32	14.00 pm - 08 vir 28
Pluto	18 cap 02	16.00 pm - 09 vir 35
		18.00 pm - 10 vir 43
Oob		20.00 pm - 11 vir 50
		22.00 pm - 12 vir 57

Saturday 9th December

Planetary Directions

Mars into Scorpio
09:00
Orcus retrograde
10 vir 10 at 04:45

Retrograde Planets

Mercury, Uranus, Pallas, Eris, Salacia, Sedna

Asteroids		Dwarf Planets	
Juno	26 cap 57	Eris	22 ar 51
Vesta	11 sco 38	Haumea	25 lib 21
Pallas	25 ar 29	Makemake	04 lib 45
Ceres	17 leo 58	Salacia	00 ar 05
Chiron	24 pis 19	Orcus	10 vir 10
N Node	16 leo 52	Quaoar	00 cap 02
S Node	16 aq 52	Sedna	26 tau 01

Phase: Disseminating
Sunrise: 07:53 GMT
Sunset: 15:52
Moonrise: 23:05
Moonset: 12:19
Voc start:
Voc end:

Planetary and Angelic Hours

Saturn	07:50	Mercury	15:53
Jupiter	08:30	Moon	17:13
Mars	09:11	Saturn	18:33
Sun	09:51	Jupiter	19:53
Venus	10:31	Mars	21:12
Mercury	11:11	Sun	22:32
Moon	11:52	Venus	23:52
Saturn	12:32	Mercury	01:12
Jupiter	13:12	Moon	02:32
Mars	13:52	Saturn	03:52
Sun	14:33	Jupiter	05:11
Venus	15:13	Mars	06:31

Aspects

Moon square Venus
Moon opp. Neptune
Moon sextile Vesta
Mercury trine Pallas
Moon sextile Jupiter
Sun trine Ceres
Mercury trine Uranus
Mercury square Chiron
Venus square Neptune
Jupiter conjunct Vesta
Uranus conjunct Pallas
Neptune trine Vesta

Planets	00:00 am	Moon
Sun	18 sag 06	00.00 am - 14 vir 04
Mercury	25 sag 16	02.00 am - 15 vir 11
Venus	10 sag 50	04.00 am - 16 vir 18
Mars	00 sco 23	06.00 am - 17 vir 24
Jupiter	12 sco 52	08.00 am - 18 vir 31
Saturn	28 sag 48	10.00 am - 19 vir 37
Uranus	24 ar 48	12.00 pm - 20 vir 43
Neptune	11 pis 33	14.00 pm - 21 vir 49
Pluto	18 cap 03	16.00 pm - 22 vir 55
		18.00 pm - 24 vir 00
Oob		20.00 pm - 25 vir 06
		22.00 pm - 26 vir 11

Sunday 10th December

Retrograde Planets

Mercury, Uranus, Pallas, Eris, Salacia, Orcus, Sedna

Asteroids		Dwarf Planets	
Juno	27 cap 20	Eris	22 ar 51
Vesta	12 sco 08	Haumea	25 lib 22
Pallas	25 ar 24	Makemake	04 lib 45
Ceres	18 leo 01	Salacia	00 ar 05
Chiron	24 pis 19	Orcus	10 vir 10
N Node	16 leo 53	Quaoar	00 cap 03
S Node	16 aq 53	Sedna	26 tau 00

Last Quarter: 07:53
Sunrise: 07:55 GMT
Sunset: 15:51
Moonrise: None
Moonset: 12:45
Voc start:
Voc end:

Planetary and Angelic Hours			
Sun	07:51	Jupiter	15:53
Venus	08:31	Mars	17:13
Mercury	09:11	Sun	18:33
Moon	09:52	Venus	19:53
Saturn	10:32	Mercury	21:13
Jupiter	11:12	Moon	22:33
Mars	11:52	Saturn	23:53
Sun	12:32	Jupiter	01:13
Venus	13:12	Mars	02:32
Mercury	13:53	Sun	03:52
Moon	14:33	Venus	05:12
Saturn	15:13	Mercury	06:32

Aspects

Moon trine Pluto
Sun square Moon
Mercury trine Uranus
Venus square Neptune
Mercury square Chiron
Moon square Mercury
Moon opposite Chiron
Moon trine Sedna
Moon trine Juno
Jupiter conjunct Vesta
Uranus conjunct Pallas

Planets	00:00 am	Moon
		00.00 am - 27 vir 17
Sun	19 sag 07	02.00 am - 28 vir 22
Mercury	24 sag 02	04.00 am - 29 vir 27
Venus	12 sag 05	06.00 am - 00 lib 31
Mars	01 sco 01	08.00 am - 01 lib 36
Jupiter	13 sco 04	10.00 am - 02 lib 41
Saturn	28 sag 55	12.00 pm - 03 lib 45
Uranus	24 ar 47	14.00 pm - 04 lib 49
Neptune	11 pis 33	16.00 pm - 05 lib 54
Pluto	18 cap 05	18.00 pm - 06 lib 58
		20.00 pm - 08 lib 02
Oob		22.00 pm - 09 lib 05

Monday 11th December

Planetary Directions

Moon into Libra 05:01

Retrograde Planets

Mercury, Uranus, Pallas, Eris, Salacia, Orcus, Sedna

Asteroids		Dwarf Planets	
Juno	27 cap 43	Eris	22 ar 50
Vesta	12 sco 39	Haumea	25 lib 23
Pallas	25 ar 20	Makemake	04 lib 45
Ceres	18 leo 04	Salacia	00 ar 05
Chiron	24 pis 19	Orcus	10 vir 10
N Node	16 leo 53	Quaoar	00 cap 05
S Node	16 aq 53	Sedna	26 tau 00

Moon Phase: Balsamic
Sunrise: 07:56 GMT
Sunset: 15:51
Moonrise: 00:16
Moonset: 13:09
Voc start: 03:02
Voc end: 05:00

Planetary and Angelic Hours			
Moon	07:52	Venus	15:53
Saturn	08:32	Mercury	17:13
Jupiter	09:12	Moon	18:33
Mars	09:52	Saturn	19:53
Sun	10:32	Jupiter	21:13
Venus	11:12	Mars	22:33
Mercury	11:53	Sun	23:53
Moon	12:33	Venus	01:13
Saturn	13:13	Mercury	02:33
Jupiter	13:53	Moon	03:53
Mars	14:33	Saturn	05:13
Sun	15:13	Jupiter	06:33

Aspects

Moon trine Juno
Moon square Saturn
Mercury trine Eris
Jupiter conjunct Vesta
Uranus conjunct Pallas

Planets	00:00 am	Moon
Sun	20 sag 08	00.00 am - 10 lib 09
Mercury	22 sag 42	02.00 am - 11 lib 13
Venus	13 sag 21	04.00 am - 12 lib 16
Mars	01 sco 38	06.00 am - 13 lib 20
Jupiter	13 sco 16	08.00 am - 14 lib 23
Saturn	29 sag 02	10.00 am - 15 lib 26
Uranus	24 ar 46	12.00 pm - 16 lib 29
Neptune	11 pis 34	14.00 pm - 17 lib 32
Pluto	18 cap 07	16.00 pm - 18 lib 35
		18.00 pm - 19 lib 38
Oob		20.00 pm - 20 lib 40
		22.00 pm - 21 lib 43

Tuesday 12th December

Retrograde Planets

Mercury, Uranus, Pallas, Eris, Salacia, Orcus, Sedna

Asteroids		Dwarf Planets	
Juno	28 cap 06	Eris	22 ar 50
Vesta	13 sco 09	Haumea	25 lib 24
Pallas	25 ar 16	Makemake	04 lib 46
Ceres	18 leo 06	Salacia	00 ar 05
Chiron	24 pis 20	Orcus	10 vir 09
N Node	16 leo 51	Quaoar	00 cap 06
S Node	16 aq 51	Sedna	25 tau 59

Moon Phase: Balsamic
Sunrise: 07:57 GMT
Sunset: 15:51
Moonrise: 01:26
Moonset: 13:31
Voc start:
Voc end:

Planetary and Angelic Hours			
Mars	07:53	Saturn	15:53
Sun	08:33	Jupiter	17:13
Venus	09:13	Mars	18:33
Mercury	09:53	Sun	19:53
Moon	10:33	Venus	21:13
Saturn	11:13	Mercury	22:33
Jupiter	11:53	Moon	23:53
Mars	12:33	Saturn	01:14
Sun	13:13	Jupiter	02:34
Venus	13:53	Mars	03:54
Mercury	14:33	Sun	05:14
Moon	15:13	Venus	06:34

Aspects

Moon sextile Venus
Jupiter conjunct Vesta
Moon sextile Ceres
Moon square Pluto
Sun sextile Moon
Moon sextile Mercury
Sun conjunct Mercury
Moon opposite Eris
Uranus conjunct Pallas

Wednesday 13th December

Planets	00:00 am	Moon
		00.00 am - 22 lib 45
Sun	21 sag 09	02.00 am - 23 lib 48
Mercury	21 sag 20	04.00 am - 24 lib 50
Venus	14 sag 36	06.00 am - 25 lib 52
Mars	02 sco 16	08.00 am - 26 lib 54
Jupiter	13 sco 48	10.00 am - 27 lib 56
Saturn	29 sag 09	12.00 pm - 28 lib 58
Uranus	24 ar 45	14.00 pm - 00 sco 00
Neptune	11 pis 35	16.00 pm - 01 sco 02
Pluto	18 cap 09	18.00 pm - 02 sco 04
		20.00 pm - 03 sco 05
Oob		22.00 pm - 04 sco 07

Planetary Directions
Moon into Scorpio
13:59
Salacia direct
00 ar 05 at 15:12

Retrograde Planets
Mercury, Uranus,
Pallas, Eris, Salacia,
Orcus, Sedna

Asteroids		Dwarf Planets	
Juno	28 cap 30	Eris	22 ar 50
Vesta	13 sco 39	Haumea	25 lib 25
Pallas	25 ar 12	Makemake	04 lib 47
Ceres	18 leo 08	Salacia	00 ar 05
Chiron	24 pis 20	Orcus	10 vir 09
N Node	16 leo 46	Quaoar	00 cap 08
S Node	16 aq 46	Sedna	25 tau 59

Moon Phase: Balsamic
Sunrise: 07:57 GMT
Sunset: 15:51
Moonrise: 02:34
Moonset: 13:54
Voc start: 12:26
Voc end: 13:58

Planetary and Angelic Hours			
Mercury	07:54	Sun	15:53
Moon	08:34	Venus	17:13
Saturn	09:14	Mercury	18:33
Jupiter	09:54	Moon	19:53
Mars	10:34	Saturn	21:14
Sun	11:14	Jupiter	22:34
Venus	11:53	Mars	23:54
Mercury	12:33	Sun	01:14
Moon	13:13	Venus	02:34
Saturn	13:53	Mercury	03:54
Jupiter	14:33	Moon	05:15
Mars	15:13	Saturn	06:35

Aspects

Moon opposite Eris
Sun conjunct Mercury
Moon opposite Uranus
Moon opposite Pallas
Moon square Juno
Moon sextile Saturn
Moon conjunct Mars
Sun trine Eris
Jupiter conjunct Vesta
Uranus conjunct Pallas

Planets	00:00 am	Moon
		00.00 am - 05 sco 08
Sun	22 sag 10	02.00 am - 06 sco 10
Mercury	19 sag 57	04.00 am - 07 sco 11
Venus	15 sag 52	06.00 am - 08 sco 13
Mars	02 sco 54	08.00 am - 09 sco 14
Jupiter	13 sco 39	10.00 am - 10 sco 15
Saturn	29 sag 16	12.00 pm - 11 sco 16
Uranus	24 ar 44	14.00 pm - 12 sco 17
Neptune	11 pis 35	16.00 pm - 13 sco 18
Pluto	18 cap 11	18.00 pm - 14 sco 19
		20.00 pm - 15 sco 20
Oob		22.00 pm - 16 sco 20

Thursday 14th December

Retrograde Planets

Mercury, Uranus, Pallas, Eris, Orcus, Sedna

Asteroids		Dwarf Planets	
Juno	28 cap 53	Eris	22 ar 49
Vesta	14 sco 10	Haumea	25 lib 26
Pallas	25 ar 10	Makemake	04 lib 47
Ceres	18 leo 09	Salacia	00 ar 05
Chiron	24 pis 21	Orcus	10 vir 09
N Node	16 leo 39	Quaoar	00 cap 09
S Node	16 aq 39	Sedna	25 tau 58

Moon Phase: Balsamic
Sunrise: 07:58 GMT
Sunset: 15:51
Moonrise: 03:40
Moonset: 14:17
Voc start:
Voc end:

Planetary and Angelic Hours

Jupiter	07:55	Moon	15:53
Mars	08:35	Saturn	17:13
Sun	09:15	Jupiter	18:33
Venus	09:54	Mars	19:54
Mercury	10:34	Sun	21:14
Moon	11:14	Venus	22:34
Saturn	11:54	Mercury	23:54
Jupiter	12:34	Moon	01:15
Mars	13:14	Saturn	02:35
Sun	13:53	Jupiter	03:55
Venus	14:33	Mars	05:15
Mercury	15:13	Sun	06:36

Aspects

Moon trine Neptune
Sun trine Eris
Moon conjunct Jupiter
Moon conjunct Vesta
Moon sextile Pluto
Moon square Ceres
Mercury trine Ceres
Jupiter conjunct Vesta
Uranus conjunct Pallas

Planets	00:00 am	Moon
Sun	23 sag 11	00.00 am - 17 sco 21
Mercury	18 sag 37	02.00 am - 18 sco 22
Venus	17 sag 07	04.00 am - 19 sco 23
Mars	03 sco 31	06.00 am - 20 sco 23
Jupiter	13 sco 51	08.00 am - 21 sco 24
Saturn	29 sag 23	10.00 am - 22 sco 24
Uranus	24 ar 43	12.00 pm - 23 sco 24
Neptune	11 pis 36	14.00 pm - 24 sco 25
Pluto	18 cap 13	16.00 pm - 25 sco 25
		18.00 pm - 26 sco 25
Oob		20.00 pm - 27 sco 26
		22.00 pm - 28 sco 26

Friday 15th December

Retrograde Planets

Mercury, Uranus, Pallas, Eris, Orcus, Sedna

Asteroids		Dwarf Planets	
Juno	29 cap 17	Eris	22 ar 49
Vesta	14 sco 40	Haumea	25 lib 27
Pallas	25 ar 08	Makemake	04 lib 47
Ceres	18 leo 11	Salacia	00 ar 05
Chiron	24 pis 21	Orcus	10 vir 09
N Node	16 leo 30	Quaoar	00 cap 11
S Node	16 aq 30	Sedna	25 tau 58

Moon Phase: Balsamic
Sunrise: 07:59 GMT
Sunset: 15:52
Moonrise: 04:45
Moonset: 14:44
Voc start: 01:42
Voc end:

Planetary and Angelic Hours			
Venus	07:56	Mars	15:53
Mercury	08:36	Sun	17:13
Moon	09:15	Venus	18:34
Saturn	09:55	Mercury	19:54
Jupiter	10:35	Moon	21:14
Mars	11:15	Saturn	22:35
Sun	11:54	Jupiter	23:55
Venus	12:34	Mars	01:15
Mercury	13:14	Sun	02:35
Moon	13:54	Venus	03:56
Saturn	14:34	Mercury	05:16
Jupiter	15:13	Moon	06:36

Aspects

Moon square Ceres
Moon sextile Pluto
Mercury trine Ceres
Moon trine Chiron
Mercury conj. Venus
Moon opposite Sedna
Venus trine Ceres
Sun trine Uranus
Sun square Chiron
Sun trine Pallas
Moon sextile Juno
Uranus conjunct Pallas

Planets	00:00 am	Moon
Sun	24 sag 12	00.00 am - 29 sco 26
Mercury	17 sag 22	02.00 am - 00 sag 26
Venus	28 sag 23	04.00 am - 01 sag 26
Mars	04 sco 09	06.00 am - 02 sag 26
Jupiter	14 sco 02	08.00 am - 03 sag 26
Saturn	29 sag 30	10.00 am - 04 sag 26
Uranus	24 ar 42	12.00 pm - 05 sag 26
Neptune	11 pis 37	14.00 pm - 06 sag 26
Pluto	18 cap 15	16.00 pm - 07 sag 25
		18.00 pm - 08 sag 25
Oob		20.00 pm - 09 sag 25
		22.00 pm - 10 sag 25

Saturday 16th December

Planetary Directions

Moon into Sagittarius 01:08

Juno into Aquarius 19:19

Ceres rx at 22:31

Retrograde Planets

Mercury, Uranus, Pallas, Eris, Orcus, Sedna

Asteroids		Dwarf Planets	
Juno	29 cap 40	Eris	22 ar 49
Vesta	15 sco 10	Haumea	25 lib 27
Pallas	25 ar 06	Makemake	04 lib 48
Ceres	18 leo 11	Salacia	00 ar 05
Chiron	24 pis 22	Orcus	10 vir 09
N Node	16 leo 20	Quaoar	00 cap 13
S Node	16 aq 20	Sedna	25 tau 57

Moon Phase: Balsamic
Sunrise: 08:00 GMT
Sunset: 15:52
Moonrise: 05:48
Moonset: 15:14
Voc start: 01:07
Voc end:

Planetary and Angelic Hours			
Saturn	07:57	Mercury	15:53
Jupiter	08:36	Moon	17:14
Mars	09:16	Saturn	18:34
Sun	09:56	Jupiter	19:54
Venus	10:36	Mars	21:15
Mercury	11:15	Sun	22:35
Moon	11:55	Venus	23:55
Saturn	12:35	Mercury	01:16
Jupiter	13:14	Moon	02:36
Mars	13:54	Saturn	03:56
Sun	14:34	Jupiter	05:17
Venus	15:13	Mars	06:37

Aspects

Moon sextile Juno
Sun square Chiron
Sun trine Uranus
Sun trine Pallas
Moon square Neptune
Uranus conjunct Pallas

Planets	00:00 am	Moon
		00.00 am - 11 sag 24
Sun	25 sag 13	02.00 am - 12 sag 24
Mercury	16 sag 14	04.00 am - 13 sag 24
Venus	19 sag 38	06.00 am - 14 sag 23
Mars	04 sco 47	08.00 am - 15 sag 23
Jupiter	14 sco 14	10.00 am - 16 sag 22
Saturn	29 sag 37	12.00 pm - 17 sag 22
Uranus	24 ar 41	14.00 pm - 18 sag 21
Neptune	11 pis 38	16.00 pm - 19 sag 21
Pluto	18 cap 17	18.00 pm - 20 sag 20
		20.00 pm - 21 sag 19
Oob		22.00 pm - 22 sag 19

Sunday 17th December

Planetary Directions

Pallas direct
25 ar 05 at 23:38

Retrograde Planets

Mercury, Uranus, Ceres, Pallas, Eris, Orcus, Sedna

Asteroids		Dwarf Planets	
Juno	00 aq 04	Eris	22 ar 48
Vesta	15 sco 40	Haumea	25 lib 28
Pallas	25 ar 05	Makemake	04 lib 48
Ceres	18 leo 11	Salacia	00 ar 05
Chiron	24 pis 22	Orcus	10 vir 09
N Node	16 leo 09	Quaoar	00 cap 14
S Node	16 aq 09	Sedna	25 tau 56

Moon Phase: Balsamic
Sunrise: 08:01 GMT
Sunset: 15:52
Moonrise: 06:49
Moonset: 15:48
Voc start:
Voc end:

Planetary and Angelic Hours

Sun	07:57	Jupiter	15:53
Venus	08:37	Mars	17:14
Mercury	09:17	Sun	18:34
Moon	09:56	Venus	19:55
Saturn	10:36	Mercury	21:15
Jupiter	11:16	Moon	22:35
Mars	11:55	Saturn	23:56
Sun	12:35	Jupiter	01:16
Venus	13:15	Mars	02:37
Mercury	13:54	Sun	03:57
Moon	14:34	Venus	05:17
Saturn	15:14	Mercury	06:38

Aspects

Moon square Neptune
Moon conj. Mercury
Moon trine Ceres
Moon conjunct Venus
Moon trine Eris
Uranus conjunct Pallas

Planets	00:00 am	Moon
Sun	26 sag 14	00.00 am - 23 sag 18
Mercury	15 sag 15	02.00 am - 24 sag 17
Venus	20 sag 54	04.00 am - 25 sag 17
Mars	05 sco 24	06.00 am - 26 sag 16
Jupiter	14 sco 25	08.00 am - 27 sag 15
Saturn	29 sag 44	10.00 am - 28 sag 14
Uranus	24 ar 40	12.00 pm - 29 sag 13
Neptune	11 pis 39	14.00 pm - 00 cap 13
Pluto	18 cap 18	16.00 pm - 01 cap 12
		18.00 pm - 02 cap 11
Oob		20.00 pm - 03 cap 10
		22.00 pm - 04 cap 09

Monday 18th December

Planetary Directions

Moon into Capricorn 13:34

Retrograde Planets

Mercury, Uranus, Ceres, Eris, Orcus, Sedna

Asteroids		Dwarf Planets	
Juno	00 aq 28	Eris	22 ar 48
Vesta	16 sco 10	Haumea	25 lib 29
Pallas	25 ar 05	Makemake	04 lib 49
Ceres	18 leo 11	Salacia	00 ar 05
Chiron	24 pis 23	Orcus	10 vir 09
N Node	15 leo 59	Quaoar	00 cap 16
S Node	15 aq 59	Sedna	25 tau 56

New Moon: 06:31
Sunrise: 08:01 GMT
Sunset: 15:52
Moonrise: 07:46
Moonset: 16:29
Voc start: 13:09
Voc end: 13:33

Planetary and Angelic Hours			
Moon	07:58	Venus	15:54
Saturn	08:38	Mercury	17:14
Jupiter	09:17	Moon	18:35
Mars	09:57	Saturn	19:55
Sun	10:37	Jupiter	21:15
Venus	11:16	Mars	22:36
Mercury	11:56	Sun	23:56
Moon	12:36	Venus	01:17
Saturn	13:15	Mercury	02:37
Jupiter	13:55	Moon	03:58
Mars	14:34	Saturn	05:18
Sun	15:14	Jupiter	06:38

Micro New Moon

Aspects

Moon square Chiron
Moon trine Uranus
Moon trine Pallas
Sun conjunct Moon
Moon conjunct Saturn
Moon sextile Mars
Venus trine Eris
Uranus conjunct Pallas

Planets	00:00 am	Moon
Sun	27 sag 15	00.00 am - 05 cap 08
Mercury	14 sag 26	02.00 am - 06 cap 07
Venus	22 sag 09	04.00 am - 07 cap 06
Mars	06 sco 02	06.00 am - 08 cap 06
Jupiter	14 sco 36	08.00 am - 09 cap 05
Saturn	29 sag 51	10.00 am - 10 cap 04
Uranus	24 ar 39	12.00 pm - 11 cap 03
Neptune	11 pis 39	14.00 pm - 12 cap 02
Pluto	18 cap 20	16.00 pm - 13 cap 01
		18.00 pm - 14 cap 00
Oob		20.00 pm - 14 cap 59
		22.00 pm - 15 cap 58

Tuesday 19th December

Retrograde Planets

Mercury, Uranus, Ceres, Eris, Orcus, Sedna

Asteroids		Dwarf Planets	
Juno	00 aq 52	Eris	22 ar 48
Vesta	16 sco 40	Haumea	25 lib 30
Pallas	25 ar 05	Makemake	04 lib 49
Ceres	18 leo 10	Salacia	00 ar 05
Chiron	24 pis 24	Orcus	10 vir 08
N Node	15 leo 50	Quaoar	00 cap 17
S Node	15 aq 50	Sedna	25 tau 55

Moon Phase: Crescent
Sunrise: 08:02 GMT
Sunset: 15:53
Moonrise: 08:37
Moonset: 17:15
Voc start:
Voc end:

Planetary and Angelic Hours			
Mars	07:59	Saturn	15:54
Sun	08:38	Jupiter	17:15
Venus	09:18	Mars	18:35
Mercury	09:58	Sun	19:55
Moon	10:37	Venus	21:16
Saturn	11:17	Mercury	22:36
Jupiter	11:56	Moon	23:57
Mars	12:36	Saturn	01:17
Sun	13:16	Jupiter	02:38
Venus	13:55	Mars	03:58
Mercury	14:35	Sun	05:19
Moon	15:14	Venus	06:39

Aspects

Moon sextile Mars
Venus trine Eris
Moon sextile Neptune
Moon sextile Jupiter
Moon sextile Vesta
Venus square Chiron
Uranus conjunct Pallas
Ceres square Vesta

Planets	00:00 am	Moon
Sun	28 sag 16	00.00 am - 16 cap 57
Mercury	13 sag 48	02.00 am - 17 cap 56
Venus	23 sag 25	04.00 am - 18 cap 55
Mars	06 sco 39	06.00 am - 19 cap 54
Jupiter	14 sco 48	08.00 am - 20 cap 53
Saturn	29 sag 58	10.00 am - 21 cap 52
Uranus	24 ar 39	12.00 pm - 22 cap 51
Neptune	11 pis 40	14.00 pm - 23 cap 50
Pluto	18 cap 22	16.00 pm - 24 cap 49
		18.00 pm - 25 cap 48
Oob		20.00 pm - 26 cap 48
		22.00 pm - 27 cap 47

Wednesday 20th December

Planetary Directions

Saturn into Capricorn
04:49

Retrograde Planets

Mercury, Uranus, Ceres, Eris, Orcus, Sedna

Asteroids		Dwarf Planets	
Juno	01 aq 16	Eris	22 ar 48
Vesta	17 sco 10	Haumea	25 lib 31
Pallas	25 ar 06	Makemake	04 lib 49
Ceres	18 leo 09	Salacia	00 ar 05
Chiron	24 pis 24	Orcus	10 vir 08
N Node	15 leo 44	Quaoar	00 cap 19
S Node	15 aq 44	Sedna	25 tau 55

Moon Phase: Crescent
Sunrise: 08:03 GMT
Sunset: 15:53
Moonrise: 09:22
Moonset: 18:08
Voc start: 15:36
Voc end:

Planetary and Angelic Hours			
Mercury	07:59	Sun	15:54
Moon	08:39	Venus	17:15
Saturn	09:19	Mercury	18:35
Jupiter	09:58	Moon	19:56
Mars	10:38	Saturn	21:16
Sun	11:17	Jupiter	22:37
Venus	11:57	Mars	23:57
Mercury	12:37	Sun	01:18
Moon	13:16	Venus	02:38
Saturn	13:56	Mercury	03:59
Jupiter	14:35	Moon	05:19
Mars	15:15	Saturn	06:40

Aspects

Moon sextile Vesta
Moon conjunct Pluto
Moon square Eris
Moon sextile Chiron
Moon square Uranua
Moon square Pallas
Moon trine Sedna
Venus square Chiron
Venus trine Uranus
Sun conjunct Saturn
Venus trine Pallas
Uranus conjunct Pallas
Pluto sextile Vesta
Ceres square Vesta

Planets	00:00 am	Moon
Sun	29 sag 18	00.00 am - 28 cap 46
Mercury	13 sag 21	02.00 am - 29 cap 45
Venus	24 sag 40	04.00 am - 00 aq 44
Mars	07 sco 17	06.00 am - 01 aq 43
Jupiter	14 sco 59	08.00 am - 02 aq 43
Saturn	00 cap 05	10.00 am - 03 aq 42
Uranus	24 ar 38	12.00 pm - 04 aq 41
Neptune	11 pis 41	14.00 pm - 05 aq 41
Pluto	18 cap 24	16.00 pm - 06 aq 40
		18.00 pm - 07 aq 39
Oob	Venus	20.00 pm - 08 aq 39
		22.00 pm - 09 aq 38

Thursday 21st December

Planetary Directions

Moon into Aquarius 02:30
Sun into Cap at 16:28

Retrograde Planets

Mercury, Uranus, Ceres, Eris, Orcus, Sedna

Asteroids		Dwarf Planets	
Juno	01 aq 40	Eris	22 ar 47
Vesta	17 sco 40	Haumea	25 lib 31
Pallas	25 ar 08	Makemake	04 lib 50
Ceres	18 leo 08	Salacia	00 ar 06
Chiron	24 pis 25	Orcus	10 vir 08
N Node	15 leo 40	Quaoar	00 cap 21
S Node	15 aq 40	Sedna	25 tau 54

Moon Phase: Crescent
Sunrise: 08:03 GMT
Sunset: 15:53
Moonrise: 10:01
Moonset: 19:06
Voc start:
Voc end: 02:29

Planetary and Angelic Hours			
Jupiter	08:00	Moon	15:55
Mars	08:40	Saturn	17:15
Sun	09:19	Jupiter	18:36
Venus	09:59	Mars	19:56
Mercury	10:38	Sun	21:17
Moon	11:18	Venus	22:37
Saturn	11:57	Mercury	23:58
Jupiter	12:37	Moon	01:18
Mars	13:17	Saturn	02:39
Sun	13:56	Jupiter	03:59
Venus	14:36	Mars	05:20
Mercury	15:15	Sun	06:40

Winter Solstice
Yule

Aspects

Moon conjunct Juno
Venus trine Pallas
Moon square Mars
Ceres square Vesta
Sun conjunct Saturn
Uranus conjunct Pallas
Pluto sextile Vesta

Friday 22nd December

Planets	00:00 am	Moon
Sun	00 cap 19	00.00 am - 10 aq 38
Mercury	13 sag 05	02.00 am - 11 aq 37
Venus	25 sag 56	04.00 am - 12 aq 37
Mars	07 sco 55	06.00 am - 13 aq 36
Jupiter	15 sco 10	08.00 am - 14 aq 36
Saturn	00 cap 12	10.00 am - 15 aq 36
Uranus	24 ar 37	12.00 pm - 16 aq 36
Neptune	11 pis 42	14.00 pm - 17 aq 35
Pluto	18 cap 26	16.00 pm - 18 aq 35
		18.00 pm - 19 aq 35
Oob	Venus	20.00 pm - 20 aq 35
		22.00 pm - 21 aq 35

Retrograde Planets

Mercury, Uranus, Ceres, Eris, Orcus, Sedna

Asteroids		Dwarf Planets	
Juno	02 aq 04	Eris	22 ar 47
Vesta	18 sco 10	Haumea	25 lib 32
Pallas	25 ar 10	Makemake	04 lib 50
Ceres	18 leo 06	Salacia	00 ar 06
Chiron	24 pis 26	Orcus	10 vir 08
N Node	15 leo 38	Quaoar	00 cap 22
S Node	15 aq 38	Sedna	25 tau 54

Moon Phase: Crescent
Sunrise: 08:04 GMT
Sunset: 15:54
Moonrise: 10:34
Moonset: 20:08
Voc start:
Voc end:

Planetary and Angelic Hours			
Venus	08:01	Mars	15:55
Mercury	08:40	Sun	17:16
Moon	09:20	Venus	18:36
Saturn	09:59	Mercury	19:57
Jupiter	10:39	Moon	21:17
Mars	11:18	Saturn	22:38
Sun	11:58	Jupiter	23:58
Venus	12:38	Mars	01:19
Mercury	13:17	Sun	02:39
Moon	13:57	Venus	04:00
Saturn	14:36	Mercury	05:20
Jupiter	15:16	Moon	06:41

Aspects

Moon sextile Mercury
Moon square Jupiter
Pluto sextile Vesta
Moon opposite Ceres
Moon square Vesta
Moon sextile Eris
Uranus conjunct Pallas
Ceres square Vesta

Planets	00:00 am	Moon
Sun	01 cap 20	00.00 am - 22 aq 35
Mercury	13 sag 00	02.00 am - 23 aq 36
Venus	27 sag 11	04.00 am - 24 aq 36
Mars	08 sco 32	06.00 am - 25 aq 36
Jupiter	15 sco 21	08.00 am - 26 aq 37
Saturn	00 cap 19	10.00 am - 27 aq 37
Uranus	24 ar 37	12.00 pm - 28 aq 38
Neptune	11 pis 43	14.00 pm - 29 aq 38
Pluto	18 cap 28	16.00 pm - 00 pis 39
		18.00 pm - 01 pis 40
Oob	Venus	20.00 pm - 02 pis 41
		22.00 pm - 03 pis 42

Saturday 23rd December

Planetary Directions

Mercury direct
13 sag 00 at 01:51
Moon into Pisces 14:42

Retrograde Planets

Mercury, Uranus, Ceres, Eris, Orcus, Sedna

Asteroids		Dwarf Planets	
Juno	02 aq 28	Eris	22 ar 47
Vesta	18 sco 40	Haumea	25 lib 33
Pallas	25 ar 12	Makemake	04 lib 50
Ceres	18 leo 03	Salacia	00 ar 06
Chiron	24 pis 27	Orcus	10 vir 07
N Node	15 leo 38	Quaoar	00 cap 24
S Node	15 aq 38	Sedna	25 tau 53

Moon Phase: Crescent
Sunrise: 08:04 GMT
Sunset: 15:55
Moonrise: 11:03
Moonset: 21:12
Voc start: 10:12
Voc end: 14:41

Planetary and Angelic Hours			
Saturn	08:01	Mercury	15:56
Jupiter	08:41	Moon	17:16
Mars	09:20	Saturn	18:37
Sun	10:00	Jupiter	19:57
Venus	10:39	Mars	21:18
Mercury	11:19	Sun	22:38
Moon	11:58	Venus	23:59
Saturn	12:38	Mercury	01:19
Jupiter	13:18	Moon	02:40
Mars	13:57	Saturn	04:00
Sun	14:37	Jupiter	05:21
Venus	15:16	Mars	06:41

Aspects

Moon sextile Eris
Moon sextile Uranus
Moon sextile Pallas
Moon square Sedna
Moon sextile Venus
Moon sextile Saturn
Sun sextile Moon
Uranus conjunct Pallas
Pluto sextile Vesta

Planets	00:00 am	Moon
Sun	02 cap 21	00.00 am - 04 pis 43
Mercury	13 sag 04	02.00 am - 05 pis 44
Venus	28 sag 27	04.00 am - 06 pis 46
Mars	09 sco 10	06.00 am - 07 pis 47
Jupiter	15 sco 32	08.00 am - 08 pis 48
Saturn	00 cap 26	10.00 am - 09 pis 50
Uranus	24 ar 36	12.00 pm - 10 pis 52
Neptune	11 pis 44	14.00 pm - 11 pis 54
Pluto	18 cap 30	16.00 pm - 12 pis 56
		18.00 pm - 13 pis 58
Oob	Venus	20.00 pm - 15 pis 00
		22.00 pm - 16 pis 02

Sunday 24th December

Retrograde Planets

Uranus, Ceres, Eris, Orcus, Sedna

Asteroids		Dwarf Planets	
Juno	02 aq 53	Eris	22 ar 47
Vesta	19 sco 10	Haumea	25 lib 34
Pallas	25 ar 16	Makemake	04 lib 50
Ceres	18 leo 01	Salacia	00 ar 06
Chiron	24 pis 28	Orcus	10 vir 07
N Node	15 leo 40	Quaoar	00 cap 25
S Node	15 aq 40	Sedna	25 tau 53

Moon Phase: Crescent
Sunrise: 08:05 GMT
Sunset: 15:55
Moonrise: 11:28
Moonset: 22:19
Voc start:
Voc end:

Planetary and Angelic Hours			
Sun	08:01	Jupiter	15:57
Venus	08:41	Mars	17:17
Mercury	09:21	Sun	18:37
Moon	10:00	Venus	19:58
Saturn	10:40	Mercury	21:18
Jupiter	11:19	Moon	22:39
Mars	11:59	Saturn	23:59
Sun	12:39	Jupiter	01:20
Venus	13:18	Mars	02:40
Mercury	13:58	Sun	04:01
Moon	14:37	Venus	05:21
Saturn	15:17	Mercury	06:41

Christmas Eve

Aspects

Moon trine Mars
Moon conj. Neptune
Moon square Mercury
Moon trine Jupiter
Venus conjunct Saturn
Uranus conjunct Pallas

Planets	00:00 am	Moon
Sun	03 cap 22	00.00 am - 17 pis 05
Mercury	13 sag 17	02.00 am - 18 pis 07
Venus	29 sag 42	04.00 am - 19 pis 10
Mars	09 sco 47	06.00 am - 29 pis 13
Jupiter	15 sco 42	08.00 am - 21 pis 16
Saturn	00 cap 34	10.00 am - 22 pis 19
Uranus	24 ar 36	12.00 pm - 23 pis 22
Neptune	11 pis 45	14.00 pm - 24 pis 26
Pluto	18 cap 32	16.00 pm - 25 pis 29
		18.00 pm - 26 pis 33
		20.00 pm - 27 pis 37
Oob	Venus	22.00 pm - 28 pis 41

Monday 25th December

Planetary Directions

Venus into Capricorn 05:26

Retrograde Planets

Uranus, Ceres, Eris, Orcus, Sedna

Asteroids		Dwarf Planets	
Juno	03 aq 17	Eris	22 ar 47
Vesta	19 sco 40	Haumea	25 lib 34
Pallas	25 ar 20	Makemake	04 lib 51
Ceres	17 leo 57	Salacia	00 ar 07
Chiron	24 pis 29	Orcus	10 vir 07
N Node	15 leo 41	Quaoar	00 cap 27
S Node	15 aq 41	Sedna	25 tau 52

Moon Phase: Crescent
Sunrise: 08:05 GMT
Sunset: 15:56
Moonrise: 11:52
Moonset: 23:27
Voc start: 02:47
Voc end:

Planetary and Angelic Hours			
Moon	08:02	Venus	15:57
Saturn	08:41	Mercury	17:18
Jupiter	09:21	Moon	18:38
Mars	10:01	Saturn	19:58
Sun	10:40	Jupiter	21:19
Venus	11:20	Mars	22:39
Mercury	12:00	Sun	00:00
Moon	12:39	Venus	01:20
Saturn	13:19	Mercury	02:40
Jupiter	13:58	Moon	04:01
Mars	14:38	Saturn	05:21
Sun	15:18	Jupiter	06:42

Christmas Day

Aspects

Moon sextile Pluto
Moon trine Vesta
Moon conjunct Chiron
Moon sextile Sedna
Venus conjunct Saturn
Moon square Saturn
Uranus conjunct Pallas

Planets	00:00 am	Moon
Sun	04 cap 23	00.00 am - 29 pis 45
Mercury	13 sag 38	02.00 am - 00 ar 50
Venus	00 cap 58	04.00 am - 01 ar 54
Mars	10 sco 25	06.00 am - 02 ar 59
Jupiter	15 sco 53	08.00 am - 04 ar 04
Saturn	00 cap 41	10.00 am - 05 ar 09
Uranus	24 ar 35	12.00 pm - 06 ar 14
Neptune	11 pis 46	14.00 pm - 07 ar 19
Pluto	18 cap 34	16.00 pm - 08 ar 25
		18.00 pm - 09 ar 30
		20.00 pm - 10 ar 36
Oob	Venus	22.00 pm - 11 ar 42

Tuesday 26th December

Planetary Directions

Moon into Aries 00:27

Retrograde Planets

Uranus, Ceres, Eris, Orcus, Sedna

Asteroids		Dwarf Planets	
Juno	03 aq 42	Eris	22 ar 46
Vesta	20 sco 10	Haumea	25 lib 36
Pallas	25 ar 24	Makemake	04 lib 51
Ceres	17 leo 54	Salacia	00 ar 07
Chiron	24 pis 30	Orcus	10 vir 06
N Node	15 leo 42	Quaoar	00 cap 30
S Node	15 aq 42	Sedna	25 tau 51

First Quarter: 09:20
Sunrise: 08:05 GMT
Sunset: 15:57
Moonrise: 12:15
Moonset: None
Voc start: 00:26
Voc end:

Planetary and Angelic Hours			
Mars	08:02	Saturn	15:58
Sun	08:42	Jupiter	17:18
Venus	09:21	Mars	18:39
Mercury	10:01	Sun	19:59
Moon	10:41	Venus	21:19
Saturn	11:20	Mercury	22:40
Jupiter	12:00	Moon	00:00
Mars	12:40	Saturn	01:21
Sun	13:19	Jupiter	02:41
Venus	13:59	Mars	04:01
Mercury	14:39	Sun	05:22
Moon	15:18	Venus	06:42

Boxing Day

Aspects

Moon square Saturn
Moon square Venus
Moon sextile Juno
Sun square Moon
Mars trine Neptune
Uranus conjunct Pallas

Planets	00:00 am	Moon
Sun	05 cap 24	00.00 am - 12 ar 49
Mercury	14 sag 07	02.00 am - 13 ar 55
Venus	02 cap 13	04.00 am - 15 ar 02
Mars	11 sco 02	06.00 am - 16 ar 09
Jupiter	16 sco 04	08.00 am - 17 ar 16
Saturn	00 cap 48	10.00 am - 18 ar 23
Uranus	24 ar 35	12.00 pm - 19 ar 30
Neptune	11 pis 48	14.00 pm - 20 ar 38
Pluto	18 cap 36	16.00 pm - 21 ar 46
		18.00 pm - 22 ar 54
Oob	Venus	20.00 pm - 24 ar 02
		22.00 pm - 25 ar 10

Wednesday 27th December

Retrograde Planets

Uranus, Ceres, Eris, Orcus, Sedna

Asteroids		Dwarf Planets	
Juno	04 aq 06	Eris	22 ar 46
Vesta	20 sco 39	Haumea	25 lib 37
Pallas	25 ar 29	Makemake	04 lib 51
Ceres	17 leo 49	Salacia	00 ar 08
Chiron	24 pis 31	Orcus	10 vir 05
N Node	15 leo 42	Quaoar	00 cap 33
S Node	15 aq 42	Sedna	25 tau 51

Moon Phase: Gibbous
Sunrise: 08:05 GMT
Sunset: 15:57
Moonrise: 12:39
Moonset: 00:38
Voc start: 20:57
Voc end:

Planetary and Angelic Hours

Mercury	08:02	Sun	15:59
Moon	08:42	Venus	17:19
Saturn	09:22	Mercury	18:39
Jupiter	10:01	Moon	20:00
Mars	10:41	Saturn	21:20
Sun	11:21	Jupiter	22:40
Venus	12:01	Mars	00:01
Mercury	12:40	Sun	01:21
Moon	13:20	Venus	02:41
Saturn	14:00	Mercury	04:02
Jupiter	14:39	Moon	05:22
Mars	15:19	Saturn	06:42

Aspects

Moon trine Mercury
Moon trine Ceres
Moon square Pluto
Moon conjunct Eris
Moon conjunct Uranus
Moon conjunct Pallas
Mars trine Neptune
Uranus conjunct Pallas

Planets	00:00 am	Moon
		00.00 am - 26 ar 19
Sun	06 cap 25	02.00 am - 27 ar 28
Mercury	14 sag 42	04.00 am - 28 ar 37
Venus	03 cap 29	06.00 am - 29 ar 46
Mars	11 sco 40	08.00 am - 00 tau 56
Jupiter	16 sco 14	10.00 am - 02 tau 05
Saturn	00 cap 55	12.00 pm - 03 tau 15
Uranus	24 ar 35	14.00 pm - 04 tau 25
Neptune	11 pis 49	16.00 pm - 05 tau 35
Pluto	18 cap 38	18.00 pm - 06 tau 46
		20.00 pm - 07 tau 56
Oob	Venus	22.00 pm - 09 tau 07

Thursday 28th December

Planetary Directions

Moon into Taurus
06:24

Retrograde Planets

Uranus, Ceres, Eris,
Orcus, Sedna

Asteroids		Dwarf Planets	
Juno	04 aq 31	Eris	22 ar 46
Vesta	21 sco 09	Haumea	25 lib 36
Pallas	25 ar 34	Makemake	04 lib 51
Ceres	17 leo 45	Salacia	00 ar 07
Chiron	24 pis 33	Orcus	10 vir 06
N Node	15 leo 40	Quaoar	00 cap 32
S Node	15 aq 40	Sedna	25 tau 51

Moon Phase: Gibbous
Sunrise: 08:06 GMT
Sunset: 15:58
Moonrise: 13:05
Moonset: 01:51
Voc start:
Voc end: 06:23

Planetary and Angelic Hours

Jupiter	08:03	Moon	15:59
Mars	08:42	Saturn	17:20
Sun	09:22	Jupiter	18:40
Venus	10:02	Mars	20:00
Mercury	10:42	Sun	21:21
Moon	11:21	Venus	22:41
Saturn	12:01	Mercury	00:01
Jupiter	12:41	Moon	01:21
Mars	13:21	Saturn	02:42
Sun	14:00	Jupiter	04:02
Venus	14:40	Mars	05:22
Mercury	15:20	Sun	06:42

Aspects

Mars trine Neptune
Moon trine Saturn
Moon trine Venus
Moon square Juno
Sun trine Moon

Planets	00:00 am	Moon
Sun	07 cap 27	00.00 am - 10 tau 18
Mercury	15 sag 23	02.00 am - 11 tau 29
Venus	04 cap 44	04.00 am - 12 tau 41
Mars	12 sco 17	06.00 am - 13 tau 52
Jupiter	16 sco 25	08.00 am - 15 tau 04
Saturn	01 cap 02	10.00 am - 16 tau 16
Uranus	24 ar 34	12.00 pm - 17 tau 28
Neptune	11 pis 50	14.00 pm - 18 tau 41
Pluto	18 cap 40	16.00 pm - 19 tau 53
		18.00 pm - 21 tau 06
Oob	Venus	20.00 pm - 22 tau 19
		22.00 pm - 23 tau 32

Friday 29th December

Retrograde Planets

Uranus, Ceres, Eris, Orcus, Sedna

Asteroids		Dwarf Planets	
Juno	04 aq 56	Eris	22 ar 46
Vesta	21 sco 39	Haumea	25 lib 37
Pallas	25 ar 40	Makemake	04 lib 51
Ceres	17 leo 40	Salacia	00 ar 08
Chiron	24 pis 34	Orcus	10 vir 05
N Node	15 leo 37	Quaoar	00 cap 33
S Node	15 aq 37	Sedna	25 tau 51

Moon Phase: Gibbous
Sunrise: 08:06 GMT
Sunset: 15:59
Moonrise: 13:34
Moonset: 03:08
Voc start: 14:00
Voc end:

Planetary and Angelic Hours			
Venus	08:03	Mars	16:00
Mercury	08:43	Sun	17:21
Moon	09:22	Venus	18:41
Saturn	10:02	Mercury	20:01
Jupiter	10:42	Moon	21:21
Mars	11:22	Saturn	22:41
Sun	12:02	Jupiter	00:02
Venus	12:41	Mars	01:22
Mercury	13:21	Sun	02:42
Moon	14:01	Venus	04:02
Saturn	14:41	Mercury	05:22
Jupiter	15:21	Moon	06:43

Aspects

Moon sextile Neptune
Moon opposite Mars
Moon opposite Jupiter
Moon square Ceres
Moon trine Pluto
Moon opposite Vesta
Moon sextile Chiron
Jupiter square Ceres

Planets	**00:00 am**	**Moon**
Sun	08 cap 28	00.00 am - 24 tau 46
Mercury	16 sag 10	02.00 am - 25 tau 59
Venus	06 cap 00	04.00 am - 27 tau 13
Mars	12 sco 55	06.00 am - 28 tau 27
Jupiter	16 sco 55	08.00 am - 29 tau 40
Saturn	01 cap 09	10.00 am - 00 gem 55
Uranus	24 ar 34	12.00 pm - 02 gem 09
Neptune	11 pis 51	14.00 pm - 03 gem 23
Pluto	18 cap 42	16.00 pm - 04 gem 38
		18.00 pm - 05 gem 53
Oob	Venus	20.00 pm - 07 gem 08
		22.00 pm - 08 gem 23

Saturday 30th December

Planetary Directions

Moon into Gemini
08:31

Retrograde Planets

Uranus, Ceres, Eris, Orcus, Sedna

Asteroids		**Dwarf Planets**	
Juno	05 aq 20	Eris	22 ar 46
Vesta	22 sco 08	Haumea	25 lib 37
Pallas	25 ar 47	Makemake	04 lib 51
Ceres	17 leo 34	Salacia	00 ar 08
Chiron	24 pis 35	Orcus	10 vir 05
N Node	15 leo 32	Quaoar	00 cap 35
S Node	15 aq 32	Sedna	25 tau 50

Moon Phase: Gibbous
Sunrise: 08:06 GMT
Sunset: 16:00
Moonrise: 14:10
Moonset: 04:26
Voc start:
Voc end: 08:30

Planetary and Angelic Hours			
Saturn	08:03	Mercury	16:01
Jupiter	08:43	Moon	17:21
Mars	09:23	Saturn	18:42
Sun	10:02	Jupiter	20:02
Venus	10:42	Mars	21:22
Mercury	11:22	Sun	22:42
Moon	12:02	Venus	00:02
Saturn	12:42	Mercury	01:22
Jupiter	13:22	Moon	02:42
Mars	14:02	Saturn	04:02
Sun	14:42	Jupiter	05:23
Venus	15:21	Mars	06:43

Aspects

Moon conjunct Sedna
Moon trine Juno
Mercury trine Ceres
Jupiter square Ceres

Sunday 31st December

Planets	00:00 am	Moon
Sun	09 cap 29	00.00 am - 09 gem 38
Mercury	17 sag 01	02.00 am - 10 gem 53
Venus	07 cap 15	04.00 am - 12 gem 08
Mars	13 sco 32	06.00 am - 13 gem 24
Jupiter	16 sco 45	08.00 am - 14 gem 39
Saturn	01 cap 16	10.00 am - 15 gem 55
Uranus	24 ar 34	12.00 pm - 17 gem 11
Neptune	11 pis 52	14.00 pm - 18 gem 27
Pluto	18 cap 44	16.00 pm - 19 gem 43
		18.00 pm - 20 gem 59
		20.00 pm - 22 gem 15
Oob	Venus	22.00 pm - 23 gem 31

Retrograde Planets

Uranus, Ceres, Eris, Orcus, Sedna

Asteroids		Dwarf Planets	
Juno	05 aq 45	Eris	22 ar 46
Vesta	22 sco 38	Haumea	25 lib 38
Pallas	25 ar 54	Makemake	04 lib 51
Ceres	17 leo 29	Salacia	00 ar 09
Chiron	24 pis 37	Orcus	10 vir 04
N Node	15 leo 26	Quaoar	00 cap 36
S Node	15 aq 26	Sedna	25 tau 50

Moon Phase: Gibbous
Sunrise: 08:06 GMT
Sunset: 16:01
Moonrise: 14:54
Moonset: 05:45
Voc start: 23:38
Voc end:

Planetary and Angelic Hours

Sun	08:03	Jupiter	16:02
Venus	08:43	Mars	17:22
Mercury	09:23	Sun	18:42
Moon	10:03	Venus	20:02
Saturn	10:43	Mercury	21:22
Jupiter	11:23	Moon	22:42
Mars	12:03	Saturn	00:03
Sun	12:42	Jupiter	01:23
Venus	13:22	Mars	02:43
Mercury	14:02	Sun	04:03
Moon	14:42	Venus	05:23
Saturn	15:22	Mercury	06:43

New Years Eve

Aspects

Moon square Neptune
Mercury trine Ceres
Moon sextile Ceres
Moon opp. Mercury
Moon sextile Eris
Moon sextile Uranus
Moon square Chiron
Jupiter square Ceres

Notes

www.ingramcontent.com/pod-product-compliance
Lightning Source LLC
Chambersburg PA
CBHW060232290526
45789CB00001B/23

* 9 7 8 1 5 3 9 6 2 6 2 4 4 *